ETHICS IN LINKED DATA

This book is number one in the Series on Critical Information Organization in LIS, Violet Fox and Kelsey George, series editors.

ETHICS IN LINKED DATA

B.M. Watson, Alexandra Provo,
and Kathleen Burlingame,
Editors

LIBRARY JUICE PRESS
SACRAMENTO, CA

Published in 2023 by Library Juice Press

Library Juice Press
PO Box 188784
Sacramento, CA 95822

http://libraryjuicepress.com/

This book is printed on acid-free paper.

Publisher's Cataloging-in-Publication data

Names: Watson, B. M., editor. | Provo, Alexandra Alisa, editor. | Burlingame, Kathleen, editor.

Title: Ethics in linked data / B.M. Watson, Aleandra Provo, and Kathleen Burlingame, editors.

Description: Sacramento, CA : Library Juice Press, 2023. | Series on Critical Information Organization in LIS ; no. 1.

Identifiers: LCCN 2023937555 | ISBN 9781634001335 (softcover)

Subjects: LCSH: Linked data--Moral and ethical aspects.

Classification: LCC Z666.73.L56 E84 2023 | DDC 025.042/7--dc23

LC record available at https://lccn.loc.gov/2023937555

Contents

Part I: Theories, Contexts, & (Infra)structures

**Part II: Ethical Considerations in the Face of
Hegemonic and Institutional Forces**

Part III: People & Communities

Introduction

B. M. WATSON, ALEXANDRA PROVO, &
KATHLEEN BURLINGAME

On a sunny, spring afternoon in 2019, a group gathered around a small conference table in an austere breakout room at the Joseph B. Martin Conference Center at Harvard Medical School. Well-caffeinated after lunch and thoughtfully energized from a day and a half of presentations and discussions organized for the inaugural LD4 Conference on linked data,[1] the group intermittently thumbed through a dog-eared copy of the recently published *Ethical Questions in Name Authority Control* that had been placed emphatically on the table as if it were a beacon.[2] The session's facilitator soon arrived and—with a determined flourish—wrote the ostensible purpose of the assembled group on a large whiteboard: "Ethics in Linking."

The animated conversations that ensued ranged from urgent professional concerns (how do we remove harm from our legacy data before it is transformed into linked data?) to personal worries (how do I protect my private information from identity theft in a linked data environment?). By the end of the allotted time, it was clear that there were no easy answers and that the GLAMS (Galleries, Libraries, Archives, Museums, and Special Collections) community would benefit from continued conversations

---

1. The LD4 Community was created to provide channels for communication and collaboration for linked data initiatives in libraries and archives. The group is open to any individuals or institutions. For more information, see https://sites.google.com/stanford.edu/ld4-community-site/home.

2. Jane Sandberg, ed. *Ethical Questions in Name Authority Control*. (Sacramento, CA: Library Juice Press, 2019).

around linked data and ethics. Subsequently, the Ethics in Linked Data Affinity Group of the LD4 community was formed to bring attention to ethical considerations around ongoing and newly proposed work using linked data technologies.

Following its establishment, the group began having monthly conversations around such topics and questions as privacy, safety, and well-being (e.g., What do you think of when you hear 'do no harm'?) and the advantages and contours of openness. These discussions benefited from participants' real-world experiences and ethical conundrums, as each brought increased awareness of the implications (both positive and negative) of linked data. The group emphasized the belief that ethics should be a priority—not an afterthought—of every initiative and that ethics are necessary to prevent, or at least reduce, harm to individuals and communities.

Over the next two years, the affinity group meetings shifted from more theoretical topics to more praxis-based considerations as the group worked towards aggregating and developing resources to guide projects and practitioners. Cross-pollination and collaboration with the LD4 Discovery Affinity Group on their white paper about knowledge panels inspired the vhecklist found in the Appendix to this volume.[3] In 2020, the Ethics Affinity Group realized the importance of capturing, documenting, and developing ideas about ethics from across the linked data community and ecosystem, and, inspired by the new Litwin Books series on Critical Information Organization in LIS, began working on the call for papers for the volume you now read.

This edited collection brings together contributions that explore the consideration (or lack thereof) of ethics in linked data initiatives. As such, it assumes that readers have a certain level of familiarity with the concepts of linked data and/or linked open data. A reader desirous of further information before proceeding

---

3. For the Knowledge Panel white paper, see http://bit.ly/ld4-kp-recipe.

should consult the footnoted resources.[4] The concepts and topics discussed in the following chapters often explicitly or implicitly apply to other information systems and concepts as well, including cataloging and classification systems, machine learning and artificial intelligence, and/or big data.

As the authors of *Linked Data for the Perplexed Librarian* define in the book's glossary, linked data refers to:

> Technologies and principles—including the use of structured data and unique identifiers to represent knowledge and resources—that, when used together, create machine-readable, extensible data that can be leveraged to expose and create relationships between datasets.[5]

---

4. Heidy Berthoud and Jeannie Hartley. "Practical Approaches to Linked Data." *The Serials Librarian*, March 9, 2021, 1–8. doi.org/10.1080/0361526X.2021.1885897; Scott Carlson, Cory Lampert, Darnelle Melvin, and Anne Washington. *Linked Data for the Perplexed Librarian* (Chicago: American Library Association, 2020); Ya-Ning Chen, "A Review of Practices for Transforming Library Legacy Records into Linked Open Data," in *Metadata and Semantic Research*, edited by Emmanouel Garoufallou, Sirje Virkus, Rania Siatri, and Damiana Koutsomiha, 755:123–33, *Communications in Computer and Information Science* (Cham: Springer International Publishing, 2017), doi.org/10.1007/978-3-319-70863-8_12; M. Hallo, S. Luján-Mora, and J. Trujillo, "Transforming Library Catalogs Into Linked Data," presented at the ICERI2014 Proceedings, 2014, library.iated.org/view/HALLO2014TRA; Ashleigh Hawkins, "Archives, Linked Data and the Digital Humanities: Increasing Access to Digitised and Born-Digital Archives via the Semantic Web," *Archival Science*, December 27, 2021, doi.org/10.1007/s10502-021-09381-0; Eero Hyvönen, "Publishing and Using Cultural Heritage Linked Data on the Semantic Web," *Synthesis Lectures on the Semantic Web: Theory and Technology* 2, no. 1 (October 17, 2012): 1–159, doi.org/10.2200/s00452ed-1v01y201210wbe003; Alexandre Passant, Philippe Laublet, John Breslin, and Stefan Decker, "A URI Is Worth a Thousand Tags: From Tagging to Linked Data with MOAT," *Int. J. Semantic Web Inf. Syst.* 5 (January 1, 2009): 71–94, doi.org/10/bnw7ck; Philip E. Schreur and Nancy Lorimer, "Linked Data in Libraries' Technical Services Workflows," in *Metadata and Semantic Research*, edited by Emmanouel Garoufallou, Sirje Virkus, Rania Siatri, and Damiana Koutsomiha, 755:224–29, *Communications in Computer and Information Science* (Cham: Springer International Publishing, 2017), https://doi.org/10.1007/978-3-319-70863-8_21; Hilary Thorsen, "Wikidata and the Linked Data for Production Project," n.d., 7; Brian M. Watson, "Linked Data," in *The Handbook of Archival Practice* (Lanham, MD: Rowman & Littlefield, 2021).

5. Scott Carlson, Cory Lampert, Darnelle Melvin, and Anne Washington, *Linked Data for the Perplexed Librarian* (Chicago: American Library Association, 2020).

Linked data platforms, ontologies, and architectures are rooted in the Resource Description Framework (RDF). Maintained by the W3C,[6] RDF is a technical standard including a data model that structures statements as triples consisting of a subject, predicate, and object. It calls for the use of Uniform Resource Identifiers (URIs) or Internationalized Resource Identifiers (IRIs) and can be serialized in various syntaxes such as XML, Turtle, and JSON-LD. Though they may store data using other structures and expand on the basic model, platforms like Wikidata take the triple and the concept of statements as their model.

Over the past two decades, many GLAMS institutions have become interested in implementing linked open data for their collections.[7] Help from major funding organizations—such as the Andrew W. Mellon grant that funded LD4P[8]— as well as programs sponsored by library cooperatives such as the Program for Cooperative Cataloging's Wikidata pilot[9] have contributed to these efforts and have increased awareness and understanding of these data models. Books like the excellent *Linked Data for the Perplexed Librarian*[10] provide accessible primers on structures and data modeling that relate linked data concepts to extant library and information science practices and traditions.

Frameworks and checklists for ethical data practice and design are well-established and continue to multiply (for example, Data

---

6. W3C or the World Wide Web Consortium is the main international standards organization for the World Wide Web.

7. For a detailed overview and literature review, see *"Ethical Explorations using Wikidata and Wikidata Tools to Expose Underrepresented Special Collection Materials"* in this volume.

8. The Linked Data for Production (LD4P) project was established in 2014 by Cornell, Harvard, and Stanford to explore the creation of native linked data in libraries' production environments. https://wiki.lyrasis.org/pages/viewpage.action?pageId=74515029.

9. See https://www.wikidata.org/wiki/Wikidata:WikiProject_PCC_Wikidata_Pilot/Wikidata_Resources.

10. Scott Carlson, Cory Lampert, Darnelle Melvin, and Anne Washington, *Linked Data for the Perplexed Librarian* (Chicago: ALA, 2020).

Feminism,[11] Design Justice Network Principles,[12] and Value Sensitive Design[13]). In addition, two reports about the use and ethical dimensions of machine learning and Artificial Intelligence (AI) in libraries have recently been published, indicating an intensifying interest in the topic.[14] Literature about inclusive metadata and reparative archival practice has also blossomed in recent years.[15]

However, scholarship and case studies about ethical and just practices in linked data contexts are still nascent. This book grew out of the observation that discussions about linked data and its potential often drift toward the utopian and technophilic, rarely examining darker implications or harmful consequences. Since technology cannot exist outside of social and environmental spheres, we believe that it is important for creators and stewards of linked data and its related systems to recognize and address the impact (whether intended or not, positive or negative) on the communities and individuals affected.

Consequently, this volume aims to address the emerging need for guidance, best practices, and lessons learned for ethical linked data. The central premise of the chapters that follow is that it is possible:

- to foreground ethics rather than apply them as an afterthought,
- to acknowledge and mitigate the damage caused by existing systems,

11. Lauren F. Klein and Catherine D'Ignazio, *Data Feminism* (Cambridge, MA: MIT Press, 2020), https://data-feminism.mitpress.mit.edu/.

12. https://designjustice.org/

13. Batya Friedman and David Hendry, Value Sensitive Design: Shaping Technology with Moral Imagination, 2019, https://ieeexplore.ieee.org/servlet/opac?bknumber=8709619.

14. Ryan Cordell, "Machine Learning + Libraries," LC Labs, 2020, https://labs.loc.gov/static/labs/work/reports/Cordell-LOC-ML-report.pdf; Thomas Padilla, "Responsible Operations: Data Science, Machine Learning, and AI in Libraries," 2020, https://www.oclc.org/research/publications/2019/oclcresearch-responsible-operations-data-science-machine-learning-ai.html.

15. Rachel Frick, and Merrilee Proffitt, "Reimagine Descriptive Workflows: A Community-Informed Agenda for Reparative and Inclusive Descriptive Practice," 2022, https://doi.org/10.25333/WD4B-BS51.

- to create a place and space of justice for the minoritized, and
- to enable more ethical outcomes in linked data projects.

To explore these possibilities, this volume collects the voices of practitioners, technologists, and developers working on linked data initiatives; scholars working at the intersection of ethics, cultural heritage, and technology; and workers in GLAMS to explore emerging and changing technical and ethical landscapes. Many authors focus on the convergence of slow libraries/archives practice, ethics of care, and foregrounding the data sovereignty, respect, safety, and dignity of the people represented in collections and their descriptions. Wikidata, with its relatively low-barrier platform for the creation of shared linked data, serves as both a test bed and a site of critique in case studies and critical readings. Labor issues, workplace contexts, and backlogs emerge as another theme across chapters. Even well-resourced projects report dealing with constraints related to time and staffing. Several chapters emphasize and provide examples of how linked data practices, standards, and technologies are decidedly not neutral.

Part I: Theories, Contexts and (Infra)structures

The first section of this volume dives into the theories, contexts, and (infra)structures of linked data and its impacts. The first chapter, "The Ethics of Sustaining Linked Data Vocabularies," by Dorothea Salo and Ruth Kitchin Tillman, is a clarion call for people, platforms, and organizations to sustain linked data vocabularies. The authors examine how, due to the interdependent nature of linked data, any decay in the integrity of a URI, vocabulary, or knowledge base can have resounding, deleterious effects throughout the data ecosystem. Using examples such as problems with the maintenance of purl.org permalinks, currency and inconsistency issues in DBpedia, as well as the many pitfalls of Wikidata, Salo and Tillman make the case that sustainability is a key ethical concern for linked data initiatives. They end their chapter with specific recommendations to help avoid unsustainable outcomes in different types of projects, including those that are grant-funded or involve crowdsourcing.

The remaining chapters in this section are arranged in pairs. The first pair offer historical examinations of linked data philosophies, policies, and platforms by examining their developments and effects on an individual level. In "Worlds in Conflict: A Dispute over Embedding Linked Data in Web Pages," Ryan Shaw examines ethical technical practice in linked data by analyzing past disputes over the design of RDFa. Reading W3C listserv discussions from the mid-2000s through the lens of pragmatic sociology and drawing on Boltanski and Thévenot's idea of common worlds, Shaw locates the underpinnings of the dispute over RDFa in disparate understandings of the common good that emerge from industrial versus connectionist worldviews. Shaw's sociological analysis of the history of RDFa reveals the hidden moral logic embedded in linked data technologies, exposing linked data standards as non-neutral. He advocates for clearer articulation of moral principles and suggests actions that can be taken to regulate injustice in linked data contexts, calling on proponents of linked data to develop reflexive practices that reveal "their own taken-for-granted assumptions about the common good."[16]

In "After Fedora: Linked Data and Ethical Design in the Digital Library," Kate Dohe also draws on publicly available discussions and her own experience to tell the story of Fedora Commons and its move to linked data in the form of the Linked Data Platform (LDP) specification. In a series of vignettes, Dohe details the Fedora platform with particular attention to Fedora 4's implementation and development. In explaining Fedora

---

16. See "Worlds in Conflict: A Dispute over Embedding Linked Data in Web Pages" in this text.

architecture and community discussions with examples drawn from her own practice, Dohe ponders what "the end of Fedora" might mean. Along the way, she raises key ethical questions about cost; skills and labor; what openness means; who has decision-making power; the role of wealthy institutions; the impacts of migrations and application performance on users; and standards adherence.

The second pair of chapters engage with the effects of linked data as a neoliberal Western technology. In "Triples and the Grammar of Control," James Kalwara and Erik Radio explain how RDF triples are predicated on Western, English language structure, hindering interoperability and multilingual inclusiveness. They argue that the subject-predicate-object RDF model (which mirrors the subject-verb-object (SVO) structure of English), does not accommodate subject-object-verb (SOV) languages well. Through close analysis of SOV sentence examples from languages such as Navajo and Mongolian, Kalwara and Radio show how forcing these statements into the RDF model can dilute and even contort their meaning. This misalignment has the potential to subsequently limit the discoverability of SOV language triples in linked data graphs. Standardization of the graph as grounded in RDF thus constitutes a hegemonic, "Western form of information coloniality."

In "Linked Data and Transindividual Ethics: An Essay in the Politics of Technology," Sam Popowich connects linked data and AI ethics through a Marxist lens, critiquing the very structures of linked data using Stuart Hall's theories of representation, ideology, and media. Popowich argues against dividing the discussion of linked data's descriptive function and its operationalization in software. Advocating for a reckoning with the socially constructed nature of both representation and encoding, Popowich explores how the transindividual perspective's prioritization of collective/community over individual rights could be relevant in a linked data context.

Part II: Ethical Considerations in the Face of Hegemonic and Institutional Forces

The second grouping of chapters focuses on ethical considerations and hegemonic, often discriminatory, influences such as colonialism, racism, and cis-centrism. These chapters examine how individuals or organizations have grappled with ethical concerns and choices within the contexts of these forces.

In "Indigenous Nationhood, Sovereignty and Linked Data: A Wikidata Case Study Examination of the Métis Nation," Stacy Allison-Cassin looks at the potentials and pitfalls of Indigenous engagement with linked data. The chapter opens with Allison-Cassin's work on the Canadian Federation of Library Association's Indigenous Matters Committee's FNMIIO (the First Nations, Métis, Inuit, Indigenous Ontology) and the process for the FNMIIO's vocabulary and authority development. The Committee soon realized that it was not possible to follow the same procedures for the Métis, who are recognized as Aboriginal, but unlike other Nations have no reserve lands, council listings, or similar authority. The rest of the chapter revolves around the "ongoing challenges around conceptualizing the Métis People" and how their complexity does not "fit into colonial epistemological systems." Allison-Cassin uses the representation of Métis identity in Wikidata as a starting point to document and explore the ethical issues and tensions around Indigenous in those systems. By examining concepts of identity, nationhood, Indigeneity, and personhood connected to the Métis Nation in Wikidata, Allison-Cassin illustrates that "naming is vitally interconnected to nationhood—to liberation, and self-determination"[17] and that the current implementation of these concepts in Wikidata does not benefit Indigenous communities. She explains that it is vitally important for users, implementers, and developers of linked

---

17. See "Indigenous Nationhood, Sovereignty and Linked Data: A Wikidata Case Study Examination of the Métis Nation" in this text.

data projects to "understand the connection between naming of Indigenous people and issues such as self-determination. It is not enough to ensure a label is correct, but that the data model, the connections within the repository and the links to external repositories must be appropriate and ethical."[18]

The chapter, "Colonial Histories of Linked Data Workflows," by Devon Murphy delves into the history and colonial residues of controlled subject vocabularies commonly used in GLAMs, revealing some of the same impulses to remove and assimilate Indigenous peoples in linked data architectures. Murphy critiques RDF structure as flattening, in that it aligns multiple vocabularies or terms on a one-to-one relationship between data. Arguing that linked data projects build on the colonial foundations of existing controlled vocabularies, Murphy cautions against a focus on terminology alone. While commending initiatives like the Manitoba Archival Information Network's (MAIN) revised LCSH subject terms and the Protocols for Native American Materials by SAA (Society of American Archivists), Murphy regards these as a "tempting trap for non-Indigenous institutions to solely amend the vocabularies, but not the protocols on how that information or the communities associated with it are treated," urging practitioners to "act preemptively and intentionally, spending the time to fully understand the colonial histories of all our linked data workflows and policies before implementation."[19]

In "Ethnological Vocabularies & GND's Authority Files: Ethical Issues & Practical Approaches," Moritz Strickert presents a two-pronged analysis centered on the Gemeinsame Normdatei (GND, the Integrated Authority File in use at German GLAMs). In the first part of his chapter, Strickert interrogates commonly-accepted principles of knowledge organization, finding that they "reflect a specifically-Western outlook in terms of both

---

18. See "Indigenous Nationhood, Sovereignty and Linked Data: A Wikidata Case Study Examination of the Métis Nation" in this text.

19. See "The Colonial Histories of Linked Data Workflows" in this text.

structure and scope" and any revisioning "require[s] a great deal of research, coordination and intellectual labor."[20] In the second part of his chapter, he discusses the collaboration and planning undertaken by the newly established Network for Sustainable Research Structures in Colonial Contexts, sponsored by the Deutsche Digitale Bibliothek (DDB, the German national digital library). Through international collaboration and direct consultation with communities of origin, these efforts aim to better represent materials in German GLAMs that were obtained under colonial regimes. Strickert concludes by arguing that "[m]ultivocality or multiperspectivity...should not be negotiated as opposites, but should be productively mediated in order to ensure the greatest possible global discoverability and accessibility."[21]

In "Non-Binary Gender Representation in Wikidata," Daniele Metilli and Chiara Paolini lay out an extensive, quantitative exploration of the history and current state of non-binary gender representation in Wikidata, mapping current data models for gender identities, outlining the history of difficulties concerning the definition and use of the Wikidata property for gender (P21), and compiling and analyzing statistical data on non-binary gender terms and demographics as represented in the database. Their chapter ends with an analysis of an English language corpus of Wikidata user discussions on gender using Latent Dirichlet Allocation (LDA) topic modeling. While Metilli and Paolini's conclusion that non-binary gender is currently not well represented in Wikidata is perhaps unsurprising, their analysis provides a baseline for assessing the continuing evolution of Wikidata, whether that be towards a more ethical inclusion of gender identities or towards more inaccuracy and insufficiency.

The "Minnesota Hip-Hop Collection And Wikidata: Ethical Considerations for a Majority White Institution," authored

---

20. See "Ethnological Vocabularies & GND's Authority Files: Ethical Issues & Practical Approaches" in this text.

21. See "Ethnological Vocabularies & GND's Authority Files: Ethical Issues & Practical Approaches" in this text.

by three University of Minnesota librarians—Kristi Bergland, Christine DeZelar-Tiedman and Patrick Harrington—explores the well-respected tradition of "lessons learned" in the digital humanities by reporting on their experience with their PCC Wikidata pilot.[22] Beginning with an introduction to the Archie Givens, Sr. Collection of African American Literature and the Minnesota Hip-Hop Collection, the authors go on to document how their initial exploration of metadata best practices for describing hip-hop creators in Minnesota was partially stymied by staffing, organizational changes, and the COVID-19 pandemic, but, more significantly, by their realization that they made some incorrect assumptions about the demographics of the collection. These roadblocks provided the authors with the opportunity to pause and question their initial approach, resulting in an exploration of ethical issues around representation and access as well as an analysis of specific points of failure and discussion of issues concerning race and cultural appropriation in hip-hop.

Part III: People and Communities

The chapters in the third section consist of case studies of linked data projects that explore issues around inclusion, privacy, and identity management for both individuals and communities represented in cultural heritage materials. Several of these chapters draw from the principles of slow libraries/archives or base their work in ethics of care.[23]

---

22. Digital Humanities Awards, "Best Exploration of DH Failure/Limitations," 2021, dhawards.org; James Cummings, "Learning How to Fail Better: Resilience in Digital Humanities Projects," presented at the Data, Culture & Society, University of Edinburgh, January 17, 2020, cdcs.ed.ac.uk/events/learning-how-fail-better-resilience-digital-humanities-projects; Max Kemman, "DH Failures vs Findings," Max Kemman (blog), February 28, 2019, maxkemman.nl/2019/02/dh-failures-vs-findings/.

23. For "slow archives", see Kimberly Christen and Jane Anderson, "Toward Slow Archives," *Archival Science* 19, no. 2 (2019): 87–116, https://doi.org/10.1007/s10502-019-09307-x. For "ethics of care," see "Information Maintenance as a Practice of Care," *The Information Maintainers*, D. Olson, J. Meyerson, M. A. Parsons, J. Castro, M. Lassere, D. J. Wright, et al, 2019, June, https://doi.org/10.5281/

In "LINCS: Ethical Considerations in the Development of Responsible Linked Open Data Infrastructure," Erin Canning, Sarah Roger, Kimberley Martin, and Susan Brown introduce readers to the Linked Infrastructure for Networked Cultural Scholarship (LINCS) project, a Canada Foundation for Innovation Cyberinfrastructure project aimed at converting datasets from humanities research into linked data for Canadian cultural research. With an emphasis on non-neutrality along with approaches from intersectional feminism and collaborative communities of practice, the project seeks to address tensions between openness and respectful limitations. The authors highlight ethical concerns and considerations for building linked open-data infrastructure and "re-platforming" humanities data (i.e., deriving or making secondary use of data) within this infrastructure. Throughout the chapter, they focus primarily on project policies and decision-making processes, including those related to prioritization of datasets, selection and adaptation of ontologies and vocabularies, dataset licensing agreements, and credit for data creators and stewards.

In "Ethical Expressions of Collective Memory: Re/presenting Central Brooklyn Jazz Oral Histories as Linked Data," Zakiya Collier and Sarah Ann Adams begin with the power of names to oppress, empower, claim, and reclaim. Sharing the work from the Linking Lost Jazz Shrines (LLJS) project, the authors foreground ethical considerations in project decision-making, name authority creation, and ontological data modeling. Working from a person-centered theory of archival care, the LLJS team consciously expands notions of the notability of those represented in the Weeksville Lost Jazz Shrines of Brooklyn (WLJSB) oral history collection. Working against the bibliographic paradigms that

zenodo.3251131; Michelle Caswell and Marika Cifor, "Neither A Beginning Nor An End: Applying An Ethics of Care to Digitizing Archival Collections in South Asia," in *The Routledge International Handbook of New Digital Practices in Galleries, Libraries, Archives, Museums and Heritage Sites*, edited by Hannah Lewi, Wally Smith, Dirk von Lehn, and Steven Cooke (New York: Routledge, 2019): 530.

privilege entities and their publication output, the team models data in a manner that conveys that "all forms of participation in Central Brooklyn's jazz culture are deemed valuable."[24] The chapter is also an invaluable window into some of the processes, philosophies, and ethical decisions guiding one of the most vibrant and significant linked open data projects today—a tremendous rethinking of the processes of cataloging, classification, description and linked data.

Oral histories are also the focus for Megan Macken, Madison Chartier, Sarah Milligan, and Julie Pearson-Little Thunder's "Oklahoma Native Artists Project: Oral Histories to Linked Open Data." As members of the Oklahoma Oral History Research Program, they detail how CARE principles (i.e., Collective Benefit, Authority to Control, Responsibility, Ethics)[25] and oral history best practices converge, and how new ethical questions arise when artists and their work are described in linked data platforms like Wikidata. The authors explore the potential benefits and difficulties of transforming unstructured oral histories into linked open data. While working toward increasing visibility of Oklahoma Native artists, they interrogate how inclusion and sovereignty can be enacted in linked data and oral history contexts. Guided by ethical checklists like the Ethical Toolkit for Engineering/Design Practice from the Markkula Center for Applied Ethics,[26] collaboration, consent, and deliberately slow process emerge as core aspects of the project's ethical practice.

In "'All We Want Are the Facts, Ma'am:' Negotiating User Needs and Creator Privacy in Name Authority Records," Hanna Bertoldi, Peggy Griesinger, and Mikala Narlock introduce readers to the University of Notre Dame's Marble (Museum, Archives,

---

24. See "Ethical Expressions of Collective Memory: Re/presenting Central Brooklyn Jazz Oral Histories as Linked Data" in this text.

25. "CARE Principles of Indigenous Data Governance." n.d. Global Indigenous Data Alliance, accessed August 21, 2022, https://www.gida-global.org/care.

26. Shannon Vallor, Brian Green, and Irina Raicu, *Ethics in Technology Practice*, The Markkula Center for Applied Ethics at Santa Clara University, 2018, https://www.scu.edu/ethics/.

Rare Books, and Library Exploration platform) project in order to surface ethical considerations related to the use of linked data for name authority records. Through user testing, Marble staff uncovered a need for more information about the creators of resources. Drawing on the framework of "slow librarianship," the authors question the ethics of leveraging linked data's technical capabilities to provide information about race and other identity affiliations, and to allow for multiple metadata values. They raise key issues such as a dearth of documentation of conversations between institutions and living creators and a lack of explanation of information sources and contexts of creation in user interfaces. The authors also question the prevalence of contingent and non-specialized labor in the creation of linked data.

In "Ethical Explorations Using Wikidata and Wikidata Tools to Expose Underrepresented Special Collection Materials," Darnelle Melvin and Cory Lampert of the University of Nevada, Las Vegas explore the use of Wikidata and its tools to expose materials related to Las Vegas's historic Westside neighborhood, a historic African American neighborhood located in Las Vegas. The authors were able to draw upon long standing community trust and partnerships built by the UNLV Oral History Research Center. By rooting their discussion in local contexts, Melvin and Lampert argue that an ethics of care should be applied to all stages of linked data projects, "in order to ensure that decision-making on all aspects of metadata design from creation through discovery to reuse is analyzed through an appropriate lens considering complex relationships and potential impacts of data in a digital world."[27] Following this argument, the authors demonstrate how

---

27. See "Ethical Explorations using Wikidata and Wikidata Tools to Expose Underrepresented Special Collection Materials" in this volume.

For the ethics of care framework, the authors cite Temi Odumosu, "The Crying Child: On Colonial Archives, Digitization, and Ethics of Care in the Cultural Commons," *Current Anthropology* 61, no. 22 and "Care Ethics | Internet Encyclopedia of Philosophy," UTM, accessed April 25, 2022, https://iep.utm.edu/care-eth/. Additionally, we would recommend Michelle Caswell and Marika Cifor, "Neither A Beginning Nor An End: Applying An Ethics of Care to Digitizing Archival Collections in South Asia," in *The Routledge International Handbook of New Digital Practices in Galler-*

each stage of their project operationalized an ethics of care, and their thinking as they navigated through the competing needs of metadata standards, system requirements, and linked data principles. Melvin and Lampert's concise and clear writing guides readers through a chapter equally technical and philosophical, producing a case study that rewards multiple re-reads.

Ethics in Linked Data Checklist

Finally, we include the LD4 Ethics in Linked Data Affinity Group's Ethics in Linked Data Checklist as an appendix to this volume. Inspired by a three-part article on fast.ai's blog titled "16 Things You Can Do to Make Tech More Ethical,"[28] the checklist was developed over the course of 2021 to 2022 in consultation with other LD4 Affinity Groups (especially the Wikidata and Discovery Affinity Groups) and attendees at multiple LD4 events and conferences. It was also circulated to the authors of the chapters in this volume for peer review and additional comments.

Divided into three major areas (Planning, Implementation, and Maintenance), the checklist presents a series of questions intended to spark reflection and action at each stage of the lifecycle of a linked data project. Questions cover topics such as Accessibility; Provenance, Sources, & Citations; Oppression & Harm; Inclusion & Diversity; Identity Management & Privacy; Data Sovereignty & Intellectual Property; and Sunsetting.

---

ies, Libraries, Archives, Museums and Heritage Sites, edited by Hannah Lewi, Wally Smith, Dirk von Lehn, and Steven Cooke (New York: Routledge, 2019).

28. The fast.ai project (tagline: "making neural nets uncool again") is a project by artificial intelligence researchers Jeremy Howard and Rachel Thomas that aims to make "deep learning" (i.e. artificial intelligence machine learning) more accessible by offering free courses, software, and other benefits. Beginning in April of 2019, Thomas authored an article with Rachel Thomas, "16 Things We can Do to Make Tech More Ethical, Part 1," fast.ai, April 2019, https://www.fast.ai/2019/04/22/ethics-action-1/#-checklist.

Final Thoughts

This book does not aim to constitute a formal treatise on ethical philosophy but rather is intended to serve as an exploration of how ethical practices can be employed in the development and management of linked data projects. Far from being pessimistic, we believe that engaging in critical and ethical analysis is ultimately an optimistic endeavor aimed at exposing problematic issues and generating best practices and guidelines for the implementation and use of linked data in GLAMs and elsewhere.

This book is not comprehensive. Each chapter brings unique insight into what it means to respect the individuals and communities that are described by linked data, and each institution or project's situation is distinct, necessarily emerging from and/or calling for localized and tailored approaches. As editors, we are also keenly aware of the limitations of our own perspectives and positionality as three white settlers. Our own gender, sexuality, dis/ability, and romantic/relationship identities informed our work as editors, and we deliberately sought out and recruited authors to speak on their own expertise and lived experiences relating to topics of race, indigeneity, and gender identity. However, there are surely perspectives missing from this volume. We also wish to acknowledge that the writing and organizing of this book has happened during the ongoing COVID-19 pandemic, which has deeply impacted the authors and editors who participated and is likely a factor that prevented others from contributing. We hope that more is published on this important topic, especially scholarship that centers minoritized perspectives and experiences.

Apart from this introduction, every chapter in this book was produced through a rigorous internal open peer review process.[29] After submission, each chapter was reviewed internally

---

29. Nature Neuroscience Editorial Board, "Pros and Cons of Open Peer Review." *Nature Neuroscience* 2, no. 3 (March 1999): 197–98, https://doi.org/10.1038/6295.;PLOS, "Open Peer Review," PLOS (blog), accessed July 15, 2022, https://plos.org/resource/open-peer-review/; Tony Ross-Hellauer, "What Is Open Peer Review? A Systematic

by authors of related chapters as assigned by the editors. For example, the authors who wrote about archives were assigned to review chapters that also discussed or focused on archives; authors who focused on Indigenous issues were assigned chapters that also focused on Indigenous issues, etc. Additionally, at least one (but more often two) external peer reviewers with relevant experience were recruited for each chapter from the linked data community. In situations where an author wrote on marginalized communities of which they are not a part, we asked them to find a qualified collaborator and ensure that the chapter was peer reviewed by someone deeply familiar with or from the community in question. Reviewers were given a month and a half to review and comment and authors were then given three to four weeks for revisions. Simultaneously, the book editors (Bri, Kathleen, and Alexandra) read and reviewed every chapter and offered substantial comments or revisions to four or five chapters each. Finally, every chapter underwent a final review and copyediting by the Series on Critical Information Organization in LIS Editors: Kelsey George and Violet B. Fox.

Acknowledgments

The editors and authors of this book would like to thank the following people for their generous contributions to the open peer review process: Sarah Ann Adams, Stacy Allison-Cassin, Suse Anderson, Kristi Bergland, Hanna Bertoldi, Susan Brown, Erin Canning, Madison Chartier, Crystal Clements, Zakiya Collier, Christine DeZelar-Tiedman, Kate Dohe, Peggy Griesinger, Jennifer Guiliano, Juliet L. Hardesty, Patrick Harrington, John Huck, James Kalwara, Effie Kapsalis, Cory Lampert, Megan Macken, Kimberley Martin, Darnelle Melvin, Daniele Metilli, Jeremy Munro, Devon Murphy, Mikala Narlock, Chiara Paolini, Sam

---

Review," F1000 Research 6 (August 31, 2017): 588, https://doi.org/10.12688/f1000research.11369.2.

Popowich, Erik Radio, Sarah Roger, Dorothea Salo, Ryan Shaw, Moritz Strickert, Ruth Kitchin Tillman, and Karly Wildenhaus.

The following people contributed to the development of the checklist via authoring, peer review, editing, or providing feedback: Alexandra Provo, Allison Bailund, Amanda Ros, Amarílis Corrêa, Brandie Pullen, Bree Midavaine, Brian M. Watson, Christine DeZelar-Tiedman, Crystal Clements, Dorothea Salo, Erin Canning, Hanna Bertoldi, Hector Correa, Hilary K Thorsen, Itza Carbajal, John Huck, Julie Hardesty, Kathleen Burlingame, Monika Soler Correa, Moritz Strickert, Naun Chew, Rhonda Super, Ruth Kitchin Tillman, Sarah Ann Adams, Sarah Osborne Bender, Stephen Hearn, and others not listed here

Finally, the editors extend their gratitude to the LD4 Ethics in Linked Data Affinity Group and the LD4 community at large for their engagement, participation, and support.

Part I:
Theories, Contexts, & (Infra)structures

The Ethics of Sustaining Linked Data Infrastructure

DOROTHEA SALO & RUTH KITCHIN TILLMAN

Introduction

The development of linked data vocabularies and infrastructure remains primarily project-based. While such experiments and short-term initiatives move the field forward, they often overlook the demands of ongoing maintenance and sustainability. Because linked data infrastructure and vocabularies are fundamentally interdependent, the deprecation or disappearance of one project cascades to damage other vocabularies and systems which had incorporated it into their design. Such losses undermine the development of a robust Semantic Web, particularly harming those who don't have the expertise or infrastructure to adapt quickly. In this chapter, we review several key cases of loss and rescue and propose maintenance and sustainability as core ethical responsibilities in linked data development.

Problem Statement

While linked data experimentation is worthwhile and necessary, it creates risk for the linked data ecosystem, which lives or dies by the reuse of URIs, vocabularies, and assertions. When maintainers abandon or destroy a trusted source of URIs, implementers must expensively retool, abandon, or accept severe feature limitations in the technology and processes relying on it. Repeated or serious source losses can even sow doubt about the entire linked data enterprise. Building a linked data vocabulary, therefore, creates an ethical commitment on behalf of downstream re-users to maintain or appropriately sunset it.

Linked data implementations rely on a stack of technologies:

- *permalink infrastructure* such as Handle, ARK, and PURL software and services;
- *infrastructure vocabularies (or ontologies)* such as Dublin Core, SKOS, BIBO, and BIBFRAME, which contain mostly classes and properties that serve as a standardized basis for triple statements; and
- *knowledge bases* such as VIAF, DBpedia, and Wikidata that contain mostly facts in the form of triples, which themselves combine permalink infrastructure, strings, and properties/classes from infrastructure vocabularies.

Breaking any of these layers has serious consequences. When permalink infrastructure breaks, any vocabulary or knowledge base relying on it also breaks, as URIs no longer resolve properly. When an infrastructure vocabulary breaks, those dependent on it may be able to manage for a time if the vocabulary is well-understood, but developers or maintainers ceasing to update documentation or letting it disappear altogether from the web will eventually drain semantic meaning from statements depending on the vocabulary. When knowledge bases are left to decay, the result can be outright misinformation.

We posit that, as a matter of best practice and responsibility to fellow professionals, the creators and funders of linked data infrastructure have an ethical responsibility to the people whose projects reuse their work and to the end users seeking out the information contained in the linked data itself. While we do not expect every experimental project to become permanent, we will demonstrate the serious impacts of broken infrastructure and share recommendations for project development, responsible funding, and clarity of maintenance commitments.

Case Studies

The threats to linked data infrastructures are not theoretical. Just as the disappearance of web content and the resulting reference rot of links in citations pervade the web, cultural heritage literature is replete with reports on exciting digital projects that no longer exist online or remain online but are no longer maintained and only partly functional. The following case studies illustrate the cascading consequences of breakdowns in linked data infrastructure, vocabularies, and knowledge bases.

BIBO and purl.org: Permalink Infrastructure and Vocabulary

In 2008, Bruce D'Arcus, a professor of human geography with an interest in citation practice, and Frédérick Giasson, a data scientist and consultant, released the Bibliographic Ontology (BIBO). BIBO is a vocabulary for structuring citations and bibliographic references for the Semantic Web. In March 2022, the Linked Open Vocabularies visualization tool identified forty other vocabularies that reuse BIBO in some way.[1] D'Arcus and Giasson followed many best practices, including minting a purl.org permalink to be used as the namespace URI.

The "Persistent Uniform Resource Locators" (PURL) service at purl.org was launched by OCLC[2] in 1995 as a permalink resolution service.[3] Like other resolver services, purl.org facilitates

---

1. Ontology Engineering Group, n.d, "Linked Open Vocabularies (LOV)," accessed March 30, 2022, https://lov.linkeddata.es/dataset/lov/vocabs/bibo.

2. A major US-based and globally active library institution which acts as a centralized MARC data aggregator, develops and supports library technology, and conducts research.

3. OCLC, n.d., "Report--CONSER PURL Pilot," accessed March 30, 2022, https://www.loc.gov/aba/pcc/conser/purl/documents/purlrept.pdf.

the relationship between a resource's identifier, which in a linked data context should not change, and its location on the web, which frequently changes for migration, branding, and other reasons. Although OCLC made the software for PURL resolution open-source, many PURL users, including the Dublin Core Metadata Initiative, relied on OCLC's own purl.org service. By the time the BIBO project launched, purl.org had been providing reliable service for 13 years.

At first, the BIBO maintainers' foresight in using purl.org paid off. Google Code, to which they had directed the PURL, announced its shutdown in 2013, necessitating a redirection. As long as the maintainers had access to the permalink resolution service, they could roll with these changes and still provide dereferenceable URIs to anyone who used BIBO. Then, toward the end of 2015, purl.org users suddenly found themselves unable to login and update their links, apparently because OCLC still considered the service "experimental," and it was maintained by a single person with other responsibilities.[4] The freeze lasted nearly a year, with the Internet Archive announcing in September 2016 that it would take over the service.

Before the service resumed, however, the BIBO maintainers lost control of their main domain (bibliontology.com) and could not update their purl.org redirections to a new domain because the purl.org infrastructure was frozen.[5] Though the situation was resolved once the handover from OCLC to the Internet Archive was complete, it points to the ethical necessity of maintaining permalink resolvers indefinitely, or at least planning for their legacy. The trust in purl.org lost through this incident has not been regained; at PIDapalooza 2020, an event dedicated to persistent identifiers, Dublin Core Metadata Initiative Managing Director Paul Walk started a discussion on risk management with respect

---

4. Frederick Giasson, "Debrief Related to the BIBO Server and Purl.Org," October 29, 2016. https://groups.google.com/g/bibliographic-ontology-specification-group/c/7WTE6VhyhMo.

5. Giasson 2016.

to purl.org, mentioning poor support from the Internet Archive among other reasons for concern.[6]

DBPedia and Wikidata: Knowledge Bases

When knowledge bases contain information about current affairs, lapses in timeliness breach the maintainers' ethical responsibility not to publish misinformation. Linked data knowledge bases such as DBpedia and Wikidata provide contextual connections that facilitate exploration of a concept or topic across the Semantic Web. They support research queries and can be used to provide enriched context for search results in commercial search engines, library databases, etc.

Launched in 2007, DBpedia is a linked data project that extracts structured data from Wikimedia sites, starting with Wikipedia, and transforms it into a queryable knowledge graph. Because the source data must undergo significant transformation to become linked data, DBpedia's knowledge graph has always been somewhat out-of-date. In 2015 and 2016, releases occurred approximately six months apart, meaning that the data released was about six months old at time of release. This caused noticeable data quality problems, such as a person's death date not appearing until six months to a year after their death. Then, after the "2016-10" release in July 2017, DBpedia releases halted. From July 2017 through the beginning of 2021, DBpedia's public resource pages and SPARQL endpoint returned results which had last been up-to-date in October 2016.

After the halt, DBpedia's factually incorrect query results increased, and critical new information failed to appear. DBpedia's data remained frozen through two United States presidential elections, changes in the Supreme Court, uprisings, and a pandemic.

---

6. Paul Walk, "What Shall We Do about PURL?" Google Docs, January 2020, https://docs.google.com/document/d/17TBUja8z8EJGx5ZEyknP3gWuPITf6lt-XkX-DHU_CKaY/edit?usp=embed_facebook.

When many updates were released at the end of January 2021, Donald Trump was finally labeled President of the United States while Joe Biden, who had been inaugurated several days before, was not (yet). At this point, incorporating DBpedia's data into another project would have inadvertently furthered the dangerous myth of a stolen election.

In their paper outlining the new DBpedia release process, Hofer et al.[7] describe how the increasing size of releases and concerns with data quality made the existing extraction, transformation, and loading processes unfeasible. Teams spent 2017 to 2019 developing new extraction/transformation processes and infrastructure such as the "Databus," where sets of DBpedia triples could be downloaded. While providing such extracts supports those who want to run their own triplestore, the divergence of Databus content from the data available through DBpedia's SPARQL endpoint risks confusion and downstream propagation of dangerous misinformation.

Actual updates to the DBpedia SPARQL querying service and public resource pages began again in early 2021, with a full data snapshot of 2021-06 data released in July 2021 alongside a promise of quarterly snapshots.[8] While this development is promising, the months between releases still allows outdated information to become misinformation, whose lethality to democracy (as with the attack on the Capitol on January 6, 2021) and to minoritized populations (as with mass murderer Dylann Roof in Charleston, SC or the genocide against the Rohingya people in Myanmar) has become starkly apparent in the years preceding this release. Knowledge bases have an ethical responsibility either to provide

7. Marvin Hofer, Sebastian Hellmann, Milan Dojchinovski, and Johannes Frey, "The New DBPedia Release Cycle: Increasing Agility and Efficiency in Knowledge Extraction Workflows," in *Semantic Systems: In the Era of Knowledge Graphs*, edited by Eva Blomqvist, Paul Groth, Victor de Boer, Tassilo Pellegrini, Mehwish Alam, Tobias Käfer, Peter Kieseberg, Sabrina Kirrane, Albert Meroño-Peñuela, and Harshvardhan J. Pandit, Vol. 12378. Lecture Notes in Computer Science. Cham: Springer International Publishing, 2020. https://doi.org/10.1007/978-3-030-59833-4.

8. Julia Holze, "Announcement: DBpedia Snapshot 2021-06 Release." DBpedia Association. July 23, 2021. https://www.dbpedia.org/blog/snapshot-2021-06-release/.

accurate data or to highlight information about their last update, which for a DBpedia release would be Wikimedia extract dates, not release dates.

While DBpedia was suspended in time, Wikidata, which permits live community editing, became a more popular choice of knowledge base in linked data communities. Although Wikidata editors can immediately address misinformation, it is not clear how often and how quickly they do (a concern we'll address further in best practices for crowdsourced projects), so we still see similar ethical pitfalls possible for Wikidata and DBpedia, as both are knowledge bases attempting to represent enormous amounts of human knowledge. One of linked data's great strengths is its distributed nature; when knowledge bases aspire to become a source for everything, they risk becoming single points of failure, as described below.

Other Infrastructure: Open Metadata Registry

Additional infrastructural services such as directories and instructional material complement the already-discussed permalink, vocabulary, and knowledge base infrastructures. For example, the Open Metadata Registry (OMR), a directory of linked data vocabularies and non-linked data "element sets," launched in 2006, was built by Diane Hillmann and Jon Phipps as part of the NSF-funded National Science Digital Library project. The NSF grant funding ended in 2010, leaving Hillmann and Phipps to run the Registry pro bono. As with many other unfunded and unsupported "passion projects,"[9] the Registry had neither succession plans in place nor a sunset plan, leaving it in limbo once its founders ceased work on it.

Although OMR is still open for contributions, contributions are unvetted; many are spam, many refer to abandoned projects,

---

9. Susan Brown, Patricia Clements, Isobel Grundy, Stan Ruecker, Jeffery Antoniuk, and Sharon Balazs, "Published Yet Never Done: The Tension Between Projection and Completion in Digital Humanities Research," *Digital Humanities Quarterly* 003, no. 2 (June 18, 2009).

and many mistake the Registry for a directory of linked data *properties* rather than whole vocabularies. Because of spam and malformed contributions, OMR is insufficiently accurate and trustworthy for downstream implementers to build upon. Moreover, OMR's existence wrongly appears to make the development, funding, and support of additional linked data vocabulary registries superfluous. Even communities wishing to develop such a registry could find themselves stymied by potential funders and contributors asking "Why not just use OMR?"

Crowdsourced Projects: Wikidata

Given the challenges of maintaining linked data work, crowdsourcing offers a promising solution. An engaged community can bring many experiences and perspectives and develop practices to ensure that maintenance work doesn't fall onto a single individual or contributing institution. In recent years, Wikidata has been a particularly successful example of crowdsourcing both infrastructure and knowledge bases. With its open participation model and a wealth of introductory tutorials, even the most underfunded cultural heritage worker or casual user can contribute, time permitting. Yet while using Wikidata allows linked data implementors to benefit from the contributions of thousands, centralizing gallery, library, archives, and museum (GLAM) contributions there raises the risk of Wikidata becoming a single point of failure.

Even when committed to supporting centralized infrastructure, institutions may struggle with its maintenance. In August 2021, Mike Pham, Senior Product Manager for Search at the Wikimedia Foundation, emailed the Wikidata listserv a request for feedback as they sought to address two threats to the Wikidata Query Service's (WDQS) ability to "provide acceptable service quality."[10] First, as more and more information is added to Wikidata, its maintainers are coming up against the technical limits of the Blazegraph software on which the query service is built. Second, Blazegraph is no longer actively maintained, meaning that bugs discovered will not be fixed and existing performance limits cannot be expanded. In this case, ironically, Wikidata's high levels of engagement and use significantly contribute to its increasing fragility.

Nor is infrastructure failure the only risk of centralization. Participating in centralized projects cedes control of data to the hosting institution. Catalogers are particularly familiar with this issue, as many of our libraries pay to contribute MARC records to OCLC, which turns around and sells them to other libraries rather than acting as an open hub for shared data. Even as our scholarly work falls under open access mandates, we cannot use these mandates to demand open licenses for our intellectual contributions to OCLC's centralized metadata store.

While Wikimedia spaces have a substantial contributor base, they demonstrate how, even with massive participation, documentation and quality of work varies widely between projects and aspects of projects. Some properties on Wikidata are primarily added by one or two contributors and have little documentation, even as other WikiProjects bring together engaged communities who create and observe best practices. Harrison's reporting on the Abstract Wikipedia project highlights concerns about Wikipedia entries which don't have enough community support for regular updates and become out-of-date (and may then be loaded into DBpedia, reinforcing its own timeliness issues).[11] Harrison

---

10. Mike Pham, "Wikidata Query Service Scaling Update Aug 2021 - Wikidata - Lists.Wikimedia.Org," August 19, 2021, https://lists.wikimedia.org/hyperkitty/list/wikidata@lists.wikimedia.org/thread/MSMKYTTWRZDD52JQLZCWPN4RSU-CLFFMZ/.

11. Stephen. Harrison, "Wikipedia Is Trying to Transcend the Limits of Human Language," *Slate Magazine*, September 1, 2021, https://slate.com/technology/2021/09/wikipedia-human-language-wikifunctions.html.

also notes the political agendas visible across different-language Wikipedia sites. Bianchini et al.[12] point out that while Wikidata and VIAF interoperate significantly, with VIAF serving as an important source of identifiers for Wikidata, the two projects' differing scope and contribution models lead to inconsistencies between them and less collaboration than might be ideal.

Although cultural heritage institutions sorely need outside voices as well, Wikidata contributors are more likely to represent a white, cisgender male perspective than they are most marginalized populations.[13] To invite crowds is to invite their implicit and explicit political views, which may directly conflict with the political agendas and goals to which GLAM institutions aspire. As notoriously has happened with Wikipedia itself,[14] this may mean Wikidata perpetuates oppressive practices leading to erasure and misrepresentation of marginalized subjects. For example, Wikidata editors disagree over the best way to describe noted synthesizer composer and transgender woman Wendy Carlos, since many of her compositions were released under her former "dead" name. Even as GLAMs seek to improve representation, their efforts may be overwritten or undermined by contributors prioritizing the oppressive status quo. Communities for whom data sovereignty is vital, as with many Indigenous communities globally, may also eschew participation in crowdsourced projects that cannot guarantee them control over representation or data reuse.[15]

12. Carlo Bianchini, Stefano Bargioni, and Camillo Carlo Pellizzari di San Girolamo, "Beyond VIAF: Wikidata as a Complementary Tool for Authority Control in Libraries," *Information Technology and Libraries* 40, no. 2 (June 17, 2021), https://doi.org/10.6017/ital.v40i2.12959.

13. The 2021 Wikidata community survey respondents reported being 75% male, 16% female, and just under 3% non-binary. https://commons.wikimedia.org/w/index.php?title=File:Wikidata_Community_Survey_2021.pdf&page=23.

14. Jackie Koerner, "Wikipedia Has a Bias Problem," Wikipedia@20, June 2019, https://wikipedia20.pubpub.org/pub/u5vsaip5/release/8.

15. Kimberly Christen, "Opening Archives: Respectful Repatriation," edited by Mary Pugh, *American Archivist* 74, no. 1 (2011): 185–210, https://doi.org/10.17723/aarc.74.1.4233nv6nv6428521.

Best Practices

How can linked data infrastructure designers, vocabulary builders, and implementers avoid either perpetrating or falling victim to the functional and ethical lapses described above?

For New Linked Data Projects

Best practices for project creators and maintainers include:
- Clearly documenting realistic maintenance, transfer, and sunsetting plans and communicating about changes.[16]
- Clearly stating whether the project is proof-of-concept or experimental.
- Giving the project its own domain name, which allows it to be transferred or rescued by a new project via owl:sameAs statements.
- Licensing the project for maximum transferability and use with minimal intellectual property worries: CC0, used by Wikidata among other projects, is an excellent choice, although we discuss below why it should not be the automatic choice for every project. European Union project creators should explicitly license or disclaim the sui generis database right.[17]
- Not inventing a vocabulary or term when an established, open, and well-supported vocabulary can fill the need. Creating a subclass or subproperty often makes more sense than inventing a class or property from whole cloth. Unnecessary vocabulary and term proliferation only

---

16. Even as we were writing this chapter, it became apparent that the SPARQL endpoint for the British Museum's linked data knowledge base had gone offline. While the endpoint has not been online for over a year (see the Twitter bot https://twitter.com/bm_lod_status which runs twice-daily checks), there has still been no statement from the British Museum on the subject.

17. Anything resembling OCLC's litigiousness with respect to the Dewey Decimal Classification (Skalbeck, 2003) is useless and unethical in a linked-open-data context.

worsens the sustainability problem and hinders communication via linked data.

Useful infrastructure that does not exist but could include:

- A permanent home for sunsetted vocabularies and (as often as possible) their domain names, a service such as perma.cc provides for websites cited in legal opinions. Such a home would have to undertake permalink redirection and creation and maintenance of any necessary owl:sameAs statements.

- Attention to the need to preserve and fund vocabularies created by and for populations without the resources or infrastructure to do it themselves.

- A way to deal with lapsed or unadoptable domain names for dead vocabularies and projects, is to avoid additional unfortunate situations like BIBO's. HTTP forwarding only works when the original domain has not been scooped up by a domain profiteer.

National libraries and standards bodies such as W3C or NISO are obvious candidates to build and maintain the above infrastructure, though such institutionalization is likely to slow further development and refinement of the vocabularies somewhat and risks the vocabulary maintainers becoming less or even not at all responsive to community needs (as happened with PURL).

At time of writing, few linked data projects had clear documentation about their maintenance and sunsetting plans. BIBO, for example, named its maintainers and provided a mailing list where its community of users could report issues. It did not, however, have a long-term plan for what would happen when its maintenance became something they could no longer commit to. Through discussions on the mailing list, maintainers identified transferring it to DCMI as the best choice they could make to ensure sufficient institutional support to remain viable. We recommend that linked data projects consider—and clearly document their decisions related to—these contingencies up front when developing and reusing infrastructure. At a minimum, maintainers should be available to answer questions and resolve issues.

For Projects Relying on Linked Data Infrastructure

We propose that implementers ask the following questions about a linked data infrastructure, knowledge base, or ontology before adopting it:

- Who sponsored this project?
    - What is their mission?
    - What is their vision for the project?
- Who owns the knowledge created by this project? Is it open?
- Who will be maintaining this project?
    - What is their track record on similar projects?
- Is there documentation for maintenance and sunsetting?
    - Is there a way to contact the maintainer? Are they responsive to such contacts? (check mailing list archives, github issues, etc)
    - Have they indicated what they commit to maintaining?
    - Have they indicated how frequently they will maintain or update it?
- Have they indicated what will happen if they are no longer able to maintain the project?

When assessing a project's sponsors, consider also whether the sponsor's mission or values differ from your own and if so, whether the disconnect raises ethical concerns about reusing their work. For example, in an August 2020 blog post, Michael Andrews discusses Google's use of schema.org to maintain its search hegemony.[18] While mission and values differences may

---

18. Michael Andrews, "Who Benefits from Schema.Org?" Story Needle (blog), August 23, 2020, https://storyneedle.com/who-benefits-from-schema-org/.

not mean that a project should not be used, they should at least shape how to engage with it.

Funding often impacts maintenance. When a project is grant-funded, find information about how the project will be maintained when the funding period ends. When considering an individual's or group's passion project or institution-specific initiative, investigate the creators' track record. Do they create exciting new products every 3-5 years without providing ongoing maintenance? If so, expect the project to lose support within a few years and plan accordingly.[19] While a commercial entity often has greater incentive and more funding to maintain linked data infrastructure that supports their business functions, they will prioritize choices that support their own agenda. Google, for example, has a long history of killing off projects[20] including Freebase, the open knowledge base it acquired and then shut down.[21]

For Grant Funders

The Open Metadata Registry illustrates how grant funding can perpetuate the creation of vocabularies and systems that die immediately or rot slowly once the grant ends. While the scale of its aspirations makes it stand out, OMR is not the only such

19. While in many cases this should mean not using the infrastructure or only doing so experimentally, you might also plan to contribute to open-source projects and even take over maintenance or "fork" a copy when the original maintainer moves on. It should also be noted that a good track record is not a reliable predictor of future developments. For example, purl.org documentation from 2014 does not even hint that OCLC might discontinue support in the future, let alone the next year. "OCLC has long been committed to facilitating access to the world's information, and that commitment stands behind PURLs, too." https://web.archive.org/web/20140705155410/http://purl.org/docs/faq.html#toc1.6. Similarly, a one-woman passion project might be well-maintained for over a decade but abandoned when life circumstances no longer allow her to support it.

20. Cody Ogden, "Killed by Google," Killed by Google, accessed March 21, 2022. https://killedbygoogle.com.

21. Although it allowed Freebase's developers to migrate Freebase's data to Wikidata, just as it had previously allowed the OpenRefine project to take over GoogleRefine (see Ontology Engineering Group, n.d., "Linked Open Vocabularies (LOV)," accessed March 30, 2022, https://lov.linkeddata.es/dataset/lov/vocabs/bibo).

project to go down this path. The OAI-PMH protocol, despite facilitating considerable interoperability between repositories and aggregators, has since fragmented into multiple incompatible implementations, and its bugs (such as lack of error messaging) have never been fixed. "Broader impact" statements facilitate this project-abandonment cycle by prioritizing novelty and hype at the expense of maintenance planning and by disincentivizing clear labeling of proof-of-concept projects and experiments.

To avoid this, grant agencies should insist that any application involving creation of linked data infrastructure, vocabularies, or knowledge bases include and properly assess a maintenance plan (analogous to a data-management plan) that includes how the vocabulary or knowledge base will be transferred or sunsetted if necessary. Project histories containing evidence of prior poorly maintained projects should count against serial project-abandoners seeking funding for new projects, and application reviewers should reject applications with impractical or missing maintenance plans. Grant agencies that fund proof-of-concept projects should insist that project staff clearly label them as such so that unsuspecting third parties do not build their own infrastructure on a foundation liable to crumble.

For Crowdsourced Projects

Defenses against commercial re-enclosure of contributed data to crowdsourced projects include open licensing, such as Wikidata's CC0 license, and strong, well-communicated community norms. Unfortunately, open licenses may deter participation from marginalized communities needing control, as discussed above. There is, as of yet, no perfectly ethical solution here, though incorporating vocabularies such as the Traditional Knowledge labels[22] may help; crowdsourced projects can only be transparent

---

22. Local Contexts, "TK Labels," accessed March 18, 2022, https://localcontexts.org/labels/traditional-knowledge-labels/.

to contributors and downstream users about the tradeoffs they faced and the reasoning behind their decisions.

Keeping a crowdsourced initiative inclusive is extraordinarily difficult; Wikipedia has clearly and repeatedly failed at it, and Wikidata's success to date may have a lot to do with its status as a niche product with a relatively small contributor base. Careful attention to the usability and accessibility of end-user contribution interfaces is fundamental to project success. Defending against e.g., white supremacists and transphobes calling themselves "trans-exclusive radical feminists" could include clearly documented contributor etiquette insisting on inclusion, with consequences for violations; "contributors" analogous to Wikipedia's notoriously non-inclusive "deletionists"[23] should be banned as quickly as possible. As patterns of harassment or other non-inclusive tactics emerge, project governance must be prepared to notice them, make rules about them, and cope with the inevitable rules-lawyering that will ensue.

Moreover, as Quinn Dombrowski has discussed[24] and the Open Metadata Registry demonstrates, crowdsourcing is not a viable maintenance model without excellent documentation for contributors, a substantial contributor base, and considerable time and effort from project leaders. Funders sponsoring crowdsourced projects should press applicants for a clear statement of who crowdsourced workers will be, and a plan for engaging and acknowledging them. Ethical crowdsourced projects must also consider labor ethics, eschewing hope labor,[25] undercompensated

23. Vasilis Kostakis, "Peer Governance and Wikipedia: Identifying and Understanding the Problems of Wikipedia's Governance," *First Monday*, March 12, 2010, https://doi.org/10.5210/fm.v15i3.2613.

24. Quinn Dombrowski, "The Directory Paradox," in *People, Practice, Power: Digital Humanities Outside the Center*, 1st ed. (Minneapolis, MN: University of Minnesota Press, 2021), https://www.upress.umn.edu/book-division/books/people-practice-power.

25. Miriam Posner, "Here and There: Creating DH Community," in *Debates in the Digital Humanities*, edited by Matthew K. Gold and Lauren F. Klein, 265–73 (Minneapolis, MN: University of Minnesota Press, 2016), https://doi.org/10.5749/j.ctt1cn6thb.25.

and under credited gig-economy labor,[26] prison labor,[27] and precarious labor.[28] Should crowdsourcing for a project not be feasible without abuse of labor, ethical project leaders must transfer or sunset the project.

Conclusion

At least some of the manifest reluctance among GLAMs to build and rebuild metadata workflows and services atop linked data has nothing to do with change resistance or even expense. Instead, potential implementers find, sometimes midway through their own project, that a project or service on which their idea relies has already degraded too much to be usable. This leads to further abandonment of projects and a breakdown in trust. Instability and degradation are not inevitable, but to prevent them, maintenance responsibilities must be planned for and taken seriously by all linked data stakeholders: funders, standards bodies, institutions, researchers, and implementers.

The linked data dream is a densely interconnected, fault-tolerant, computer-traversable network of individual data sources available for the building of any number of production-quality services. For this dream to become reality, however, project creators must supervise and maintain projects properly, sunset them as needed, and communicate their desired and actual reliability clearly. Similarly, funders, standards bodies, and other non-creator stakeholders must demand and facilitate adequate project maintenance and communication, and refuse to fund, maintain, and use vocabularies whose maintainers do not employ best practices.

---

26. Dhruv Mehrotra, "Horror Stories from Inside Amazon's Mechanical Turk," *Gizmodo*, January 8, 2020, https://gizmodo.com/horror-stories-from-inside-amazons-mechanical-turk-1840878041.

27. Alexis Logsdon, "Ethical Digital Libraries & Prison Labor?" October 2019, https://osf.io/w7xe3/.

28. South Asian American Digital Archive, "Against Precarity: Towards a Community-Based Notion of Fiscal Sustainability," Sustainable Futures (blog), July 30, 2018, https://medium.com/community-archives/against-precarity-towards-a-community-based-notion-of-fiscal-sustainability-815d1d889309.

Worlds in Conflict: A Dispute over Embedding Linked Data in Web Pages

RYAN SHAW

"Linked data" is a way of publishing data on the Web as a network of hyperlinked resources representing entities and relationships among them. Using Uniform Resource Locators (URLs) to identify and link to individual chunks of data results in federated networks of data that can be authored and updated in a distributed fashion. That authoring and updating can be done not only by people, but also by software, which can query the networks of data and process the results to produce new data. Libraries, archives, museums and initiatives for open science and open civic data are adopting this approach to collaboratively author and maintain federated datasets. So too are large companies seeking to federate data across their disparate internal subdivisions and external partners. Platform companies like Google and Facebook use linked data to integrate federated data into their "knowledge graphs," taking data from other companies and organizations and further processing it in order to "seamlessly" answer simple questions and automate routine transactions. As these public and private networks of data are being extended further and interlinked more densely, there are increasing concerns about the potential for harmful consequences and calls for the establishment of ethical principles.

Ethical codes aim to connect human conduct to moral principles. Discussions of ethical technical practice often focus on codifying those connections rather than clarifying the moral principles themselves, which are either left implicit or gestured to with abstract terms like *justice*, *equity*, *dignity*, or *agency*. A general sense of "the common good" is taken for granted, and attention quickly turns to the formulation of rules for ensuring that it is realized.[1] But there are a number of ways to specify the common good, and these different specifications are not necessarily compatible. Abstract appeals to justice can obscure these differences. Rather than examining abstract and flattening codes of technical conduct to understand what justice means to different people, it can be more fruitful to look at *disputes* in which participants attempt to justify some technical practice. An advantage of this strategy is that it does not assume a distinction between ethics and technics: a technical concern for effective and efficient functioning is treated as just one more way of specifying the common good, rather than something different in kind from ethical concerns about the ends to which effective and efficient functioning may be applied.

In this chapter I examine a dispute over RDFa, a proposed extension to the HTML standard intended to ease the authoring and publishing of linked data by allowing it to be embedded in Web pages. I begin by summarizing the theoretical motivation for examining disputes in order to find clues about the moral frameworks informing technical practice. Next, I provide historical context for the dispute, specifically the transfer of control over the HTML standard from the World Wide Web Consortium (W3C) to a consortium of companies developing Web browsers—a conjuncture that significantly shaped the subsequent development of the Web and the rise of the platforms that consume it. After describing the traces left by the dispute in public mailing list archives, I show that distinct and incompatible visions of the common good—not disagreement over technical issues—underlay the dispute. I

---

1. An excellent example is the W3C TAG Ethical Web Principles, ed. Daniel Appelquist and Hadley Beeman (W3C TAG Finding, October 6, 2021), https://www.w3.org/2001/tag/doc/ethical-web-principles-20211006.

conclude by considering implications for the ethical use of linked data. Organizations implementing linked data projects must consider whether their values are compatible with the moral order implied by linked data and, if so, they must take up the challenge of further strengthening and clarifying that order.

Pragmatic Sociology and the Common Worlds

Let's examine the dispute over RDFa through the lens of pragmatic sociology. Pragmatic sociology emerged in the 1980s and 1990s in response to the then-dominant programs of sociology that sought to reduce explanations of social behavior either to embedded biological or economic dispositions on the one hand, or to hegemonic sociocultural structures on the other.[2] While in those programs sociologists tended to reserve for themselves the right to formulate critique, pragmatic sociologists sought to avoid a "deep asymmetry between deluded actors and the clear-minded sociologist" by taking seriously the critical facilities people exhibit in ordinary life.[3] The modifier "pragmatic" was inspired by the study of pragmatics in linguistics. Where other branches of linguistics focus on explaining the abstract semantic or syntactic structures of language, pragmatics is the study of how people actually speak in concrete situations.

The goal of pragmatics is to infer something about people's linguistic competence: their subconscious, intuitive knowledge

---

2. For an overview of pragmatic sociology and how its exponents distinguish it from other sociological stances, see Luc Boltanski and Laurent Thévenot, *On Justification: Economies of Worth*, trans. Catherine Porter (Princeton, NJ: Princeton University Press, 2006), 1–18; Thomas Bénatouïl, "A Tale of Two Sociologies: The Critical and the Pragmatic Stance in Contemporary French Sociology," *European Journal of Social Theory* 2, no. 3 (1999): 379–96, https://doi.org/10.1177/136843199002003011; Luc Boltanski, *On Critique: A Sociology of Emancipation*, trans. Gregory Elliott (Cambridge: Polity Press, 2011), 18–49; Luc Boltanski, "A Journey Through French-Style Critique," in *New Spirits of Capitalism? Crises, Justification, and Dynamics*, ed. Paul du Gay and Glenn Morgan (Oxford: Oxford University Press, 2013), 43–59, https://doi.org/10.1093/acprof:oso/9780199595341.003.0002.

3. Boltanski, "Journey," 44.

of the more general rules governing speech. Likewise, pragmatic sociologists study what people do and say, especially in situations—such as disputes—where they are justifying their own actions or criticizing the actions and intentions of others. In such situations people typically try to transcend the specific contingencies of the immediate situation by appealing to more general ideas of what the world should be like.

The pragmatic study of disputes has deeply influenced social and historical studies of science and technology through the work of Bruno Latour, Michel Callon, and others.[4] But here I rely primarily on the pragmatic sociology of justification and critique developed in the work of Luc Boltanski with his collaborators Laurent Thévenot and Ève Chiapello. Boltanski and Thévenot observed that people try to settle disagreements by appealing to some higher common principle.[5] A higher common principle reduces complexity by providing clarity about what matters and what does not: some people, things, and arrangements are deemed more worthy of concern because they more clearly manifest the higher common principle, while others that do not are deemed less worthy. That sense of what matters—what Boltanski and Thévenot call a *sense of justice*, or *moral sense*—is not something constantly renegotiated in every concrete situation, but rather something that works more like a language, providing a continuity and stability that transcends specific moments of performance.

Like languages, intuitive understandings of moral order are learned not by studying grammar but through participation in social life. And just as more-or-less continuous and stable linguistic traditions can be identified within the kaleidoscopic variety of actual language use, so can traditions of moral justification be identified: what Boltanski and Thévenot call *common worlds*. A common world is not a "culture" that pervades every aspect of

---

4. Bénatouïl, "Tale," 380.
5. Boltanski and Thévenot, *On Justification*, 138.

a person's life and therefore ostensibly explains their behavior. Just as people may speak one language at home and another at work, "code switching" as they deem appropriate to the situation at hand, so can people fluidly transition from one world to another.[6] In the analysis that follows, I focus specifically on two of these common worlds: the *industrial* world identified by Boltanski and Thévenot and the *connectionist* world later identified by Boltanski and Chiapello.[7]

Prelude to a Dispute

Linked data is structured as a network of nodes and links between them. While there are many ways to define such a structure,[8] the definition endorsed by the W3C is the Resource Description Framework (RDF). RDF was designed to be an abstract model of (or way of structuring) data rather than a concrete syntax for (or way of writing down) data. In theory, RDF was "syntax-neutral,"

6. Were there no hope of moving between worlds, there would be no point in attempts to criticize or compromise with other orders of worth.

7. Boltanski and Thévenot, *On Justification,* 118–123, 203–211; Luc Boltanski and Ève Chiapello, *The New Spirit of Capitalism*, trans. Gregory Elliott (London: Verso, 2018), 103–163.

8. Structuring data as a network of nodes and links has a long history. Hogan et al. trace the lineage of knowledge graphs back to late nineteenth century attempts by Peirce, Frege and others to develop diagrammatic systems for facilitating formal reasoning. Aidan Hogan et al., *Knowledge Graphs* (Morgan & Claypool, 2022), 157–158, https://doi.org/10.2200/S01125ED1V01Y202109DSK022. In the 1970s, before the relational model came to dominate, many database management systems were based on network models, e.g., Charles W. Bachman, "Data Structure Diagrams," DATA BASE: A Quarterly Newsletter of the Special Interest Group on Business Data Processing 1, no. 2 (1969): 4–10, https://doi.org/10.1145/1017466.1017467. In the 1990s, work on publishing hypertextual indexes to technical documentation developed into Topic Maps, a generalized standard for describing knowledge structures. Steve Pepper, "Topic Maps," in *Encyclopedia of Library and Information Sciences*, ed. John D. McDonald and Michael Levine-Clark, 4th ed. (Boca Raton: CRC Press, 2018), 4611–4623. More recently, databases organized around a "property graph" model have become popular. Josep Lluís Larriba-Pey, Norbert Martínez-Bazán, and David Domínguez-Sal, "Introduction to Graph Databases," in *Reasoning Web: Reasoning on the Web in the Big Data Era*, ed. Manolis Koubarakis et al. (Cham: Springer, 2014), 171–194, https://doi.org/10.1007/978-3-319-10587-1_4.

meaning that the same data modeled using RDF could be written down or "encoded" in different ways. But in practice, the only syntax described in the initial RDF specification was RDF/XML, which used the Extensible Markup Language (XML) to encode RDF-structured data.[9] This would prove to be a barrier to the adoption of RDF, as RDF/XML syntax is hard for humans to read and requires sometimes-complicated XML libraries and tools for programmatic manipulation.[10] Simpler alternatives were discussed and developed, but by 2006, when Tim Berners-Lee introduced the term "linked data" to encourage the publication of useful data on the Web as RDF, none of these alternatives had yet become official standards.[11] One of the alternatives envisioned early on was a way to embed RDF-structured data in HTML pages as a way of piggybacking on the success of the HTML format. Various techniques for embedding RDF in HTML were considered,[12] one of which was to use existing HTML syntax (specifically, HTML attributes) to encode RDF structures.

As early as 2005, the microformats initiative had successfully demonstrated that HTML attributes could be used to embed structured data in Web pages.[13] A microformat is an agreed-upon convention for using the HTML class attribute to indicate that an HTML element contains a certain type of data value. While microformats can be used only to embed specific kinds of data such as contact information and calendar events, their success bolstered support for a similar effort at the W3C called RDFa

---

9. Resource Description Framework (RDF) Model and Syntax Specification, ed. Ora Lassila and Ralph R. Swick (W3C Recommendation, February 22, 1999), https://www.w3.org/TR/1999/REC-rdf-syntax-19990222/.

10. Furthermore, standard tools for validating XML documents cannot be used to check that RDF/XML documents are valid RDF, which begs the question of why to use XML at all.

11. Tim Berners-Lee, "Linked Data," Design Issues, last modified October 25, 2006 (archived November 15, 2006 at https://web.archive.org/web/20061115043657/https://www.w3.org/DesignIssues/LinkedData.html).

12. RDF in XHTML, ed. Ben Adida (W3C Task Force Document, October 12, 2004), https://www.w3.org/2001/sw/BestPractices/HTML/2004-10-12-tf.

13. Wikipedia contributors, "Microformat," Wikipedia, https://en.wikipedia.org/w/index.php?title=Microformat&oldid=1057681034 (accessed December 14, 2021).

(for "RDF attributes").[14] However, the RDFa designers found that it was not possible to encode all possible RDF data using existing HTML attributes without running the risk of misinterpreting ordinary HTML as embedded data. Thus, their design called for extending the HTML specification by adding five new attributes. In their view, this was not a problem, as the W3C had been working for several years on a "modular" version of HTML—called XHTML—that would allow precisely this kind of extensibility. But then something happened that made it a problem: the W3C lost control of HTML.

XHTML was part of the W3C's long-term plan to replace HTML with something (in their view) better-suited to the kinds of complex, dynamic "applications" that were beginning to supplant simple "pages" on the Web. With the rise of the commercial Web, more and more developers had been turning to Flash and other proprietary technologies to create richer "user experiences." HTML had been carefully designed to give browsers control over content rendering, something crucial for people with visual impairments, living in areas with low bandwidth, or simply wanting to access the Web on their own terms. Catering to corporate interests more concerned with brand identity and intellectual property than universal access, these new technologies put content publishers firmly in control and threatened the vision of an open Web. W3C experts believed that replacing HTML documents with "compound documents" constructed from modules defined in different XML-based markup languages would provide a viable open alternative to these proprietary technologies, allowing developers to build more complex Web applications in a way consistent with the success of HTML.[15] HTML allows people to create interactive, multimedia hypertext declaratively,

---

14. RDFa in XHTML: Syntax and Processing, ed. Ben Adida, Mark Birbeck, Shane McCarron, and Steven Pemberton (W3C Working Draft, October 18, 2007), https://www.w3.org/TR/2007/WD-rdfa-syntax-20071018/.

15. Compound Document Use Cases and Requirements Version 2.0, ed. Steve Speicher and Petri Vuorimaa (W3C Working Draft, December 19, 2005), https://www.w3.org/TR/2005/WD-CDFReqs-20051219/.

by learning a set of tags and attributes (i.e., a markup language) rather than procedurally, by using a full-fledged programming language, and the W3C hoped to do the same for the new generation of Web applications.[16]

But the ease of authoring HTML comes at the price of complexity in the software responsible for interpreting and rendering HTML: the Web browser. The W3C's vision for modular compound documents implied a quantum leap in the complexity of Web browsers—or so it seemed to the engineers responsible for those browsers. Rather than take on the unprecedented challenge of developing a rendering engine for compound documents, these engineers preferred to focus on improving the performance, consistency, and capabilities of browsers' JavaScript engines, thus allowing developers to build Web applications procedurally.[17] In response to a 2004 W3C workshop that sought to build consensus on a way forward for Web applications and compound documents, engineers from Apple, Mozilla, and Opera openly rejected the W3C vision and, behind the leadership of Opera (and soon-to-be Google) employee Ian Hickson, announced their intention to continue work on new HTML-related specifications outside the purview of the W3C.[18] The new standards organi-

---

16. When programming procedurally, one provides a specific set of steps to be executed. Writing code in a language such as JavaScript or Python is procedural programming, giving the machine specific instructions to be carried out. When programming declaratively, one provides a description of a desired outcome. The machine then determines the specific steps to be carried out to achieve that outcome. Authoring a Web page using HTML and CSS is declarative, because one provides a description of the desired layout and style rather than the specific set of steps necessary to achieve that layout and style in a browser window on some particular device.

17. Wanda Cox (AC Representative for Apple), "RE: Apple's XForms CFR Response," www-forms-editor@w3.org mailing list archives, W3C, September 3, 2003, https://lists.w3.org/Archives/Public/www-forms-editor/2003Sep/0006.html; The Mozilla Foundation and Opera Software, "Position Paper for the W3C Workshop on Web Applications and Compound Documents" (position paper, The W3C Workshop on Web Applications and Compound Documents, San Jose, CA, June 1–2, 2004), https://www.w3.org/2004/04/webapps-cdf-ws/papers/opera.html.

18. "What is the WHATWG and Why Did It Form?" WHATWG and HTML 5 FAQ, The WHATWG Blog (archived December 7, 2006 at https://web.archive.org/web/20061207215558/http://blog.whatwg.org/faq/#whattf)

zation was dubbed the Web Hypertext Application Technology Working Group (WHATWG), and Hickson became the editor of the HTML specification, with ultimate responsibility for deciding what would be included in it.

Reading the WHATWG Mailing List

In June 2004 the WHATWG established a publicly archived, open mailing list through which to develop the HTML specification.[19] It was primarily on this mailing list that the dispute over RDFa examined here took place. The dispute began in August 2008, when a member of the list pointed out that a proposal submitted to the W3C for embedding licensing metadata in Web pages depended on the use of new attributes—those required to encode RDFa—not provided for in the WHATWG version of the HTML specification.[20] The immediate response was that there was "absolutely no reason to extend html to accomodate [*sic*]" the proposal,[21] a sentiment with which the editor of the HTML specification agreed.[22] This in turn led to the editors of the RDFa specification and other proponents of RDFa joining the WHATWG mailing list to advocate for their point of view, leading to a dispute over RDFa that would continue, off and on, for approximately the next year.

---

19. Ian Hickson, "WHAT open mailing list announcement," whatwg@whatwg.org mailing list archives, W3C, June 5, 2004, https://lists.w3.org/Archives/Public/public-whatwg-archive/2004Jun/0000.html.

20. Matt Bonner, "Creative Commons Rights Expression Language," whatwg@whatwg.org mailing list archives, W3C, August 20, 2008, https://lists.w3.org/Archives/Public/public-whatwg-archive/2008Aug/0300.html.

21. Tab Atkins Jr., reply to "Creative Commons Rights Expression Language," whatwg@whatwg.org mailing list archives, W3C, August 20, 2008, https://lists.w3.org/Archives/Public/public-whatwg-archive/2008Aug/0301.html.

22. Ian Hickson, reply to "Creative Commons Rights Expression Language," whatwg@whatwg.org mailing list archives, W3C, August 20, 2008, https://lists.w3.org/Archives/Public/public-whatwg-archive/2008Aug/0305.html.

As a "lurker" on the WHATWG mailing list during the period
of the dispute, I observed it unfold in real time. I have worked
with linked data, RDF, and their predecessor technologies since
1997, and so I am deeply familiar with both linked data and the
types of arguments made for and against it. For the purposes of
this study, however, I did not rely solely on that familiarity but
re-immersed myself in the archives of the mailing list in order to
attend to the details of how the dispute unfolded in writing.

The WHATWG hosts a public archive of its (no longer
active) mailing list, but it is incomplete and not easily searchable. Fortunately, the W3C maintains a searchable and complete
archive, which was used to carry out this study.[23] I began by
using the W3C archive's search functionality to find every message posted to the WHATWG mailing list between August 2008
and July 2009 that contained the terms *RDFa*, *RDF*, *metadata*, or
microdata anywhere in the subject line or body of the message.
I was then able to identify the thread (tree of messages created
by senders replying to earlier messages, typically all having the
same subject line) to which each message belonged and read it
in its entirety. As I read, I took note of arguments that appealed
to concepts beyond the immediate technical details of RDFa
implementation. I identified five major themes: collaboration
and coordination, expertise and consensus, community and scale,
human labor and machine labor, and the role of search engines. In
my analysis below, I interpret these themes in terms of Boltanski
and Thévenot's common worlds model. While I did not initially
set out to apply the common worlds model to the RDFa dispute,
after completing the process described above, I began to see how
their model could be applied to the themes I had identified.

The Industrial Case against RDFa

The WHATWG discussions I read often revolved around questions of proper process. Ian Hickson (founder of the WHATWG

---

23. whatwg@whatwg.org mailing list archives, W3C, https://lists.w3.org/Archives/
Public/public-whatwg-archive/.

and editor of the HTML specification) repeatedly outlined the WHATWG's process for evaluating RDFa or any other proposed addition to the HTML specification. First, the problem to be solved by the proposed addition must be clearly stated in the form of a "use case."[24] Next it must be demonstrated that the problem is "is one that needs solving,"[25] which can be done by presenting evidence that "the bulk of users"[26] face the problem and that current solutions are inadequate "hacks."[27] If the proposed problem passes these tests, the next step is to enumerate all possible solutions in order to identify the one that most effectively and efficiently solves the problem. Finally, "the relevant implementors"—browser vendors, search engine companies, or creators of HTML authoring and validation tools—must show a willingness to implement the identified solution.[28] At each stage, participants in the process must "use rational debate, back up their opinions with logical arguments, present research to justify their claims, and derive proposals from user needs."[29] These arguments were to be evaluated solely "based on their technical merits and on what supporting research they have, and not on the number of times they were made" or the number of people making them.[30]

According to the criteria outlined above, in the eyes of many members of the WHATWG, human-authored metadata on the

24. Ian Hickson, reply to "RDFa is to structured data, like canvas is to bitmap and SVG is to vector," whatwg@whatwg.org mailing list archives, W3C, January 18, 2009, https://lists.w3.org/Archives/Public/public-whatwg-archive/2009Jan/0210.html.

25. Ian Hickson, reply to "Creative Commons Rights Expression Language," whatwg@whatwg.org mailing list archives, W3C, August 21, 2008, https://lists.w3.org/Archives/Public/public-whatwg-archive/2008Aug/0315.html.

26. Ian Hickson, reply to "Creative Commons Rights Expression Language," www-archive@w3.org mailing list archives, W3C, August 24, 2008, https://lists.w3.org/Archives/Public/www-archive/2008Aug/0073.html. Note that this message was posted to a part of the thread that spilled out of the WHATWG mailing list onto another mailing list—a not uncommon occurrence.

27. Hickson, reply to "RDFa is to structured data," https://lists.w3.org/Archives/Public/public-whatwg-archive/2009Jan/0210.html.

28. Ibid.

29. Ibid.

30. Ian Hickson, reply to "Self-imposed RDFa cool-down period," whatwg@whatwg.org mailing list archives, W3C, August 29, 2008, https://lists.w3.org/Archives/Public/public-whatwg-archive/2008Aug/0604.html.

Web had already failed to pass muster as a reliable and useful technology: "We have shown time and time again that when metadata mechanisms face the wider Web community, they fail."[31] The case against human-authored metadata on the Web goes as follows: such metadata only works in "controlled environments" such as "a small coherent community where all the participants have compatible goals."[32] Within these controlled environments, it is possible to ensure that people create and use metadata honestly, conscientiously, and intelligently. But in the absence of mechanisms for enforcing this discipline, some people's "inherent greed and evilness" will lead them to author metadata dishonestly.[33] Others will be lazy, not caring enough "to bother doing a good job"[34] and content to live with "terrible metadata hygene [sic]."[35] And even among those people who work diligently and honestly, many will be incompetent, unable to create and use metadata without "making huge mistakes."[36] As a result, outside of controlled environments, "the metadata becomes an utter mess, misused, wrong, missing, syntactically incorrect, semantically incorrect, unusable."[37]

31. Ian Hickson, "RDFa," whatwg@whatwg.org mailing list archives, W3C, August 22, 2008, https://lists.w3.org/Archives/Public/public-whatwg-archive/2008Aug/0345.html.

32. Hickson.

33. Ian Hickson, reply to "RDFa Problem Statement (was: Creative Commons Rights Expression Language)," whatwg@whatwg.org mailing list archives, W3C, August 26, 2008, https://lists.w3.org/Archives/Public/public-whatwg-archive/2008Aug/0416.html.

34. Ian Hickson, reply to "Creative Commons Rights Expression Language," www-archive@w3.org mailing list archives, W3C, August 21, 2008, https://lists.w3.org/Archives/Public/www-archive/2008Aug/0024.html.

35. Hickson, "RDFa," https://lists.w3.org/Archives/Public/public-whatwg-archive/2008Aug/0345.html.

36. Ian Hickson, reply to "RDFa," whatwg@whatwg.org mailing list archives, W3C, August 22, 2008, https://lists.w3.org/Archives/Public/public-whatwg-archive/2008Aug/0354.html.

37. Hickson, "RDFa," https://lists.w3.org/Archives/Public/public-whatwg-archive/2008Aug/0345.html.

The arguments marshaled against human-authored metadata on the Web by WHATWG participants closely followed a template established by influential tech pundit and science fiction author Cory Doctorow in his 2001 essay "Metacrap."[38] Doctorow began his argument against reliable human-authored metadata by observing that "people lie," "people are lazy," and "people are stupid."[39] An implicit assumption of Doctorow's argument was that the Web is an environment that is uncontrolled and inherently uncontrollable—a tenet among libertarian Web evangelists since its inception.[40] The uncontrollable nature of the Web means that reliable human-authored metadata is "a pipe-dream," Doctorow argued, but there is an alternative that works reliably: implicit, observational metadata, derived through statistical analysis of human behavior.[41] The premise that aggregation and analysis of large-scale data could work reliably in uncontrolled environments where human-authored metadata was destined to fail was picked up a few years later by tech pundit and consultant Clay Shirky, who incorporated it into a just-so story purporting to explain the success of Google and the decline of its competitor Yahoo.[42] Both Shirky and Doctorow advocated addressing the problem of the uncontrolled Web through the carefully controlled creation, analysis, and extraction of value from large datasets, derived from the Web but not part of it. Their exemplar was the Google search index: impossible to construct without the Web, but not itself available as a resource openly published on the Web. It would

---

38. Doctorow, "Metacrap: Putting the Torch to Seven Straw-Men of the Meta-Utopia," August 26, 2001 (archived August 31, 2001 at https://web.archive.org/web/20010831024354/http://www.well.com/~doctorow/metacrap.htm).

39. Doctorow, "Metacrap."

40. John Perry Barlow, "A Cyberspace Independence Declaration," February 9, 1996 (archived December 20, 1996 at https://web.archive.org/web/19961220115636/http://www.eff.org/pub/Publications/John_Perry_Barlow/barlow_0296.declaration).

41. Doctorow, "Metacrap."

42. Shirky, "Ontology is Overrated: Categories, Links, and Tags," Clay Shirky's Writings About the Internet (archived May 18, 2005 at https://web.archive.org/web/20050518032708/http://shirky.com:80/writings/ontology_overrated.html).

provide a blueprint for today's machine learning models, trained on data from the open Web but only rarely open to inspection themselves.

Echoing Doctorow and Shirky, RDFa critics on the WHATWG mailing list asserted that the success of web search engine companies obviated the need for human-authored metadata, since "search engines probably already 'understand' pages with far more accuracy than most authors will ever be able to express."[43] While acknowledging limits to that understanding, they argued that investment of technical effort should focus on transcending those limits through advances in natural language processing: "Google's experience is that natural language processing of the actual information seen by the actual end user is far, far more reliable than any source of metadata. Thus from Google's perspective, investing in RDFa seems like a poorer investment than investing in natural language processing."[44] Human authoring of metadata is a poor investment because it "require[s] us to solve a fundamentally unsolvable pair of problems (making humans not be lazy and making humans not be evil)."[45] Rather than technical resources being squandered on unsolvable problems of human nature, they should be invested in ventures more likely to result in effective functionality: "To scale to the whole Web, the only thing I can see working is the computers understanding human language."[46]

The arguments made against RDFa and in favor of natural language processing reflect a system of values characteristic of

---

43. Hickson, reply to "RDFa Problem Statement," https://lists.w3.org/Archives/Public/public-whatwg-archive/2008Aug/0416.html.

44. Ian Hickson, "Trying to work out the problems solved by RDFa," whatwg@whatwg.org mailing list archives, W3C, December 31, 2008, https://lists.w3.org/Archives/Public/public-whatwg-archive/2008Dec/0404.html.

45. Hickson, reply to "RDFa Problem Statement," https://lists.w3.org/Archives/Public/public-whatwg-archive/2008Aug/0416.html.

46. Ian Hickson, reply to "Creative Commons Rights Expression Language," whatwg@whatwg.org mailing list archives, W3C, August 28, 2008, https://lists.w3.org/Archives/Public/public-whatwg-archive/2008Aug/0476.html.

what Boltanski and Thévenot identify as an *industrial* world in which the common good is equated with efficient functioning.[47] In this world, expert technicians are valued for the responsibility they assume over the planning and execution of realistic projects for the future.[48] The valorization of technicians is linked to their ability to exercise *control*, not through the direct exercise of power over others but through decomposing complexity into less complex elements and "predicting less complex actions by integrating them into a larger overall plan."[49] This decomposition and re-integration is achieved by marshaling lists of use cases and requirements, tools of definition, measurement, and planning, "the instruments for defining and measuring [that] constitute the situation of action as a *problem* leading to the formulation of *hypotheses* and calling for a solution."[50] Immorality in the industrial world is associated with laziness and inefficiency due to a lack of motivation or qualifications. These vices lead to waste, pollution, and deterioration—"mess" and "crap"—all symptoms of a poorly controlled system.[51] But harmonious functioning can be restored through the introduction of carefully controlled machinery and "operations of *standardization* and *formalization* [making] it possible to see the world through data *expressed* in numbers, *quantified*, ready to be *processed*, combined, *added up*."[52]

The Connectionist Case for RDFa

The arguments made by proponents of RDFa and linked data reflect a system of values characteristic of what Boltanski and Chiapello refer to as a *connectionist* world.[53] In this world,

47. Boltanski and Thévenot, *On Justification*, 118–123, 203–211.
48. Boltanski and Thévenot, 206.
49. Boltanski and Thévenot, 209.
50. Boltanski and Thévenot, 208.
51. Boltanski and Thévenot, 205.
52. Boltanski and Thévenot, 210.
53. Boltanski and Chiapello, *New Spirit*, 103–163.

project managers are valued for their ability to tap into their personal networks and quickly assemble teams with complementary knowledge and skills.[54] The status of project managers is linked to their role as redistributors of information and links, putting formerly separated people into contact by integrating them into new networks.[55] This redistribution of links is achieved through the cultivation of informal relations with trusted partners from past projects. These relations are maintained through savvy use of new communication technologies, so that they may be kept in reserve and re-engaged when necessary for new projects.[56] Immorality in the connectionist world is associated with an inability to engage in new projects, due either to a failure to communicate effectively or an unwillingness to reciprocally share information and links. These vices lead to the monopolistic hoarding of information within closed networks: silos that benefit privileged insiders but do not extend the network for the greater good.[57] Hence the importance of lowering barriers to communication and coordination, allowing links to proliferate and ensuring that the network will be able to flexibly support innovative projects.

The dispute over RDFa on the WHATWG mailing list was instigated by a proposal[58] submitted to the W3C by Creative Commons, a nonprofit founded in 2001 to provide "flexible, customizable intellectual-property licenses" that people posting work on the Web could use to legally define acceptable uses of that work.[59] The proposal described the Creative Commons Rights Expression Language (ccREL), a method for embedding

---

54. Boltanski and Chiapello, 115–116.

55. Boltanski and Chiapello, 121–122.

56. Boltanski and Chiapello, 117–118.

57. Boltanski and Chiapello, 119–120.

58. ccREL: The Creative Commons Rights Expression Language, ed. Hal Abelson, Ben Adida, Mike Linksvayer, and Nathan Yergler (W3C Member Submission, May 1, 2008), https://www.w3.org/Submission/2008/SUBM-ccREL-20080501/.

59. Hal Plotkin, "All Hail Creative Commons / Stanford Professor and Author Lawrence Lessig Plans a Legal Insurrection," SFGate, February 11, 2002 (archived November 5, 2012 at https://web.archive.org/web/20121105090944/http://www.sf-gate.com/news/article/All-Hail-Creative-Commons-Stanford-professor-2874018.php).

these licenses in Web pages using RDFa. As ccREL was one of the first major applications envisioned for RDFa, Creative Commons also became involved in the design of RDFa itself: as the proposal puts it, "RDFa was designed by the W3C with Creative Commons' input."[60] This is relevant because, as the ccREL proposal demonstrates, the Creative Commons vision was deeply rooted in the connectionist world. Boltanski and Chiapello note that the innovative project managers of the connectionist world are modeled on artists and scientists.[61] Creative Commons also centers artists and scientists as subjects: the ccREL proposal concludes by asserting that "Creative Commons wants to make it easy for artists and scientists to build upon the works of others when they choose to."[62] Artistic and scientific collaboration is framed as network-building activity to be stimulated through the provision of technological tools and infrastructure that lower barriers to sharing information and making mutual connections: "the minimal infrastructure required to enable collaboration and invention, while letting it flourish as an organic, distributed process."[63]

In the artistic-scientific model of collaboration valorized by Creative Commons, small groups work autonomously while maintaining an openness to opportunistic links with other groups. Maintaining local autonomy without foreclosing on opportunities for connection is repeatedly emphasized by advocates for RDFa and linked data: "... there are a very large set of very small problem spaces relevant to a small group at a time. Like RDF itself, RDFa is meeting the problem of allowing these people to share machine-processable data without previously coordinating

60. ccREL, RDFa and concrete syntax for Work properties, https://www.w3.org/Submission/2008/SUBM-ccREL-20080501/#SECTION00051000000000000000.

61. Boltanski and Chiapello, *New Spirit*, 115–116.

62. ccREL, Conclusion, https://www.w3.org/Submission/2008/SUBM-ccREL-20080501/#SECTION00080000000000000000.

63. ccREL, Conclusion.

their approach."[64] Linked data exemplifies the close association between connections and information in the connectionist world: "Information is at once the result and the condition of multiplying connections ... To succeed in discovering good connections, such information must be integrated into a representation of the universe to be explored. In a network world, however, there can be no question of an overarching representation. Useful representations are local, singular, circumstantial ..."[65] To cultivate relations of interdependence and trust, people in the connectionist world need "fine-grained, open information" rather than comprehensive standardization.[66] Fine granularity means that representations can be local but overlapping: "... what RDF is really about is publishing data in a fine-grained enough matter that applications can easily overlap. That's why you can ignore parts of the data if you don't need it. You get a much more loosely-coupled, opportunistic Web, that way ..."[67]

The loose coupling of small autonomous groups is essential to how innovation and creativity are conceived in the connectionist world. Rather than being associated with inspired genius, in the connectionist world "creativity is a function of the number and quality of links. Moreover, it is a matter of *recombination*, rather than creation *ex nihilo*, and readily assumes a 'distributed' form (as one talks of 'distributed intelligence'), with responsibility for innovation being allocated between different actors."[68] "Distributed innovation" is a recurrent theme of linked data advocates, who argue that adding support for RDFa to the HTML specification "will help make many small communities happy,

64. Charles McCathieNevile, reply to "Trying to work out the problems solved by RDFa," whatwg@whatwg.org mailing list archives, W3C, January 1, 2009, https://lists.w3.org/Archives/Public/public-whatwg-archive/2008Dec/0416.html.

65. Boltanski and Chiapello, *New Spirit*, 113.

66. Boltanski and Chiapello, 130.

67. Ben Adida, reply to "Creative Commons Rights Expression Language," whatwg@whatwg.org mailing list archives, W3C, August 29, 2008, https://lists.w3.org/Archives/Public/public-whatwg-archive/2008Aug/0568.html.

68. Boltanski and Chiapello, *New Spirit*, 129.

each in their own way ... That's the power of RDF, and the idea behind RDFa is to enable that distributed innovation within HTML."[69] Making an argument against central planning similar to that made by the Austrian economist Friedrich Hayek[70]—but with fine-grained, open data playing the role of information about prices—linked data advocates argue that an unknown future is best prepared for by enabling distributed intelligence. Creative Commons argues that needs "not yet envisioned" must be addressed through innovation that proceeds "in a distributed fashion in different communities,"[71] just as Hayek argued that "decentralized planning by many separate persons," by making use of each individual's "special knowledge of circumstances of the fleeting moment not known to others," would outperform centralized industrial planning.[72]

Tim Berners-Lee identified "non-centralisation" as a core requirement for the Web, asserting that it "must allow existing systems to be linked together without requiring any central control or coordination."[73] This specter of a "central bottleneck" is frequently invoked by linked data advocates. For example, in the RDFa dispute, critics of linked data often pointed to microformats as a superior alternative to RDFa. As explained above, microformats are an alternative means of embedding metadata in HTML, the main difference being that microformat metadata vocabularies[74] are developed through a centralized standardiza-

---

69. Ben Adida, reply to "RDFa," whatwg@whatwg.org mailing list archives, W3C, August 22, 2008, https://lists.w3.org/Archives/Public/public-whatwg-archive/2008Aug/0366.html.

70. Hayek, "The Use of Knowledge in Society," *The American Economic Review* 35, no. 4 (September 1945): 519–530.

71. ccREL, Creative Commons and RDF, https://www.w3.org/Submission/2008/SUBM-ccREL-20080501/#SECTION00021000000000000000.

72. Hayek, "Use of Knowledge," 522.

73. Tim Berners-Lee, "Information Management: A Proposal," March 1989, https://www.w3.org/History/1989/proposal.html.

74. A metadata vocabulary is a fixed set of terms for naming the kinds of things to be described, what properties those things may have, and (in some cases) the values that those properties can take. A metadata vocabulary that is designed to support formal reasoning and inference about the described things is known as an "ontology." Meta-

tion process very similar to the one WHATWG adopted for the HTML specification.[75] RDFa advocates repeatedly rejected this process as "unworkable"[76] for the distribution innovation they envisioned, as it would introduce a point of centralized control:

> It seems "bloodtype" is more important in Japanese culture than in Western Europe, but that the toolset and design provided by RDFa allows independent extension of FOAF in Japan without expensive central bottlenecks.[77]

> Who decides what the right due diligence is? One organization for *all* topics, ever? An RDF vocabulary can be created by the proper community … rather than assuming that one central group should be the centralized bottleneck for all development. In other words, RDF vocabularies function like the web does: decentralized, let the best sites/vocabs win.[78]

> What happens when the people you're justifying your design to are the gatekeepers? What happens when they don't understand the problem you're attempting to solve? Or they disagree with you on a philosophical level? Or they have some sort of political reason to not allow your vocabulary to see the light of day (think large multi-national vs. little guy)?[79]

---

data vocabularies defined using RDF support formal reasoning and inference, and this was often cited by advocates as a point in favor of RDFa over alternatives such as microformats. Critics of RDFa, on the other hand, expressed doubts that formal reasoning was either effective or necessary.

75. "So You Wanna Develop a New Microformat?" Microformats Wiki, last modified October 6, 2005 (archived October 19, 2005 at https://web.archive.org/web/20051019000344/http://microformats.org/wiki/process).

76. Ben Adida, reply to "Creative Commons Rights Expression Language," whatwg@whatwg.org mailing list archives, W3C, August 21, 2008, https://lists.w3.org/Archives/Public/public-whatwg-archive/2008Aug/0331.html.

77. Dan Brickley, reply to "RDFa Problem Statement," whatwg@whatwg.org mailing list archives, W3C, August 26, 2008, https://lists.w3.org/Archives/Public/public-whatwg-archive/2008Aug/0414.html.

78. Ben Adida, reply to "'Just create a Microformat for it' - thoughts on micro-data topic," whatwg@whatwg.org mailing list archives, W3C, May 5, 2009, https://lists.w3.org/Archives/Public/public-whatwg-archive/2009May/0039.html.

79. Manu Sporny, reply to "'Just create a Microformat for it' - thoughts on micro-data topic," whatwg@whatwg.org mailing list archives, W3C, May 6, 2009, https://lists.w3.org/Archives/Public/public-whatwg-archive/2009May/0045.html.

For similar reasons, linked data advocates also rejected natural language processing and machine learning as potential network-killers. Since these technologies require expensive investments in expertise and computation power that few organizations are in the position to make, relying on them introduces another potential point of central control. RDFa advocates repeatedly expressed concern about making connection and collaboration on the Web dependent on Google or other "big tech" intermediaries:

I'm not sure a web design should be predicated on the existence of Google ...[80]

We can reasonably assume the existence of large search engines covering a good part of the public Web, Google being a well-known example. But we can't necessarily assume their owners will offer reliable machine-friendly APIs [application programming interfaces] to that data, with terms of service that are sufficiently unconstrained ... the constraints are significant. And may change at any time ...[81]

It would seem important that the Web easily enable small-time users of data to efficiently communicate with one another, without the need to have one of the giants as an intermediary ... Google ... can afford to run a huge organisation with massive computer power and many engineers ... there are many others who find that processing structured data is more efficient for their needs than doing free-text analysis of web pages ... these are the people whe [*sic*] have decided that investing in RDFa is a far more valuable exercis [*sic*] than trying to out-invest Google in natural language processing.[82]

These concerns reflect the characteristic moral sense of the connectionist world, which condemns "the networker [who] keeps information to himself, weaves connections in secret ...

---

80. Ben Adida, reply to "RDFa," whatwg@whatwg.org mailing list archives, W3C, August 22, 2008, https://lists.w3.org/Archives/Public/public-whatwg-archive/2008Aug/0370.html.

81. Dan Brickley, reply to "RDFa," whatwg@whatwg.org mailing list archives, W3C, August 23, 2008, https://lists.w3.org/Archives/Public/public-whatwg-archive/2008Aug/0375.html.

82. McCathieNevile, reply to "Trying to work out," https://lists.w3.org/Archives/Public/public-whatwg-archive/2008Dec/0416.html.

avoiding a situation where others can pursue them without going through him … [whose] monopolistic conduct leads fairly rapidly to the closure of the network" such that it no longer serves the common good.[83]

Worlds in Conflict

Conflicting visions of the common good, not disagreement over technical issues, precipitated the dispute over RDFa. Technical disagreements can be resolved through an industrial test of strength such as the process prescribed by the WHATWG. But such a resolution is impossible when "the very reality of the common good underlying the legitimacy of the test is contested," as it was in this case.[84] The WHATWG appealed to RDFa advocates to submit to an industrial test, insisting that "it is important to actually make sure the problem you are solving is one that needs solving,"[85] but RDFa advocates denounced the test as invalid: "Who gets to decide which problems need solving?"[86] Having to justify RDFa by demonstrating that it would solve a problem for "the bulk of users" ran counter to the fine granularity linked data advocates required to enable distributed innovation: "Are we only trying to solve problems that the *bulk* of users know they have? What about enabling new solutions that will provide a new category of solutions that the bulk of users can't quite put their finger on?"[87] Linked data advocates' focus on small communities made no sense to the WHATWG: "There are thousands of small communities with their own needs, we can't possibly

83. Boltanski and Chiapello, *New Spirit*, 120.

84. Boltanski and Thévenot, *On Justification*, 223.

85. Hickson, reply to "Creative Commons," https://lists.w3.org/Archives/Public/public-whatwg-archive/2008Aug/0315.html.

86. Adida, reply to "Creative Commons," https://lists.w3.org/Archives/Public/public-whatwg-archive/2008Aug/0331.html.

87. Ben Adida, reply to "Creative Commons Rights Expression Language," www-archive@w3.org mailing list archives, W3C, August 24, 2008, https://lists.w3.org/Archives/Public/www-archive/2008Aug/0076.html.

address each one in HTML. Indeed, we have design principles that make addressing the needs of small communities an explicit non-goal."[88] Those principles, linked data advocates countered, could not be applied to metadata vocabulary design: "A somewhat strained analogy would be bringing in representatives from all of the cultures of the world and having them agree on a universal vocabulary. It is an untenable prospect, there is too much diversity in the world to agree on one master vocabulary."[89] In the connectionist world, a universal solution is untenable, but in the industrial world it is the very definition of the common good: "That's pretty much exactly what Unicode did. Or what we're doing with HTML. That doesn't seem untennable [*sic*], it seems quite reasonable."[90]

RDFa advocates' disagreement with the WHATWG exemplifies how people in the connectionist world call the industrial world into question:

> ... flexibility, their ability to adapt and learn continuously, become major advantages, which take precedence over their technical expertise (knowledge changes so quickly) and their experience. Personality make-up, the qualities of communication, listening and openness to differences, thus count for more than efficiency as measured by the ability to achieve predefined objectives. Work methods are developed in line with constantly changing needs: people organize themselves and invent local rules that are not amenable to totalization and comprehensive rationalization by some putative organization department.[91]

Ultimately, this disagreement was resolved through an uneasy compromise. Of the use cases identified for RDFa, only two were

---

88. Hickson, "RDFa," https://lists.w3.org/Archives/Public/public-whatwg-archive/2008Aug/0345.html.

89. Manu Sporny, "RDFa Problem Statement (was: Creative Commons Rights Expression Language)," whatwg@whatwg.org mailing list archives, W3C, August 25, 2008, https://lists.w3.org/Archives/Public/public-whatwg-archive/2008Aug/0410.html.

90. Hickson, reply to "RDFa Problem Statement," https://lists.w3.org/Archives/Public/public-whatwg-archive/2008Aug/0416.html.

91. Boltanski and Chiapello, *New Spirit*, 135.

deemed efficiently solvable through changes to the HTML specification: providing metadata to search engines that could be used
to enhance the presentation of search results[92] and "annotat[ing]
structured data that HTML has no semantics for, and which
nobody has annotated before, and may never again, for private
use or use in a small self-contained community."[93] The latter was
an attempt to reformulate the values of the connectionist world
in the form of a "problem" acceptable to the industrial world—
part of the process of working out a compromise between two
worlds.[94]

RDFa itself, however, was rejected as a solution to these problems in favor of an alternative, dubbed "microdata," designed by
Ian Hickson to better agree with his engineering sensibilities.
Microdata was simpler and less flexible than RDFa, making
it easier to write efficient microdata parsers. But from the perspective of the connectionists, the most significant difference
was that microdata rejected the use of URLs as identifiers, thus
eliminating the one feature of RDF that promotes visions of a
globally distributed network of data. Hickson made it clear that
microdata was designed not to enable the construction of this network but instead "for private use or use in a small self-contained
community."[95]

Two years later, microdata would become the initial focus
of schema.org, a consortium founded by Google, Microsoft, and
Yahoo to manage one master vocabulary that website administrators could use to "help search engines and other applications
better understand your content and display it in a useful, relevant

92. Ian Hickson, "Providing enhanced search results," whatwg@whatwg.org
mailing list archives, W3C, May 19, 2009, https://lists.w3.org/Archives/Public/pub-
lic-whatwg-archive/2009May/0269.html.

93. Ian Hickson, "Annotating structured data that HTML has no semantics for,"
whatwg@whatwg.org mailing list archives, W3C, May 10, 2009, https://lists.w3.org/
Archives/Public/public-whatwg-archive/2009May/0116.html.

94. Boltanski and Thévenot, *On Justification*, 281.

95. Hickson, "Annotating structured data," https://lists.w3.org/Archives/Public/
public-whatwg-archive/2009May/0116.html.

way."[96] Schema.org was a response to what became the first major use of RDFa: Facebook's Open Graph Protocol, intended to ease the process of incorporating Web content into Facebook's "social graph."[97] Ironically, rather than devolving power to small independent communities, embedding linked data in Web pages accelerated the centralized hoarding of information by providing a way for "content producers" to make themselves more legible to these platforms' data processing regimes. In retrospect, linked data advocates undermined their own vision by focusing on technical standards for encoding metadata rather than the much harder problem of establishing a framework of general conventions within which independent groups could define their own vocabularies in a decentralized-yet-loosely-connectable way. As a result, organizations often choose to use linked data not in order to exercise local autonomy, but in exchange for preferential treatment on centralized platforms, to whom they relinquish control over vocabulary design decisions rather than investing in the labor and expertise necessary to retain control themselves.[98]

By making these observations, I am not suggesting that practitioners considering the use of linked data should necessarily adopt connectionist values. Instead, I am emphasizing that linked data is not a neutral technology: it comes equipped with its own moral logic, a logic that may not sit easily with the values espoused by organizations implementing it. For example, linked data and the Web are sometimes assumed to be "democratizing" forces well-suited to the aims of civic institutions like libraries and local governments. But the common good understood as a collective good, realizable through democratic expression of the

---

96. "Why Use Microdata?" Getting Started with Schema.org, Schema.org (archived on June 6, 2011 at https://web.archive.org/web/20110606061323/http://www.schema.org/docs/gs.html#microdata_why).

97. "The Open Graph Protocol," last modified December 10, 2010 (archived on December 11, 2010 at https://web.archive.org/web/20101211091635/http://ogp.me/).

98. Erik Radio and James Kalwara, "The Trajectory of Linked Data in Late Capitalism," *Journal of Documentation* 78, no. 3 (2022): 597–612, https://doi.org/10.1108/JD-02-2021-0037.

general will, is not how the common good is understood in the connectionist world.[99] Nor does the connectionist world, despite its reliance on the maintenance of local connections, respect communitarian rootedness, traditional ways of knowing, or the authoritative wisdom of elders and ancestors—calling into question the idea that linked data is particularly well suited to organizing indigenous cultural heritage or projects of decolonization.[100] Boltanski and Chiapello argue that, beginning in the 1970s, critiques of capitalist institutions were successfully defused through the deployment of a connectionist grammar that elides the differences between putting on a play, organizing a protest, and closing a factory: all become "projects."[101] The appeal of linked data may be due in part to the ease with which the connectionist grammar can assimilate such a variety of activities.

On the other hand, it may be that linked data advocates do, in fact, believe in the connectionist ideals that Creative Commons and others have made seem so attractive. If this is the case, then there is still a need for clearer articulation of, and mechanisms for enforcing, the principles of justice native to the connectionist world—principles that Boltanksi and Chiapello refer to as the "projective city." Boltanski and Chiapello identify three ways that unjust exploitation in the connectionist world might be regulated:

1. frameworks for inventorying contributions to the network so as "to put an end to exploitation that is bound up with the low visibility of certain contributors";[102]

2. fairer rules of remuneration, modeled after the collective agreements pursued by unionized workers, but where

99. Boltanski and Thévenot (*On Justification,* 107–117, 185–193) name the *civic* world as the one that identifies the common good as democratic expression of a collective will. For how connectionist goods can be mistaken for civic ones, see Alejandro Diaz, "Through the Google Goggles: Sociopolitical Bias in Search Engine Design," in *Web Search: Multidisciplinary Perspectives,* ed. Amanda Spink and Michael Zimmer (Berlin: Springer-Verlag, 2008), 11–34.

100. Boltanski and Chiapello, *New Spirit,* 133–135.

101. Boltanski and Chiapello, 111.

102. Boltanski and Chiapello, 382.

"remuneration" is understood not only in terms of fairer pay for participation in individual projects, but also as fairer opportunities to acquire and maintain the skills and reputation necessary to ensure participation in future projects;[103] and

3. equality of opportunity for mobility, through mechanisms intended to provide everyone (not only those who are already well-integrated into the network) with opportunities to cultivate new links and reestablish those that have withered.[104]

Their analysis suggests that linked data advocates should focus on:

1. standards and methods for comprehensively crediting contributions to the network of linked data projects, no matter how small;
2. rules for providing contributors with rewards in forms besides public recognition or the warm feelings yielded by volunteering; and
3. programs for ensuring that not just the already-well-connected (e.g., the Wikimedia Foundation, Yale University, or the Getty Research Institute) have the opportunity to grow their networks.

Alongside these efforts (and particularly in relation to #2 above), there needs to be recognition and renewed critique of how linked data, by facilitating the process of analyzing and codifying resources into distinctive but re-combinable features,[105] potentially renders all kinds of resources newly amenable to commodification: "ideas ... and information about other people's [social] relations or ... their state of health, their political, aesthetic, intellectual, etc., inclinations" and so on.[106]

---

103. Boltanski and Chiapello, 384–391.
104. Boltanski and Chiapello, 392–398.
105. Boltanski and Chiapello, 445–446.
106. Boltanski and Chiapello, 378.

Toward Diplomacy among Reflexive Technical Institutions

Distinct and incompatible visions of the common good led to the dispute over RDFa and prevented its resolution through the WHATWG specification process. That process allowed for the evaluation of competing designs with respect to an industrial ideal of efficient and effective functioning, but did not allow for consideration of any competing ideals. Hence the frustration of RDFa advocates, who sought in vain to promote their ideal of greater network connectivity in solely technical terms. Rather than repeat that mistake, proponents of linked data might reflect on how their rhetoric reveals their own taken-for-granted assumptions about the common good. If upon reflection they decide to re-confirm their commitment to connectionist ideals, then they can address the challenge of enunciating and advocating for a connectionist ethics. Alternatively, they might conclude that their conception of the common good requires facilities not afforded by linked data and seek alternative ways of building the world they envision.

The ethical use or non-use of linked data cannot be assured by formulating rules of conduct without clarifying the moral principles underlying those rules. Even once those moral principles are clarified, ethical considerations cannot be treated as independent from the technical evaluation of possible architectures for arranging and relating people, technologies, protocols, expressions, and ideas—among which linked data is just one possibility. Deciding how and how not to connect and arrange things is not a separate activity to be carried out before or after moral questions have been addressed; it is *how* moral questions are addressed. Ethically deploying or dismantling technological systems such as linked data depends not on finding the right moral framework beforehand, but on building better technical institutions. Good technical institutions are reflexive, attempting as best they can to provide stability and continuity according to some specific conception of the common good. But they are also aware of that conception's limitations and open to the possibility of transformation in response to critiques born of other conceptions.[107] This implies that good technical institutions need other good technical institutions willing to critique, confront, and occasionally compromise with them. Perhaps we need to redirect effort away from developing yet more ethical frameworks for technology, and toward developing more diplomatic ones.

107. Ryan Shaw, "The Missing Profession: Towards an Institution of Critical Technical Practice," in Proceedings of CoLIS, the Tenth International Conference on Conceptions of Library and Information Science, Ljubljana, Slovenia, June 16-19, 2019, Information Research 24, no. 4 (2019), http://informationr.net/ir/24-4/colis/colis1904.html.

After Fedora: Linked Data and Ethical Design in the Digital Library

KATE DOHE

Introduction

A common application of linked data technology within the library community is within digital library projects, many of which are deep into their second decade. For nearly as long, practitioners have raised implementation concerns about linked data in digital projects:

- that transforming and maintaining linked data requires expensive programming expertise,
- that the application stack is complex and fragile with many interdependencies, and
- that the maintenance communities are often made up of only a handful of qualified volunteers.

Such technical issues present very real ethical dilemmas for digital library practitioners – is the cost of implementing linked data systems so high as to be inaccessible to all but the wealthiest organizations? Do the decision makers in these open source projects accurately reflect the needs of a variety of libraries and cultural heritage organizations? Is the meticulous nature of designing around linked data worth the inevitable slowdowns in making digital content accessible? Is the level of effort of large-scale migration to linked data and maintenance over time actually sustainable in cash-strapped academic libraries? On balance, can these applications meet the needs of users as they evolve over time? Are these projects and their user communities truly "open" and egalitarian? These questions took on new urgency in the digital library community in 2015, when the newly-released Fedora 4 repository application implemented native linked data architecture,[1] and initiated a sea change in the digital library application landscape.

Any conversations about the practical applications of linked data are inevitably shaped by the design, features, and functionality of the systems that store and serve that data to end users. Many aspects of digital librarianship and its technologies are not widely understood within the profession at large, and as a result practitioners rely heavily on community-driven professional networks for information sharing, open-source application development, and informal support and consulting. In particular, this chapter will explore digital repository management and the small, semi-formal practitioner communities built around specific systems, and how implementation decisions about open source technical projects might be made by a handful of individuals. Repository software is frequently difficult to explain from both a usability and infrastructure perspective, especially when those systems are rarely seen or directly accessed by end users. The complexity and breadth of our professional mission—to make as much of our most unique and valuable content discoverable and available to anyone in the world, preserve it for future generations, and deliver an inclusive end user experience for both novice browsers and expert researchers—means our digital infrastructure has vastly expanded to meet our requirements. However, the nuances of the digital library ecosystem requires both individual and institutional participants to possess a level of technical expertise that often functions in an exclusionary way, limiting meaningful

---

1. Tom Cramer, "Fedora Update at CNI 2013 Fall Meeting." 12/10/2013. https://www.slideshare.net/Tom-Cramer/2013-12-cni-fedora-updatebuilding-community-building-software.

participation within these communities to only those with time, resources, training, and experience.

Systems and application design is itself an expression of values by the people and organizations who build and maintain these products,[2] and consequently, the choices and practices of those communities directly influence the creators and consumers of linked data. This chapter will explore the landscape of linked data applications in digital libraries, with particular focus on the Fedora Commons community and related projects after the move to linked data. The project is more than middleware repository software—it's a community with its own values and relationships and ethics and, ultimately, it will be those ethics that shape the project's future long after the shift to Linked Data Platform (LDP) specification[3] shook its foundations. More urgent for the digital library community, and Fedora in particular, is the extent to which its community seeks to expand beyond only the wealthiest research libraries and institutes. "When maintenance work is enacted without critical interrogation of the power structures within which its objects are embedded, that work can lead to the maintenance of harmful systems such as patriarchy or white supremacy," the authors of "Information Maintenance as a Practice of Care" explain,[4] and embracing an inclusive, feminist, critical perspective to complement technical expertise will be vital to the survival of digital repository projects in the long term.

Fedora, A Personal Story

It wasn't working.

---

2. Sasha Costanza-Chock, "Design Values: Hard-Coding Liberation?" in Design Justice, 2020, https://design-justice.pubpub.org/pub/3h2zq86d/release/1.

3. Andrew Woods, "Linked Data Platform - Fedora 4.7.5 Documentation - LYRASIS Wiki," Wiki. LYRASIS Wiki., February 16, 2018, https://wiki.lyrasis.org/display/FEDORA475/Linked+Data+Platform.

4. "Information Maintenance as a Practice of Care: An Invitation to Reflect and Share | Maintainers," 2019, accessed December 20, 2021, https://themaintainers.org/information-maintenance-as-a-practice-of-care-an-invitation-to-reflect-and-share/.

In early 2017, I stared at a whiteboard in one of my library's nondescript conference rooms, looking at the options identified by our loose band of developers and librarians as they worked on our first digital collection destined for our new Fedora 4 repository. I was less than a year into my role as department head for Digital Initiatives at the University of Maryland Libraries, still getting my feet under me and my head around our portfolio, and pushing hard to deliver on the promise of our brand new technology stack to get our digitized content accessible at scale with our first collection of digitized student newspapers. We had a terabyte of files, and 3,500 newspaper issues dating from 1911 ready for ingest. Our team had built the first version of our command-line interface (CLI) loader, defined the content models, and run our initial test loads. Then we began to encounter significant performance problems when the rubber met the road and we attempted to load the whole batch.[5] I expected this, given that we were among the first universities to put Fedora 4 into production, and I knew from experience that life on the bleeding edge inevitably involves some bumps. What I didn't expect, at the bottom of the whiteboard, was the half-joking final option to "Put the collection in DSpace," in reference to our venerable institutional repository.

We didn't throw our hands up and load the collection in DSpace, which is a great solution for published products but often a poor one for complex digital collections. I am fortunate enough to work at an institution with the resources and talent to tackle hard problems, and in what felt to me like an 11th hour save, my team came up with a solution that allowed us to load the content by temporarily turning off indexing during content ingest. I came away from the experience with a more skeptical view of the Fedora platform and its implementation of the LDP specification,

---

5. UMD Libraries, Digital Systems & Stewardship Division, "Stew of the Month: February 2017," Digistew (blog).,March 13, 2017, https://dssumd.wordpress.com/2017/03/13/stew-of-the-month-february-2017/.

but a continued commitment to the project. After all, I reasoned, we were early adopters, and this was to be expected as part of the learning process.

Five years later, my institution remains one of fewer than twenty-five self-reported institutions that went into production with Fedora 4 for a major digital library initiative.[6] While this number is certainly an undercount of Fedora 4-based projects, it is an illustrative indicator of a broader challenge encountered in the digital library community in recent years. For many institutions, Fedora 4 wasn't working. Other established digital repository programs also encountered considerable complexities when attempting to move forward with digital library migration projects. According to an IMLS grant statement of need by Duraspace in 2019,[7] nearly two thirds of the Fedora community (estimated at 240 institutions, the overwhelming majority of which are academic institutions and research libraries) were still using older versions of Fedora four years after its release. Fedora 4, as the first version of the Fedora digital repository platform to implement linked data, initiated a rift in the digital library community. Application communities split, debates erupted in the community over the validity of the project, and many of my digital librarian peers and I found ourselves on what Ruth Tillman termed "The Repository Ouroboros"[8]—eternally planning a migration that never quite gets behind us. Over dinners, in the back rooms at conferences, during breakout sessions—the places where the Fedora community is a *community*—we engaged in sustained conversations about what we ask of our software projects, what we are obligated to deliver, and whether the technologies we

6. "Fedora 4 Deployments - Fedora Repository," DuraSpace Wiki, June 11, 2018.,https://wiki.duraspace.org/display/FF/Fedora 4 Deployments.

7. LYRASIS, "Fedora Migration Paths and Tools: A Pilot Project," Institute of Museum and Library Services, 2020, http://www.imls.gov/grants/awarded/lg-246264-ols-20.

8. Ruth Kitchin Tillman, "Repository Ouroboros." Ruth Kitchin Tillman, July 30, 2019, https://ruthtillman.com/post/repository-ouroboros/.

make and champion are fulfilling our ethical standards. In short, whether they're *working*, both for us and our users.

Many of the events and decisions outlined in this chapter are described in publicly available documentation and contemporaneous sources, and involve a small group of committed software developers, digital repository librarians, and library administrators. This community is extremely technical and frequently reflects the resources and needs of North American, predominantly white research institutions. Often, the work is poorly understood and intimidating to other librarians, but the values and choices of the digital library community have outsized impacts on the accessibility, usability, durability, and discoverability of our digital cultural heritage materials. Over the course of this chapter, I hope to shed light on what happened, why, and what an ethically-considered path forward for the digital library community might be. I am myself an outside observer on the events of this chapter; while my institution's experience with Fedora 4 informs my own perspective, and UMD Libraries have a long history of engagement with the Fedora community, I was not a formal member of the project's technical or leadership groups at the time (in other words, I was not in the room where it happened, but I was loitering in the hallway).

Fedora, The Product

Running Fedora can be a complicated business. Explaining the entire ecosystem of Fedora, its architecture, and its full history is outside the scope of this chapter. Instead, this chapter focuses on the intersection of product decisions related to linked data and the impact those choices have on Fedora adopters and the digital library community at large. For those outside this practitioner community, the differences between repository architectures are obscure and highly technical, but they have significant impacts on the ability of a given institution to preserve and facilitate access to their digital materials.

Some digital repository solutions (such as Veridian, ContentDM, and Tind, among others), are commercial, closed-source, all-in-one applications, using either the Software-as-a-Service business model or licensed and self-hosted. However, most digital library products have their roots in the open source software community, and numerous commercial services implement open standards and software as part of their service offerings, like services such as Tind that implement the open International Image Interoperability Framework (IIIF) specification. Openness, whether in source code or digital content, is commonly understood as a state of egalitarian access—a removal of the financial, social, and political barriers to knowledge and tools that any person may consume, use, and transform. The preamble to the 2007 GNU GENERAL PUBLIC LICENSE,[9] one of the most widely used open source code licenses, references "freedom" eight times in as many paragraphs, positioning open source code as a type of natural right. Within this framework, code is more than a set of instructions for a computer; it is a form of communication—one that transmits and manifests values and ideas from programmers to users. Fedora is one of these open source projects.

Fedora is not an all-in-one or "turnkey" digital library application like other open source projects such as Dspace,[10] which, by default, provides adopters with a public user interface for create/read/update/delete functions, a database, and administrative services to manage metadata and binaries.[11] Rather, Fedora is a middleware repository solution designed to manage large or highly complex digital content libraries, without its own public interface. In order to fulfill organizational goals of presenting content via user interfaces, institutions that adopt Fedora for this purpose need to also make choices about the public and staff application layers. This approach facilitates flexibility (the F in

---

9. "The GNU General Public License v3.0 - GNU Project - Free Software Foundation," n.d., accessed November 23, 2021, https://www.gnu.org/licenses/gpl-3.0.html.

10. https://dspace.lyrasis.org.

11. A binary in this context is a non-text computer file like an image, PDF, or audio recording.

the old FEDORA acronym) but shifts the development and maintenance burden increasingly to personnel at local institutions.

As a result, the "Fedora ecosystem" can be categorized by a handful of prominent application choices:

- Islandora,[12] which uses Drupal as the foundation for the public and administrative interfaces and provides a turnkey digital library solution for adopters.
- Samvera[13] (formerly Hydra), which is a set of community-developed Ruby on Rails gems that can create, update, delete, and display data housed in a Fedora repository. Some fully packaged applications do exist that are built atop Samvera, although their use cases are somewhat specific (Avalon[14] for audiovisual materials, Hyku[15] primarily for institutional repositories).
- Custom applications, which may pick and choose services such as search and discovery interfaces, image browsers and servers, or preservation management tools based on local needs and resources available. This group encompasses a high percentage of Fedora's international users.

These components of the Fedora portfolio are not mutually exclusive. For example, at UMD we run Avalon for audiovisual materials, as well as fully customized interfaces for our primary Fedora repositories. However, increasing the complexity of the ecosystem also inherently raises annual costs for management, maintenance, and feature development. Thus, "Fedora" is a platform with a wide range of applications and services built atop it, with their own requirements and methods for interacting with Fedora repository data. Notably, while the user communities for these systems overlap with each other and have many common institutional members, developers, and leadership, few formal agreements or communication channels exist regarding

---

12. https://www.islandora.ca/.
13. https://samvera.org/.
14. https://www.avalonmediasystem.org/.
15. https://hyku.samvera.org/.

coordination of efforts and strategic direction. Significant changes to Fedora's design—like the move to linked data—inevitably necessitate substantial updates to applications relying on it, which in turn impacts locally-maintained custom features or functionality.

Fedora 4, The Event

At the 2014 Coalition for Networked Information (CNI) Fall Meeting, representatives from Stanford University, UCSD, and Penn State presented on the Fedora 4 project as the earliest adopters and founding members of the initiative.[16] Within only five years, Stanford publicly announced in a technical analysis document[17] that they had not adopted Fedora 4 and had no plans to do so. While Stanford has been uniquely transparent and detailed in their assessment, they were hardly the only university library in the community to shelve their Fedora 4 plans. What ethical and architectural issues surfaced in those five years to bring the most enthusiastic early supporters to this point? What impact did system design choices have within the digital repository community?

The initial announcement of Fedora 4 was met with enthusiasm, particularly for its embrace of the World Wide Web Consortium's (W3C) Linked Data Platform (LDP) specification.[18] In order to align with this specification, Fedora's development and leadership governance groups made four key choices, spelled out in its API Specification,[19] which define how Fedora must use linked data to internally manage repository resources, version

---

16. "Fedora 4 Early Adopters," CNI: Coalition for Networked Information (blog), December 6, 2014, https://www.cni.org/topics/repositories/fedora-4-early-adopters.

17. "Stanford and Fedora (Public-Facing) — 2019," n.d., Google Docs, accessed November 23, 2021, https://docs.google.com/document/d/1uFxZ5MwVY7qVEHTY rFsNHA5WbMe_1iTcmTTlxACbwQo/

18. "Linked Data Platform 1.0 | W3C Recommendation 26 February 2015." https://www.w3.org/TR/ldp/, accessed November 19, 2021.

19. "Fedora API Specification," n.d., accessed November 27, 2021, https://www.w3.org/TR/fedora-api/.

those resources, facilitate access, and issue notifications. On the face of it, these changes deliver on the promise of linked data—complex resource management at scale, with open standards, to power the next generation of digital library technology! In reality, these design choices created significant challenges in local implementations. First, the use of LDP containers for digital resource management represents a considerable increase in data model complexity from previous digital library implementations. A framework known as the Portland Common Data Model (PCDM) provides repository managers with a flexible method for representing these containers, but in practice this makes it both more challenging to migrate legacy content from older versions of Fedora (or other repository architecture that may require more custom development) and introduces new user experience challenges when representing even fairly simple digital objects.

For example, at the University of Maryland, our first Fedora project with student newspapers highlights the challenges for the end user with this approach. In our model for newspapers,[20] which is an implementation of the National Digital Newspaper Program (NDNP) specification, an "Issue" of a newspaper has member pages that have image files associated with them, as well as Optical Character Recognition annotation text stored as XML. In addition, the conceptual model of the "Issue" also has member "Articles," which may appear on noncontiguous pages. While Issues and Articles are searchable by end users, as well as Annotations that belong to a given page, there are no links in the software between Articles and the Annotation text, or even Articles and pages. A common pain point for users is selecting a relevant-looking "Article" from search results, and then being deposited onto the first page of the newspaper issue without any indication where a given article may appear. This is a data-model

---

20. Mohamed Mohideen Abdul Rasheed, Peter Eichman, Joshua Westgard, Kate Dohe, Xiaoyu Tai, and Ben Wallberg, "Newspapers Re-Issued: Developing a Custom IIIF Based Newspaper Viewer at the University of Maryland Libraries," March 2017, https://doi.org/10.13016/M21847.

limitation with no easy solution, but a very real problem to end users all the same.

The prospects for transforming and migrating our tens of thousands of books, diaries, postcards, audiovisual materials, and other content types, many of which have custom access rules, from our considerably older Fedora 2 repository into linked data represented a daunting migration project. Moreover, the project represented a considerable institutional investment in content that, to many external eyes, was already available and safely housed in a repository. Like many American research libraries, Maryland has far more desired digital projects and content in urgent need of digitization than we have capacity and funding to execute. The pressures of releasing new content—particularly in a time period when we were pursuing more mass-digitization funding initiatives—squeezed expensive and less visible mainte- nance projects onto the back burner. However, such projects are vital to averting catastrophic outcomes like security exploits that threaten our digital content, users, and institutional systems; con- tinuously kicking the can down the road has hard consequences.

Another common complaint from the Fedora community revolved around performance problems with the repository, specifically regarding its database's performance at ingest time. Fedora opted to implement a data store (the underlying persistent storage layer of the repository) called ModeShape in the produc- tion release of Fedora 4, which managed the storage of repository files. Furthermore, Fedora 4 did not include its own search and query services, choosing instead to allow for external imple- mentations of these services. Some readers may be familiar with traditionally structured, relational databases for web applications like PostgreSQL or MySQL. To support storage and querying of linked data resources, applications can use a type of database called a triplestore—as in linked data triples—and Fedora 4 opted to support this as an external service, as well as external search index services like Solr Triplestores are newer technology than relational databases, are not as widely utilized, and can be prone to performance problems that require specialized expertise to troubleshoot. In the community, performance problems related to these architectural decisions became known as a "many members" problem, in which ModeShape's performance drops off steeply once there are about a thousand direct children of a node, such as a digital collection with a large number of objects or a book with many scanned page images. While this specific issue was resolved by the Fedora technical community, the problem surfaced again with the addition of shortcuts in Fedora to see all children nested under more hierarchical structures. This problem was also exacerbated by technical recommendations early in Fedora 4's development to adhere to Semantic Web "Cool URI" principles[21] and keep repository structures as flat as possible.[22]

What do these architectural issues mean in practical terms? Loading content—particularly lots of it or more complicated content types—into Fedora 4 could encounter timeouts, slow response times, and "lost" actions, depending on the methods, services, and applications in use by a local institution. Complicated object modeling choices could complicate user experience refinements. Migration analysis from older versions of Fedora would require a significant amount of technical expertise at individual institutions, spanning developers, curatorial staff, technical librarians, metadata specialists, and other key stakeholders in a months-long focused effort.

These problems are all surmountable, and no complex application is free from implementation problems, but they do require highly specialized talent to solve:

- Software developers with deep expertise in back-end languages like Java (which Fedora is written in), *and* a

---

21. W3C Interest Group, Danny Ayers, and Max Völkel, "Cool URIs for the Semantic Web," Worldwide Web Consortium (W3C), March 12, 2008, https://www.w3.org/TR/cooluris/.

22. From consultation with Peter Eichman, UMD Libraries Senior Software Developer and former Fedora Committer.

strong understanding of cultural heritage requirements. At the University of Maryland, we attempted to hire a contract developer to assist with this work prior to my arrival, who "spent several months attempting to learn a digital library toolkit. Ultimately the developer left before accomplishing any significant milestones."[23]

- Functional specialist librarians with experience in linked data, system dependencies, user experience and discovery analysis, repository design, metadata transformation processes, and institutional knowledge of the content and collections being migrated.
- Project and product management experts to oversee and coordinate this level of large-scale technical migration work.

This depth of talent is frequently only found at the wealthiest universities and research institutes in the country. Even at those institutions, as at UMD, a fairly wealthy research library, it is common to find one person occupying multiple roles in this process—spreading themselves very thin across intellectually demanding work and risking significant migration delays in the event of one personnel departure. It is important to note as well that, while digital initiatives often loom large in those wealthy library strategic plans, the site visitors and users of those projects are dwarfed by less-flashy core library services like reference, access, lending, maintenance, and instruction, creating cognitive dissonance in personnel who need to support all those services and organizational priorities that may not reflect on-the-ground realities. Moreover, the extremely technical nature of that talent means that the primary participants in these conversations are developers and IT managers rather than librarians (though many in the Fedora community are both). The level of expertise required

---

23. Kate Dohe, Babak Hamidzadeh, and Ben Wallberg, "Doing More, With More: Academic Libraries, Digital Services, and Revenue Generation," Ithaka SR Issue Brief, January 24, 2019, p. 11, https://doi.org/10.18665/sr.310917.

for even accessing the conversation, let alone contributing to it or supporting implementation, functions as an exclusionary barrier to entry.

In this scenario, "Fedora" conceptually becomes a black box to outside observers who nevertheless rely on the repository, one which appears to them (rightly or wrongly) to have substantial problems. In early 2019, I provided a departmental update at a library-wide meeting on our digital collections' efforts, and the first question from one of my colleagues after I finished my presentation was "Why is Fedora terrible?" Is the question pointed and reductive? Certainly. If the question is born from a lack of understanding, then it is imperative to contemplate why this is so difficult for even technical librarians to grasp and explain. It reflected broader frustration with the way that the complexity of our digital collections stack gets in the way of the work of our curators and digitization personnel, frustrations I'd heard echoed at conferences and in conversations with my peers at other institutions.

Fedora, Fractured

As described earlier, much of the broad Fedora user community can be further bifurcated by the two primary application communities that rely on the Fedora repository for metadata and binary management services—Hydra (at the time) and Islandora. Fedora 4's launch coincided with a series of additional technical changes in both communities, which further complicated the digital library landscape.

The version of Islandora available at the time of Fedora 4's release used Drupal 7 for its public and administrative management interfaces. Drupal 7 had been plagued by multiple high-profile security exploits demanding urgent IT group attention, notably the 2014 Drupalgeddon exploit that allowed anonymous attackers to compromise administrator accounts in

Drupal,[24] and Islandora community members were advocating for the next version of Islandora to use the more recently released Drupal 8 instead, *in addition* to changing the repository architecture to Fedora 4. This raised the complexity of the project substantially, making it effectively a completely new application. Islandora CLAW was the name of the in-development Drupal 8/ Fedora 4 project, which formally began in June 2016.[25] Islandora 8, the final production implementation with Drupal 8 and Fedora 5 support, was released four years later in summer of 2020.

Facing legal action, the Hydra Project changed their name to Samvera in 2017.[26] While this was happening, substantial project and code changes were occurring with a number of Samvera's "core" community gems (gems are code packages for Ruby on Rails developers to install and implement without needing to create application functions completely from scratch). This level of "churn" made it time-consuming and expensive for personnel at the local level to keep up with upstream changes as numerous gems and projects consolidated, then split apart, dropped functionality, introduced new functionality, upgraded underlying versions of Rails, and re-merged in a dizzying fashion.[27]

One of those core community gems central to implementation of Samvera is ActiveFedora, which enables creation and management of objects within a Fedora repository. ActiveFedora is itself modeled on a widely used and foundational Ruby on Rails method called ActiveRecord, which is designed for interaction

24. "Drupal Vulnerability: Mass Scans & Targeted Exploitation | Volexity," accessed May 1, 2022, https://www.volexity.com/blog/2014/10/16/drupal-vulnerability-mass-scans-targeted-exploitation/.

25. "Introduction to Islandora CLAW - Islandora CLAW," n.d., accessed November 28, 2021, https://clawkim.readthedocs.io/en/latest/user-documentation/intro-to-claw/.

26. Christopher Awre and Richard Green, "From Hydra to Samvera: An Open Source Community Journey," *Insights* 30, no. 3 (2017): 82–88, https://doi.org/10.1629/uksg.383.

27. Jonathan Rochkind, "Performance on a Many-Membered Sufia/Hyrax Show Page," Bibliographic Wilderness (blog), October 19, 2017, https://bibwild.wordpress.com/2017/10/19/performance-on-a-many-membered-sufiahyrax-show-page/.

with traditional relational databases. Over the course of 2016 and 2017, it became apparent in test deployments at numerous institutions[28] that ActiveFedora exhibited considerable performance problems due to the complex modeling changes required by Fedora 4 and its linked data implementation, which substantially complicated maintenance, migration, and upgrade choices at institutions that had heavily invested in Samvera. The change in modeling turned simple steps for item creation or updating into a long sequence of tasks. An institutional investment in Samvera almost inevitably requires expensive institutional investment in Ruby on Rails developers, therefore restricting community participation and decision-making to the research libraries and cultural heritage organizations that can afford such talent. In response to these technical pressures, a handful of institutions led by Princeton University developed a new gem called Valkyrie,[29] which crucially allowed technical teams to choose from a variety of backend database options, of which Fedora 4 was only one of several. In practical terms, this meant it was possible for developers and institutions to run a Samvera-based digital library application *without the Fedora repository underpinning it*, thus backing away from a commitment to linked data and, in many ways, the philosophical concept of repositories in favor of straightforward Rails web applications.

Even the Valkyrie project leaders understood the implications these options would have on the digital library community at large. "Using Fedora has been *the* defining aspect of the Samvera community, with Samvera defined in relation to Fedora," wrote Esme Cowles, Assistant Director of Information Technology at Princeton University Library, in his remarks at Open Repositories in 2018. "As using different backends becomes a core part of the Samvera stack, it means we should rethink Samvera, and

---

28. Adam Wead, "Benchmark Testing with Valkyrie and Hyrax," @awead, August 29, 2017, https://awead.github.io/fedora-tests.

29. "Princeton University Library Systems by Pulibrary," n.d., accessed November 27, 2021, https://pulibrary.github.io/2017-07-06-valkyrie.

how it relates to other technologies. And like the renaming from Hydra to Samvera last year, it gives us an opportunity to think about who we are and who we want to be."[30]

Valkyrie promised choices, but who has the power and depth of expertise to choose? The question of whether to build a digital library on top of a SQL database or a linked data platform may seem like a deeply technical decision for library IT departments to argue about, and in many ways it is. However, this seemingly obscure, highly localized decision had very serious impacts across the community and posed a risk to the financial stability of the Fedora project overall. Fedora's software is open source and free for anyone to use, but Fedora (as well as DSpace, Samvera, and many other open digital library projects) is funded through membership fees by participating institutions, with several tiers of membership ranging from $500 to $20,000 per year. Importantly, those membership fees often function to define who may participate in governance and leadership discussions for the project, with higher membership tiers having more "seats at the table."[31] Furthermore, Fedora relies upon developers and technical personnel at member universities to maintain, test, and update the system's code base and documentation; some of these contributors become formal "committers" on the project.[32] As noted earlier, participation in Samvera necessitates considerable resources to hire or contract expensive software development talent, and Samvera community members disproportionately occupied higher financial tiers of membership within Fedora and participation as committers. Suddenly, their contributions could not be relied upon.

---

30. Esme Cowles, "Valkyrie, Reimagining the Samvera Community," Princeton University Library Newsletter, 2018, accessed November 23, 2021, https://library.princeton.edu/news/digital-collections/2018-06-05/valkyrie-reimagining-samvera-community.

31. "Membership Value and Benefits," accessed May 1, 2022, https://www.lyrasis.org/programs/Pages/membership-value-and-benefits.aspx.

32. "Fedora Committers - Fedora Repository - LYRASIS Wiki," December 13, 2021, https://wiki.lyrasis.org/display/FF/Fedora+Committers.

If enough Samvera institutions withdrew their financial and technical support for Fedora, that certainly would have very real implications for the *entire* Fedora community, regardless of their participation in Samvera, and could potentially sink the entire community. This is a direct function of the economic privilege of those organizations, with wealthy, predominantly white institutions making technical choices and elevating use cases that may not serve cultural heritage institutions without those considerable resources in hand.[33] While this may come across as alarmist, the similarly membership-driven Digital Preservation Network collapsed in late 2018, partly due to a large simultaneous exodus among institutional members (the University of Maryland Libraries was one of those departing members).[34] Indeed, between 2018 and 2021, former "Platinum" Fedora members Northwestern University, Princeton University Library, Stanford University Libraries, the University of Michigan Library, the University of New South Wales, the University of Oxford, and the University of Toronto all dropped or reduced their financial contributions to Fedora—though it must be noted that not all of these institutions are Samvera institutions, and the financial effects of the pandemic are of course also a variable in this situation.

What would the end of Fedora mean? This is a question that has kept me up on more than one evening (including now, while I write this chapter), as I contemplate the implications for my university library. We would be left with not merely one, but *two* unsupported, high volume digital collections repositories in urgent need of migration. We would likely embark on a costly research project to identify an alternative digital strategy and potentially not find any other solutions that fit our available resources, expertise, and specialized user requirements. There

---

33. Kate Dohe, "Linked Data, Unlinked Communities," Lady Science, 2018, https://www.ladyscience.com/essays/linked-data-unlinked-communities

34. David Rosenthal, "Digital Preservation Network Is No More," 2019, accessed December 12, 2021, https://blog.dshr.org/2019/01/digital-preservation-network-is-no-more.html.

are few systems that offer the long-term preservation, complex object management, scalability, and metadata functionality that digital repositories like Fedora provide—features that support our Libraries' central mission to preserve and make accessible our unique digital content. At UMD, I could not shake the impression that the "choice" to implement a Valkyrie-based Samvera system *without* Fedora meant deprioritizing permanence and authenticity in favor of theoretically easier development and short-term content management—a decision that prompted me to reflect on my own professional values at length in discussions with my team. With any new system we chose, we would be staring down considerable tradeoffs in functionality, an increase in costs, a significant hit to staff morale, and no certain ability to make new digital collections content available in the interim. The University of Maryland Libraries is an unambiguously *wealthy* research library, and the prospective failure of the Fedora project could have been catastrophic for our own program. Smaller institutions without our staffing levels and in-house technical expertise would have found themselves with even fewer options.

And yet, could I say with confidence that our Fedora-first strategy was working for us? Our Fedora 4 repository, in and of itself, continues to be stable and perform well. Our internally created and maintained command-line tools[35] for adding new content in batches are fairly reliable, and while we encounter occasional quirks with the public user interface and have challenging strategic questions regarding search and discovery for end users, the overall experience for patrons and researchers is at least functional. However, in 2018, ingesting and managing content was still a cumbersome process that relied heavily on our most technical (and overextended) personnel, and we lacked a web-based administrative interface for curators and digitization specialists to create and update content. The pressure for this small team to work on releasing new content—much of which

---

35. https://github.com/umd-lib/plastron.

had been trickling through project queues for years, to the vocal frustration of users, donors, curators, and administrators—meant that migration plans kept being pushed back, especially as it seemed apparent that we would undertake our move from Fedora 2 to 4 with little community support compared to the attention paid to institutions moving from Fedora 3, or who had previously adopted one of the primary application platforms. The fractures in the Samvera community over its commitment to Fedora did not fill us with confidence in the long-term ability of the project to meet our needs as Fedora adopters. Islandora CLAW was still in development, with no clear release timeline, and UMD Libraries had only limited experience with Drupal at that time. With no community to join, we elected to build our own staff interface for Fedora 4 called Archelon.[36] This approach allowed us to prioritize our own articulated stakeholder needs, and I am proud of this application: proud of the locally inclusive way we built it, and certainly proud of my colleagues. Yet Archelon is also undeniably expensive, far from feature complete, and continues to have reliability and interface design issues that prevent it from being used by our curators and digitization personnel for their activities or for batch ingest.

I am uncertain whether it's working, or if it's only the best of bad choices.

Fedora's Future

2018 and 2019 were pivotal years for the Fedora community in multiple ways. As the Valkyrie project was debuting at the first international digital repository conference after its production launch, Fedora community leadership met at Open Repositories to discuss the strategic future of the product and plan for

---

36. https://github.com/umd-lib/archelon.

Fedora 6.[37] Notes and documents from this meeting,[38] and a sub-sequent leadership meeting in April 2019 at CNI in St. Louis, reflect the anxieties of project leaders. How can Fedora better support migrations? What is the value-add of Fedora to a digital library program? How can the community better articulate this to library professionals outside the development groups? What, fundamentally, are the values of the Fedora community, and could it be made more inclusive at both an institutional and individual level? These conversations coincided with the initial design and planning for Fedora 6, as well as a merger between Fedora's parent organization Duraspace and LYRASIS. The community's struggles to move to Fedora 4 were self-evident by this point, and the future of the repository rode on the choices and values of project developers and governance.

Fedora 6 redoubled the project's commitment to digital preservation services, with the replacement of the problematic ModeShape with the community-driven Oxford Common File Layout (OCFL) specification.[39] OCFL is a software-independent standard for digital repository file layouts that ensures data are stored in a transparent, human-parse-able, and predictable manner independent of any particular software, and can be reconstructed without the original software. Removing the requirement for a repository application to define and manage file layout has substantial benefits for both digital preservation and migration planning—theoretically reducing the staff resources necessary to move content between repositories *and* making the content

37. Carol Minton Morris, "NOW AVAILABLE: Fedora 5.0.0," Duraspace.org, December 20, 2018, https://duraspace.org/now-available-fedora-5-0-0/. Fedora 5, released in 2018, served largely as a technical alignment release. As Daniel Bernstein, the technical lead for the project, stated in all-caps, "The move from Fedora 4.x to 5.x DOES NOT represent the same scope of change."

38. "2018-06-03 - OR2018 Fedora Leadership Group Meeting - Fedora Repository - LYRASIS Wiki," n.d., accessed December 12, 2021, https://wiki.lyrasis.org/display/FF/2018-06-03+-+OR2018+Fedora+Leadership+Group+Meeting.

39. https://ocfl.io/.

repository safer in the long term. OCFL also emphasizes transparency in design and implementation—lowering some of the highest technical barriers to understanding and participating in the digital library community. That said, OCFL is still a new specification—achieving 1.0 status in 2020—and the choice to implement it in Fedora 6 represented a gamble on the success of the spec. Additionally (and critically), OCFL's community leaders draw disproportionately on representatives from wealthy, predominantly white research institutions,[40] and does not resolve the harder and more fundamental questions about who gets to drive community infrastructure and how the barriers to participation might be lowered. With Fedora 6's recent (as of the time of this writing) release in 2021, it's still too early to say whether this implementation change and the community focus on easing the migration path will push Fedora forward.

What does it mean for Fedora to work? The project is more than middleware repository software—it is a community, with its own values, relationships, and ethics; ultimately, it will be those ethics that shape the project's future, long after the shift to linked data shook its foundations. More urgent for many digital library projects and networks, and Fedora in particular, is the extent to which these communities seek to expand beyond only the wealthiest research libraries and institutes. If Fedora continues to only be a project for technical personnel at American R1s and elite private universities to engage with meaningfully, then that choice and its consequences should be made intentionally—not as a byproduct of neglect. Yet such a choice would be a disservice to the digital library community—a reinforcement of the elitism and stratification that led to Fedora being perceived as and treated like a status symbol for libraries—a complicated nuisance and not an essential piece of infrastructure. A future without robust and open

---

40. Andrew Hankinson, Donald Brower, Neil Jefferies, Rosalyn Metz, Julian Morley, Simeon Warner, and Andrew Woods, "The Oxford Common File Layout: A Common Approach to Digital Preservation," *Publications* 7, no. 2 (June 2019): 39, https://doi.org/10.3390/publications7020039.

source digital repositories would ultimately shift the emphasis of digital libraries away from *permanence*—the idea that access to our digital materials should survive us; that our work is more than just building websites for today with no consideration of long-term maintenance; that our content is as ephemeral and fragile as the rest of the web. Digital library infrastructure is inextricable from its user and adopter communities, and for Fedora to work, the rest of us in this community must as well.

Triples and the Grammar of Control

JAMES KALWARA & ERIK RADIO

Introduction

The decomposition of documents into linked data raises a concern for the types of control that are enacted through what is essentially a new grammar for describing information resources. In 2004, the World Wide Web Consortium's (W3C) Resource Description Framework (RDF) Working Group established RDF as a standardized data model for describing, publishing, and exchanging data across the Web.[1] The key feature of the RDF model is the triple statement, which is the standard approach for expressing relationships in order to create descriptions about a resource, an entity, or a thing. These RDF triple statements create the foundation for serializing RDF data and allow data descriptions to be machine readable in the RDF model. However, when reviewing the construction of a triple statement, which consists of a subject, a predicate, and an object, it is important to note that this construction is rooted in English language grammar and Western linguistics. From this, we ask: how might development in linked data initiatives be overly influenced by Western research, thought, and semantics? Further, does the triple represent a new type of colonial grammar in that it necessitates articulating resource descriptions according to Western syntax? With interoperability being a core tenet of linked data, how might the linked

---

1. "RDF Primer," W3C, accessed December 12, 2021, https://www.w3.org/TR/2004/REC-rdf-primer-20040210/.

data community best support international and multilingual participation when various knowledge organization systems are not always expressed in the English language? How does this hinder a fuller representation of resources for non-Western knowledge organization systems? Whom do graphs serve? In this chapter, we examine interoperability issues that stem from the structure of the RDF triple statement and provide a critique of the triple to illuminate latent tendencies in its structure that colonize resource descriptions according to Western grammars and lenses.

Hegemony, Neocolonialism

Before we can examine the implications of triple statement structure, we need to briefly examine two ideas relevant to how power and control are enacted in the 21st century. The first, hegemony, was popularized by Antonio Gramsci in the early 20th century who outlined it generally as:

> ...the spontaneous consent given by the great masses of the population to the general direction imposed on social life by the dominant fundamental group.[2]

Alternatively, it can be understood as the set of ideas or beliefs designed by a dominant group to attain the consent of the population to govern in a particular way. It is not surprising that Gramsci's writings on the subject coincided with the rise of fascism in Italy. And while hegemony is closely linked to the relation between capitalism and fascism, its effects permeate society far outside economic and legislative arenas, in turn making its ability to gain consent dependent on the strength of its messaging to various groups. As Lears notes, consent is rarely achieved in any sort of totalizing way; individuals respond to ideology with a mix of

---

2. Antonio Gramsci, *Selections from the Prison Notebooks*, ed. and trans. Quentin Hoare and Geoffrey Nowell Smith (New York: Columbia University Press, 1971): 12.

resignation, resistance, and apathy.[3] This last point is critical for understanding that hegemonic practices are rarely static, as there is an ongoing tension between what the subjugated group will acquiesce to and how the dominant group must adapt to maintain control. So, if hegemony represents a critical tool for controlling society, how it is enacted depends on the specific places it is used. Of particular interest for our discussion are those former colonies of imperial powers.

Neocolonialism is a concept examining how colonial practices persist in reinforcing the dominance over former colonies by (generally) Western powers. Writing in 1965, Nkrumah identified this new iteration of imperialism as one focused on the continuation of exploitative practices, but through covertly subversive means that, on the surface, may appear benevolent, with his analysis focusing primarily on post-war Africa:

> The essence of neocolonialism is that the State which is subject to it, is in theory independent and has all the outward trappings of international sovereignty. In reality, its economic system and thus its political policy is directed from outside.[4]

It is impossible to separate the actions of neocolonialism and its antecedents from the engine of capitalist accumulation which, through the latter half of the 20th century, found new points of extraction as barriers that insulated countries from capitalist expansion were removed in service of global free-trade. Concomitant with the forced opening of new markets was the invention of information economies and commodities under a banner retrospectively understood as a new spirit of capitalism.[5] This shift can also be viewed as the rise of the network as the operating

---

3. T.T. Jackson Lears, "The Concept of Cultural Hegemony: Problems and Possibilities", *American Historical Review*, 90:3 (1985): 570.

4. Kwame Nkrumah, *Neo-Colonialism: The Last Stage of Imperialism* (London: Thomas Nelson and Sons, 1965), ix.

5. Luc Boltanski and Eva Chiapello, *The New Spirit of Capitalism* (London: Verso, 2018): 10.

technique of capitalistic expansion into new information economies. The network necessitates a decomposition (rehashing?) of
existing information into more readily commodifiable forms. As
Deleuze observed:

> The numerical language of control is made of codes that mark access
> to information,or reject it. We no longer find ourselves dealing with
> the mass/individual pair. Individuals have become "dividuals," and
> masses, samples, data, markets, or "Banks."[6]

To give one example, Tan has already identified this digital
neocoloniality present with the export of MOOCs to non-Western
countries,[7] but for our purposes we are interested in looking
closely at the decomposition of information into triples. As we
will see, this represents its own form of subversive imperialism
in that it purports to do so in the service of making information
more readily available, which, while partially and situationally
true, comes at a problematic cost. But before we can explore that,
we must examine in detail the nature of the decomposition of
information, specifically resource description, into triples.

Triple Syntax

The nature and origin of the triple statement, or triple, is rooted
within the RDF model, which was adopted by the W3C in
February 2004.[8] The RDF model was chosen as a language to
describe, publish, and exchange information on the Web.[9] Moreover, the RDF model was seen as taking concrete steps to helping
develop the Semantic Web, which has the ultimate goal of

---

6. Gilles Deleuze, "Postscript on the Societies of Control." October 59 (1992): 5.

7. Taskeen Adam, "Digital neocolonialism and massive open online courses
(MOOCs): colonial pasts and neoliberal futures." *Learning, Media and Technology*,
44:3 (2019): 377.

8. "Resource Description Framework (RDF): Concepts and Abstract Syntax,"
W3C, this version modified February 10, 2004, http://www.w3.org/TR/2004/REC-rdf-
concepts-20040210/.

9. W3C, "RDF: Concepts and Abstract Syntax."

supporting a web of data that can be queried and shared beyond the hypertext document web.[10] Some of the core design principles behind RDF were to support simplicity in the way that practitioners would easily make any kind of statement about a resource, entity, or thing.[11] Furthermore, this principle was intended to also support automated processing by machines whereby "RDF provides a world-wide lingua franca for these processes."[12] Another important design principle for the RDF model was that it should adhere to a graph data model and work to establish an RDF graph.[13] The RDF graph consists of a set of triple statements that work to designate relationships among resources in the graph and the RDF framework defines the syntax and semantics that are to be used for it.[14, 15] The goal in establishing an RDF graph is to support a data storage model in which all triple statements can be queried and shared more easily across different knowledge bases.

The construction of the RDF triple statement consists of three parts: a subject, a predicate, and an object.[16] Each of these parts plays an integral role in creating a statement about a resource. Another important aspect of a triple is the role of nodes and arcs. Within an RDF graph, the subject and the object serve as nodes while the predicate serves as the arc to direct the relationships from the subject to the object.[17] An example of an RDF triple statement using natural language in English would be as follows: "The book was published by Verso Press." In this example, "book" is the subject; "was published by" serves as the predicate; and "Verso Press" represents the object of the triple statement. In using this example, "book" serves as a subject node, while

10. Tim Berners-Lee, "Linked data - Design issues," last modified June 18, 2009, https://www.w3.org/DesignIssues/LinkedData.html.

11. W3C, "RDF: Concepts and Abstract Syntax."

12. Ibid.

13. Ibid.

14. Ibid.

15. W3C, "RDF: Concepts and Abstract Syntax."

16. Ibid.

17. Ibid.

"was published by" serves as the arc and directs the subject node "book" to the object node "Verso Press." From this example, we can see how the nodes and arcs in the triple statement specifically flow in one direction in order to assert that the subject points towards the object.

However, in order for an RDF graph to fully support data querying and sharing across different knowledge bases, and to help create new ones from established graphs, inferencing needs to take place. Inferencing is defined as the mechanism that can produce or connect new resource relationships by drawing on a combination of already established data sets (or triples) and existing vocabularies/ontologies.[18] For example, a computer program can make inferences about a discipline/domain by generating new triple statements based on existing triple statements from another existing domain ontology. RDF Schema (RDFS) and OWL are two ontology languages that can be used with the RDF model to conduct inferencing.[19] [20] Both RDFS and OWL use sets of classes, subclasses, properties, subproperties, and datatypes in order to "describe groups of resources and relationships between them" to support inferencing.[21] Of particular note within OWL is the inclusion of inverse object properties that support bidirectionality in triple statements under class expressions.[22] The capacity to support bidirectionality in triples is important in that one can query for the statement: the book (subject) → was published by (predicate) → Verso Press (object) and the graph database will also query for its inverse statement: Verso Press (subject) →

18. "Inference," W3C, accessed March 30, 2022, https://www.w3.org/standards/semanticweb/inference.

19. "RDF Schema 1.1," W3C, accessed March 30, 2022, https://www.w3.org/TR/rdf-schema/.

20. "OWL 2 Web Ontology Language Document Overview," W3C, accessed March 30, 2022, https://www.w3.org/TR/owl-overview/.

21. Jose Emilio Labra Gayo, Eric Prud'hommeaux, Iovka Boneva, and Dimitris Kontokostas, Validating RDF Data, 1st ed., vol. 16 (San Rafael, California: Morgan & Claypool, 2017), 20-23, https://doi.org/10.2200/S00786ED1V01Y201707WBE016.

22. "OWL 2 Web Ontology Language Structural Specification and Functional-Style Syntax (Second Edition)", W3C, accessed March 30, 2022, http://www.w3.org/TR/2012/REC-owl2-syntax-20121211/.

published (predicate) → the book (object). These are the basic building blocks for supporting an RDF graph.[23] In the following sections, we attempt to illustrate how triple syntax from both a linguistic and technical sphere is intertwined in shaping how the RDF model works to connect and create resource descriptions.

Implications of the Tripled World

As previously mentioned, there is a specific directionality for RDF triples whereby the subject is directed by the predicate towards the object. This construction and directionality also follows the same syntax as the English language, which adheres to a subject-verb-object (SVO) syntax.[24] While there are various languages throughout the world that do not solely adhere to the SVO syntax, we can see from the previous section how RDF triples mandate usage of a similar subject, predicate, object syntax to generate its graphs. For instance, Japanese, Korean, Mongolian, Navajo, Quechua, and Hindi are examples of languages that use a subject-object-verb (SOV) word order.[25] With this, how do RDF triples accommodate or map resource descriptions that do not adhere to English SVO syntax?

23. For a more detailed overview of the RDF ecosystem, please see Jose Emilio Labra Gayo, Eric Prud'hommeaux, Iovka Boneva, and Dimitris Kontokostas, Validating RDF Data, 9-25.

24. Gerard Kempen and Karin Harbusch, "Mutual Attraction between High-Frequency Verbs and Clause Types with Finite Verbs in Early Positions: Corpus Evidence from Spoken English, Dutch, and German," *Language, Cognition and Neuroscience* 34, no. 9 (2019): 1141, https://doi.org/10.1080/23273798.2019.1642498.

25. Yong-Seok Choi, Yo-Han Park, Seung Yun, Sang-Hun Kim, and Lee Kong-Joo, "Factors Behind the Effectiveness of an Unsupervised Neural Machine Translation System between Korean and Japanese," *Applied Sciences* 11, no. 16 (2021): 7662, 1, https://doi.org/10.3390/app11167662; Dalai Zayabaatar, Vanchinsuren Dashdavaa, Dagvasumberel Enkhjargal, and Tsulbaatar Onon, "Genitive Case-Marked Subject in Modern Mongolian," *Advances in Language and Literary Studies* 7, no. 2 (2016): 185, http://dx.doi.org/10.7575/aiac.alls.v.7n.2p.183; Ellen H. Courtney and Muriel Saville-Troike, "Learning to Construct Verbs in Navajo and Quechua," *Journal of Child Language* 29, no. 3 (2002): 629–31, https://doi.org/10.1017/S0305000902005160; Debajyoty Banik, "Phrase Table Re-Adjustment for Statistical Machine Translation," *International Journal of Speech Technology* 24, no. 4 (2021): 904, https://doi.org/10.1007/s10772-020-09676-0.

Looking at certain sentence structures found in the Navajo language, for example, one can see how semantic nuances might be lost when attempting to map them into a triple statement. An example sentence in Navajo is as follows: "dibé łį́į́' yitah yíghááh."[26] In this example, "dibé" translates in English to "sheep," "łį́į́'" translates to "horse," "yitah" represents the third-person form in English of "among," and "yíghááh" represents the third-person present tense form in English of "to join."[27] It is also important to note that with the word "yitah," "yi" is serving as a prefix to indicate *direct* voice construction.[28] Together, the sentence translates into English as "the sheep is joining the horses."[29] In looking at another Navajo sentence, "dibé łį́į́' bitah yíghááh," which appears similar to the above example but introduces the important role of the prefix "bi" to the word "tah" to denote an *inverse* voice third person present tense construction.[30] Here the verb phrase "bitah yíghááh," which translates into English as "are being joined," is still placed *after* the subject and object nouns "dibé / sheep" and "łį́į́' / horse."[31] Together, the sentence translates into English as "the sheep are being joined by the horse."[32]

Attempting to map the aforementioned Navajo example into an RDF triple, we are left with the following construction: dibé (subject) → bitah yíghááh (predicate) → łį́į́' (object). However, in order to properly convey the original semantic meaning that "bitah yíghááh" carries, one would need to establish clear inference rules to denote the usage of the verb prefix "bi" with the word "tah" in order to create an inverse voice third person present tense construction. Additionally, by assigning bidirectionality to the subject and object nodes, "dibé / sheep" and "łį́į́' / horses"

---

26. Mary Ann Willie, "The Inverse Voice and Possessive yi-/bi- in Navajo," *International Journal of American Linguistics* 66, no. 3 (2000): 367.

27. Ibid.
28. Ibid.
29. Ibid.
30. Ibid.
31. Ibid.
32. Ibid.

respectively, we lose some of the original Navajo meaning whereby "łį́į́' / horses" and "dibé / sheep" are simply joining among each other instead of the dibé / sheep specifically being joined by the łį́į́' / horse. These examples illustrate the important nuances verb phrase prefixes take in shaping the meaning of a sentence. Furthermore, it highlights how vital the subject and object syntax are in an SOV language such as Navajo since they retain their SO directionality within a sentence despite changes in verb phrases (such as with introducing yi-/bi- prefixes), in order to establish semantic meaning with *direct* and *inverse* voice. Lastly, while it may be subtle, the above Navajo examples aim to illustrate how mapping the SOV syntax into the context of an RDF triple statement breaks up the original syntax and with that also leads to a change and loss in the semantic meaning of the natural language.

Mongolian is another SOV language that can reveal mapping limitations when attempting to map with RDF triple statements. For instance, Mongolian includes genitive case-marked sub-jects that are presented in various forms.[33] The genitive case marker for subjects denotes possession and additional roles such as theme and agent.[34] An example sentence in Mongolian is as follows: "Bat**iin** nom**iin** orchuulga."[35] In this example, "Bat**iin**" and "nom**iin**" are presented in the genitive case form whereby "**iin**" serves as the case marker to denote "Bat" as the subject agent of the sentence.[36] The sentence translates into English as "Bat's translation of the book."[37] Here, the Mongolian genitive case-marked subject is vital in establishing semantic meaning in

---

33. Dalai Zayabaatar, Vanchinsuren Dashdavaa, Dagvasumberel Enkhjargal, and Tsulbaatar Onon, "Genitive Case-Marked Subject in Modern Mongolian," *Advances in Language and Literary Studies* 7, no. 2 (2016): 183-84, http://dx.doi.org/10.7575/aiac.alls.v.7n.2p.183.

34. Dalai Zayabaatar, Vanchinsuren Dashdavaa, Dagvasumberel Enkhjargal, and Tsulbaatar Onon, "Genitive Case-Marked Subject in Modern Mongolian," 186.

35. Ibid.
36. Ibid.
37. Ibid.

that it defines the specific role of the subject noun.[38] With the genitive case marker in Mongolian serving as a critical function in defining the different types of possession subject roles (agent, possessor, and theme), mapping these into an RDF triple may not always be viable, as the SVO orientation of the triple would most likely dilute the possession role established within the subject nouns.

Attempting to map the aforementioned Mongolian example into an RDF triple, we are left with the following construction: Batiin (subject) → orchuulga (predicate) → nomiin (object). However, by disrupting the original syntax that comes from the genitive case-marked subject in the Mongolian noun phrase "Batiin nomiin," we now have lost semantic meaning with this RDF mapping. This also presents challenges for bidirectionality querying for the nodes since the subject node, "Batiin," has been specifically determined by its subject genitive case marker and would have to be specified under different case markers (i.e., accusative or nominative) when querying for other resource description statements that use the word "Bat." Ultimately, the example of genitive case-marked subjects in Mongolian illustrates that SOV syntax can be quite different from SVO syntax and with this, the semantics too will change when attempting to map to an SVO syntax, such as English, or to a linked data model, such as an RDF triple statement.

These examples of SOV syntax illustrate that attempting to assert the same semantic meaning by using an English SVO syntax, or mapping to an RDF triple, for SOV languages would be difficult and could lead to an obfuscation of the original meaning. Furthermore, asserting semantic meaning from the above Navajo and Mongolian example sentences in an RDF context would be especially difficult given that it specifically relies on a one directional arc from the subject to the object node; it also does not account for how case-markers may change the semantics of a subject node.

---

38. Ibid.

Taking a step back to reflect on how the RDF triple statement and its SVO syntax were adopted, it is important to understand that, while the W3C is committed to translating Web standards and other W3C documentation, the English language serves as the default language for conducting its work.[39, 40] With this in mind, one can see how it might be a natural development that English SVO syntax would also be reflected within the RDF data model. Tracing the lineage further back, another complicating feature is RDF's roots in predicate calculus, which, as was noted several decades ago, does not match well to the ways that humans reason.[41] Furthermore, predicate calculus contains its own unique set of rules and that preclude certain articulations. Over time, how might these rules and preferences affect the way information and data is created and networked?

In and Out of Graphs

The decomposition of information from documentary forms into triples is the foundation of linked data. We have also demonstrated how this particular syntax is biased towards Western languages and structures, especially English. While this is problematic on a semantic level (in that meaning can be warped by the structure of the triple), it also points to a scenario in which the willingness and ability to conform to linked data grammar will determine the degree of availability and findability of resources. Crucially, as Galloway observes, the point of power today resides in networks and their hiddenness.[42]

From a bibliographic perspective, adding triples that describe information resources, or participating in the graph, makes the

39. "Facts About W3C," W3C, accessed December 12, 2021, https://www.w3.org/Consortium/facts.

40. "W3C Process Document," W3C, last modified November 2, 2021, https://www.w3.org/Consortium/Process/.

41. Harry Halpin, "The Semantic Web," in *Social Semantics. Semantic Web and Beyond*, vol. 13 (Boston: Springer, 2013), 53.

42. Alexander Galloway, 'Are some things unrepresentable?' *Theory, Culture & Society* 28:7-8 (2012): 95.

graph richer and allows for resources to be more readily found (at least in theory). But the inversion of this is that those resources not in the graph are made even less available because there is no way to see what is outside of the graph. As Ortolja-Baird and Nyhan argue, 'righting' the absence of data often perpetuates various dominant subjectivities.[43] Participating in the graph can represent the same impulse. The serendipitous search described by Quan-Haase and Martin becomes even harder in this scenario.[44] While visualizations of networks do exist, we should be careful not to equate those with the actual network itself, which can be queried but not seen. That this obfuscation of non-graph resources can be avoided only by adherence to a specific syntax makes its dominance quietly subversive.[45]

One cannot really 'look' at a database either, only query it. We might even say that the bits that inscribe a network or database can only ever be enacted through some sort of mediation, which adds a layer of ideological complexity to any sort of interaction with it. That there is no fixed representation but, rather, undulating incompleteness in how the data can be perceived is true and enacts the precepts of a society of control as Deleuze envisioned it. The cataloger's impulse towards standardization has always meant that some information can get left out if there is no element in the schema, no term in the vocabulary, etc. In contrast to documents, the triple (as a standard and inherently normative) represents an intensification of control down to the syntactic level. Through the combining and linking of more triples into the

---

43. Alexandra Ortolja-Baird and Julianne Nyhan. "Encoding the haunting of an object catalogue: on the potential of digital technologies to perpetuate or subvert the silence and bias of the early-modern archive." *Digital Scholarship in the Humanities* (2021): 19.

44. Anabel Quan-Haase and Kim Martin. "Rethinking Tradition: The Loss of Serendipity and the Impact of Technology on the Historical Research Process." *Proceedings of the American Society for Information Science and Technology* 48, no. 1 (2011): n.p.

45. For further reading see Alexander Galloway's *Protocol: How Control Exists After Decentralization* (Cambridge, MA: MIT Press, 2004).

graph, new information structures can emerge. While some may see this as an acceptable compromise, our purpose here has been to demonstrate that networks/graphs are an information construction embedded with their own ideological inflections that may be at odds with equitable information description and access.

We should avoid thinking about networks and graphs as objects with their own agency separate from human interventions. Rather, we need to illuminate those human goals that shape graphs and the data within them to particular ends. Who does the graph serve? We have already demonstrated the neocolonial impulses present in linked data technologies. But as the erasure of the difference between Kittler's "files and facts" from records to triples continues, what becomes of that data?[46]

> Increasingly, data flows once confined to books and later to [sound] records and films are disappearing into black holes and boxes that, as artificial intelligences, are bidding us farewell on their way to nameless high commands.[47]

While sensitive to the post-human concern Kittler describes for machinic autonomy, we argue that it is a mistake to minimize the impact of human agents behind these engines. Blaming Capitalism or the West, though generally accurate, is not enough. The Graph is not inevitable and its content can be changed by people. Until then, one must ask about the consequences of being in or out of The Graph. Standardization in linked data comes at a high price when it comes to information loss. Triples, as materially inscribed statements, change the meaning of the graph as a *techne* into a pure *telos* or end in itself.

There is a subtle eschatological undercurrent around the joining of graphs into The Graph, or an object formed of and by perfect informational praxis. It is fitting that this comes at the

---

46. Friedrich Kittler, *Gramophone, Film, Typewriter.* (Palo Alto, CA: Stanford University Press, 1999): xxxix.

47. Ibid.

cost of what de Sousa Santos describes as "epistemicide," though we note here that this type of destruction is no longer relegated to just non-Western countries.[48] For many cultures, the end of the world has already arrived, sometimes several times. What participation in The Graph requires is yet another subsumption but with a greater level of control, no longer just through erasure but by reconstituting other non-Western knowledges according to Western epistemology.

If linked data is to reverse this current trajectory, it needs to move away from positivistic ideas of itself. At present, it can seem as though linked data is the end in itself, and as we have noted, this comes at significant costs for how information is shaped and shared. It would be better then to reconsider it as a type of *techne* (or tool) accomplishing some end and to orient it towards concrete, material goals rather than to use it for its own sake. Only then will it be able to accommodate those other epistemological frameworks that it currently stands poised to overshadow. Instead of eliminating them, it could establish them as valuable alternatives to the current epistemic traditions that inform the Internet and the way information is organized.

Conclusion

Western forms of informational coloniality are clearly a problem. Rather than being informed by other epistemic traditions, the current trajectory of linked data in GLAM suggests a future in which alternative models are subsumed by the syntax of the Western graph. Indeed, as academic libraries are currently an important driver behind these initiatives, critical reflection on the hegemonic practices they are supporting through this technology is warranted. Homogeneity is not the way forward. As Mbembe observes:

---

48. Boaventura de Sousa Santos, *Epistemologias del sur.* (Mexico: Siglo XXI, 2010).

In order to set our institutions firmly on the path of future knowledges, we need to reinvent...a university that is capable of convening various publics in new forms of assemblies that become points of convergence of and platforms for the redistribution of different kinds of knowledges.[49]

While academic libraries are not always well positioned to direct international web standards such as W3C, they are in a unique position to collectively create a pathway for their own information ecosystem through its wide range of consortia, alliances, associations, and organizations. Moreover, as the cataloging community continues its trajectory towards implementing linked data, it has reached a crucial point where critical reflection is needed to assess what potential impacts our proposed data models might have. Are we simply recreating another form of informational coloniality that we are purportedly trying to remove ourselves from? How do the data models we adopt perpetuate or dismantle previous hegemonic practices? In order to move away from such hegemony, the library community first needs to collectively recognize this as an issue. Without this step, the way we describe resources will continue under the same hegemonic grammars and lenses.

---

49. Achille Mbembe, "Decolonizing Knowledge and the Question of the Archive," lecture, University of Witswatersrand, Cape Town, South Africa, 2015.

Linked Data and Transindividual Ethics: An Essay in the Politics of Technology

SAM POPOWICH

Introduction

Linked data is a particular form of Artificial Intelligence. This statement will likely be a well-known and obvious fact to some readers but completely new to others. In this chapter, I am referring to linked data in a broad sense to include not only the actual data (e.g., RDF in its graph structure or in a given serialization),[1] but also the technologies that enable that data to be operationalized in the form of a graph data structure as well as rules of inference and a logic/reasoning engine.[2] It is important to explicitly situate linked data not only within the larger context of AI and AI ethics but also within the ethical context of GLAMS (Galleries, Libraries, Archives, Museums, and Special Collections),

---

1. Resource Description Framework (RDF) is a data model for exchanging data on the web; RDF consists of atomic data elements or statements consisting of a subject, an object, and a relationship (predicate). RDF exists as a graph data structure in memory, but can be serialized for storage and exchange using a number of different formats (e.g., Turtle, JSON-LD).

2. The insistence on linked data as a form of AI requires that we not separate description from operationalization or action. For example, Kenneth Craik's model of a "knowledge-based agent" has three components: the creation of internal representations, the manipulation of these representations by internal rules (e.g., inference, reasoning), and the "retranslation" of representations back into action. See Stuart J. Russell and Peter Norvig, *Artificial Intelligence: A Modern Approach* (Englewood Cliffs, NJ: Prentice Hall, 1995): 13.

issues around settler-colonial and racist language in descriptions, dehumanizing controlled-vocabulary classifications,[3] and other issues which Hope Olson has summarized under "the power to name."[4]

I approach this work from a Marxist perspective, naming liberalism as the hegemonic, often-unconscious "common sense" ideology of capitalism. Stuart Hall and Paolo Virno's theories of language come out of structuralism. Both Marxism and structuralism challenge the fundamental and foundational individualism of liberal social theory. This individualism in turn underpins positivism, which I see as privileging what is immediately and empirically present, seeing phenomena in isolation and dismissing both larger context and integral interrelationships between things or people. Positivism, in this chapter, is linked to the "reflective" view of language, where "meaning is thought to lie in the object, person, idea or event in the real world, and language functions like a mirror, to *reflect* the true meaning as it already exists in the world."[5] This reflective view underpins a naive conception of description and modeling that I will describe below. The Marxist approach adopted here rejects both positivism and the reflective view of language/description.

AI critic Hubert Dreyfus noted that early AI researchers took for granted the rationalist assumptions of Hobbes, Leibniz, and

---

3. See, for example, Sanford Berman, *Prejudices and Antipathies: A Tract on the LC Subject Heads Concerning People* (Lanham, MD: Scarecrow Press, 1971); Alissa Cherry and Keshav Mukunda, "A Case Study in Indigenous Classification: Revisiting and Reviving the Brian Deer Scheme," *Cataloguing & Classification Quarterly* 53, no. 5-6 (2015): 548-567; Raegan Swanson, "Adapting the Brian Deer Classification System for Aanischaaukamikw Cree Cultural Institute," *Cataloguing & Classification Quarterly* 53 no. 5-6 (2015): 568-579.

4. Hope Olson, *The Power to Name: Locating the Limits of Subject Representation in Libraries* (New York: Springer, 2002).

5. Hall, "The Work of Representation," in *Representation*, Second Edition, ed. Stuart Hall, Jessica Evans, and Sean Nixon (Milton Keynes: The Open University, 2013):10. In the philosophy of language this is often called the "referential" theory of language. See William G. Lycan, *Philosophy of Language: A Contemporary Introduction* (Abingdon, UK: Routledge, 2018): 3-5.

others, seeing cognition as simply the manipulation of propositions and the inference of new data according to explicit rules,
essentially "turning rationalist philosophy – inextricably linked
with the development of capitalism—into a research program."[6]
One goal of rationalist philosophy, deeply inscribed within AI
research, was the power to dispense with human contestation
over meanings and to fix meaning once and for all.[7] The rational-
ists eventually realized that there is no way to do this without a
transcendental sovereign power capable of fixing meaning. However, this contradicted the liberal/capitalist desire for individual
freedom not subject to sovereign and all-powerful authority.
Liberal ideology—the ideology I argue is encoded in the very
structure of linked data—is marked by the contradiction between
requiring a sovereign authority to fix meaning and requiring the
individual freedom to choose.[8] Liberalism has always sought to
remove the absolute power of the sovereign, to make space for
a pluralism of meanings, while avoiding social anarchy—and
maximizing profit through domination of natural and human
worlds—through the hegemonic power to fix meanings.

One of the reasons AI has such deep ethical problems is that
the messy, biased, or contested meanings in the social world of
humans are made concrete and fixed or stabilized (in Marxist
terms, are "reified") within AI systems. This appears to be a

---

6. Hubert Dreyfus, "Why Heideggerian AI Failed and How Fixing It Would Re-
quire Making It More Heideggerian," in *Philosophy of Technology: The Technological
Condition, An Anthology*, 2nd ed., ed. Robert C. Scharff and Val Dusek (Chichester,
UK: Wiley-Blackwell, 2014): 597.

7. Fixed meaning is required for the scientific/capitalist control over the natural and
social worlds needed for the extraction of profit.

8. Liberal political thought reproduces the figure of "the sovereign" at many different levels, from the sovereignty of the King or the Constitution, to the sovereignty
of capital, to the sovereignty of the individual, each claiming the authority to define
terms, fix language, and create order. In GLAMS, sovereignty is often centralized in the
authority of cataloguing, classification, or description rules which take on the force of
a law. In linked data terms, sovereignty is vested in an ontology, and the contradiction
between the fixed authority of an ontology and the openness of a given knowledge base
is one of the ethical contradictions I am exploring here.

neutral, objective, and positivist process, but in fact encodes an implicit social background in software. As metadata work adopted linked data, it also inherited this set of ethical problems.

From this perspective, it is important not to divide the descriptive data aspect of linked data from its operationalization in software. As will become clear, such a distinction obscures the ethical commitments that linked data entails; not only does this separation hide the way linked data is implicated in all the contemporary ethical debates in AI—around facial recognition[9] and algorithmic bias,[10] for example—but it produces an ambiguity at the heart of linked data use in GLAMS institutions. On the one hand, metadata workers produce ontologies and knowledge bases[11] as an act of *description*, while, on the other hand, these ontologies and knowledge bases are the data models operationalized in particular pieces of software. By dividing description from the operationalization of linked data, an ambiguity is produced, and it is this ambiguity that allows particular interpretations of reality to be encoded not only in the *content* of ontologies, but in the very form of linked data itself. The linked data model does not merely include biased content, it also represents a (necessarily ideological) socially constructed worldview in its very structure.

These issues are not limited to particular ontologies, systems, or linked data platforms. Rather, they are baked into the concepts and specifications of linked data itself. The openness of linked data, for example, is not a function of its public or private accessibility but refers instead to the ability of any knowledge base, public or private, open or closed, to include new statements, whether those are added by a metadata worker or inferred

9. Joy Buolamwini and Timnit Gebru, "Gender Shades: Intersectional Accuracy Disparities in Commercial Gender Classification," *Proceedings of the 1st Conference on Fairness, Accountability and Transparency* (2018): 77-81.

10. Safiya Umoja Noble, *Algorithms of Oppression: How Search Engines Reinforce Racism* (New York: NYU Press, 2018).

11. Throughout this chapter, I use "knowledge base" to refer to any operationalized, filled-in linked data structure (i.e., a graph) rather than any specific instance or application.

by the logic engine. Openness in this sense is a characteristic of linked data as a whole rather than of particular "linked open data" instances.

In this chapter, I draw heavily on the work of cultural theorist Stuart Hall, whose work on race, representation, and politics provides a useful framework for dealing with the larger social issues around the encoding and decoding of social messages in "objective" data structures. In 1973, Hall described the ways television programs encode social, cultural, and political perspectives, values, definitions and discourses—that is, *conceptual models* of the social world—not only through the content but also the formal conditions of television production.[12] A television program sends an encoded message alongside or beneath its surface content, that is then decoded by viewers who may or may not share the socio-cultural and political context of the producers. For Hall, the encoding process allows discursive and symbolic rules to "intervene" in order to "transform and naturalize" a specific historical moment with the goal of reconciling and making that history palatable to an audience. The end result of this reconciliation is the production of ideology, the maintenance of hegemonic control, and the dissemination and reproduction of particular social and political values.[13]

In 1981, Hall wrote that the media, far from simply reflecting an objective, external reality, in fact produces "representations of the social world, images, descriptions, explanations and frames for understanding how the world is and why it works as it is said and shown to work."[14] Hall's primary concern was the media's creation and reproduction of racist discourses that "help to classify out the world in terms of the categories of race," but his

---

12. Stuart Hall, "Encoding and Decoding in the Television Discourse," in *Writings on Media: History of the Present*, ed. Charlotte Brunsdon (Durham, NC: Duke University Press): 251-252.

13. Hall, "Encoding and Decoding," 262.

14. Stuart Hall, "The Whites of their Eyes: Racist Ideologies and the Media," In *Selected Writings on Race and Difference*, ed. Paul Gilroy and Ruth Wilson Gilmore (Durham, NC: Duke University Press, 2021): 103-104.

insight applies to all forms of classification: binary sex and gender classifications, disability, neurodiversity, etc. The significance of Hall's theory to linked data is that, if we conceive of linked data along Hall's lines—as the encoding of representational systems—then we have to take account of the ways linked data, like the media, performs this ideological function, allowing us to get at linked data ethical issues more precisely.

In addition to Hall's work, arguments in this essay are also situated within the humanist tradition of hermeneutics or interpretation rather than taking a more positivist social science, computer science, or information science approach.[15] linked data as a representational system encodes a "political unconscious"[16] that reproduces structures and dynamics of oppression in linked data technology as such, just as it does with other AI technologies. For example, when the title "doctor" is inextricably related to the gender "male" in a software system.[17] This requires seeing Linked Data as a kind of language—the social product of historically situated human minds—rather than as a data model rationally constructed on timeless mathematical principles or as transparent descriptions of the real world.

In the rest of the chapter, we look at how ideology relates to AI, then takes a step back to understand how Hall's theory of language and representation connects to ideological discourse. Then we will consider the specific mechanisms by which ideology is encoded in linked data, before turning to a non-individual (or transindividual) way of understanding language and society that will necessarily inform any ethical conception of linked data in the future.

---

15. For a brief introduction to, and defence of, this approach, see Edward W. Said, *Humanism and Democratic Criticism* (New York: Columbia University Press, 2004).

16. Fredric Jameson, *The Political Unconscious: Narrative as a Socially Symbolic Act* (Ithaca: Cornell University Press, 1981).

17. This was the case of Dr Louise Selby, who was locked out of the women's changing room at her gym, because the data model used by the swipe-card made precisely this "Dr"="Male" equation. See Victoria Turk, "When Algorithms Are Sexist," *Vice* (March 20, 2015), https://www.vice.com/en/article/ezvkee/when-algorithms-are-sexist.

Ideology and Artificial Intelligence

Using Hall's framework to analyze linked data technology provides a useful way to unite the ethical fields of ideology and AI and sheds light on the broader relationship of politics to technology. From the perspective of Hall's theory, linked data is not only a symbolic, conceptual, or descriptive system, it is also a *representational* system that encodes not just descriptions but meanings. linked data, therefore, is immediately (not accidentally) implicated in the construction, dissemination, and reproduction of social power relations and values—that is, ideologies—outside and beyond concrete information systems.

Hall identified three important aspects of ideology as representation: (1) "ideologies do not consist of isolated and separate concepts, but in the articulation of different elements into a distinctive set or chain of meanings"[18] (a linked data knowledge base is just such an articulation);[19] (2) "ideological statements are made by individuals: but ideologies are not the product of individual consciousness or intention"; (3) "ideologies 'work' by constructing for their subjects (individual and collective) positions of identification and knowledge which allow them to 'utter' ideological truths as if they were their authentic authors."[20] This last aspect illustrates the way software systems authoritatively reproduce ideological positions ("biases") as unquestionable truths, even when the linked data knowledge base itself is informed by openness and pluralism.

---

18. Hall, "Whites of Their Eyes," 100.

19. It is hard to suggest specific, well-defined examples, because what is being described is the totality of a conceptual system. However, in Wikidata the description of "liberalism" in different languages articulates liberalism, ideology, doctrine, movement, individual, and state differently. Alternatively, the Wikidata description of 'individual entity" articulates a contestable claim as an authoritative one: "[an] entity, be it a thing, a person or any other agent, which is identifiable by its determined characteristics, as contrasted to a class whose characteristics may be varying among its instances".

20. Hall, "Whites of Their Eyes," 101.

This kind of ideological reproduction is made possible by the separation of description from operationalization. Because GLAMS description has its own history, the adoption of Semantic Web technologies was one-sided, focusing on linked data as a descriptive technique without paying enough attention to its role as a data layer for software systems.[21] The ambiguity at the heart of linked data in GLAMS arises out of its dual history in AI and in information science.[22]

There are two main research programs within AI: *symbolic AI*, which understands knowledge as the manipulation of discrete symbols within the mind; and *connectionist AI*, which sees knowledge as arising out of configuration and strengths of synaptic connections.[23] linked data is an example of symbolic AI, while neural networks are examples of connectionism. While the history of AI has come to favour the connectionist model (e.g., neural networks and machine learning) at the expense of symbolic or "good old fashioned" AI,[24] symbolic AI has formed the basis of Expert Systems since the 1960s and gained a new impetus through the development of the Semantic Web by Tim Berners-Lee in the 1990s.[25] The move towards adoption of Semantic Web technologies in GLAMS in the early 21st century reframed linked data from a data model for a software system to a descriptive technology, essentially understood as the "next generation"

---

21. This division is often reflected organizationally, with description taking place in cataloguing and metadata departments and operationalization the responsibility of systems departments.

22. For an excellent recent analysis of the history of linked data and its political context, see Erik Radio and James Kalwara, "The Trajectory of Linked Data in Late Capitalism," *Journal of Documentation* ([preprint], 2021). https://doi.org/10.1108/JD-02-2021-0037

23. Within AI research, these two approaches "were seen as rival fields, rather than as mutually supporting approaches to the same problems." Russel and Norvig, *Artificial Intelligence*, 25.

24. Hubert Dreyfus, *What Computers Still Can't Do: A Critique of Artificial Reason* (Cambridge, MA: MIT Press, 1992): ix.

25. Tim Berners-Lee and Mark Fischetti, *Weaving the Web: The Original Design and Ultimate Destiny of the World Wide Web* (New York: Harper, 1999): 213.

methodology of metadata, description, cataloguing, and classification. With this move, the Semantic Web was brought into GLAMS and the end result was that description became severed from operationalization.

At the same time, the move to use linked data as a descriptive technology broke apart the long hegemony of the document or the record[26] in favour of flexible, reusable, atomic data elements and, thus, for the first time integrated GLAMS description and metadata with a sophisticated computer data model.[27] Where MARC, for instance, had been shoehorned into the role of a data model for library technologies, it was designed for printing Library of Congress catalogue cards, and was never implemented as a proper data model within library cataloguing systems.[28] The separation of description and data model, which are really part of a single technology, exposes, though it does not create, a very real ambiguity at the heart of the system: a single description—ontology or knowledge base—is the *encoding* of a conceptual model for metadata workers but acts as a *conceptual model as such* for a software system. This is a very important distinction

---

26. The fact that selections or aggregations of triples are still combined into particular "record views" suggests that the document or record is still dominant in certain areas of information retrieval and access, but I think this supports my distinction between a conceptual model and its encoding. The construction of records or documents from triples is yet another locus of the encoding of social structure.

27. The reason why linked data has gained the kind of traction that relational databases did not is, I suspect, down to the division between the implementers of databases in integrated library systems (ILSs) and cataloguers/data modelers. MARC records were not operationalized as proper (atomic, normalized) data models within ILSs, but rather were stored as text fields with some indexes created on some fields. There was also no standard database representation of MARC data; every vendor had their own proprietary schema. This prevented FRBR (Functional Requirements for Bibliographic Records) from successfully transforming the underlying data model. The openness and standardization of linked data technologies has meant that metadata workers/data modelers work more closely with linked data implementations than they were able to with proprietary, locked down ILS databases.

28. By "proper" I mean normalized in a database sense in order to reduce redundancy and improve data integrity. For the leveraging of MARC to make computerized catalogues possible, see Karen Coyle, *FRBR, Before and After: A Look at Our Bibliographic Models* (Chicago: ALA Editions, 2016): 50.

which we will explore in the rest of this chapter. In order to fully understand this distinction, however, we need to look a bit more closely at a few different theories of language.

Language, Description, and Meaning

Some theories of language see it as directly reflecting the real world, without any kind of interpretation or social mediation.[29] This reflective view understands words as having a one-to-one relationship with phenomena which can then simply be "read off" the world into a particular description. Traditionally, data modeling in computer science and metadata work take this positivist or reflective approach, thinking of symbols or data elements as having a simple one-to-one relationship to phenomena.[30] This relationship is conceived as unproblematic, transparent, and unmediated, as when Sandi Metz writes that "it's easy to describe the combination of parts that make up a specific bike."[31] While this kind of data modeling may appear easy and unproblematic in terms of concrete items like bicycles, it becomes extremely problematic when applied to social formations, structures, and dynamics. This is because modeling human or social phenomena requires taking account not only of surface description, but of *meaning*, which should be understood as a social relationship made possible through the negotiation of shared codes. In this

---

29. Hall, "The Work of Representation," 24-25.

30. The proliferation of new information formats caused problems for the positivist approach. Coyle and Hillman note that "descriptive rules based on predictable, stable and named 'sources of information' (title pages, colophons, etc.) about a resource, with a prescribed order of preference, were not adaptable to resources without title pages or pages, and not suitable for resources that existed in a state of constant change" (Karen Coyle and Diane Hillman, "Resource Description and Access (RDA): Cataloguing Rules for the 20th Century," *D-Lib Magazine*, January-February 2007). The tendency towards positivism also causes problems for the interpretive question of "warrant." See Brian Dobreski, "Common Usage as Warrant in Bibliographic Description," *Journal of Documentation* 76, no. 1 (2020): 49-66.

31. Sandi Metz, *Practical Object-Oriented Design in Ruby: An Agile Primer* (Boston: Addison-Wesley, 2012): 176.

view, words and other descriptions are not direct, immutable references to objects but rather encode social relations in a constantly negotiated (and contested) way.

Meaning never enters into the naïve modeling process and, as a result, contemporary issues in AI and GLAMS ethics share a common problem: that "common sense" ("obvious" or "easy") mappings of phenomena to symbols tend to reproduce hegemonic oppression and unjust structures of race, gender, sexuality, class, and disability that already exist in the conceptual maps (languages/minds) of the people who do the description and modeling. In this view, the concept of "bias" is inadequate to describe the complex processes of encoding that take place.[32] Attempting to isolate one part of reality from the rest has serious ethical repercussions bound up with the individualism of liberal-capital itself. In Hall's theory of ideology (drawing on Marx), the unquestionable ubiquity of one element of social reality—the market is the classic example—determines how we think and feel about other elements: the market becomes an exemplar, epitome, and metaphor for all other aspects of social relationships. Similarly, the capitalist view of society as made up of isolated, atomic individuals[33] determines, say, science's view of the natural and social worlds as composed of isolated elements.

However, other theories of language, derived, for example, from Ferdinand de Saussure or, later, Wittgenstein,[34] see language

---

32. "To interpret what are in fact essential elements in the systematic distortions of a socio-communications system as if they are technical faults in transmission is to misread a deep-structure process for a surface phenomenon." Hall, "Encoding and Decoding," 264.

33. This derives originally from social contract theory and carries through classical liberalism, utilitarianism, and neoliberalism. In the "Introduction" of 1857, Marx argues that social contract theory posited social atomism as an origin when it was, in fact, the outcome of a long process of capitalism's corrosion of social relations. Karl Marx, *Grundrisse* (London: Pelican Books, 1973): 84.

34. I.e., the Wittgenstein of the Philosophical Investigations. It is possible to connect linked data modeling with Wittgenstein's earlier position in the *Tractatus Logico-Philosophicus* if we interpret proposition 1.1, "the world is the totality of facts, not of things" as suggesting the subject-object-predicate triple as the ontological basis of a

rather as encoding certain social relations that construct a view of the world for us. Words encode social meanings—not labels or descriptions. Hall and Virno argue, as we will see, that because we are born into already-existing languages, the resulting socially constructed conceptual map exists transindividually (though never identically) in the mind of every person in a given culture. This theory of language explicitly rejects the foundational individualism of capitalist social thought in favour of a *transindividual* view that sees language and other aspects of social life as existing prior to the individual and producing the individual through a common set of social experiences and structures.[35]

But while meaning is not individual—read off the world by an autonomous subject—it is also not perfectly transmitted from one generation to another. Hall writes that "the codes of encoding and decoding may not be perfectly symmetrical."[36] Encodings change, interpretations vary, which makes meaning, interpretation, and communication inescapable realities for the human sciences, but causes problems for positivist data modeling and metadata work. The conceptual map we (i.e., anyone who engages in language and knowledge-exchange) have in our heads is an interpretation of the world that we must subsequently encode in words, in metadata, or in data models for any kind of communication or common activity to take place, and the asymmetry is what allows for what we tend to think of as individual agency or freedom. The encoding of signs in human societies is historical, contextual, always contested, and never fixed. Exploring these codes is the way "children learn, and how they become not simply biological individuals but cultural subjects."[37]

---

system. Indeed, while Wittgenstein later rejected the view held in the Tractatus, that view does seem to me to conform very strongly with logical/mathematical/conceptual systems like linked data graphs.

35. For more detail on Paolo Virno's concept of transindividuality, see Sam Popowich, "Compound Brain or General Intellect? Paolo Virno's Transindividualism," *New Proposals* 12, no. 1 (2021).

36. Hall, "Encoding and Decoding," 250.

37. Hall, "The Work of Representation," 8.

The main consequence of this for metadata workers and data modelers is that the creation of any representational system cannot be understood as reflecting a fixed description of the world (even the necessarily selective and simplified world of artefacts, archives, and bibliographic objects). "Meaning does not inhere *in* things, in the world," Hall writes, "it is constructed, produced. It is the result of a signifying practice, a practice that *produces* meaning, that *makes things mean*."[38] The recognition that cataloging, classification, description, and data modeling is such a practice, and that its work does not lie in accurately reflecting the world but, rather, in the *production* of its meanings has deep ethical implications for GLAMS workers.

The conceptual map we have is, however, only one aspect of representation. The second element, as Hall explains, is the encoding in a language of the conceptual map in order for the arranged and classified meanings/concepts/objects to be communicated or operationalized. In linked data terms, in addition to the act of constructing a knowledge base as a set of descriptions, the knowledge base must also be operationalized in a data layer that allows a software application to act, in a sense, like a speaker. Just as two humans must encode their own conceptual maps in a common language in order to communicate, so a software system operationalizes its knowledge base/conceptual model in order to communicate with a user. However, as we shall see below, the software package is unable to perform the complex cognitive movements that human beings do as they *negotiate* shared meaning.

It is important to bear in mind the distinction between a conceptual map and its encoding. For a given metadata worker, speaking about the world and constructing an ontology are two different encodings of the same conceptual map. In Hall's view, the meanings we share in a given culture are "constructed by the system of representation [and] constructed and fixed by the *code*,

---

38. Hall, "The Work of Representation," 10.

which sets up the correlation between our conceptual system and our language system."[39] From the perspective of a metadata worker, an ontology is one language system out of many. The ontology is an encoding of the metadata worker's conceptual map.

But for a software system, this *encoding* of a conceptual map becomes a conceptual map *in its own right*. When the conceptual map is operationalized as a data model, the ontology acts as a kind of hinge between the representation system of the wider (political, ethical) culture and the encoding of those representations in static, fixed descriptions for a software application to use. If linked data modeling is naively considered as simply reflecting existing reality (with the main concerns being accuracy and absence of bias), it obscures the fact that both representation and its encoding are socially constructed.

Encoding, Decoding, and Linked Data Mechanisms of Representation

Linked data ontology, or knowledge base, is at the same time (1) an *encoding* of a representational system (a culture, a language, a form-of-life) *for humans* and (2) a representational system *in itself* for the software that uses it. This has the ambiguous effect of presenting the openness, flexibility, and negotiability of all encodings (languages) for data modelers while presenting fixed, immutable meanings to users of the software systems. It separates the socially constructed meanings encoded by metadata workers from their social context, presenting them as isolated, atomic, naturally given and uncontestable facts when presented to individual users. In this, the structure of linked data itself—like any data model—erases the always-contested, never-finalized struggle for meaning among human beings by presenting an

---

39. Hall, "The Work of Representation," 7.

authoritative, fixed meaning to end users.[40] What makes linked data different from other data modeling systems is that, situated as it is at the intersection of AI and GLAMS histories, it includes a commitment to openness and pluralism alongside a static and closed authority.

But how does this encoding actually work? How are social, political, and ethical interpretations represented in symbolic systems like languages or ontologies? Hall's work on encoding/ decoding in television helps us to understand the way the production process (i.e., the social relations and institutions that produce a representation) gets encoded as a hidden message in the representation itself. From a very limited set of underlying social realities, a large number of surface-level visual signs or symbols can be produced.[41] The hidden messages "transform and naturalize" particular elements of our social structures in order to reproduce them as common-sense understandings in the decoders. But one of Hall's vital insights into this process was that the "correct" decoding is never guaranteed to be identical to the encoded meaning.[42] For Hall, this opens up political space, space for resistance, as misreadings can signify "at the 'message' level, the structural conflicts, contradictions and negotiations of economic, political, and cultural life."[43] The struggle to "fix" meanings once and for all becomes a cultural and ideological imperative, but this in turn creates a tension between the openness and flexibility of *our* encodings and the fixity and authority of the conceptual map used by a software system.

---

40. This struggle finds its clearest expression in the work of Hobbes, who "concluded that the solution to linguistic instability, and any disputes resulting from instability, could only be found in the determinations of the sovereign who could fix meaning and (therefore) morality." Amanda Dickens, "An 'Intercourse of Sentiments' and the Seductions of Virtue: The Role of Conversation in David Hume," in *The Concept and Practice of Conversation in the Long Eighteenth Century, 1688-1848*, eds. Katie Halsey and Jane Slinn, 20-39 (Cambridge, UK: Cambridge Scholars Publishing, 2006): 26.

41. Hall, "Encoding and Decoding," 253.

42. Hall, "Encoding and Decoding," 250.

43. Hall, "Encoding and Decoding," 261.

This tension has deep ethical and political implications. linked data ontologies and knowledge bases appear to be realms of freedom and openness for metadata workers, while also being a realm of fixed and unquestionable meanings for users of software. One of the proposed benefits of linked data modeling over other kinds of description (document- or record-based description in GLAMS, object-oriented modeling in programming, for example) is that it seems to build human flexibility and contestation of meaning into the modeling technology itself. By reducing the data model to atomic, granular triples—themselves modeled on the "atomic propositions" of positivist analytic philosophy—isolated "facts" could be inscribed in a given knowledge base independent of a structural role in a document or a record. The open-world assumption[44] says that a new fact can always be added to the conceptual map, and the AAA principle ("Anyone can say Anything about Any topic")[45] attempts to reify liberal openness and pluralism within linked data. Both are made possible by the granularity of triples that attempts to overcome the problem of meaning by reducing description to its simplest, most computationally tractable, elementary units.

There are two major problems with the open-world and AAA perspectives: (1) openness and flexibility only apply to our *encoding* of the conceptual map, not to the map as operationalized in a given software system; and (2) these principles are themselves not neutral descriptions of the world or of representational systems, but are part of the *liberal-capitalist* representation, liberalism's ideological interpretation of the world. As such, both open-world and AAA are themselves intensely political and expose deep ethical issues.

The tension between claiming and rejecting the "power to name" is at the heart of the linked data ambiguity discussed so far.

---

44. Dean Allemang and James Hendler, *Semantic Web for the Working Ontologist: Effective Modeling in RDFS and OWL*, 2nd Ed. (Burlington, MA: Morgan Kauffmann, 2011): 10.

45. Allemang and Hendler, *Semantic Web*, 6-8.

The distinction made between linked data as a representational encoding *for us* but a representational system as such *for machines* makes linked data appear to solve liberalism's problem: human contestation over meaning takes place within metadata work[46] but is in any event fixed once and for all when it is operationalized in software. Social anarchy is displaced onto and resolved in the sovereignty of the machine. This kind of displacement was very clear to Saussure, Jameson, Hall and others: it is the problem of diachronic change and synchronic fixity.[47] This will be looked at more closely below, but at this stage it is important to bear in mind that, from the perspective of metadata workers and programmers, a linked data ontology or knowledge base is not fixed; i.e., it can change over time (via the open-world assumption, the AAA principle, and other mechanisms). From the perspective of a user of a software system, however, the ontology or knowledge base *is* fixed; that is, it is only ever present at a *single, static* moment in its history, thus only a single, fixed meaning can be communicated and shared between machine and user. There is no ability for a user to negotiate or contest the meanings in the machine's representational system, even though for metadata workers, the encoding of the representational system appears to change over time.

Hall argues that understanding how representational systems can be synchronically static but diachronically shifting "opens up meaning and representation, in a radical way, to history and change."[48] The fact that, from a diachronic perspective, meanings shift and change makes interpretation a necessary element of the processes of communication and understanding. Meanings have to be "read" (that is, interpreted) out of the world before they can

---

46. Even when metadata work adopts the positivist, reflective, or naive view of description, this contestation or discursive struggle still takes place but is often displaced onto higher-level hegemonic systems.

47. See Hall, "The Work of Representation," 17 as well as Fredric Jameson, *The Prison House of Language: A Critical Account of Structuralism and Russian Formalism* (Princeton, NJ: Princeton University Press, 1972): 5-7.

48. Hall, "The Work of Representation," 17.

be encoded in a representational system, and they must be read out again in order to be understood. This means that, contrary to the naive or reflective view of description, not only is the act of interpretation foundational to classification and data modeling—with all the ethical obligations that entails—but that no interpretation can ever be correct or accurate from all perspectives or for all time. Interpretation is ethical because it is historical.

However, by looking at a single, synchronic moment in the history of a representational system, meanings *appear* to be fixed and unchanging, and therefore, they *appear* to be an authoritative, accurate, and "true" reflection of the world as it is. This appearance of true reflection is what gives representational systems their ideological power when reified in particular software applications and machines.[49] The machine forecloses interpretation and cannot engage in the contestation of shared meaning, which is a key component of human social life. Maurizio Lazzarato, in describing the way choice is reduced to the options offered by a user-interface, calls this process "machinic subjection"[50]—the power of an immovable assemblage of fixed meanings that frustrates and constrains human agency.

The obscuring of fixity within linked data systems is, as we have seen, itself ideological. Liberal political thought requires the illusion of freedom, change, flexibility, and debate while in reality enclosing them within concrete social and technological structures. We can take as a classic example the formal (rather than real) freedom of labour under capital—the freedom of a worker

---

49. The "naive" data modeling described above fits with the rationalist philosophy Dreyfus described as lying at the heart of Symbolic AI, in which description carries with it the power to overcome the struggle or contestation over meaning, to fix meaning once and for all in an exercise of unchallengeable sovereign authority. Liberal ideology sees its role—as liberal politics originally did—as removing the absolute power of the sovereign and making space for a pluralism of meanings, while still holding the reins of a legitimate sovereign power, the hegemonic power to fix meanings.

50. Maurizio Lazzarato, *The Making of the Indebted Man: An Essay on the Neoliberal Condition* (Cambridge, MA: MIT Press, 2012). See also Sam Popowich, "Proxying the Data Body: Artificial Intelligence, Federated Identity, and Machinic Subjection," *Journal of Contemporary Issues in Education* 15, no. 1 (2020).

to enter into a labour contract—which, because of the separation of worker from means of production, really means nothing but the forced sale of labour-power for a wage.[51] What follows from this is that both the open-world assumption and the AAA principle must also be recognized as ideological: they obscure the very real effects of power in capitalist societies through the privileging of openness and pluralism themselves. Open-world and AAA represent the utopian self-image of liberal ideology itself.

We know, for example, that some facts/interpretations find it easier to enter the world than others. Likewise, we know that not everyone has equal power to speak in heteropatriarchal, racial-capitalist society.[52] The idea that the best way to counter false arguments is by better arguments (which follows from both open-world and AAA) is patently false under white supremacy, under patriarchy, or in the contexts of homomisia and transmisia.[53] Those who possess the power to name do not need to enter into contests over meaning or discursive struggle; they inherently have the power to silence and exclude.[54]

These problems are made especially clear when we consider logically incommensurable statements. Incommensurable statements cause no problems for the human mind, or human social interaction. But in a logical system like a linked data ontology or knowledge base, incommensurable statements (trans women

---

51. Marx, *Capital*, 272.

52. Miranda Fricker calls this "epistemic injustice." Both kinds of epistemic injustice—testimonial and hermeneutic—that Fricker describes are implicated in the kind of linked data ethical problems I am exploring. See Miranda Fricker, *Epistemic Injustice: Power and the Ethics of Knowing* (Oxford, UK: Oxford University Press, 2007).

53. The use of the suffix -misia (hatred) rather than -phobia (fear) is gaining ground, particularly within disability advocacy, as a way to resist confusing anti-Black racism, anti-queer or trans bigotry, and other forms of hatred with mental illness.

54. One of the most important sources of linked data, Wikidata, thus inherits the contradiction between ostensible pluralism and silencing of marginalized people from the Wikipedia project. Leigh Gruwel sees such silencing as a product of "Wikipedia's positivist epistemology" (Leigh Gruwel, "Wikipedia's Politics of Exclusion: Gender, Epistemology, and Feminist Rhetorical (In)action," *Computers and Composition* 37 (2015): 120).

are women and its opposite, for example) introduce a logical contradiction which has to be resolved in order for the inference rules and logic engine to function.[55] That such contradictions can be introduced follows from the AAA principle; the only way to resolve the contradiction, according to the open-world assumption and following Mill's argument in *On Liberty*, is through the addition of new propositions. However, Georg Lukacs criticized this idea as early as 1927. In liberalism, he argued, the presence of contradictions requires the discovery/production of new knowledge in order to perfect our understanding and overcome the contradictions. But "in the case of social reality… these contradictions are not a sign of the imperfect understanding" but indicate real points of ethical and political struggle within capitalist society.[56] The addition of new propositions cannot lead to the resolutions of contradictions and the long-awaited fixity of meanings; ethical struggle for social justice in full awareness of the always-contested nature of meanings is called for. Just as we weed material for outdated, dangerous, or patently unjust content, so unjust propositions need to be actively removed from a given ontology. Adding *more* propositions does not solve the problem, and this commits us to ethico-political struggle within the field of Linked Data itself.

Transindividualism

Such struggle—like meanings themselves—must be understood as transindividual. We have to reject the individualism of the social contract and liberalism that have determined the design and implementation of linked data (and AI more broadly). There

---

55. If we separate data modeling/description from its operationalization, then such contradictions would not need to be resolved, but because our descriptions are operationalized in software systems, the contradictions have to be removed for the illusion of fixed, non-contradictory meaning to be presented to software users.

56. Georg Lukacs, *History and Class Consciousness: Studies in Marxist Dialectics* (Cambridge MA: MIT Press, 1971): 10.

is no fact that is not already a social interpretation; there are no pure individuals arising out of a state of nature and entering into social relations after the fact. Rather, human beings are produced by their parents, their culture, their language; we can struggle against these determinations, but there is no point at which we are primordially free of their influence. There is no individuality outside of social relations and communal obligations, and an ethical technology must reflect that reality.

Linked data, like the liberalism that produced it, assumes that people are always/already independent individuals. Judith Butler remarks that "the individual who is introduced to us... is posited as if he was never a child; as if he was never provided for, never depended upon parents or kinship relations, or upon social institutions, in order to survive and grow and (presumably) learn."[57] Various theories of social construction have explored what it means to reject this view but, in closing, I want to touch briefly on the work of Italian philosopher Paolo Virno. Virno explores theories of language and child development to express a view of human subjectivity as transindividual, using the example of "maternal language" which, he argues "belongs to everyone and no one; it is a public and collective dimension. It shows with great clarity the preliminary sociality of the speaker."[58] The child's introduction to language is through listening to and absorbing the pre-existing language of the family.[59] As the child learns to speak on its own, it gradually individuates itself from its pre-individual attachment to and reliance on its parents, while retaining indelible traces of its pre-individual life. In this way, the child gradually learns, as Hall put it, how to become a cultural subject and not just a biological individual.

---

57. Judith Butler, *The Force of Non-Violence: An Ethico-Political Bind* (New York: Verso, 2021): 37. Butler uses the masculine pronoun here because in her view social contract theory always postulates the individual as a man.

58. Paolo Virno, *When the Word Becomes Flesh: Language and Human Nature* (Cambridge, MA: MIT Press, 2015): 65.

59. This need not indicate only the bourgeois nuclear family, but can be interpreted as broadly as necessary, while still maintaining the idea of a preliminary sociality.

Virno's insistence on transindividuality leads to particular ethical and political commitments. By destroying the illusion of individual subjectivity, we are required to think of people always as part of a community, to subsume individual rights to collective rights where that makes sense, and (in the language of linked data) to prioritize predicates over nodes. Facts are always already a social interpretation, and this would need to be reflected in an ethical linked data. In Butler's meditation on non-violence, she argues that full recognition of our interdependency, our transindividuality (like that of the child) requires us to understand violence not as an act of one individual or set of individuals against another, but an act against social relations themselves.[60] And this, in the end, is where the ethical problems with the atomic, granular, immediate descriptions of linked data become clear. By reifying an individualistic social theory, by paying lip-service to pluralism and change from a diachronic perspective while foreclosing these from a synchronic perspective, linked data in its very structure provides the basis for ongoing racial, transmisic, misogynistic, and ableist violence. Its "links" become, in the framing of dialectics, only external relations between standalone, autonomous things rather than real internal relations of change, conflict, and resolution. They are relations of fixity intended to ensure the stability of the capitalist world for the maintenance of the social order and the guarantee of profit.

Only a changed social order, only the full recognition of the mutual dependency of transindividualism, only a technology developed in a radically egalitarian society can have a chance of overcoming the ethical problems of AI and linked data. But such a state of affairs can never be static or given once-and-for all. Hall argued that there were two ways of understanding human rights.

> The "language of rights" is frequently deployed to obscure and mystify [the] fundamental basis which rights have in the struggle between contending social forces. It constantly *abstracts* rights from their real

---

60. Butler, *Force of Non-Violence*, 16.

historical and social context, ascribes to them a timeless universality, speaks of them as if they were "given" rather than *won*, and as if they were given once and for all, rather than having to be constantly secured.[61]

The ambiguity between the synchronic and diachronic aspects of linked data, between linked data as an open and flexible descriptive system and linked data as a static and reified, closed, representation of reality, plays a role in this kind of ethical and political construction. Only by fully understanding the way these tensions play out in linked data can we begin to construct a just and ethical politics of technology. However, this requires understanding our often unconscious political and ethical commitments, being transparent about them, and rejecting the "neutral" reflective view of description in favour of a politically and ethically committed practice. This goes against many of the "common sense" principles and values of the GLAMS professions, and will require confrontation and discursive struggle to make headway. However, it is this struggle, and the social and ethical lessons learned from it, that will lay the groundwork for a social order in which ethical linked data—indeed, any ethical cultural work at all—will be possible.

61. Stuart Hall, "Drifting into a Law and Order Society: The 1979 Cobden Trust Human Rights Day Lecture," in *Selected Writings on Race and Difference*, ed. Paul Gilroy and Ruth Wilson Gilmore (Durham, NC: Duke University Press, 2021): 84.

Part II:
Ethical Considerations in the Face of
Hegemonic and Institutional Forces

Indigenous Nationhood, Sovereignty and Linked Data: A Wikidata Case Study Examination of the Métis Nation

STACY ALLISON-CASSIN

The discussion in this chapter is informed by the work I undertook on the First Nations, Métis, Inuit, Indigenous Ontology (FNMIIO) as a member of the Joint Working Group on Subject Headings and Classification of the Canadian Federation of Library Associations Indigenous Matters Committee and through the National Indigenous Knowledge and Language Alliance (NIKLA). The FNMIIO is a project to create a vocabulary of respectful terminology to be used in cataloguing and knowledge organization in relation to Indigenous peoples. The initial focus of the project was on the names of First Nations, Métis, Inuit communities. Much of the work undertaken on collecting the names of First Nations and Inuit communities proceeded in a straightforward manner. We relied on listings of First Nations reserves, band council listings, and Inuit hamlets and settlements. However, it was not possible to follow the same route to the documentation of Métis communities, even though the Métis are a recognized Aboriginal people within Canada. The Métis Nation has no reserve lands or contemporary, easily identifiable settlements or hamlets outside of a small number of formal settlements in Alberta; because of this, the Métis communities could not be defined in the same way as other Indigenous groups in the FNMIIO.[1] The ongoing challenges

1. Métis communities exist and there are lands that have been designated as homelands, but as will be discussed later in the chapter, these communities are historical, overlap with First Nations communities, and are challenging to define.

around conceptualizing the Métis People draw their complexity from trying to fit into colonial epistemological systems.

While discussions around Métis identity have received increased attention within legal and Indigenous studies in Canada, there has been little discussion in Library and Information Studies (LIS) literature, critical data studies, or within digital humanities and related literature of Métis people. The exclusion of Métis concerns from within LIS and other literature echoes wider political and cultural exclusions of the Métis people, the relatively recent recognition of Métis rights within Canada, and the recent rise of Métis studies.[2]

Situating and Self-Location

The challenges felt within this problem of "fit" echoes my own challenges with my own identity. As a white-passing person of Indigenous and Settler ancestry, I have struggled with understanding my Indigenous identity my whole life. In a situation that is common amongst many people, my grandmother strongly prohibited any discussion of our background, and I grew up confused about how to understand this part of myself. The confusion I have, and continue to feel, is further complicated by growing up in Winnipeg, Manitoba—an area strongly connected to the birth of the Métis Nation, but with more recent kinship connections to the Georgian Bay "half breed" community in Ontario—a community that has been contested as belonging to the Métis Nation.[3]

---

2. Jennifer Adese and Chris Andersen, eds., *A People and a Nation: New Directions in Contemporary Métis Studies* (Vancouver: UBC Press, 2021); Yvonne Boyer, Larry Chartrand, and Tony Belcort, eds., *Bead by Bead—Constitutional Rights and Métis Community* (Vancouver: UBC Press, 2021).

3. Ashley Brandson, "MNC Passes a Motion Declaring the Official Homeland of the Métis People." APTN News, November 30, 2018. https://www.aptnnews.ca/national-news/mnc-passes-a-motion-declaring-the-official-homeland-of-the-metis-people/; Métis Nation of Ontario, "MNO Sets the Record Straight about Its History within the Métis Nation and the Métis National Council," Métis Nation of Ontario, November 26, 2020, https://www.metisnation.org/thefacts/; Dennis Ward, "Métis National Council

Later in life, after talking to family, researching my background, and becoming a Citizen of Métis Nation of Ontario, I have come to connect with my culture and kin more fully. However, I also more fully understand the frictions and fractures within communities and the struggles for recognition, as well as the resiliency and the joys of connection. My involvement in my own community, including within community governance, has led me to think more deeply about what we mean when we say "community," the weakness of the standard conceptual structures surrounding naming and nations, and a frequent conflation of "community" with a "land" or "ethnicity" that tends to be overly simplistic in most knowledge organization systems.

My inability to move forward in a way that felt appropriate within the FNMIIO was connected to my own self-location as both a Citizen of the Métis Nation and as a researcher and practitioner within metadata work. The need to figure out how to accomplish the practical work of developing terminology in an ethical and responsible way formed the motivational basis for the conceptual and practical explorations in this chapter. This chapter presents a critical analysis and discussion of ethical tensions in the documentation of Indigenous identity, firstly through a discussion of concepts of identity, nationhood, and peoplehood, particularly in relation to the Métis Nation, and secondly through a case study of the description of the Métis Nation within the open, structured data knowledge base Wikidata. The scope of the discussion is centered primarily in the country now known as Canada and is nation-specific; however, the larger ethical issues can be related to other situations. Naming is vitally interconnected to nationhood—to liberation and self-determination—and implementations do not necessarily benefit Indigenous communities. Labels alone, without locating such terms into a larger framework

Moving Forward Says MNO President." APTN News, March 22, 2022, https://www.aptnnews.ca/facetoface/metis-national-council-moving-forward-after-years-of-dysfunction-says-mno-president/.

of Indigenous liberation, do not do the necessary work to support such ambitions and community responsibilities.

Respectful and Ethical Practice in Relation to Indigenous Naming

A key challenge for anti-colonial and ethical naming within linked data systems and repositories is ensuring the expression of situatedness and context of appropriate respectful names. Exposing problematic issues of terminology and naming within library and other formal descriptive practices and vocabulary systems is not new: library practitioners such as Sandy Berman have been pointing to inaccurate and harmful subject headings for well over fifty years, and researchers such as Adler, Turner, and Olsen have made clear the history, power and problematic nature of description and vocabularies, especially in relation to systems of oppression, exclusion, and control.[4] Recent initiatives, such as OCLC's *Reimagine Descriptive Workflows* report, name racism and colonialism as historic and ongoing elements of descriptive practice, but it is an open question whether any evidence of real action toward reparations and systemic change within practice will result.[5] Those responsible for creating and supporting linked data ontologies, datastores, and systems have an obligation to ensure a move beyond "correct" terminology to fully align linked data practices with anti-colonial or justice-focused work.

4. Melissa Adler, *Cruising the Library: Perversities in the Organization of Knowledge* (New York: Fordham University Press, 2017); Sanford Berman, *Prejudices and Antipathies: A Tract on the LC Subject Heads Concerning People* (McFarland & Company Incorporated, 1993); Hope A. Olson, *The Power to Name: Locating the Limits of Subject Representation in Libraries* (Kluwer Academic, 2002); Hannah Turner, *Cataloguing Culture: Legacies of Colonialism in Museum Documentation* (Vancouver: UBC Press, 2020).

5. Rachel L. Frick and Merrilee Proffitt. "Reimagine Descriptive Workflows: A Community-Informed Agenda for Reparative and Inclusive Descriptive Practice." OCLC, June 6, 2022. https://www.oclc.org/research/publications/2022/reimagine-descriptive-workflows.html.

Naming not only denotes belonging and identity in relation to community and kin, but it is also connected to Indigenous peoples' political aspirations, self-determination, and liberation. However, deep historic and ongoing problems with the terminology used for Indigenous peoples, cultures, and territories are present within mainstream library and interrelated vocabulary systems.[6] The myriad problems extend from misnaming and colonial renaming, to inappropriate placement within hierarchies, to using terminology inappropriate to the territory of their adoption. Turner has pointed to problematic issues of colonial misnaming as tangled up with colonial collecting practices, mundane bureaucracies, and a scientific practice wrapped up with universal and Western approaches to knowledge construction present in the founding of the Smithsonian.[7] For Indigenous people, the use of incorrect names is related to a lack of political recognition that is intimately tied to settler colonialism and ongoing moves toward erasure.

Nuances of Indigenous Identity

Those working within knowledge organization systems, such as linked data repositories, must be aware of the layered realities of Indigenous identity categories, relationships, kinship

---

6. Alissa Cherry and Keshav Mukunda, "A Case Study in Indigenous Classification: Revisiting and Reviving the Brian Deer Scheme," *Cataloging & Classification Quarterly* 53, no. 5–6 (July 4, 2015): 548–67, https://doi.org/10.1080/01639374.2015.1008 717; Ann M. Doyle, Kimberley Lawson, and Sarah Dupont, "Indigenization of Knowledge Organization at the Xwi7xwa Library," *Journal of Library and Information Studies* 13, no. 2 (December 1, 2015): 107–34, https://doi.org/10.6182/jlis.2015.13(2).107; Sandra Littletree and Cheryl A. Metoyer, "Knowledge Organization from an Indigenous Perspective: The Mashantucket Pequot Thesaurus of American Indian Terminology Project," *Cataloging & Classification Quarterly* 53, no. 5–6 (July 4, 2015): 640–57, https://doi.org/10.1080/01639374.2015.1010113; Heather Moulaison Sandy and Jenny Bossaller, "Providing Cognitively Just Subject Access to Indigenous Knowledge through Knowledge Organization Systems," *Cataloging & Classification Quarterly* 55, no. 3 (April 3, 2017): 129–52, https://doi.org/10.1080/01639374.2017.1281858.

7. Turner, *Cataloguing Culture: Legacies of Colonialism in Museum Documentation.*

connections, and categories. As stated above, ethical naming must include the encoding of appropriate contextual relationships. Furthermore, awareness of both contemporary and historical issues in identity are vital to ensuring both appropriate use of identity categories and related support for Indigenous self-determination and sovereignty. In Canada, contemporary debates surrounding Indigenous identity have come to the fore with several cases of Indigenous identity fraud. Winona Wheeler, an Associate Professor in the Department of Indigenous Studies at the University of Saskatchewan, states that Indigenous identity fraud "occurs when non-Indigenous people pose and represent themselves as Indigenous."[8] Indigenous identity fraud or "raceshifting" is self-indigenization practiced by settler individuals—typically for financial gain.[9] Recent and historic cases of fraud are prevalent enough to be a consideration of ethical practice.

Indigenous Identity, Erasure, and Control

Those responsible for or engaged with the development or deployment of linked data projects with a relationship to Indigenous people must be aware that ethical and appropriate determination of identity is complex, but also deeply important. D'Arcy Vermette, in defining Métis identity, centers definitions of Métis identity within a legal framework, noting categories such as "Indian" are used by the settler state to the advantage of colonial needs to control resource extraction and exert control over land.[10] While the increase in attention on Indigenous research, digital

---

8. Winona Wheeler, "Indigenous Identity Fraud in the Academy," Vox, November 15, 2021, https://usaskfaculty.ca/wp-content/uploads/2021/11/Indigenous-Identity-Fraud-in-the-Academy.pdf.

9. Darryl Leroux, *Distorted Descent: White Claims to Indigenous Identity* (Winnipeg: University of Manitoba Press, 2019).

10. D'Arcy Vermette, "Colonial Ideologies: The Denial of Métis Political Identity in Canadian Law," in *Bead by Bead—Constitutional Rights and Métis Community*, ed. Yvonne Boyer, Larry Chartrand, and Tony Belcort (Vancouver: UBC Press, 2021), 131–55.

projects, collections, and other initiatives are positive, the flip side is that the rapid development of such activity has put pressure on systems not created for Indigenous peoples. Furthermore, such initiatives may be curated by those lacking in deep knowledge of Indigenous identity and nationhood. Data structures should be attentive to the ways the nations, communities, and identity categories are structured and regulated, and how they are not. In their *Protocol for Working with Indigenous Communities and Peoples*, Lawford and Coburn suggest that, "Every individual has a right to self-identify based on culture, identity, ethnicity, gender, sexuality, or other facet of their life. This right is adjoined with responsibility and accountability to all Indigenous Peoples and is relational, ethical, and contextual."[11] Furthermore, and vital to this conversation,

> Existing paradigms, approaches, frameworks, legal definitions, etc. for confirming or validating identity are fraught with colonial underpinnings, racism, and discriminations. On their own, these approaches may be relationally unethical and contribute to race-shifting, secrecy, and the state's ongoing legal erasure of our Peoples.[12]

Considering the relationship between colonization, nation-states, and the ongoing regulation of identity is vital to creating an ethical and just linked data environment for data related to Indigenous peoples.

Colonial Entanglements and Identity Categories

Littletree, Belarde-Lewis and Duarte document the "colonial entanglements" of knowledge organization, finding that

---

11. Karen Lawford and Veldon Coburn, "Research, Ethnic Fraud, and the Academy: A Protocol for Working with Indigenous Communities and Peoples" (Yellowhead Institute, August 20, 2019), https://yellowheadinstitute.org/2019/08/20/research-ethnic-fraud-and-the-academy-a-protocol-for-working-with-indigenous-communities-and-peoples/.
12. Ibid.

colonialism is tied to statecraft and to the denial of "Indigenous peoples' existence, experiences, and rights to representation."[13] In their discussion of relationality and Indigenous knowledge organization practices, Littletree, Belarde-Lewis, and Duarte invoke Hobbes and Hegel to point to the intersections between law, citizen, and the state, and the conceptualization of citizens and Indigenous peoples within the North American context. Furthermore, the authors contextualize Hegel's connection between law, philosophy, ethics, and the connection to the "tree of knowledge" as part of the disciplining of knowledge within the settler state.[14] The connection between law and knowledge extends to the disciplining of categories of citizenship and identity within the settler state, and an attentiveness to colonialism requires recognition of the role of nation-states within the determination of identity and knowledge. These conceptualizations are deeply embedded within Western societal structures, going unnoticed by most settler citizens, but for Indigenous peoples, these structures are more visible and felt due to the regulation of Indigenous identity by the state. For example, the nation-state of Canada provides, or doesn't provide, access to services and education depending on one's identity.

Grammond points to the fact that, "For Indigenous peoples, identity issues are particularly fraught. This is so because their identity has often been defined by non-Indigenous settler society, for purposes associated with the colonial project. Indeed, categories such as 'Indian,' 'Indigenous,' or 'Aboriginal' did not exist before the Europeans came to the Americas."[15] Identity categorization is linked to legal concerns, and to ensure vocabulary

---

13. Sandra Littletree, Miranda Belarde-Lewis, and Marisa Duarte, "Centering Relationality: A Conceptual Model to Advance Indigenous Knowledge Organization Practices," *Knowledge* 47, no. 5 (2020): 410–26, https://doi.org/10.5771/0943-7444-2020-5-410: 411

14. Ibid.

15. Grammond, "Métis Identity Captured by Law: Struggles over Use of the Category Métis in Canadian Law," in *Bead by Bead—Constitutional Rights and Métis Community*, ed. Yvonne Boyer, Larry Chartrand, and Tony Belcort (Vancouver: UBC Press, 2021): 15.

related to Indigenous identity is ethical, it cannot be divorced from the collective. Ethical naming asserts: "political projects cannot be divorced from identity. Whether we are talking about a country, a nation, or a smaller political entity, collective action assumes a definition of the collective that is acting."[16] However, as Grammond goes on to assert, the challenge of definitions of identity cannot be only legal and only be imposed by the outside: "legal definitions are typically framed in terms of binary either-or classifications, whereas identity is often a matter of degree or of multiple allegiances."[17] Thus, for Indigenous naming to be ethical, it cannot simply use a label to recognize the names peoples call themselves; rather, it should understand, support, and advance (including through technological means) the political rights of Indigenous peoples.

Colonial legal regimes categorize Indigenous people for the purposes of control, and the experiences of colonization—both historical and present day—are different depending on one's situation and experiences. Just as universal categories and systems are problematic, and at their heart unethical, so too are systems which foreground pan-Indigeneity, document Indigenous identity on hardened, unmoving categories and labels, and refuse nuance and contextual depth. Montenegro points to the problems that exist between universal systems of knowledge organization and Indigenous knowledge:

> Indigenous collections are often managed using major national languages such as English, and according to western and universalist documentation and classification systems, ignoring and disavowing Indigenous ontologies, epistemologies and local language ideologies. Furthermore, western classification and documentation practices typically assimilate living Indigenous cultures into existing schemes designed to treat collections as fragmented and static materials preserving "frozen" knowledge.[18]

---

16. Grammond, "Métis Identity," 15-16.
17. Grammond, "Métis Identity," 16.
18. María Montenegro, "Subverting the Universality of Metadata Standards: The TK Labels as a Tool to Promote Indigenous Data Sovereignty," *Journal of Documenta-*

With the roots of control of collections in colonial govern-ment bureaucracy, there is an intimate and insidious link between the development of standards of control and efficiency and the methods by which Indigenous people continue to be treated within numerous cultural heritage collections.[19]

Terminology for the Representation of Self-Determination & Rights

Terminology used within knowledge organization systems must be mindful of the political implications of word usage. Self-de-termination for Indigenous peoples remains under threat or non-existent in many jurisdictions within Canada. Those working and creating linked data must understand and work toward the deep connections between naming and political power. The United Nations Declaration on the Rights of Indigenous Peoples (UNDRIP) calls for the recognition of rights of self-determination of Indigenous peoples in all areas of Indigenous experience.[20] For example, in his discussion of terminology in *Elements of Indig-enous Style*, Younging lists the term *band* as an inappropriate or offensive term in relation to Indigenous people.[21] He compares the definition of *band* to Oxford English Dictionary definitions for terms for *nation, people,* and *society*. The crux of his argu-ment is that the word *band* refers to a "confederation of persons" but without "political or national structure" or reference to territo-rial connections that is found with terms like *nation, people,* and *society*. Younging states that, while *band* is used by the govern-ment of Canada, it should not be used in general terms because it lacks a connection to concepts of nation, culture, and politics.[22] For those seeking to create linked data systems, consideration

tion 75, no. 4 (January 1, 2019): 734, https://doi.org/10.1108/JD-08-2018-0124.

19. María Montenegro, "Subverting the Universality of Metadata Standards"; Turner, Cataloguing Culture: Legacies of Colonialism in Museum Documentation.

20. United Nations General Assembly, "United Nations Declaration on the Rights of Indigenous Peoples" (United Nations, October 2, 2007).

21. Gregory Younging, *Elements of Indigenous Style,* 53.

22. Ibid.

of the term "band" in relation to Indigenous nations should be approached with the knowledge of these issues. Younging further unpacks how terminology used in writing needs to uphold Indigenous sovereignty. The same practice must extend to the selection and development of terminology within metadata and vocabulary work as a whole. Ethical practice means giving full consideration and knowledge of the impacts and situatedness of terminology and the thoughtful ways it is leveraged and deployed.

Terminology and the Métis Nation

The Métis Nation presents a particular challenge in relation to categorization and documentation of nation, people, and society. Métis scholar Adam Gaudry states: "The use of the term Métis is complex and contentious and has different historical and contemporary meanings."[23] The implications of an important identity term like Métis in the context of Indigenous data and knowledge organization practice in Canada are cause for concern and caution. While the Métis are not a new people in relation to the history of Canada, the means to define and demarcate and discipline Métis identity as understood through Canadian law, education, and culture are not as entrenched as those for First Nations and Inuit communities. This lack of widespread understanding and consciousness is a result of the deliberate exclusion of the Métis. Recognition of the Métis as one of the three groups of Aboriginal peoples by the government of Canada is very recent, and recognition of Métis rights even more so. While this history and context is unique to the Métis, it demonstrates the vital need to understand context in order to support Indigenous self-determination within ethical practice and linked data. To understand this context requires a further examination of the history of Métis rights and the term usage.

---

23. Adam Gaudry, "Métis," in *The Canadian Encyclopedia* (Historica Canada, January 7, 2009), https://www.thecanadianencyclopedia.ca/en/article/metis.

Métis is a French term that means "mixed." It is important to note that while *métis* means mixed, the Métis Nation is not a people defined only as mixed race. While the bounds and definitions of the Métis Nation may be disputed and complex, there are common understandings of what is not the definition of Métis identity—and that is a definition which promulgates the connection between Métis and mixed descent. The 1996 Report of the Royal Commission on Aboriginal People defines Métis: "Métis' means a person who self-identifies as Métis, is distinct from other Aboriginal peoples, is of historic Métis Nation Ancestry and who is accepted by the Métis Nation. Many Canadians have mixed Aboriginal/non-Aboriginal ancestry, but that does not make them Métis or even Aboriginal ... What distinguishes Métis people from everyone else is that they associate themselves with a culture that is distinctly Métis."[24] On the term métis, Gaudry notes: "The term is used to describe communities of mixed European and Indigenous descent across Canada, and a specific community of people—defined as the Métis Nation—which originated largely in Western Canada and emerged as a political force in the 19th century, radiating outwards from the Red River Settlement."[25] The Métis Nation emerged through a process of ethnogenesis, a process whereby a group, over time, develops its own distinct ethnic boundaries.[26] Frequently the usage of the capital "M" indicates the Métis Nation, while the usage of a lower case "m" indicates "any community of European-Indigenous ancestry."[27] However, this distinction is not common or well-enough known to depend on.

While Indigenous scholars and Métis experts may wish to use such nuances to keep the boundaries of terminology firm, it is not a dependable means of distinction and, in the context of knowledge organization systems, such distinctions might be

---

24. Royal Commission on Aboriginal Peoples, "Report of the Royal Commission on Aboriginal Peoples" (Ottawa, Canada, October 4, 2016):
25. Adam Gaudry, "Métis."
26. Ibid.
27. Ibid.

rendered invisible or unusable in any meaningful way. The use of the term "mixed" for the Métis people has had implications for problematic understandings of definitions of identity, problems that have been caught up in mainstream systems of documentation—including linked data repositories. It is vital to understand the Métis Nation as a distinct nation. The challenge of ethical deployment of linked data means pragmatism must be constantly evaluated against ethical frameworks to assist with aims of doing work that is just.

Métis scholar and lawyer Grammond makes it clear that "...Canadian law treats the Métis Nation quite differently from other Indigenous groups. The origins of that distinctiveness may be traced back to the nineteenth century."[28] As settlement moved westward, the system and treaties, and later the formalized system of control of Indigenous people through the Indian Act, were means of asserting and controlling who was, and who was not, Indigenous.[29] Métis people, by and large, were excluded from treaty processes and the Indian Act though, at the same time, recognized as not white settlers. The Red River Resistance, the Battle of Batoche, and the execution of Métis leader and founder of Manitoba, Louis Riel, by the Canadian government in 1885 for treason, are examples of events that situated the Métis people as resistant to mainstream settler colonial society.[30] The lack of

28. Grammond, "Métis Identity," 19.

29. The Indian Act became law in Canada in 1876. It is "is the primary law the federal government uses to administer Indian status, local First Nations governments and the management of reserve land. It also outlines governmental obligations to First Nations peoples." The Indian Act has been used to determine who has status as an "Indian" in Canada. Those with status are entitled to certain rights; however, the Act was also used as the basis for the Residential School System and, until very recently, women who married non-Status men lost their Status. Its purpose was to assimilate and disappear First Nations people in Canada. Métis and Inuit people are not subject to the Indian Act and therefore do not have "Status." Zach Parrott, "Indian Act," in *The Canadian Encyclopedia* (Historica Canada, February 7, 2006).

30. There is not enough space within this chapter to relate the whole history of the Métis Nation. Many excellent sources exist, including Jean Teillet's *The North-West Is Our Mother: The Story of Louis Riel's People, the Métis Nation* (Patrick Crean Editions, 2019).

easy fit extends to a lack of easy terminology. Vermette notes that the use of "Indian" is different in Canadian law at different times, making matters confusing even in areas where they should be clear. He uses natural resources extraction agreements (NRTAs) as an example of this. He finds that in the 1930s, the agreements do not include Métis people and yet, in the Daniels decision of 2016, the Supreme Court of Canada determined Métis people were included as part of a broader definition of "Indian." Vermette critiques the imprecise nature and "flexibility" of legal definitions of Métis as being "divested from reality" and the ways the "court has constructed Métisness will undermine Métis political aspi-rations and legal recognition in other areas of law (treaties)."[31] Using identity terms such as Métis within linked data systems requires careful consideration of how such a term is derived and defined, as well as its relation to other terms.

Despite the problems outlined by Vermette, legal definitions may provide vital aid in clarifying and fixing terms within a colonial system that requires textual documentation for validity. Grammond writes: "legal definitions of Indigenous identity may also serve as a tool of justice. They may ensure fairness in the allocation of resources aimed at compensating the wrongs of the past. They may help mainstream a group's distinctiveness. They may also contribute to the functioning of the political insti-tutions of an Indigenous community or nation."[32] By extension, legal terms may also assist those in information organizations to understand terminology relating to Indigenous peoplehood and the connected expression of sovereignty. Métis peoples were not recognized as Aboriginal by the Government of Canada until the passing of Section 35 of the Canadian Constitution Act in 1982.[33]

---

31. D'Arcy Vermette, "Colonial Ideologies: The Denial of Métis Political Identity in Canadian Law," in B*ead by Bead—Constitutional Rights and Métis Community*, ed. Yvonne Boyer, Larry Chartrand, and Tony Belcort (Vancouver: UBC Press, 2021): 143.

32. Grammond, "Métis Identity Captured by Law," 17.

33. The 1982 Canadian Constitution Act was a landmark moment in the history of the Canadian state as it marked full independence from the United Kingdom and allowed Canada to make changes to its constitution without requiring permission from

A further significant legal gain was the 2003 Canadian Supreme Court case R. v. Powley, [2003] 2 S.C.R. 207, 2003 SCC 43.[34] The case, which centered around harvesting rights in the Sault Ste. Marie area of Ontario, clarified ambiguous language in Section 35 regarding Métis identity and rights. The resulting definition has been dubbed the "Powley test" and is widely used to determine a claim of Métis identity which, in part, states that one must: "self-identify as Métis, have an ancestral connection to a historic Métis community and be accepted by the modern Métis community."[35] Furthermore, it is vital to understand the legal implications and sets of rights related to Indigenous identity that are substantially different from other kinds of ethnicity or racialized terms often used as identity markers. Understanding and being mindful of the location and legal frameworks of Indigenous identities matter when it comes to supporting Indigenous sovereignty and political aspirations within linked data systems. Where the vocabularies and terminologies we use are situated in relation to such categories matters.

Métis Citizenship, Membership and Rights

In Canada there are several Métis organizations that have established Nation-to-Nation relationships with Her Majesty, the Queen in Right of Canada, through the Canada-Métis National Accord signed in 2007.[36] The accord was signed by five provin-

---

the United Kingdom. Andrew McIntosh and Stephen Azzi, "Constitution Act, 1982," in The Canadian Encyclopedia (Historica Canada, February 6, 2012), https://www.the-canadianencyclopedia.ca/en/article/constitution-act-1982.

34. Supreme Court of Canada, "Supreme Court of Canada—SCC Case Information—Search," January 1, 2001, https://scc-csc.lexum.com/scc-csc/scc-csc/en/item/2076/index.do.

35. Métis Nation of Ontario, "Establishing a Métis Right," Métis Nation of Ontario, accessed June 18, 2022, https://www.metisnation.org/registry/the-powley-case/establishing-a-metis-right-the-powley-test/.; Heather Conn, "Powley Case," in The Canadian Encyclopedia (Historica Canada, December 3, 2018), https://www.thecanadianencyclopedia.ca/en/article/powley-case.

36. "Canada-Metis Nation Accord," Prime Minister of Canada, April 20, 2017, https://pm.gc.ca/en/canada-metis-nation-accord.

cial Métis affiliate organizations: the Manitoba Métis Federation (MMF), Métis Nation of Ontario, Métis Nation of Saskatchewan, Métis Nation of Alberta, and Métis Nation of British Columbia. These provincial associations are located within the geographic territories considered to be connected to historic communities of the Métis Nation. Each association maintains a membership list, and members (also known as Citizens) must meet criteria based on genealogical/kinship ties. Adese and Anderson find that these associations "position the descendants of the Métis Nation as being represented" by the Métis National Council and its provincial affiliates.[37] Anderson and Adese acknowledge representation by the MNC and the provincial bodies as being imperfect; however, these entities, "born from the sustained effort of the Métis" should be acknowledged as having an ability to determine membership, following the Powley test and other legal frameworks, and engage in self-determination.[38] Members, also referred to as Citizens, must submit documentation of ancestry that demonstrates a link to established kinship and lineage. While there are other groups claiming to be representatives of Métis people, typically in geographic areas east of Ontario, none have so far been successful in testing the rights of their members in court, and they are generally unrecognized by the associations listed here and by the provincial and national governments of Canada.[39] The complexities of the ongoing work of the Métis Nation in establishing citizenship, self-determination, and work such as writing constitutions are important because this context is typically absent in knowledge organization systems.

In cataloguing, metadata, linked data, and other descriptive work, there is a lack of connection between terms designating

37. Jennifer Adese and Chris Andersen. "Introduction: A New Era of Métis Studies Scholarship," in *A People and a Nation: New Directions in Contemporary Métis Studies* (Vancouver: UBC Press, 2021): 11.

38. Ibid.

39. Rhiannon Johnson, "Exploring Identity: Who Are the Métis and What Are Their Rights?," CBC, April 28, 2019, https://www.cbc.ca/news/indigenous/metis-identity-history-rights-explainer-1.5098585.

peoplehood and the advancement and upholding of principles and rights as expressed through these documents. While Indigenous data sovereignty is an area of concern and attention, the focus tends to be on Indigenous cultural expressions, Indigenous knowledge, and data related to Indigenous peoples, such as health or genomic data. Digital collection and linked data work tends to focus on considerations for respectful and responsible care and protocols for holding and accessing data and digital objects. However, this focus leaves out, or is less concerned with, some of the structural issues related to sovereignty and naming.

What is Wikidata?

Wikidata "is a free and open knowledge base that can be read and edited by both humans and machines" and is a free crowdsourced, multilingual, structured data repository.[40] Wikidata is a "sister project" to Wikipedia and other Wikimedia projects such as Wikimedia Commons. While Wikipedia is supported by the not-for-profit Wikimedia Foundation, Wikidata is hosted and supported by Wikimedia Deutschland, an "arm's length" German branch of the Foundation. Wikidata was initially developed and launched in October 2012 as a means of supporting and connecting the thousands of Wikipedia articles in different languages and as a means of supporting some integration and deployment of structured data on Wikipedia.[41] Wikidata allows information well-supported by structured data, such as birthdates, to be updated in one place and have that data updated across Wikipedia pages. Unlike many linked data repositories, Wikidata is crowdsourced, with data structures determined through community consensus on an ongoing basis. According to a study comparing several major linked data repositories, Wikidata had

---

40. "Wikidata," accessed June 18, 2022, https://www.wikidata.org/wiki/Wikidata:-Main_Page.
41. Ibid.

the "the highest degree of schema completeness, population completeness and timeliness frequency" and was "the most diverse
in having labels in multiple languages"[42] However, Wikidata has
grown well beyond its scope as an internally Wiki-focused tool
to become a linked data hub interlinking content from many data
stores because the platform allows for the addition of URIs. As of
this writing, Wikidata contains 98,617,349 data items.[43]

Because Wikidata's structured data allows for both easy
integration into other repositories and the ability to support
URIs, Wikidata is increasingly becoming part of library linked
data workflows for numerous projects. Such projects include
the LD4L's support and development of the Wikidata Affinity
group, and the Program for Cooperative Cataloging (PCC)
Wikidata pilot program. The Association of Research Libraries
(ARL) white paper working group, that I was a member of, made
numerous recommendations for the integration of Wikidata into
library workflows, including the use of library authority data:
"These data are the most readily usable and linkable as linked
data on the open web. Implementing authority data in the form of
uniform resource identifiers (URIs) connected to collections is a
powerful way to link to related collections through Wikidata, as
well as opening the possibility of enriching library bibliographic
systems with external data sources."[44] One of the main library
applications for Wikidata is as a linking hub for library authority
data. The platform's ease of use and ontological flexibility give it
an advantage over other linked data tools, making it a low-barrier
tool for linked data work and, potentially, opening opportunities

42. Timothy Kanke, "Knowledge Curation Work in Wikidata WikiProject Discussions," *Library Hi Tech* 39, no. 1 (January 1, 2020): 64–79, https://doi.org/10.1108/
LHT-04-2019-0087.

43. "Wikidata:Statistics—Wikidata," accessed June 18, 2022, https://www.wikida-
ta.org/wiki/Wikidata:Statistics.

44. ARL Task Force on Wikimedia and Linked Open, "ARL White Paper on Wikidata: Opportunities and Recommendations," Report (Association of Research Libraries, April 18, 2019): 11.

for lower resourced organizations to participate in linked data initiatives.[45] Many projects and researchers, including myself, felt Wikidata would hold great opportunity for handling metadata in a more equitable way. However, while Wikidata may yet provide opportunities to create and engage in linked data work that supports the aspirations of Indigenous peoples, it currently does not.

Wikidata and Indigenous Peoples

Wikidata's deep structural and ontological ties to Wikipedia cause problems with the ways Indigenous knowledge, peoples, localities, and relations are encoded within the platform. Wikipedia is an encyclopedia where individuals are helping to create "a world in which everyone can freely share in the sum of all knowledge."[46] The Wikipedia mission statement and the puzzle globe icon points to a presumption that with encyclopedic impulse, all the world can and should be documented and made available—the globe of knowledge must be filled in.[47] Within the aims of the Wikipedia project, no knowledge in the world is to be kept secret or excluded from the sum. Many of the members of the Wikipedia community are focused on "filling in" missing areas as well as "collecting" knowledge, rather in the way of 18th-century encyclopedists, and this attitude and framework has been transferred to the structure and community culture of Wikidata. This universalist and universalizing approach to knowledge is at odds with ethical practices that recognize that not all knowledge is available for the taking.

---

45. Stacy Allison-Cassin and Dan Scott, "Wikidata: A Platform for Your Library's Linked Open Data," *The Code4Lib Journal,* no. 40 (May 4, 2018), https://journal.code4lib.org/articles/13424.

46. "Wikimedia Foundation," Wikimedia Foundation, accessed June 18, 2022, https://wikimediafoundation.org/.

47. "Wikipedia Logo," in Wikipedia, June 13, 2022, https://en.wikipedia.org/w/index.php?title=Wikipedia_logo&oldid=1092861848.

Systematically subduing and documenting the world's knowledge, even when done in the pursuit of equity, cannot be separated from colonialism. The community ethos of Wikipedia, and by extension Wikidata, tends toward the "gathering of all knowledge."[48] This same push toward completion and openness and "collection," while less obvious in Wikidata, still imbues projects where the focus is on "gaps" and "data donations" rather than examinations of data structures themselves for inequities or unethical practice. Kimberly Christen critiques the information freedom movement for its lack of nuance and lack of recognition of the need for care and sensitivity in relation to Indigenous knowledge.[49] The crowdsourced nature of the project means Wikidata lacks both rigorous monitoring and rules around what can be added, aside from ambiguous conditions of notability. A major issue in relation to Indigenous data is that there are no protocols in place to either recognize Indigenous sovereignty over data or to ensure that materials that are legal to share under colonial concepts of copyright (for example, public domain materials) are treated ethically. Hopefully, this is something that can be developed in the future.

Land, Territory, and Nation

In the case of Indigenous communities and peoples, the use of Wikipedia articles as the basis for the generation of Wikidata items has meant a conflation between land as territory, nation, and a people. For example, the "Mississaugas of the Credit First Nation" Wikipedia article describes: the history and culture of the Misi-zaagiwininiwag, prominent members, the history of

---

48. Roy Rosenzweig, "Can History Be Open Source? Wikipedia and the Future of the Past," *Journal of American History* 93, no. 1 (2006): 117–46, https://doi.org/10.2307/4486062.

49. Kimberly Christen, "Does Information Really Want to Be Free? Indigenous Knowledge Systems and the Question of Openness," 2012, https://research.libraries.wsu.edu:8443/xmlui/handle/2376/5705.

movement, and Land Title, as well as the geographic boundaries of the present-day reserve. At the time of writing this chapter, however, the Wikidata item Q6878995 linked to the article only contains statements regarding geography and is only an instance of an "Indian reservation of Canada." There are no other items in Wikidata for the Mississaugas of the Credit First Nation. The issue may in large part be due to the automated creation of Wikidata items from Wikipedia articles and an inability of the process to appropriately map data items. For example, the movement between land and peoples is not an issue for the narrative text, but because only one Wikidata item is generated through a bot process, the contextual richness and nuance of the original Wikipedia article is lost. While the automated generation of Wikidata items is not problematic for items such as the majority of biographies, numerous articles on Indigenous communities present conceptual and political challenges that are not addressed or acknowledge within this process.

Furthermore, there is currently no way to encode traditional territory, treaty, or other Indigenous-specific properties and data structures. For example, I currently reside in Oakville, Ontario, but there are not appropriate statements that allow for stating that Oakville is the treaty territory of the Mississaugas of the Credit First Nation, nor are there any properties that allow for the encoding of traditional territory or that Oakville is within the lands of the Dish With One Spoon territory.[50] The conflation of communities and land in this way is perhaps not intended, but it is unethical nonetheless. As of the writing of this chapter the Wikidata item generated for the Wikipedia articles on the Dish With One Spoon covenant, item Q3904875, has an English label stating that it is a "law used by Indigenous people" but it has no

---

50. Town of Oakville, "Indigenous Culture and Community," Town of Oakville, accessed July 17, 2022, https://www.oakville.ca/culturerec/indigenous-community.html; I also wish to acknowledge students in the Fall 2021 class of INF1321 at the University of Toronto for pointing out the lack of support within Wikidata for expressing information linking geographic locations, treaties, and traditional territories.

"instance of" or value, making it of limited use as a data point. The lack of connection between what is considered to be an important law or covenant covering a highly populated area within Canada, and further a covenant cited in many institutional and municipal land acknowledgements and cities, towns, and organizations, highlights a lack of attention to the recognition of Indigenous rights, protocols, and land. This one example is representative of an issue relating to the ways many First Nations communities are documented in Wikidata. The automatic generation of entities from Wikipedia articles and the lack of attention to treaty and territory recognition is something that bears further examination in order to ensure more ethical practice within Wikidata, and libraries, archives, or other organizations using Wikidata as a linking hub need to be mindful of such problematic structures.

Wikidata, URIs, and Ethics

Ethical practice in linked data systems must also consider the use of identifiers and the appropriateness of "same as" relationships when linking entities. Universal Resource Identifiers (URIs) are the backbone of semantic systems, as they identify a unique resource or entity, create meaningful relationships, and are one of Tim Berners-Lee's four general guidelines for linked data.[51] External identifiers are defined as "strings that represent identifiers used in external systems (databases, authority control files, online encyclopedias, etc.) and they will display as external links in Wikidata items if a formatter URL (P1630) is defined." External identifiers are listed as being useful to Wikidata in several ways: "Data quality: cross-checking statements with other, academic sources; Identifying missing notable items; Popularise and motivate the use of Wikidata; Supporting sister projects: for example, providing references, further information links, etc., for

---

51. Tim Berners-Lee, "Linked Data—Design Issues," July 27, 2006, https://www.w3.org/DesignIssues/LinkedData.html.

Wikipedia."[52] Many in cultural heritage institutions, and libraries more specifically, see the ability to create meaningful links between repositories as one of the biggest opportunities for the use of Wikidata for linked data work.[53] However, while the idea of Wikidata as a linking hub is attractive, care must be taken to ensure that the encoding of URIs is ensuring appropriate relationships within the data.

For example, the Wikidata item for Métis people contains a URI for the Library of Congress Subject Heading for Métis people. The Library of Congress authority record for this heading states: "Here are entered works on Canadians of mixed European and Indian descent."[54] Clearly, returning to definitions in the first section of this chapter, this heading is at best lacking in nuance, and at worst is harmful. As discussed above, members of the Métis Nation are not simply people of "mixed" ancestry, and it is therefore inappropriate to encode "same as" relationships using identifiers with faulty or problematic definitions and usage in the Wikidata item for Métis people. While there is currently some legal flexibility around the usage of the term, the Library of Congress definition is not in keeping with the political or ethical concerns of the Métis Nation. The notes in the authority file indicate that the source of this definition comes from a phone call to "Indian Affairs" in 1988 where the cataloguer was told "Mixed bloods is still common terminology, but also means mixed descent among Indian groups. Metis is being used." Wikipedia is cited as a source in 2009, which does not lend great credibility to the accuracy of the subject heading. Ensuring links are accurate

---

52. Wikidata, "Wikidata:External Identifiers—Wikidata," accessed June 18, 2022, https://www.wikidata.org/wiki/Wikidata:External_identifiers.

53. ARL Task Force on Wikimedia and Linked Open, "ARL White Paper on Wikidata: Opportunities and Recommendations," Report (Association of Research Libraries, April 18, 2019); Effie Kapsalis, "Wikidata: Recruiting the Crowd to Power Access to Digital Archives," Journal of Radio & Audio Media 26, no. 1 (January 2, 2019): 134–42, https://doi.org/10.1080/19376529.2019.1559520.

54. Library of Congress, "Métis," MARC Display (Library of Congress Authorities), accessed June 18, 2022, https://id.loc.gov/authorities/subjects/sh88007566.html.

in terms of scope and definitions are important given the ways Wikidata is being integrated or consumed by other systems.

Projects and initiatives that focus on creating linked data concerning Indigenous peoples, including identity, communities, and localities, should involve Indigenous people. Many of the other URIs present link to equally problematic URIs. While it is easy to point to quality issues related to the crowd-sourced nature of Wikidata, this is not a satisfactory answer. When organizations or individuals take on Wikidata work in relation to Indigenous peoples, there needs to be great attention paid to the accurate use of URIs and the "same as" relationship within Wikidata. The same attention is required in other linked data projects seeking to link disparate linked data stores such as the numerous projects that have come out of the Program for Cooperative Cataloging (PCC) Wikidata Pilot Project, or the LINCS Project.[55]

Ethnicity Versus Nationhood

The challenges of documenting Indigenous people within Wikidata are related to the kinds of properties available, and the lack of modelling and definitions across multiple languages in relation to the meaning of race, ethnicity, ancestry, nationhood and community belonging. Another example of a problematic data structure is the Wikidata property for ethnicity. The property "ethnic group" is a known issue among some members of the Wikidata community. "Ethnic group," property P172, is a property that, unlike most of the properties on Wikidata, has a constraint. A constraint means that there are encoded limitations on how it can be applied to items and applications that do not follow the rules as set out by the constraint are flagged with a "violation" tag. As

55. This author is a research theme lead on the LINCS project. The aim of the project is to use linked data to connect cultural data from researchers as well as cultural data organizations. "LINCS—Linked Infrastructure for Networked Cultural Scholarship." Accessed July 17, 2022. https://lincsproject.ca/.

of this writing, the description in English for this property states: "subject's ethnicity (consensus is that a VERY high standard of proof is needed for this field to be used. In general this means 1) the subject claims it themselves, or 2) it is widely agreed on by scholars, or 3) is fictional and portrayed as such)"[56] "Ethnic group" isn't defined beyond the description of usage. While there is a link to WikiProject Ethnic Group, that group defines ethnicity in connection to a longer article in Wikipedia where: "An ethnic group or ethnicity is a grouping of people who identify with each other on the basis of shared attributes that distinguish them from other groups. Those attributes can include common sets of traditions, ancestry, language, history, society, culture, nation, religion, or social treatment within their residing area. Ethnicity is sometimes used interchangeably with the term nation, particularly in cases of ethnic nationalism, and is separate from the related concept of races."[57] Note that within this definition there is a wide set of attributes bundled under the concept of ethnic group, and the conflation of "ethnic group" with "nation." Indigenous sovereignty and peoplehood are not adequately captured in concepts related to ethnicity. For example, one may be Irish Canadian and feel oneself to be part of a particular ethnic group and even nationality, but this is not the same, conceptually, as being a member of the Métis Nation within Canada. The *Report of the Royal Commission on Aboriginal Peoples* makes the connection between Indigenous identity and nationhood clear, while also dissuading connections between such identities and racial categories, stating: "The term Aboriginal peoples refers to organic political and cultural entities that stem historically from the original peoples of North America, rather than collections of individuals united by so-called 'racial'

---

56. Wikidata, "Ethnic Group," accessed June 18, 2022, https://www.wikidata.org/wiki/Property:P172.

57. "Wikipedia:WikiProject Ethnic Groups," in Wikipedia, September 6, 2021, https://en.wikipedia.org/w/index.php?title=Wikipedia:WikiProject_Ethnic_groups&oldid=1042644386.

characteristics."[58] Therefore, using properties such as ethnicity for Indigenous nations and tribal groups is not appropriate or ethical.

Adese and Anderson see concepts of Métis identity rooted in racialized discourse as being problematic with the potential to create claims based on historical narratives and understandings.[59] Such claims, bolstered by academic writing, the formation of organizations, and even court cases, are seen as false and potentially harmful to the Métis. In the context of Wikidata, the use of the property of "ethnicity" for Métis people is problematic and unethical. For example, the Wikidata item for the author Maria Campbell, Q1895752, as of this writing has the statement "Ethnic identity" with the value "Métis."[60] Ethnicity items, such as Métis, lack a nuanced and developed connection to a shared sense of nationhood or peoplehood, self-determination, territory, and kinship connections that are necessary in the context of Indigenous identity. Hancock states, "For Indigenous peoples recognition of personhood requires a profound challenge to the ideology of the nation state, and must recognize Indigenous relationships (including relationships to land), belonging, citizenship, community, and territory."[61]

---

58. Royal Commission on Aboriginal Peoples, "Report of the Royal Commission on Aboriginal Peoples" (Ottawa, October 4, 2016): iii.

59. Jennifer Adese and Chris Andersen, eds., *A People and a Nation: New Directions in Contemporary Métis Studies* (Vancouver: UBC Press, 2021).

60. Wikidata. "Maria Campbell." Accessed July 17, 2022. https://www.wikidata.org/wiki/Q1895752.

61. Robert I.A. Hancock, "The Power of Peoplehood: Reimagining Metis Relationships, Research, and Responsibilities," in *A People and a Nation: New Directions in Contemporary Métis Studies*, ed. Jennifer Adese and Chris Andersen (Vancover: UBC Press, 2021); A sense of the ways of considering kinship connections and connections to land and the considerations of issues such as scrip and treaties in the following discussion featuring Maria Campbell and Tony Belcourt is illuminating: Toronto Metropolitan University. Metis Identity Webinar 1. Métis Identity, 2021. https://www.youtube.com/watch?v=KxyJ0b97TIE.

Wikidata References, or Lack of References

The inclusion of references, or data sources, is an excellent practice within Wikidata. References strengthen linked data by ensuring that the provenance of a data point is clear and can be verified. References also ensure a Wikidata user can decide on the veracity of a data point. However, data can be added to Wikidata without references. Furthermore, and problematically, references must be in the form of formal textual documents from notable sources, an issue that penalizes those from communities with oral traditions or alternate forms of community documentation. In the case of Indigenous identity, the instruction on the use of the property for ethnic group privileges self-identification. While self-identification is important, in the case of application of Indigenous identity categories, more nuances may be required. Naming connected to identity is an issue of authority and sovereignty of the community and nation in question.

Conclusion

It is unclear as to how ethical work related to Indigenous nationhood can be undertaken within Wikidata. At this time, it is not possible to wholly recommend Wikidata as a truly ethical and just space for linked data work in connection to the Métis Nation, and likely other Nations as well. However, an organized project to consider how to ensure the expression of Indigenous identity in Wikidata is part of Indigenous nations' self-determination and sovereignty. Ethical use and deployment of Indigenous identity categories and names within linked data projects must include structures that allow for the full expression and documentation of the complexity of expressions of Nationhood and Peoplehood. The inclusion of Indigenous-related initiatives within linked data work must acknowledge and advance the political aims of the nations they represent.

It is vital that those working on linked data projects understand the connection between the naming of Indigenous people and issues such as self-determination. It is not enough to ensure a label is correct—the data model, the connections within the repository and the links to external repositories must be appropriate and ethical. This may mean that some data connections are "lost" in the case of not connecting to data stores with heavily colonial or problematic naming, and it may mean creating data models that do not align with data structures used for other people.

For those working either within platforms such as Wikidata, or on other linked data repositories, it is imperative that expressing Indigenous identities relates to understanding the multidimensionality of such identification and what the purpose of such data is. Questions to be asked include: Is your project advancing the political aims of Indigenous peoples? Do you appropriately and fully understand the implications of the work you are doing? Inclusion of Indigenous materials, identities, or persons does not necessarily or automatically benefit Indigenous people. Linked data holds within its technological possibilities the potential to support the collective aspirations of Indigenous nations. Métis scholar Chris Andersen has stated, "nations—at least in their modern sense—are not things but political projects produced through the collective efforts of...claims makers."[62] Nation building is a collective effort, and Indigenous and non-Indigenous people can work together to uphold Indigenous sovereignty and self-determination.

---

62. Chris Andersen, "Indigenous Nationhood," in *Native Studies Keywords*, ed. Stephanie Nohelani Teves, Andrea Smith, and Michelle H. Raheja, *Critical Issues in Indigenous Studies* (Tucson, AZ: The University of Arizona Press, 2015): 23.

The Colonial Histories of Linked Data Workflows

DEVON MURPHY

Introduction

The foundations of American classificatory systems or knowledge organization (KO) systems were inextricably part of the colonial project to remove and assimilate Indigenous people; I argue that these features persist within current linked data workflows.[1] This chapter focuses on these colonial systems as the object of dissection and analysis, turning past practice on its head as an effort of unsettling.[2] In turn, I encourage other White cultural heritage workers to deeply examine the infrastructure that many linked data work tasks rest upon, peeling back extant

---

1. I am forever grateful for the instruction and guidance provided by my late advisor/mentor, Dr. Jenny Tone-Pah-Hote (Kiowa). It is from her belief and encouragement that I am here offering this work now. I also want to thank Dr. Andrea Snow for her patient and empathetic guidance with this article. Linked data is defined here as a series of recommendations on how to create structured information online, generally by using URIs that link descriptive materials together. "LinkedData." W3C, August 1, 2016. https://www.w3.org/wiki/LinkedData.

2. Unsettling has been used in various ways to convey the reinsertion of Indigenous understandings into scholarship and social life, as well as the displacement of White colonial systems, as in Natchee Blu Barnd, *Native Space: Geographic Strategies to Unsettle Settler Colonialism* (Corvallis, OR: Oregon State University Press, 2017). Some, like Paulette Regan in *Unsettling the Settler Within: Indian Residential Schools, Truth Telling, and Reconciliation in Canada* (Vancouver, BC: Crane Library, 2015), 13, define unsettling as a personal act to reckon with Indigenous and settler histories. Here, I am using it in both senses to convey the institutional and individual worker roles in this process.

colonial residue.[3] Jumping in at current practice precludes us from seeing historical connections between current work methods, like mass data harvesting, and superannuated extractive actions, like mass collecting.

From "Indians of North America" to "Slaveholders," the subject terms and classification schemas used by cultural heritage workers throughout the United States have long needed revision.[4] While the voices of workers and community members, largely non-White, have called for changes since the mid-20th century with varying success, it has only been within the last ten years that a large, concerted effort to update terminology used in library, archive, and museum systems has been meaningfully initiated across disciplines.[5] This discourse has centered

3. This work, as well as following practice in Indigenous Studies to capitalize "Indigenous," will also capitalize "White" when referring to it as a racial or cultural descriptor. This follows from a suggestion during the peer reviewing process and from growing convention, as seen in the National Association of Black Journalists' guidelines and the tacit acceptance of this practice from the Chicago Manual of Style. As this work's central focus is classification practices from Euro-American professionals and their roots in colonialism, it is key that Whiteness is identified as the source. "NABJ Style Guide - National Association of Black Journalists." June, 2020. https://www. nabj.org/page/styleguide, "Black and White: A Matter of Capitalization." 2020. CMOS Shop Talk. June 22, 2020. https://cmosshoptalk.com/2020/06/22/black-and-white-a-matter-of-capitalization/.

4. Marisa Elena Duarte (Pascua Yaqui) and Miranda Belarde-Lewis (Zuni/Tlingit), "Imagining: Creating Spaces for Indigenous Ontologies," *Cataloging & Classification Quarterly* 53, no. 5–6 (2015): 677–702, 677-678, 680-683; Melissa A. Adler, "'Let's Not Homosexualize the Library Stacks': Liberating Gays in the Library Catalog." *Journal of the History of Sexuality* 24, no. 3 (September 2015): 478–507, doi:10.7560/ JHS24306, 486-489.

5. Duarte and Belarde-Lewis, "Imagining: Creating Spaces for Indigenous Ontologies," 677-678; A catalog of more recent efforts can be found at https://cataloginglab. org/category/critcatenate/, maintained by Violet Fox. Under the varying banners of "critical cataloging," "critcat," "conscious cataloging," "ethical description," or "reparative description," librarians, students, scholars, and community members have sought to amend the biases and stereotypes baked within vocabularies used for a myriad of cultural heritage work tasks. Bri Watson, "CritCat.Org," Accessed 2021, https://critcat.org/; Utah Historical Society, "Statement on Socially Conscious Cataloging and Archival Descriptions," Utah Division of State History, 2021, https://history.utah.gov/ statement-on-socially-conscious-cataloging-and-archival-descriptions/; "Reparative Description." Dictionary of Archives Terminology, Society of American Archivists, 2021. https://dictionary.archivists.org/entry/reparative-description.html); "Toward Ethical and Inclusive Descriptive Practices in UCLA Library Special Collections,"

on cataloging and its relationships to the interpersonal work of GLAMS (gallery, library, archive, museum, special collections) institutions, making the connection from the catalog record and its creation to the feelings and understandings of the researcher, student, or community user. However, there is limited scholarship utilizing similar analysis on linked data workflows.[6] Such work is especially vital as linked data is increasingly pushed as a possible improvement to descriptive metadata work tasks, such as the rising use of Wikidata by archives and universities, the deployment of linked data projects at major institutions like the Library of Congress and the Getty Vocabularies, and OCLC's timely research into creating linked data infrastructure for archival description.[7] Especially for museums, archives, and special col-

---

Library Special Collections, UCLA Library, 2021, https://www.library.ucla.edu/location/library-special-collections/discover-collections/toward-ethical-inclusive-descriptive-practices-ucla-library-special-collections.

6. Karen Li-Lun Hwang, "Minding and Mending the Gaps: A Case Study in Linked Open Data / Karen Li-Lun Hwang," The Design for Diversity Learning Toolkit, Northeastern University Library, 2018, https://des4div.library.northeastern.edu/minding-and-mending-the-gaps-a-case-study-in-linked-open-data/; OCLC Research Archives and Special Collections Linked Data Review Group. "Archives and Special Collections Linked Data: Navigating between Notes and Nodes." (Dublin, OH: OCLC Research, 2020); Jennifer Walker, Bonnie Healy, Chyloe Healy, Tina Apsassin, William Wadsworth, Carmen Jones, Jeff Reading, et al. 2018, "Perspectives on Linkage Involving Indigenous Data," *International Journal of Population Data Science* 3 (4). https://doi.org/10.23889/ijpds.v3i4.999; Michelle Futornick and Christine Fernsebner Eslao, "Ethics in Linked Data Affinity Group." LYRASIS, 2021. https://wiki.lyrasis.org/display/LD4P2/Ethics+in+Linked+Data+Affinity+Group, and Kelly J. Thompson, "More than a Name," *Library Resources & Technical Services* 60, no. 3 (07, 2016): 140-155 represent some of the research and projects available on this subject. See also chapters in this volume by Stacy Allison-Cassin and by Megan Macken, Madison Chartier, Sarah Milligan, and Julie Pearson-Little Thunder.

7. Greta Bahnemann, Michael Carroll, Paul Clough, Mario Einaudi, Chatham Ewing, Jeff Mixter, Jason Roy, Holly Tomren, Bruce Washburn, and Elliot Williams, "Transforming Metadata into Linked Data to Improve Digital Collection Discoverability: A CONTENTdm Pilot Project," OCLC Research Report, Accessed 2022, https://www.oclc.org/content/dam/research/publications/2021/oclcresearch-transforming-metadata-into-linked-data.pdf; "ID.LOC.GOV - Linked Data Service," Library of Congress, 2021, https://id.loc.gov/; "Getty Vocabularies as Linked Open Data," Getty Research Institute, 2021, https://www.getty.edu/research/tools/vocabularies/lod/index.html; ARL Task Force on Wikimedia and Linked Open Data, "ARL White Paper on Wikidata Opportunities and Recommendations," Association of Research Libraries, April 18, 2019, https://www.arl.org/wp-content/uploads/2019/04/2019.04.18-ARL-wh

lections that overwhelmingly employ localized terminology and methods, linked data promises "higher-quality and richer metadata…with greater efficiency" by way of standardized and openly available content, whether through quick standardization of subject terms or linking associated collections.[8] For GLAMS with large backlogs or institutional pressure to make more content digitally available, these capabilities are understandably attractive.[9] Linked data's standardization and automation, however, relies upon an earlier strata of cataloging machinery, including the same problematic terms and organizational schemas under critical cataloging review.[10] Harmful vocabularies can inhibit the ability of individuals to find materials, perpetuate harmful stereotypes, and release sensitive information.[11] Linked data workflows, then,

ite-paper-on-Wikidata.pdf, 10-11, 42-43, https://doi.org/10.25333/4gtz-zd88.

8. Bahnemann, et al., "Transforming Metadata into Linked Data," x; OCLC Research Archives and Special Collections Linked Data Review Group, "Archives and Special Collections Linked Data: Navigating between Notes and Nodes" (Dublin, OH: OCLC Research, 2020); Ed Jones and Michele Seikel, eds. *Linked Data for Cultural Heritage* (Chicago, IL: ALA Editions, 2016), 1-8.

9. OCLC, "Archives and Special Collections Linked Data," 6-11; Rob Sanderson and David Newbury, "Linked.Art: Our Linked Open Usable Data Model," Getty Research Institute, 2017. https://www.getty.edu/research/tools/vocabularies/sanderson_newbury_linkedartgetty.pdf; Itza Carbajal and University of Texas at Austin Libraries Linked Data Learning Group, "Linked Data & Its Application," UT Linked Data Learning Group, September 24, 2018, https://wikis.utexas.edu/display/UTLinkedDataLearning/UT+Linked+Data+Learning+Group+Home?preview=/281806835/281821541/UTDiscussion3Slides_LinkedDataApplication2018.pdf; Ashleigh Hawkins, "Archives, linked data and the digital humanities: increasing access to digitised and born-digital archives via the semantic web." *Arch Sci* (2021), https://doi.org/10.1007/s10502-021-09381-0, 1-5. This view also stems from my professional experience as a metadata analyst and librarian, previously working with Getty Vocabularies and linked data at the Getty Research Institute and currently at the University of Texas at Austin. In both institutions, linked data is employed to allow for easier sharing of descriptive metadata and to enable faster basic metadata creation so that more attention can be devoted to more complicated tasks (ex. translation.)

10. For example, both the Library of Congress's and the Getty Vocabularies' linked data services utilize older thesauri. "ID.LOC.GOV - Linked Data Service," Library of Congress, 2021. https://id.loc.gov/; "Getty Vocabularies as Linked Open Data." Getty Research Institute, 2021. https://www.getty.edu/research/tools/vocabularies/lod/index.html.

11. Duarte and Belarde-Lewis, "Imagining: Creating Spaces for Indigenous Ontologies," 677-678; Melissa Adler and Joseph Tennis, "Toward a Taxonomy of Harm,"

demand the same ethical critique that subject terms and classification schemas have been subjected to, if not one more rigorous,
to ensure we, as White metadata workers, do not reenact the
same harm our past colleagues have already wrought with subject
headings, classification, and information policy.

First, I will look at the development of United States colonial policy towards Indigenous people and its entanglements with
the Library of Congress and other institutions, such as museums
and university departments, by arguing that the government's
efforts to understand and control Indigenous populations shaped
the GLAMS work tasks we continue to use today. These include
descriptive and classificatory practices, mass collecting, and
information use policies. I connect these practices to their current evolutions in the cultural heritage workplace, emphasizing
that it is not just the terminology but the structuring of our work
and our knowledge that have allowed these colonial residues to
persist. I then demonstrate these linkages with current linked data
practice, critiquing the work practices of data validation and data
modeling, large-scale data collection, and open access policies
as echoes of past practice. I do not offer specific prescriptions on
how to amend this situation but, instead, point to Indigenous-led
efforts and theory, emphasizing data sovereignty and "digital
repatriation" of knowledge and methods back to Indigenous communities.[12] To comply with these protocols will require changes,
not just in linked data practice, but in how White and Euro-American GLAMS institutions are organized as a whole.

This argument draws on and utilizes institutional ethnography methods as defined by Dorothy Smith, as well as KO
definitions provided by information science scholars Marisa

NASKO 4 no. 1 (2013): 3-5.

12. "Qualla Arts and Crafts Turns 75." Cherokee One Feather Tsalagi Soquo
Ugidahli. 2021. https://theonefeather.com/2021/08/16/qualla-arts-and-crafts-turns-75/.
Digital repatriation is used in this article to describe the return of the knowledge and
digital collections material associated with content as well as the object itself, recognizing the proliferation of content that can be created and shared from a digital surrogate
of an object. This understanding of the phrase is used in this chapter.

Duarte (Pascua Yaqui), Miranda Belarde-Lewis (Zuni/Tlingit), and Melissa Adler, using the work task and its particular ways of organizing information as the unit of analysis.[13] This chapter also draws upon and acknowledges the long history of Indigenous Studies scholarship on non-Indigenous GLAMS institutions and their informational practices, including work by Amy Lonetree (Ho-Chunk) and Karen Coody Cooper (Cherokee), as well as contributions by Indigenous librarians such as Sandra Littletree (Diné/Eastern Shoshone) and Cheryl Metoyer (Eastern Band of Cherokee).[14] My argument echoes these more established efforts by Indigenous scholars and workers, adding to this discourse by focusing directly on linked data work tasks and using my positionality to encourage my White colleagues to do their own critical review.

Recognizing that the workers stewarding Indigenous information in GLAMS spaces are largely White, due to systematic oppression of Indigenous professionals and removal of Indigenous

---

13. Melissa Adler, "The Case for Taxonomic Reparations." *Knowledge Organization* 43, no. 8 (2016): 630-640; Duarte and Belarde-Lewis, "Imagining: Creating Spaces for Indigenous Ontologies," 677–702. https://doi.org/https://doi.org/10.1080/0 1639374.2015.1018396; Marisa Elena Duarte, Morgan Vigil-Hayes, Sandra Littletree, and Miranda Belarde-Lewis, "Of Course, Data Can Never Fully Represent Reality: Assessing the Relationship Between 'Indigenous Data' and 'Indigenous Knowledge,' 'Traditional Ecological Knowledge,' and 'Traditional Knowledge,'" *Human Biology* 91, no. 3 (2020): 163–178; Dorothy E. Smith, *Institutional Ethnography as Practice* (Lanham, MD: Rowman & Littlefield, 2006). A small note on terminology. Following practice in other Native North American scholarship, I designate nation/tribal affiliation using parentheses. I also use Indigenous to refer to Indigenous people across the world/Americas and Native or Native American to refer to Indigenous people within the United States. Indigenous is also used in favor of Native when speaking about Nations/communities existing before the formalization of today's contemporary Nations within the United States. When speaking about specific people or communities, their specific titles are used as much as possible. For examples of similar practice see Amy Lonetree, *Decolonizing Museums: Representing Native America in National and Tribal Museums* (Chapel Hill, NC: University of North Carolina Press, 2012) and in Damon B. Akins and William J. Bauer (Round Valley Indian Tribes), *We Are the Land: A History of Native California* (Oakland, CA: University of California Press, 2021).

14. Lonetree, *Decolonizing Museums*; Karen Coody Cooper (Cherokee), *Spirited Encounters: American Indians Protest Museum Policies and Practices* (Lanham, MD: AltaMira Press, 2008).

knowledge to White institutions, we must understand our first encounters, our first creations of these colonial systems. This work will always have limitations based on my position; I cannot speak for any Indigenous community or with any authority on Indigenous issues. I can only unsettle my own culture's practices. In turn, I will sometimes use our/I statements as I am directing this work to other White cultural workers. As White settlers and in colonial institutions, we cannot decolonize, but we can re-engage in relationships and reciprocity, and bend our institutions to non-White ways of knowing, using this knowledge to stop current practice and engage respectfully with our non-White partners. We must work to undo ourselves.

Colonialism, Anthropology, and our Classificatory Systems

My use of the word *colonial* for American classificatory systems is intentional. The formation of the United States upon sovereign Indigenous land was (and continues to be) a violent act; explicitly, it is a project to take Indigenous territory and exert White control. Indigenous communities were frequently classed as obstacles to the continued expansion of the American colonies.[15] Beginning in the 1700s, the departments of the Interior and of War often utilized military action against Indigenous communities, using the categorization of Indigenous peoples as "savages" or as "tribes" to justify land seizure.[16] Seeking to expand into western Indigenous territories, the U.S. government spent a large part of its early years in the 1700s fighting and creating—and breaking—treaties with Indigenous tribes in Kentucky, Ohio, the Midwest/Great

---

15. Susan Sleeper-Smith, *Indigenous Prosperity and Conquest: Indian Women of the Ohio River Valley, 1690-1792*, (Chapel Hill, NC: UNC Press, 2018), 3-5; Pauline Turner Strong, *American Indians and the American Imaginary: Cultural Representation Across the Centuries* (Abingdon, UK: Routledge, 2016), 23.

16. Ibid., 8, 215; Strong, *American Indians and the American Imaginary*, 24.

Lakes area, and in the Southeast.[17] One of the first conflicts under the banner of the new American State was a series of wars against Shawnee communities living in Kentucky, southern Indiana, and Ohio in the 1780s-1790s, with colonizers gaining Kentucky and pushing Shawnee communities north past the Ohio River in the process.[18] This war, as well as conflicts against other Southeastern and Midwestern tribes at this time, set the stage for U.S.-backed colonial policy and the ever-shifting legal and scholarly definitions applied to Indigenous people.[19] While this is a complex history, as all Indigenous communities experienced colonialism differently, sometimes even within the same tribal community, the end goal, driven by the American government, was to seize land and to control Indigenous people seen as political threats.[20] This work was made possible through various diplomats, federal agents, and even artists, using maps, paintings, and treaties to categorize Indigenous Nations as static entities with discrete lands and borders that could be fought, contained, and dissected.[21]

17. Sleeper-Smith, *Indigenous Prosperity and Conquest*, 1-8; Sarah H. Hill, *Weaving New Worlds: Southeastern Cherokee Women and Their Basketry* (Chapel Hill: University of North Carolina Press, 1997), 87-90, 106-109; Strong, *American Indians and the American Imaginary*, 23-26.

18. Sleeper-Smith, *Indigenous Prosperity and Conquest*, 1-8, 211-215; Sami Lakomäki, "'Our Line'," *Journal of the Early Republic* 34, no. 4 (Winter 2014): 601-604. Shawnee people living in Kentucky and the wider Ohio River Valley region were under constant conflict with Anglo/Anglo-American colonizers; Clark's War was simply an evolution of the conflict to include nascent United States military assistance and presidential backing.

19. Resources such as Sleeper-Smith, *Indigenous Prosperity,* and Hill, *Weaving New Worlds* provide a deeper look into this history.

20. Lakomäki, "'Our Line." 597-605. For example, the experiences of Shawnee people vary widely from genocide in Kentucky, to receiving land plots from colonial Spain across the Mississippi, to various treaties signed with different Shawnee communities and towns, to forced removal to Oklahoma. Akins and Bauer, *We Are the Land*, and Jenny Tone-Pah-Hote, *Crafting an Indigenous Nation: Kiowa Expressive Culture in the Progressive Era* (Chapel Hill, NC: University of North Carolina Press, 2019), 9-11, provide examples of complicated Indigenous experiences with colonialism in other areas of the United States.

21. Ibid., 1-12, 170-180, 210-216; Conn, History's Shadow, 49-59; Jennifer Guiliano, and Carolyn Heitman, "Difficult Heritage and the Complexities of Indigenous

From the earliest formulations of the American state, politicians, generals, and intellectuals struggled to make sense of Indigenous peoples who had existed on the land long before their arrival. Indigenous people were seen as both central to nascent views of American national identity and as a foil to them.[22] This was keenly felt during the United States' early years, with scholars and government officials alike seeking to build a national identity that could compete with those of other nations in Europe.[23] As Steven Conn provides:

> "[T]rying to answer questions posed by the very existence of American Indians and the astonishing variety of their cultures forced Americans to confront...their own history."[24]

Thomas Jefferson was an especially prominent figure in these efforts, both collecting an extensive library of materials relating to Indigenous peoples as well as writing prolifically on the subject of creating an American national character from these roots.[25] With his collection donated to the newly formed Library of Congress, the first major organization for collating bibliographic

---

Data," *Journal of Cultural Analytics* 4, no. 1 (2019), https://doi.org/10.22148/16.044, 4-7; C. Joseph Genetin-Pilawa, *Crooked Paths to Allotment: The Fight over Federal Indian Policy after the Civil War* (Chapel Hill, NC: University of North Carolina Press, 2012), 11-20.

The U.S. government, as well as earlier European traders/colonies, classified Indigenous communities as nations or nation-states, applying this definition across the board to tribes that had varying kinship, land, and governing structures. In doing so, treaties applied to tribes did not always include all parties, nor were they overseen by the appropriate authorities, while in other cases, ceremonies or speeches by Indigenous figures were purposely misunderstood to incite conflict and gain land. Whether intentional or not, this categorization served colonial purposes, not Indigenous ones.

22. Steven Conn, *History's Shadow: Native Americans and Historical Consciousness in the Nineteenth Century* (Chicago: University of Chicago Press, 2004), 4-10; Strong, *American Indians and the American Imaginary*, 17-19, 30-31.

23. Ibid, 88-89.

24. Ibid., *History's Shadow*, 6.

25. Ibid, 88-89; John Y. Cole, *Jefferson's Legacy: A Brief History of the Library of Congress* (Washington DC: Library of Congress, 1993), 11-13; James Conaway, *America's Library: The Story of the Library of Congress, 1800-2000* (New Haven, CT: Yale University Press, 2000), 8-9, 16-17, 25.

and scholarly knowledge in the United States, scholarship about Indigenous people was clearly defined as central to American intellectual understanding.[26]

For the U.S. government, land seizure from Indigenous people and national identity building were intertwined. A panoply of institutions formed to accomplish this work, creating knowledge organization systems that redefined Indigenous identities. Growing from the Department of War's violent policies towards Indigenous people, the U.S. government formed the Indian Office (OIA) in 1832, which continued to draft treaties, gather information on Indigenous people, handle trade, and conduct war.[27] The OIA was later transformed into the Bureau of Indian Affairs (BIA) in the 1860s.[28] In this same period of systemic land seizure and genocide of Indigenous communities, the Bureau of Ethnology (also known as the Bureau of American Ethnology or BAE) was created in 1879, headed by John Wesley Powell, to record Indigenous peoples' ceremonies and material culture and to map territories in an effort to fix fluid Indigenous identities and borders into discernable research outputs.[29] During the mid-19th to early 20th centuries, vast quantities of objects and information from Indigenous communities were collected—variously stolen or taken under duress—by these two institutions, competing fiercely with other colonial empires who were also fueled by their universities and museums practicing "museum anthropology," which placed primacy in object collections as sites of knowledge.[30] Central to museum anthropology was the belief in

26. Cole, *Jefferson's Legacy*, 11; Duarte and Belarde-Lewis, "Imagining: Creating Spaces for Indigenous Ontologies," 684-685, 694-695.

27. Genetin-Pilawa, *Crooked Paths to Allotment*, 43-45, 175.

28. Ibid., 69-71.

29. Conn, *History's Shadow*, 10, 107-8, 176-179; Hannah Turner, *Cataloguing Culture: Legacies of Colonialism in Museum Documentation* (Vancouver: UBC Press, 2020), 57-60. The BAE was formally part of the Smithsonian but largely acted as its own entity, conducting anthropological research as part of a larger federal effort to collate information about Indigenous people.

30. Conn, *History's Shadow*, 107-117, 178-185; H. Glenn Penny, *Objects of Culture: Ethnology and Ethnographic Museums in Imperial Germany* (Chapel Hill, NC:

comparing similar items in order to understand human behavior and "progress," driving collectors and scholars to purchase all known examples of an item or, in some cases, to commission them from source communities.[31]

As overseas collectors were snapping up whole Indigenous communities' material culture, the United States joined in with the same ferocity to ensure an American cultural heritage.[32] Conn posits in his study of American intellectual institutions that anthropology in the United States formed out of the desire to create a national heritage.[33] Similar motivations drove the Library of Congress's development, with John Y. Cole noting that "...the growth of the institution [is] tied to the growth and ambitions of the entire American nation."[34] As Indigenous Nations increasingly lost land to violence driven by the U.S. military and private citizens, as well as to legislation like the Dawes Act of 1887 and the Burke Act of 1906, BIA policy shifted from conflict and negotiation with "domestic dependent nations" to community control, implementing residential school systems, reservations, and Indian Agents.[35] These systems sought to recategorize and assimilate Indigenous people using ever-shifting blood quantum and genealogical rules.[36] Control of cultural practices was also part of this program, though there was significant resistance from

University of North Carolina Press, 2002), 60-65; Andrew Zimmerman, *Anthropology and Antihumanism in Imperial Germany* (Chicago: University of Chicago Press, 2001), 150-155; Turner, *Cataloguing Culture*, 57-59;

31. Lonetree, *Decolonizing Museums*, 26-27; Devon Murphy, "Matter That Matters: A Study of Cherokee Baskets and the Museums that Display Them," (Master's thesis, University of North Carolina at Chapel Hill, 2019), https://doi.org/10.17615/n45h-n793, 20-26.

32. Penny, *Objects of Culture*, 60-65; Zimmerman, *Anthropology and Antihumanism in Imperial Germany*, 150-155; Turner, *Cataloguing Culture*, 57-59.

33. Conn, *History's Shadow*, 88-89.

34. Cole, *Jefferson's Legacy*, 12.

35. Genetin-Pilawa, *Crooked Paths to Allotment*, 64; Tone-Pah-Hote, *Crafting an Indigenous Nation*, 20-25.

36. Susan Labry Meyn, *More than Curiosities: A Grassroots History of the Indian Arts and Crafts Board and Its Precursors, 1920-1942* (Lanham, MD.: Lexington Books, 2001), x-xv, 4; Lonetree, *Decolonizing Museums*, 22, 27-29.

Indigenous communities, from taking advantage of White anthropological visits to preserve cultural heritage, like Will West Long and other Eastern Band of Cherokee members working with BAE staff, or Kiowa communities using collectors and fairs to continue beadwork and regalia.[37] All of these colonial systems relied on steady flows of information about Indigenous lands, populations, customs, and key figures, much of this collected not just from federal agents but also from universities, museums, and libraries, by way of epistemic networks.

Major American institutions, such as the Library of Congress, benefited greatly from colonial knowledge bodies like the BAE and the BIA, as well as universities, anthropological museums, and natural history collections like the University of Pennsylvania Museum of Archeology and Anthropology, the Peabody Museum of Archeology and Ethnology, and the Museum of the American Indian, as well as many others.[38] The accrued information, ranging from languages to ethnobotany to typologies of basket forms, was organized to document lifeways considered lost and to exploit that information for various government reform projects.[39] Scholars at these institutions deposited their written findings into the aforementioned Library of Congress, which received a high volume of materials through its status as a major depository library, its government printing office's

---

37. Murphy, "Matter that Matters," 21-23; Tone-Pah-Hote, *Crafting an Indigenous Nation*, 4-5, 12, 25-30.

38. George W. Stocking Jr., "Introduction," in *Objects and Others: Essays on Museums and Material Culture*, ed. George W. Stocking Jr. (Madison, WI.: University of Wisconsin Press, 1985), 3-13; Curtis Hinsley, *The Smithsonian and the American Indian: Making a Moral Anthropology in Victorian America* (Washington D.C.: Smithsonian Institution Press, 1994), 19-29; Ira Jacknis, "Franz Boas and Exhibits: On the Limitations of the Museum Method of Anthropology," in *Objects and Others: Essays on Museums and Material Culture*, 75-86; Cole, *Jefferson's Legacy*, 14, 19. This drive to explore and understand the continent is also credited as the birth of American museology and museum anthropology.

39. Erik Trump, "'The Idea of Help': White Women Reformers and the Commercialization of Native American Women's Art," in *Selling the Indian: Commercializing and Appropriating American Indian Cultures*, eds. Carter Jones Meyer and Diana Royer (Tucson, AZ: University of Arizona Press, 2001), 167-168, 174-177; Meyn, *More than Curiosities*, 30-32, 36.

publishing program, and its later acquisition of the Smithsonian's collection in 1867.[40] Anthropologists and ethnologists also sold their research—to collectors like Charles Jewett, head librarian at the Smithsonian—and shared informants and valuable locations with fellow scholars dispersed in other museums, universities, and at the BAE.[41]

James Mooney, one of the more prominent anthropologists working for the BAE, provides an example of these information-sharing networks. During the late 1800s, Mooney traveled to the Qualla Boundary in western North Carolina. The Qualla Boundary is Cherokee land, bought by Cherokees so that they could remain on their land during the U.S government's forced Removal of Southeastern Nations in the 1830s.[42] Only roughly fifty years after Removal, Mooney collected hundreds of baskets, masks, and other material culture from Cherokees and shared this information in BAE Bulletins that were collected by the Library of Congress.[43] His work put forth a typology of baskets based on utilitarian uses, disregarding the aesthetic, community, and cultural aspects of Cherokee basketry.[44] His research laid

40. Stocking, "Introduction," 3-13; Hinsley, *The Smithsonian and the American Indian*, 19-29; Ira Jacknis, "Franz Boas and Exhibits," 75-86; Cole, *Jefferson's Legacy*, 14, 19. This drive to explore and understand the continent is also credited as the birth of American museology and museum anthropology.

41. Cole, *Jefferson's Legacy*, 14, 19; Conn, *History's Shadow*, 107-117, 178-185. The government printing project ended for a brief period before restarting in the latter half of the 1890s, though Indigenous content was always central to the library's collections.

42. "Frequently Asked Questions," Museum of the Cherokee Indian, Accessed 2022, https://mci.org/learn/faq; Hill, *Weaving New Worlds*, 132.

43. Ibid., 169-176.

44. Ibid, 169-177; Examples can be seen in the Smithsonian National Museum of Natural History's collections, such as "Ethnology: Double Walled Basket; Catalog Number E209218-0," Smithsonian National Museum of Natural History, Accessed 2022, http://n2t.net/ark:/65665/34247d79e-9bde-442b-b659-5849b45ad450. Similar practices were used by other major anthropological figures like Franz Boas, which Aaron Glass explores in his article, "Plural provenances and the Kwakwa̱ka̱'wakw Collection in Berlin and beyond," in which Boas focuses his typology of Kwakwa-ka'wakw material culture on physical appearance, not on the familial roles that Kwak-waka'wakw would consider paramount to understanding them. Aaron Glass, "Plural

groundwork for other scholars, either for contemporaries like independent researcher Dr. Edward Palmer, or for later 20th-century scholars like university-based anthropologists Arthur Kelly and Frank G. Speck, who categorized baskets in a similar manner.[45] At the same time, Cherokee informants like Will West Long and his mother Ayasta were also heavily involved in these information exchanges; Long provided information and created material culture for Mooney, Speck, and many other anthropologists in the interest of preserving Cherokee culture, often issuing corrections to their work.[46] It is important to note, though, that this information was still filtered through White anthropological understandings. Speck's work in particular became highly circulated amongst museum bulletins and other anthropological scholars, with museum catalogs today using similar terms and classification.[47] These scholarly works, which were often derived from troubled "salvage anthropology" tactics, helped develop the Library's collection and its standing as a national institution, as well as creating the strata of literary warrant—which later, problematic subject headings would be sourced from.[48] As

provenances and the Kwakwa̱ka 'wakw Collection in Berlin and beyond," in *Museum as Process: Translating Local and Global Knowledges*, ed. Raymond A. Silverman (Abingdon, UK: Routledge, 2015), 28-30.

45. Murphy, "Matter that Matters," 19-26. Speck and Kelly also corresponded with each other, sharing information on recently-purchased Cherokee items and on fieldwork methods, as well as imparting similar information to students and worked collaboratively with Cherokee scholars and culture bearers like Will West Long.

46. Ibid., 19-28; Anna Fariello, "People: Will West Long (1870-1947)" From the Hands of Our Elders: Cherokee Traditions, Western Carolina University, 2013,https://www.wcu.edu/library/DigitalCollections/CherokeeTraditions/People/Carvers_WillWestLong.html.

47. Murphy, "Matter that Matters," 22. Speck's *Decorative Art and Basketry of the Cherokee* (1920), for example, was published within the Bulletin of the Milwaukee Public Museum. Examples of catalog records can be seen in collection records at the Georgia Museum of Art, Athens, GA, Lossie Welch, Agnes, "Basket," Accessed 2022, https://emuseum.georgiamuseum.org/objects/21378/basket and the Gregg Museum of Art and Design, Raleigh, NC, Panther, Katie, "Fruit Basket," Accessed 2022. http://searchgreggcollection.arts.ncsu.edu/mDetail.aspx?rID=TD366.338&db=objects&dir=GALLERY%20OF%20ART.

48. Cole, *Jefferson's Legacy*, 14, 19; Lonetree, *Decolonizing Museums*, 27.

Marisa Duarte and Miranda Belarde-Lewis state, "...these are not unrelated and inconvenient phenomena endemic to Indigenous knowledge, but rather the evidence of systemic colonial marginalization."[49]

The Library of Congress's collection is significant here in that it illuminates the epistemic networks connecting BIA/BAE fieldwork, university sponsorship, and library collection development. These linkages led to the creation of literary warrant, the scholarly proof of the use of a term or concept.[50] Literary warrant became a central tool for organizing text collections, especially at the Library of Congress which was implementing its first iteration of subject headings during the 1890s-early 1900s, drawn from a mixture of terms derived from anthropological and natural history scholarship and headings used by other major library systems like the Boston Public Library.[51] These terms indexed text collections on similar themes, reinforcing White knowledge systems about Indigenous life, imparting different names, categories, and relationships that often ignored or misrepresented Indigenous knowledges. One example is available in the "List of subject headings for use in dictionary catalogs," published in 1898 by the American Library Association. These guides were published for small and regional libraries as well as institutions as large as the Library of Congress, who used this information to construct the basis for their subject headings, highlighting knowledge-sharing between institutions.[52] This iteration of the list is the first to contain the term "Totems," with additional references

49. Duarte and Belarde-Lewis. "Imagining: Creating Spaces for Indigenous Ontologies," 678.

50. Patricia Harpring, "7. Constructing a Vocabulary or Authority" in "Introduction to Controlled Vocabularies: Terminology for Art, Architecture, and Other Cultural Works," Getty Research Institute, 2010, https://www.getty.edu/research/publications/electronic_publications/intro_controlled_vocab/constructing.html.

51. Cole, *Jefferson's Legacy*, 27. This replaced a system created by Jefferson that consisted of 46 general categories.

52. American Library Association, *List of Subject Headings for Use in Dictionary Catalogs*, 2nd Ed. (Boston.: Pub. for the A.L.A. Publishing Section by the Library Bureau, 1898), 180.

to "Indian" culture and mythology.[53] These reference terms indicate knowledge of current anthropological scholarship at the time, which utilized the Ojibwe noun stem "doodem," or totem, for materials considered to have a symbolic spirit, with the totem pole, a communication and material culture form belonging to Northwest Coast Indigenous communities, being the most emblematic of these.[54]

By using "totem," non-Indigenous scholars collapsed the complex roles and active agency totem poles contained into a singular, static identity applied across diverse Indigenous materials.[55] The new appearance of this term also hints at the concurrent collecting frenzy of totem poles initiated by White collectors, anthropologists, and governmental bodies. Collectors and anthropologists like Franz Boas took advantage of repressive legislation, like the potlatch ban in Canada (1885-1951) and the Dawes Act in the U.S., that forced Northwest Coast communities like the Kwakwaka'wakw and Tsimshian into selling cultural heritage items like totem poles to survive.[56] This violent dispossession of

---

53. Ibid., 180.

54. "Gidoodem," Ojibwe People's Dictionary, 2021, https://ojibwe.lib.umn.edu/main-entry/gidoodem-nad; Loriene Roy (White Earth Nation), "Ojibwe." in *Gale Encyclopedia of Multicultural America*, 3rd ed., edited by Thomas Riggs, 359-373. Vol. 3. (Detroit, MI: Gale, 2014.), 367.

55. Emily L. Moore, "The Seward Shame Pole: A Tlingit Counter-Monument to the Alaska Purchase," in *Unsettling Native Art Histories on the Northwest Coast*, Kathryn Bunn-Marcuse and Aldona Jonaitis, eds. (Seattle, WA: University of Washington Press, 2020), 26-27, 31; Aldona Jonaitis, "Northwest Coast Totem Poles," in *Unpacking Culture*, 107-110. Totem poles have comprised complicated roles ranging from the communication of familial and political information to being created for the anthropological and tourist trade.

56. Facing twin pressures of active colonization of the Pacific Northwest Coast area and of legal discrimination through the potlach ban in Canada (1885-1951), which outlawed creation of material culture like totem poles, and the Dawes Act (1887) and Indian Reorganization Act (1934) in the United States that sold off land in Oregon and Washington, Pacific Northwest Coast Indigenous communities like the Kwakwaka'wakw and Tsimshian, amongst many others, were forced to part with items like totem poles. Sometimes they were stolen, or their makers were pressured by buyers, or Indigenous carvers created new totem poles specifically for the market in an effort to physically and culturally survive. Chip Colwell, *Plundered Skulls and Stolen Spirits: Inside the Fight to Reclaim Native America's Culture* (Lincoln, NE: Universi-

Indigenous material cultures and knowledge is crystallized into one subject term used to index other related scholarship created and fueled by the same colonial systems. As Indigenous communities and their cultures became known to White, American systems, they were assigned terms and disseminated within various KOs built to make sense of them—as ethnographic objects and as literary subjects.

Current Evolutions

As demonstrated in the previous section, White anthropological/ethnological scholarship about Indigenous people, rooted in colonial assumptions, shaped broader descriptive and classificatory practice. Like the term "Totems," described earlier, many more harmful terms exist from these same evolutions, like "Indians of North America" and its many permutations within Library of Congress subject headings.[57] Many of these outdated or pejorative subject terms persist today within the Library of Congress's thesauri and name authority files (LCSH, LCNAF), using old literary warrant or 20th-century scholarship that continued use of these harmful terms.[58] In turn, the collections that these scholars amassed required description of their own within universities, museums, and archives, and a professional staff to do the work. Faced with the pressure to describe and classify thousands upon thousands of items derived from these collectors,

ty of Nebraska Press, 2017), 138-142, 208-215; Candice Hopkins (Carcross/Tagish), "Outlawed Social Life," *Documenta* 14 (2014), https://www.documenta14.de/en/south/685_outlawed_social_life; Meyn, *More than Curiosities*, 4, 40; Lonetree, *Decolonizing Museums*, 28-29; Jonaitis, "Northwest Coast Totem Poles," 110-116.

    57. Duarte and Belarde-Lewis, "Imagining: Creating Spaces for Indigenous Ontologies," 684-685, 694-695.

    58. "Indian Captivities," Library of Congress Authorities, Library of Congress, Accessed 2021, https://lccn.loc.gov/sh85065218 and "Indians of North America—California," Library of Congress Authorities, Library of Congress, Accessed 2021, https://lccn.loc.gov/sh85065440 serve as some examples. The latter also contains "Mission Indians," an unhelpful term lumping together distinct Indigenous communities in Southern California.

curators and cataloging staff alike employed time-saving measures, writing brief descriptions, repeating terms across varying
items, and copying content directly from buyer or anthropologist
records.[59] From Turner's assessment of cataloging practices at the
Smithsonian, to Yve Chavez's (Tongva) research into miscatego-
rized California Native baskets across Western U.S. collections,
to my thesis research on the description of Cherokee material
culture by BIA agents and museums in the Southeast U.S., the
staggering amount of Indigenous collections in American scholarly institutions enabled expedient, poor quality recordkeeping.[60]
As H. Glenn Penny states in his study of museum anthropology,
museum staff were aware of the logistical chaos and impossibility
of comprehensive collecting efforts, but pursued this endeavor
all the same.[61] It is from these foundations that resources like
LCSH, LCNAF, and the Getty Vocabularies were built with the
aim of being as comprehensive as the legacy collections were
that needed their terms.

As the GLAMS world grew its professional infrastructure
in the 20th century and began to require advanced degrees or
training, Indigenous scholars faced structural, systemic hurdles
to achieving the type of professional status that would enable
them to access their cultural heritage in these spaces.[62] The perceived lack of such knowledge was also used as an excuse to bar
research visits or repatriation requests by Indigenous people.[63]

---

59. Turner, *Cataloguing Culture*, 57, 106-107, 115; Murphy, "Matter That Matters," 32-36.

60. Turner, *Cataloguing Culture*, 49, 102-114; Yve Chavez (Tongva), "Basket
Weaving in Coastal Southern California: A Social History of Survivance," *Arts* 8, no. 3
(2019): 1-2, 5-9; Murphy, "Matter That Matters," 19-26.

61. Penny, *Objects of Culture*, 163-164.

62. Coody Cooper, *Spirited Encounters*, 6-7; Hill, *Weaving New Worlds*, 212-221,
283-285; Mary Jo Tippeconnic Fox (Comanche), Shelly C. Lowe (Navajo) and George
S. McClellan, "Where We Have Been: A History of Native American Higher Education," *New Directions for Student Services* 109 (2005): 9-11. These include lack of
access to education required by GLAMS institutions, thanks to decades of residential
schools whose programs rarely included comprehensive academic programs, as well as
oppressive conditions within GLAMS for Indigenous workers.

63. Ibid., 2-7.

While some Indigenous people, like Will West Long and Gladys Tantaquidgeon (Mohegan), worked as co-researchers in these ventures, most Indigenous people were barred from their cultural heritage and the data derived from it.[64] Many scholars viewed Indigenous informants and culture bearers as knowledgeable, but also paradoxically as incapable of stewarding their cultural heritage due to assumed decline and assimilation into White, American culture.[65] These assumptions rested on a complex bed of anthropological and art historical thought that organized cultures by civilizational types, observing the rapid changes undergone by Indigenous communities as evidence of a whole-sale decline of Indigenous life.[66] Indigenous people that adopted modern crafting tools or utilized non-Indigenous land practices (often forced by government policy like the Dawes Act) were no longer considered to be Indigenous by White anthropologists, art historians, and government workers.[67] For many White scholars, documenting and taking control of cultural heritage materials perceived to be free of White influence was the only way to save such knowledge.[68]

As early as the 1920s, when collecting Indigenous material culture by scholars, art collectors, and hobbyists was at its

---

64. Margaret M. Bruchac and Melissa Tantaquidgeon Zobel (Mohegan), "Indian Stories: Gladys Tantaquidgeon and Frank Speck." In *Savage Kin: Indigenous Informants and American Anthropologists* (Tucson, AZ: University of Arizona Press, 2018): 140-45, https://doi.org/10.2307/j.ctt2050vr4.12; Murphy, "Matter that Matters," 20-26. Both Long and Tantaquigeon worked with anthropologist Frank G. Speck, who made it part of his practice to form close relationships with his Indigenous informants and to include them in the research process more than his contemporaries or predecessors did.

65. Lonetree, *Decolonizing Museums*, 22-29; Monique Tyndall (Stockbridge-Munsee Band of Mohicans), "Menominee Collaborative Curation Model for Allies," Menominee Tribal Archives, Menominee Indian Tribe of Wisconsin, 2021, https://www2.archivists.org/sites/all/files/NAAS%20Reparative%20Description.pdf.

66. Lonetree, *Decolonizing Museums*, 31.

67. Ibid., 26-28; Flannery Burke, *From Greenwich to Taos: Primitivism and Place at Mabel Dodge Luhan's* (Lawrence, KS: University of Kansas Press, 2008), 5-6, 8-12.

68. Elizabeth Hutchinson, *The Indian Craze: Primitivism, Modernism, and Transculturation in American Art, 1890-1915* (Durham, NC: Duke University Press, 2009), 94-98; Jonaitis, "Northwest Coast Totem Poles," 107-110.

height, Indigenous leaders and culture bearers sought to retain control over their cultural heritage and associated data or have it returned. Several Haudenosaunee leaders, for example, petitioned for the return of a wampum belt from the New York State Historical Society and requested that information about the False Face Society be removed from publicly available records.[69] These struggles continued into the 20th and 21st centuries fueled by the purchase of Indigenous materials (such as baskets or pottery) by White art and hobby collectors during the 1920s-50s and the anthropological collecting of Indigenous materials and data that extended into the 1960s.[70] The rise of tribe-administered museums in the 1960s-70s and focused efforts like the Hopi government ban on ceremony recordings were often seen as the only options in the face of uncooperative scholarly institutions.[71] Only recently have some museums made moves to repatriate collection objects back to source communities, motivated, in part, by the passing of NAGPRA in 1990, which attached a legal requirement to the return of a limited set of Indigenous material culture (human remains, funerary objects, and some sacred materials).[72] Even fewer have considered the "digital repatriation" of metadata associated with Indigenous collections outside of any

---

69. Ibid., 33-34; Chief Leon Shenandoah (Onondaga), "Haudenosaunee Confederacy Announces Policy on False Face Masks," 1995, http://www.nativetech.org/cornhusk/maskpoli.html.

70. Hutchinson, *The Indian Craze*, 92-95; Murphy, "Matter that Matters," 11, 20-25; "History of Anthropology at the Smithsonian," Smithsonian National Museum of Natural History, Accessed 2022, https://naturalhistory.si.edu/sites/default/files/media/file/history-anthropology-si_0.pdf, 3-5.

71. Lonetree, *Decolonizing Museums*, 34-35; Molly Torsen and Jane Anderson, Intellectual Property and the Safeguarding of Traditional Cultures: Legal Issues and Practical Options for Museums, Libraries and Archives. World Intellectual Property Organization, 2010. https://www.sustainableheritagenetwork.org/system/files/atoms/file/Anderson&Torsen_IntellectualPropertyandtheSafeguardingofTraditionalCultures(WIPO).pdf, 77.

72. Colwell, *Plundered Skulls and Stolen Spirits*, 7-8, 46-47. NAGPRA remains a difficult process for tribes to utilize in order to repatriate cultural heritage, being limited to a small set of materials and with little enforcement.

legal imperative.[73] These issues are not simply caused by poor descriptive metadata alone, but are fundamentally part of institutional workflows that historically have prioritized and organized information through Euro-American KOs, instead of respecting Indigenous communities' protocols.[74]

Even as GLAMS missions have shifted, these legacies persist through databases, physical labels, and organizational policy. It is vital to view cultural heritage institutions as knowledge organization systems because of these histories of categorization, which can highlight what narratives are being constructed. Immense collecting, information harvesting, and anthropological classification can be seen today in linked data practices, such as the same anthropological terms used in API (Application Programming Interface) retrieval workflows and the large-scale data harvesting of cultural heritage content without explicit community consent.

Colonial Residues in Linked Data

Pejorative terminology and classification, large backlogs of poorly recorded materials, and little community review comprise much of the colonial strata that many institutions are struggling to reconcile with today.[75] In turn, these issues comprise the same strata that linked data projects rely on to function, from the subject terms that are retrieved by APIs to the data models that structure information. While linked data can be a powerful tool to repair or enrich cultural heritage information, as seen in Karen Li-Lun Hwang's work to add missing or amend existing Asian American artist names in name authority files, it is imperative

---

73. "Qualla Arts and Crafts Turns 75," Cherokee One Feather Tsalagi Soquo Ugidahli, 2021, https://theonefeather.com/2021/08/16/qualla-arts-and-crafts-turns-75/; Guiliano and Heitman, "Difficult Heritage and the Complexities of Indigenous Data," 13-16.

74. Duarte and Belarde-Lewis, "Imagining Ontologies", 682.

75. As the Guidelines for Collaboration, facilitated by Landis Smith, Cynthia Chavez Lamar, and Brian Vallo, indicate, when community review is sought by GLAMS institutions, compensation or proper attribution is rarely provided.

that its relationships to these practices are carefully reviewed and revised so as to not reenact the same harm.[76] Data validation and data modeling, large-scale data collection, and open access policies will be considered here based on their centrality to linked data work in cultural heritage spaces.

Data validation has long been part of cataloging and metadata work, though usually consigned to a particular collections system or conducted through ad hoc methods. With linked data, one can review batches of information, such as subject terms or author records, to ascertain correctness or make updates, operationalizing exposed APIs and RDF-formatted metadata to:

> check[ing] to see what elements/properties/attributes are present, see[ing] if information is correct and factual (to the best of our abilities), see[ing] if information adheres to our expectations, and that values are consistent within our domain, elements are represented in a consistent manner.[77]

Any kind of cultural heritage content, from subject terms to names to whole item records, can be reviewed in this manner if consistent RDF and URIs are applied and an API is available, along with a reconciliation service to help query the data.[78] Several major institutions, such as the Library of Congress, the Getty Vocabularies, and VIAF (Virtual International Authority File), have their vocabularies available as linked data, and the Getty offers their own reconciliation service as well.[79] While data validation can function well with general items like generic subject

---

76. Hwang, "Minding and Mending the Gaps."

77. Gretchen Gueguen, "OpenRefine Workshop, DPLA Members Meeting, March 14, 2018," Metadata Analysis Workshop. Digital Public Library of America, 2018, https://github.com/dpla/Metadata-Analysis-Workshop/blob/master/OpenRefine.md.

78. Julia Marden, Carolyn Li-Madeo, Noreen Y. Whysel, and Jeffery Edelstein, "Linked Open Data for Cultural Heritage: Evolution of an Information Technology," in SIGDOC '13: Proceedings of the 31st ACM International Conference on Design of Communication, September 2013,107-109, https://doi.org/10.1145/2507065.2507103.

79. For the Getty Vocabularies, see http://vocab.getty.edu/; for the Library of Congress, see https://id.loc.gov;/; for VIAF, see http://viaf.org/viaf/data/.

or name terms, they can also just as easily retrieve pejorative terms that still persist within thesauri and name authorities such as the LCSH, LCNAF, and the Getty Vocabularies. As Duarte and Belarde-Lewis assert:

> Challenges include identifying authoritative names of tribes and peoples, such as Navajo or Diné; historical periodization within Anglo-American cataloging and classification schemes; and identifying accurate terms to reflect the unexpected diversity of Indigenous topics.[80]

While there have been some efforts to amend Indigenous terms in these large vocabularies, many still depend on outdated literary warrant, utilizing 20th or even 19th century scholarship; for example, the term "Nootka" is used in both the Getty Vocabularies and in the Library of Congress's thesauri to refer to the Nuu-Chah-Nulth.[81] Nootka is a pejorative name that is not used by the Nuu-Chah-Nulth community.[82] Yet, there are existing headings with IDs that can and will be retrieved by linked data services, perpetuating harm through their use in public-facing resources like digital collections portals or finding aids. And while more updated tribe names are being added to the Getty Vocabularies, they are usually stored as "variant" terms, creating additional issues for retrieval.[83] In turn, as linkages between

---

80. Duarte and Belarde-Lewis, "Imagining: Creating Spaces for Indigenous Ontologies," 677-678.

81. Turner, *Cataloguing Culture*, 115; Murphy, "Matter that Matters," 32-35; "Nootka (Culture or Style)," Art and Architecture Thesaurus Online, Getty Vocabularies, Accessed 2021, http://vocab.getty.edu/page/aat/300017616; "Nootka Indians," Library of Congress Authorities, Library of Congress, 2021, https://lccn.loc.gov/sj2021055118. As of August 2021, a new heading for "Nuu-Chah-Nulth Indians" has been added to the Library of Congress, an improvement but still including "Indians."

82. "Nuu-chah-nulth (Nootka)" in *Great Basin, Pacific Northwest, Arctic*, 3rd ed., Laurie J. Edwards, Ed., Vol. 5 of *UXL Encyclopedia of Native American Tribes* (Detroit, MI: UXL, 2012), 1943-1962; "History," Nuu-Chah-Nulth Tribal Council, 2021, https://nuuchahnulth.org/history.

83. For ULAN queries, variant tribe names can be retrieved by using "skosxl:altLabel" in a SPARQL query, but this complicates queries searching for multiple tribes or

thesauri, controlled vocabularies, and other open datasets are forged, incorrect or outdated information can spread quickly and be aggregated uncritically, as seen for example in Wikidata's entry for Nuu-Chah-Nulth.[84] Wikidata's record uses the correct term, but its listing of identifiers still highlights the incorrect LCSH and Getty terms alongside other sources that use "Nuu-Chah-Nulth." With no accompanying information, these terms appear to have equal usage. In response, many resources have been created by Indigenous librarians and scholars to replace these problematic thesauri, such as the MAIN (Manitoba Archival Information Network) Indigenous subject headings, created by a coalition of Indigenous and non-Indigenous librarians, the FNMIIO (First Nations, Métis, and Inuit Indigenous Ontologies) terminology list, and the many tribe-owned websites that detail proper terminology.[85] Their creation and protocols of use highlight the shortcomings of non-Indigenous materials. In addition to pejorative terms, the classification systems used within thesauri also fall short of Indigenous concepts, ranging from the incorrect use of broader headings to limiting items and concepts that have multiple relationships to exist as one term.[86]

---

by wider guide terms/hierarchies. This process can burden the searcher, and continues to highlight the pejorative term.

84. "Nuu-Chah-Nulth People (Q537784)," Wikidata, 2021, https://www.wikidata.org/wiki/Q537784.

85. Xwi7xwa Library, "Indigenous Knowledge Organization," March 28, 2018, https://xwi7xwa.library.ubc.ca/collections/indigenous-knowledge-organization/, Christine Bone, Brett Lougheed, Camille Callison, Janet La France, and Terry Reilly, "Changes to Library of Congress Subject Headings Related to Indigenous Peoples," University of Manitoba, 2015, https://mspace.lib.umanitoba.ca/xmlui/handle/1993/31177; National Indigenous Knowledge and Language Alliance (NIKLA) and CFLA-FCAB Indigenous Matters Committee – Red Team Joint Working Group on Classification and Subject Headings, "First Nations Metis and Inuit Indigenous Ontology," 2021, https://docs.google.com/spreadsheets/d/e/2PACX-1vSOKcm9HB-28iSqNN3sQd5hV7bM-LMGpCeGL0dkQgyg2AiZAMWUF0sp98GyxIvLXYIWqSZ3nX_j_q4UN/pubhtml.

86. As one example, Cherokee baskets exist in multiple roles; as utilitarian object, art piece, trade good, and as an ancestor or active agent in a community, as argued in Murphy, "Matter that Matters," 19-29; Multiple values exist in other material culture, such as at.oow as discussed by Tlingit and Inupiaq scholar Ishmael Hope in "Tlingit

The latter highlights problems within data validation work-flows, which assume a one-to-one relationship between data. Assets are modeled as singular items, matching and validating to one other sole concept, and while an asset's RDF statements contain multiple threads of information, it still assumes one stable identity for that item through a non-hierarchical structure.[87] This structure flattens complex information about the asset and inhibits the ability to easily review complex relationships, such as those between Indigenous knowledge and communities, or between the asset and the sources used to describe it, which can lead to verification problems.[88] In turn, the ontologies and data models that structure linked data retrieved in these workflows, such as CIDOC-CRM (Conceptual Reference Model), were constructed with largely Euro-American conceptions of assets in mind, as seen in CIDOC-CRM's definition of a work as something that must be measured or sensed, or the classing of objects as solely inanimate.[89] As Belarde-Lewis and Duarte provide, these KO systems do not account for the varied ways Indigenous knowledge systems organize items, with some objects conceptualized as active agents or the inclusion of non-tangible materials as a work.[90]

Art," in *Unsettling Native Art Histories on the Northwest Coast*, Kathryn Bunn-Marcuse and Aldona Jonaitis, Eds. (Seattle, WA: University of Washington Press, 2020), 289.

87. Jones and Seikel, eds., *Linked Data for Cultural Heritage*, 24-29.

88. For example, Wikidata has a ranking feature, but it is inconsistently used, community-defined, and mostly employed to indicate multiple links between records when doing queries, not to show a preferred/non preferred relationship. When validating terms or descriptive metadata in Open Refine, the data returned is still flattened with no clear hierarchy or relationships between sources or links, making data validation difficult without prior knowledge of the terms or descriptive metadata being reviewed. "Help:Ranking," Wikidata, January 22, 2022, https://www.wikidata.org/wiki/Help:Ranking.

89. Chryssoula Bekiari, George Bruseker, Martin Dorr, Christian-Emil Ore, Stephen Stead, and Athanasios Velios, "Volume A: Definition of the CIDOC Conceptual Reference Model," CIDOC ICOM International Committee for Documentation, 2021, 1–232, https://cidoc-crm.org/sites/default/files/cidoc_crm_v.7.1.1_0.pdf, 25-26, 37.

90. Marisa Elena Duarte, et al., "Of Course, Data Can Never Fully Represent Re-

Colonial residues remain not just in the composition of the corpus, but also in its size and methods of processing. The copious collecting of material into museum collections also included collecting information about that material, leading to the need for large KO systems to accommodate it. The Library of Congress' thesauri, the Getty Vocabularies, as well as other systems like Nomenclature for Museum Cataloging, were created to keep up with the organization of these vast collections, and their maintenance structures today reenact those old workflows. The Getty Vocabularies, for example, originated as a large base of terms created by Getty staff beginning in the 1970s. These terms were meant to assist in the standard description of all possible art collections, expanding outwards to cultural heritage more generally through increased partner contributions.[91] The desire to make the Getty a comprehensive resource is rooted in the colonial realities of the collections it was built to serve, as well as in the Euro-American scholarly tradition of encyclopedic collecting, whether that goal is possible or not. Other thesauri and name authority files replicate this impulse, whether through attempts to catalog all possible items (LCSH, LCNAF) or as efforts to fill in gaps not attended to by other resources (Nomenclature, Rare Books and Manuscripts Section Controlled Vocabularies, etc.). Technical interventions, like SPARQL endpoints and APIs, with their promise of collecting all information from a source, echo these earlier histories, offering up only limited content from predominantly White institutions.[92] Linked data, then, is only the most recent effort to deal with colonial legacy collections of

---

ality," 166; Duarte and Belarde-Lewis. "Imagining: Creating Spaces for Indigenous Ontologies," 684-685.

91. "Getty Vocabularies Frequently Asked Questions," Getty Research Institute, 2021, https://www.getty.edu/research/tools/vocabularies/faq.html.

92. Examples of such projects, beyond the Getty's and Library of Congress's efforts, include the American Art Collaborative, which combines 14 art institutions' collections data into one SPARQL endpoint, as well as the increased use of Wikidata by archival and museum institutions. See http://browse.americanartcollaborative.org/ and https://www.wikidata.org/wiki/Q5671855.

objects and data. These projects, whether intentional or not, are reflective of 19th and early 20th century scholarship that suggests that all items can be collected to understand a culture—one need only link all data for full understanding.

Open access policies, defined as linked open data in this application, undergird these processes, stating that all information can be shared to further scholarly understanding.[93] However, this precept is not a universally held value; in some Indigenous KO systems, information may need varying protocols based on the content, season, or viewer.[94] Historically, these protocols have not been respected, with spiritual items on display and sensitive information shared freely in object labels and in collections databases.[95] As noted in the previous section, many institutions simply did not view Indigenous people as experts of their own knowledge, placing White, Euro-American KO systems above that of the community. As institutions are only now slowly addressing these issues, the risk of sensitive content being shared within linked data is high.[96]

93. "Linked Open Data (LOD)," W3C eGovernment Wiki, W3C, 2010, https://www.w3.org/egov/wiki/Linked_Open_Data.

94. "TK Labels," Local Contexts, Accessed 2021, https://localcontexts.org/labels/traditional-knowledge-labels; Kim Christen, " Indigenous Knowledge Systems and Mukurtu CMS / Kim Christen," The Design for Diversity Learning Toolkit, Northeastern University Library, 2018, https://des4div.library.northeastern.edu/indigenous-knowledge-systems-and-mukurtu-cms/; Kayla Lar-Son, (Métis). "Data as Relation: Indigenous Data Sovereignty and Ethic of Care," IASSIST Webinar Series, January 27, 2020, https://docs.google.com/presentation/d/e/2PACX-1vQJK1N-bvFmX9NUvJnmmLi_BQiIwBQrJ5RhEJTToscAD0DaOAa1rcYIlYgLwpqk4tQ/pub?start=false&loop=false&delayms=3000&slide=id.p30.

95. Coody Cooper, *Spirited Encounters*, 32-33, 40-47, 65-84.

96. While reasons for the slow adoption of Indigenous partners and knowledges in predominantly White institutions are varied, little state or institutional support, perceived high difficulty, and presumed incompatibility between informational norms comprise some of these cases. Coody Cooper, *Spirited Encounters*, 2-10; Gwyniera Isaac, "Mediating Knowledges: Zuni Negotiations for a Culturally Relevant Museum," *Museum Anthropology*, 1, no. 28 (2005): 9-12, https://doi.org/10.1525/mua.2005.28.1.3; Amy Yurkanin, "Tribes Ask University of Alabama to Return Artifacts from Moundville," Al.com, October 11, 2021, https://www.al.com/news/2021/10/tribes-ask-university-of-alabama-to-return-artifacts-from-moundville.html.

For example, controlling information about the "False Face Society," a religious practice belonging to the Haudenosaunee, has long been a problem for Haudenosaunee communities.[97] Images, descriptions, and terms about the False Face Society are not meant to be shared outside of the group's membership due to its sacred content, and while Haudenosaunee leaders have been successful in taking down most physical and online displays, descriptions persist, such as those linked in Wikidata's record of the term.[98] Offering up linked data uncritically runs the risk of exposing sensitive information and reenacting the same colonial harms as those done by GLAMS institutions in the distant and recent past; in turn, data scraping methods used without Indigenous consultation also run these risks, multiplying content to spaces they were possibly not intended for. It is a necessary, vital act to stop, contact communities, and review information collaboratively instead of bowing to the pressure to produce and share.[99] As scholars like Stephanie Russo Carroll (Ahtna-Native Village of Kluti-Kaah), Desi Rodriguez-Lonebear (Northern Cheyenne/Chicana), and Andrew Martinez (Salt River Pima-Maricopa Indian Community) have argued, "Indigenous data sovereignty," or the ability of Indigenous people to enact their specific protocols and controls on information, is an inherent right, based in the political identities and realities of Indigenous people.[100] Those

97. Chief Leon Shenandoah (Onondaga), "Haudenosaunee Confederacy Announces Policy on False Face Masks," 1995, http://www.nativetech.org/cornhusk/maskpoli. html; Coody Cooper, *Spirited Encounters*, 32-33.

98. Ibid., "Haudenosaunee Confederacy Announces Policy on False Face Masks"; "False Face Society," Wikidata, 2021, https://www.wikidata.org/wiki/Q260890. This link serves as a citation of proof, but I do not encourage its further circulation.

99. Julia Glassman, "The Innovation Fetish and Slow Librarianship: What Librarians can Learn from the Juicero," In The Library with The Lead Pipe, 2017, http://www.inthelibrarywiththeleadpipe.org/2017/the-innovation-fetish-and-slow-librarianship-what-librarians-can-learn-from-the-juicero/, for more on the problems of excessive working and workflows.

100. Stephanie Russo Carroll (Ahtna-Native Village of Kluti-Kaah), Desi Rodriguez-Lonebear (Northern Cheyenne/Chicana), and Andrew Martinez (Salt River Pima-Maricopa Indian Community), "Indigenous Data Governance: Strategies from

controls are "constrained by their position in the problematic settler colonial paradigm of recognition and acknowledgment."[101]
As such, non-Indigenous workers must, at the very least, insert
Indigenous partners in full, non-exploitative collaborations, with
the understanding that previous institutional practices should
not apply, and at best, turn over administration to Indigenous
partners.[102]

The automation that linked data can bring to cultural heritage
work tasks can be leveraged positively. With less manual work
spent on data validation for more simplistic terms (think names of
White collectors or American city names), one can devote more
attention to the relationship-building and consultation aspects
of the work. At the same time, with the rise of projects like the
United States Indigenous Data Sovereignty Network, co-founded
by Rodriguez-Lonebear and Russo Carroll, institutions have a
unique opportunity to collaboratively build data models and protocols with Indigenous partners, making the linked data pushed
out by institutions more informed and complete than previous
content.[103]

Towards Unsettling

The creation and growing use of the Manitoba Archival Information Network's (MAIN) revised LCSH subject terms, the
recent recognition of the Protocols for Native American Materials by SAA (Society of American Archivists), and the adoption
of various Indigenous-made classification and citation schemes

---

United States Native Nations," *Data Science Journal* 18, no. 1 (2019): 1–15, https://
doi.org/ http://doi.org/10.5334/dsj-2019-031, 3-4.

101. Russo Carroll, et al., "Indigenous Data Governance: Strategies from United
States Native Nations," 3.

102. The Guidelines for Collaboration provide an example of how to begin such
partnerships, though it is geared specifically towards museums with object collections.
See https://guidelinesforcollaboration.info/.

103. "About," United States Indigenous Data Sovereignty Network, Accessed
2021, https://usindigenousdata.org/.

are just some examples of steps made by Indigenous and non-Indigenous information professionals to loosen the colonial hold on Indigenous information.[104] These projects allow for multiple ways of knowing to overlap, utilizing the knowledge organization systems of Euro-American, colonial GLAMS in order to insert Indigenous frameworks and protocols. However, some of these projects can offer a tempting trap for non-Indigenous institutions to solely amend the vocabularies, but not the protocols on how that information or the communities associated with it are treated. The myriad information-seeking initiatives spurred by Indigenous professionals, such as the Searching for Our Heritage project which combines digital collections of Yukon First Nations' materials, the Indigenous Digital Archive which collates residential school archives, and the Baskets 2 Bytes initiative which creates 3D examples of California Native basketry, further illustrate that the power balances have not fully shifted.[105] These projects, amongst many other efforts, demonstrate that once again Indigenous cultural heritage workers shoulder the greatest burden to retrieve their own information, instead of non-Indigenous institutions doing the searching and relationship building to undo their colonial wrongs.[106] To reverse course on our harmful

---

104. Bone, et al., "Changes to Library of Congress Subject Headings Related to Indigenous Peoples"; First Archivist Circle, "Protocols for Native American Archival Materials," 2007, https://www2.nau.edu/libnap-p/protocols.html; Lorisa MacLeod (James Smith Cree Nation), "More Than Personal Communication Templates for Citing Indigenous Elders and Knowledge Keepers," *KULA: Knowledge Creation, Dissemination, and Preservation Studies* 5, no. 1 (2021), https://doi.org/https://doi.org/10.18357/kula.135.

105. "Find Artifacts of Yukon First Nations Origin around the World," Yukon, Accessed 2021, https://yukon.ca/en/searching-for-our-heritage; "The Indigenous Digital Archive," Museum of Indian Arts & Culture, New Mexico, 2021, https://omeka.dlcs-ida.org/s/ida/page/home; "Baskets 2 Bytes: Indigenous California Heritage Preservation," University of California Merced, Accessed 2021, https://phds.ucmerced.edu/projects/community-engagement/henry-luce-foundation-projects/building-research-partnerships-san-5.

106. Charity Bacon, "The Stone Soup Approach to Building a Tribal Archive," California Institute for Community, Art, & Nature, March 24, 2021, https://californiaican.org/california-indian/savingourstoriessurvey/cherity-bacon-building-a-tribal-archive;

practices we must act preemptively and intentionally, spending the time to fully understand the colonial histories of all our linked data workflows and policies before implementation. As Duarte and Belarde-Lewis demonstrate in their "Stages in the Technique of Imagining" model, with historical understanding, we can identify what practices, or whole parts of our workflows, to strip away.[107] Is it just the terms one uses? Or is it also the lack of community oversight of descriptive practice? Or is it also that one's institution values high volumes of digitally published content? With linked data, we have a unique opportunity to thoughtfully put aside these past ways of working, carefully review the past structures our technologies are built on, and create systems that center relationships first.

Meghanlata Gupta, "Regaining Control: Indigenous-Owned and Operated Archives," *Indian Country Today*, January 29, 2022, https://indiancountrytoday.com/news/regaining-control-indigenous-owned-and-operated-archives.

107. Duarte and Belarde-Lewis, "Imagining: Creating Spaces for Indigenous Ontologies." 688. Understanding the process of colonization is the first step to creating new Indigenous ontologies and systems in Duarte and Belarde-Lewis's model, and while written for Indigenous practitioners, I believe it is necessary for us non-Indigenous workers to also understand this history so that we can use our privilege to assist those efforts.

Ethnological Vocabularies and GND's Authority Files: Ethical Issues and Practical Approaches

MORITZ STRICKERT

Introduction

In the context of growing digital data holdings, linking of previously separate data silos and information systems has become increasingly important. Data stewards now interconnect many resources together, aiming to make them available for reuse with as few technical restrictions as possible. The Internet provides the infrastructure to create this globally-linked database using machine-readable data in the form of linked data.[1] However, in order to establish these connections and make material reliably searchable and findable, users require nodes in the form of permanently-maintained and accessible authority files. These nodes can serve as a basis for indexing a wide range of materials and as search entry points.

This chapter focuses on ethical issues of naming within controlled vocabularies (especially authority files) on both a theoretical and a practical level by drawing from real-world examples. The first part of the chapter engages with theoretical issues. I will interrogate controlled vocabularies as a form of knowledge

---

1. Natalja Friesen and Christoph Lange, "Linked Data und Digitale Bibliotheken," in *Linked Enterprise Data: Management und Bewirtschaftung vernetzter Unternehmensdaten mit Semantic Web Technologien, ed. Tassilo Pellegrini, X.media.press* (Berlin: Springer, 2014), 241–42.

organization because they reflect a specifically-Western[2] outlook
in terms of both structure and scope. In the field of authority
control, automated solutions for revising and improving the
vocabularies alone are often not possible but, rather, require a
great deal of research, coordination and intellectual labor.

The second part of the chapter turns to real-world and practical issues and presents two connected projects, reflecting on
the procedures and problems encountered therein. These projects
involve the revision and supplementation of the Gemeinsame
Normdatei (the Integrated Authority File, abbreviated as the
'GND'), the central authority file in the German-speaking library
world. Narrowing the focus to the topic of ethnology and cultural
anthropology, I will also discuss my participation in the Thesauri
Working Group of the Network for Sustainable Research Structures in Colonial Contexts (established in the winter of 2020–21).
Both projects aim to identify gaps in their respective authority
files, missing links (i.e. connections), and outdated or problematic terminology, and to correct these grievances if possible.

The GND revision project focuses on ethnological terms covering six fields: 1. ethnic terms (terms created by anthropologists
or groups themselves); 2. languages (terms defining languages);
3. personal datasets (datasets for individuals relevant to the field
of social and cultural anthropology); 4. research branches (academic specializations, etc.); 5. research methods (used in the
field of social and cultural anthropology); and 6. discipline-specific subject terms (thematic research foci). Newly-created and
changed terms are used to index and link ethnological research
data and are intended to serve as a basis for linking data sets from
different sources in order to improve search results for users.

The newly established Network for Sustainable Research
Structures in Colonial Contexts deals with the management of

---

2. Below I will use the terms Western, Global North and Eurocentric interchangeably, though I recognize that they may have slightly different contextual meanings for
English readers.

collections and holdings from colonial contexts and seeks to ensure respectful handling of culturally sensitive data while establishing transparency and accessibility.[3] In the second phase of the project (starting June 2022), network members will work on a shared controlled vocabulary and make additional revisions to the GND in order to make collections originating from colonial contexts more accessible. Ultimately, the project aims to improve the metadata, linkage and searchability of materials from colonial contexts. One possible point of access for the combined resources will be the Deutsche Digitale Bibliothek (DDB), a platform where different materials from colonial contexts will be linked and made available based on a controlled vocabulary.[4] Actors at different levels—both in the holding institutions and experts from the colonial regions—can then discuss proper terminology, material provenance, and ways to improve discoverability with each other. The discussion below will demonstrate how different stakeholders can be a part of the revision process. First, I will introduce the GND in greater detail before moving on to an introduction of Deutsche Digitale Bibliothek (DDB).

---

3. For further information see: https://www.evifa.de/en/about/fid-projects/network-colonial-contexts?set_language=en.

4. The DDB is a virtual platform that connects resources from German cultural and scientific institutions and makes them accessible to the public via its online presence. At the European level, integration takes place in the Europeana platform (https://www.deutsche-digitale-bibliothek.de/content/ueber-uns/fragen-antworten?lang=en). With the project data.europeana.eu, the metadata is intended to be made accessible to interested parties as Linked Open Data as well. Haslhofer and Antoine summarize the goal as follows: "It allows others to access metadata collected from Europeana data providers via standard Web technologies. The data are represented in the Europeana Data Model (EDM) and the described resources are addressable and dereferencable by their URIs. Links between Europeana resources and other resources in the Linked Data Web will enable the discovery of semantically related resources." Bernhard Haslhofer and Antoine Isaac, "Data.Europeana.Eu: The Europeana Linked Open Data Pilot," in *Dublin Core Conference* (2011), 94.

Materials from colonial contexts can be searched through the following portal: https://ccc.deutsche-digitale-bibliothek.de.

Gemeinsame Normdatei (GND)

Generally, authority files aim to establish standardized forms of names in order to enable consistent indexing. They achieve this by collocating alternative spellings, synonyms, and/or translations of persons, places and things. Such linking makes it possible to use name variants (e.g., different city name variants such as Breslau, Wrocław, Wrotizla, Breßlau, and Breßlaw) for the unambiguous identification and search of resources, resulting in new research possibilities. The more information and relationships included in an authority file, the more useful it is as linked data.[5] Through many years of maintenance, authority files usually contain high-quality information that is well-suited for linked data use cases.

In the German-speaking world, the Gemeinsame Norm-datei is central—it is similar to the LCNAF (authorities.loc.gov) and VIAF (viaf.org) in importance. The GND consists of four different authority files that have been maintained for several decades, including more than nine million interdisciplinary records that have to walk the fine line between general and discipline-specific usages.[6] Via mappings, the GND overlaps with other authority files (e.g., Library of Congress Subject Headings, or 'LCSH'), meaning that search results in other languages are also possible.[7] A cooperative editorial system consisting of numerous German-speaking library associations in Austria, Germany, and Switzerland has been responsible for the maintenance of the GND. Historically, the primary focus was on cataloging

---

5. Friesen and Lange, "Linked Data und Digitale Bibliotheken," 235. For a quantitative analysis of the retrieval advantages of subject headings over resorting to keywords, see: Tina Gross, Arlene G. Taylor, and Daniel N. Joudrey, "Still a Lot to Lose: The Role of Controlled Vocabulary in Keyword Searching," *Cataloging & Classification Quarterly* 53, no. 1 (2015), https://doi.org/10.1080/01639374.2014.917447.

6. These include standardized entries for geographic information, corporate bodies, congresses, persons, subject headings, and work titles.

7. For more information regarding the MACS (Multilingual Access to Subjects) project, see: Genevieve Clavel-Merrin, "MACS (Multilingual Access to Subjects): A Virtual Authority File Across Languages," *Cataloging & Classification Quarterly* 39, 1-2 (2004), https://doi.org/10.1300/J104v39n01_02.

within a library context although, in the past few years, the project has expanded to include archives, museums, and other projects, including web-based ones. Currently, about 1,000 institutions use the GND in their work.[8] A 2016 survey on indexing in libraries, museums, and archives, revealed that GND was by far the most widely used controlled vocabulary throughout these cultural heritage institutions.[9]

Until now, most of the GND's authority files were based on published works, and subject headings were only added if the newly-cataloged item could not be described with terms already available. This is otherwise known as literary warrant. As a result, the usefulness of the controlled vocabulary for representing entities and concepts that are not referenced in published bibliographic materials is limited. Additionally, the coverage and applicability of the GND is limited because it originated within the library community. For example, many subject terms from museums have not yet been integrated into the GND.[10] There is a need for an increased cross-disciplinary terminology that addresses different needs.[11]

Since 2010, the German National Library has provided free access (Creative Commons Zero CC0 1.0) to all national bibliographic and authority files through its linked data service. For interoperability purposes, their ontology (GNDO) defines classes and relations that describe the data with reference to Resource

---

8. For German-speaking countries, the GND for Cultural Data (GND4C) project, which is funded by the German Research Foundation (DFG) and aims to expand and connect various types of institutions, should be mentioned in particular. Jens Lill, "Gemeinsam neu definiert – Das Projekt „GND für Kulturdaten (GND4C)," *AKMB-news* 25, no. 1 (2019).

9. Barbara Marković, Olga Kmyta, and Irina Sucker, "Objekterschließung an Bibliotheken, Museen und Archiven in Österreich. Ergebnisse einer Erhebung," *Mitteilungen der VÖB* 69, 3-4 (2016): 418 f.

10. Lill, "Gemeinsam neu definiert – Das Projekt GND für Kulturdaten (GND4C)", 20.

11. Jürgen Kett, Detlev Balzer, et al., "Content Kuratieren: Das Projekt „GND Für Kulturdaten" (GND4C)," *o-bib. Das offene Bibliotheksjournal*, no. 4 (2019): 59.

Description Framework (RDF) vocabularies.[12] The GND as a linked database thus enables semantic interoperability and the possibility of data reuse. Thus, records from different sources can be found by potential users and an interdisciplinary use becomes easier. In this way, linked data creates the possibility for bridges between different user communities.

In the future, the GND intends to make the process for suggesting new terms or changes to terms less complicated than it is currently. However, a workflow has yet to be developed for how this will be handled from an editorial point of view. For example, one central question is "which rights and roles should be granted to individual editors?" Another series of questions revolve around how much power individual actors or members of the public should have to edit the GND directly. While crowd-sourcing and open access would aid the GND in its process of opening up, procedures to protect against false, and/or malicious edits or errors due to lack of knowledge of how the individual system components work are needed to ensure that data records cannot be randomly altered.

One possibility is the use of the Wikibase platform. Wikibase, the software platform that underlies Wikidata, is a powerful and scalable software used to manage linked open data. While Wikidata is the largest and best-known instance of Wikibase, it is possible for individual institutions to host their own Wikibase platform, thereby allowing for a measure of control over editing. Based on the demonstrated success and ease-of-use of the wiki model, Wikibase enables easy editing by experts and members of the public alike. GND's instance of Wikibase, known as 'GND meets Wikibase' (hereafter GNDmW) is still in development, but developers have begun the process of importing GND data into it. Once the platform is launched publicly, data from GNDmW

---

12. An overview of the current state of the linkages, which are based on external mappings as well as concordances and so far have a focus on the German-speaking domain and the Global North, respectively, can be found here: https://wiki.dnb.de/display/LINKEDDATASERVICE/Anreicherungen.

will be synchronized with the GND on an ongoing basis. The aim of this project is to improve ease of linking to GND data by increasing the variety of fields represented and means of mappings and concordances. Next, I will turn to one large user of GND data, the Deutsche Digitale Bibliothek (DDB).

Deutsche Digitale Bibliothek (DDB)

The Deutsche Digitale Bibliothek (DDB) is a virtual library that links German cultural and scientific institutions and has been making their holdings publicly accessible via a common online platform since 2012. The DDB has been integrated into Europeana at the European level.[13] The online portal of the DDB is one application for linked data reconciliation based on the GND. Reconciling collections and making them interoperable is labor-intensive due to the variety of different data formats and indexing vocabularies used. Computer scientists Natalja Friesen and Christoph Lange have characterized automated reconciliation as the "most important challenge given the size of digital libraries."[14] Thus, initial attempts have been made by the DDB to automatically determine the degree to which a person in the DDB is identical to a person record in the GND. In addition, when new items are connected to the GND by the DDB, several runs of automatic string matching are performed against the subject

---

13. For more information see: https://www.deutsche-digitale-bibliothek.de/content/ueber-uns/fragen-antworten?lang=en. Integration takes place in the Europeana platform. With the project data.europeana.eu, the metadata is intended to be made accessible to interested parties as Linked Open Data as well. Haslhofer and Antoine summarize the goal as follows: "It allows others to access metadata collected from Europeana data providers via standard Web technologies. The data are represented in the Europeana Data Model (EDM) and the described resources are addressable and dereferencable by their URIs. Links between Europeana resources and other resources in the Linked Data Web will enable the discovery of semantically related resources." Bernhard Haslhofer and Antoine Isaac, "Data.Europeana.Eu: The Europeana Linked Open Data Pilot," in *Dublin Core Conference* (2011), 94.

14. Friesen and Lange, "Linked Data und Digitale Bibliotheken," 241 (author's translation).

headings in the GND. This matching procedure is supplemented by other procedures (e.g., searching for base-word stems or distance metrics).[15] If no match exists for a term, it is considered novel, and can therefore be added to the GND.[16] The following section deals with the potentials and problems that arise with the use of vocabularies (authority files) that have already been established for some time.

Potential and Perils of Authority Files

Problems with the use and reuse of authority files and their content has been discussed in library literature for decades, and those outlined here are no different. These issues persist and, in the context of linked data, are becoming more significant in general because the circle of users is expanding globally beyond the (German-speaking) library context due to growing openness and interconnectedness. In principle, the criticism is not limited to the use and form of authority files but includes debates about inadequate and exclusionary indexing and representation practices.[17] Although large-scale linking of data enables a great gain in accessibility of resources, many questions cannot be solved by simple technical means. The lack of marking up of synonyms and homonyms has thus far been the main reason why the automatic

---

15. Friesen and Lange, "Linked Data und Digitale Bibliotheken," 241.

16. Kett, et al., "Content kuratieren," 76.

17. Guimarães et al. mention the following problems in the context of knowledge organization and issues of (resource) representation at a more general level: „negligence of the indexer in choosing indexing terms (Dahlberg 1992), damage suffered by the author when his/her work is not compiled by an international publication due to inadequate or insufficient indexing (Van der Waalt 2002), bias in the representation of concepts in knowledge organization systems (KOSs) (Berman 1971; Gogh and Greenblatt 1990) and problems arising from prejudice, dichotomous categorizations, too specific vision of the world, lack of terminological precision, polysemy and indiscriminate use of political correctness in representations." José A. C. Guimarães, Fabio A. Pinho, and Suellen O. Milani, "Theoretical Dialogs About Ethical Issues in Knowledge Organization: García Gutiérrez, Hudon, Beghtol, and Olson," *Knowledge Organization* 43, no. 5 (2016): 339–40, https://doi.org/10.5771/0943-7444-2016-5-338.

matching of terms with the same meaning in the GND and the GLAM facilities does not work.[18] This means that terms that have a similar meaning (synonyms) are not connected to each other and therefore preexisting links to other datasets cannot be verified. At the same time, terms that have the same spelling but different meanings (homonyms) cannot be clearly distinguished from each other and therefore cannot be correctly assigned to other pre-existing datasets. Since synonyms and homonyms are not explicitly marked or defined, they are therefore not applicable for reconciliation. This leads to the possibility of data reconciliation failure despite the use of the same terminology in different institutions.

The matching procedures described above have their limits (e.g., lack of control, issues arising from homonyms and synonyms), particularly in the case of subject headings, although problems can also arise with personal data records.[19] In many cases, groundwork in the form of time-consuming editing of datasets is necessary in order to make these datasets usable for more advanced applications such as linked data environments. Other issues include addressing missing terminology, the subjectivity of knowledge, the data's completeness, and how frequently update cycles occur.

Historically, the literature critiquing biases in authority files has taken two different points of view. The first aims to identify biases within the vocabulary, for example, in the form of problematic or absent terms and to rectify those terms by changing or

---

18. Kett, et al., "Content kuratieren," 76.

19. Thus, in addition to the question of transliteration of non-Western languages and thus the question of correct spellings, Rigby and Gallant point out that: "Traditionally, Inuit did not have surnames, and Inuit naming practices differed significantly from English ones, including a lack of gender bias." Carol Rigby and Riel Gallant, "Creating Multilingual and Multiscript Name Authority Records: A Case Study in Meeting the Needs of Inuit Language Speakers in Nunavut," in *Ethical Questions in Name Authority Control*, ed. Jane Sandberg (Sacramento, CA: Library Juice Press, 2019), 363. This issue is also potentially relevant with regard to format issues, for example, when systems require the mention of first and last names.

enhancing the vocabulary.[20] The second, more fundamental critique of authority files highlights the basic limitations of a system based on standardizations and emphasizes that representation and polyphony are always limited in such systems.[21]

The supposed universalizing language of the authority files, which are expected to be highly comprehensive, is characterized by a substantial perspectivity and historicity of knowledge and

20. This approach includes, among others, the work of Sanford Berman, *Prejudice and Antipathies: A Tract on the LC Subject Heads Concerning People* (Metuchen, NJ: Scarecrow Press, 1971). For an overview of the movement to correct problematic assumptions and the changes made based on Berman's proposals over several decades, but also the Racism and Sexism in Subject Analysis Subcommittee, based at the Library of Congress, see: Steven A. Knowlton, "Three Decades Since Prejudices and Antipathies: A Study of Changes in the Library of Congress Subject Headings," *Cataloging & Classification Quarterly* 40, no. 2 (2005), https://doi.org/10.1300/J104v40n02_08.

Recently, especially, the discussion about the term "Illegal Aliens" and its possible modification has generated a lot of attention. For a compact overview regarding the debate cf.: Grace Lo, "'Aliens' Vs. Catalogers: Bias in the Library of Congress Subject Heading," *Legal Reference Services Quarterly* 38, no. 4 (2019), https://doi.org/10.108 0/0270319X.2019.1696069.

In the course of this, Lacey points out fundamental issues and problems of classification and naming that play an important role in the author's work context: "The classification of migration must struggle with both the difficulties of a politically contentious subject, and legally fraught and ever-changing terminology. As things stand, libraries cannot move fast enough to keep up with natural language, particularly in areas such as sexuality, ethnicity, and migration, in which terms are more likely to pejore, lose relevance or be reclaimed over time. In addition to these linguistic challenges, librarians working within standardized classification schemes will find that they are governed by an epistemology that Wimmer and Schiller (2002, 301) describe as "methodological nationalism," a theoretical outlook that naturalizes the nation as the primary category for sorting and collecting data." Eve Lacey, "Aliens in the Library: The Classification of Migration," *Knowledge Organization* 45, no. 5 (2018): 358–59, https://doi.org/10.5771/0943-7444-2018-5-358.

21. The creation of distinct definitions of terms always involves distortions and exclusions, since elements are not included in the definition. Melissa Adler, *Cruising the Library: Perversities in the Organization of Knowledge* (New York: Fordham University Press, 2017), 157.

In principle, this process is incomplete, since it is not possible to comprehensively arrive at a final objectivity by means of more correct terms, especially because category forming and definitions always show contingency and movement in view of discursive, political and social change. Emily Drabinski, "Queering the Catalog: Queer Theory and the Politics of Correction," *Library Quarterly: Information, Community, Policy* 83, no. 2 (2013): 104.

concepts.[22] In other words, terms used in authority files appear neutral and timeless at first glance. However, they are both time-specific, meaning their meaning and usage can change over time, and are based on the worldview of those who produced them, mostly persons of the Global North.

Controlled vocabularies and their associated taxonomy are not neutral and objective. They are based on rules or decisions that have to be discussed in light of their historical-ideological embedding. Hannah Turner has described the effects of these decisions as "data legacies."[23] For a historical framing of indexing practices, as well as knowledge organization systems and the interweaving of power in naming and classification practices, the work of information scholar Hope Olson is instructive.[24] Rules and regulations create a high degree of standardization for the purpose of data collection and exchange but, at the same time, are culturally specific. Consequently, the rules and structures under-lying cataloging and classification appear arcane and are difficult for outsiders to understand, making (public) participation more difficult. It is also not always clear in which context terms are applied, and terms often lack the cross-references needed to apply them to different contexts.

In many cases, there is a lack of multiple perspectives and flex-ibility in authority systems. Historically, formal considerations, such as rules and regulations in the construction of authority systems, have often taken precedence over ethical ones. Pablo

22. For a more in-depth discussion of this issue, see: Richard Gartner, *Metadata: Shaping Knowledge from Antiquity to the Semantic Web* (Basel: Springer, 2016), 42.

23. Hannah Turner, *Cataloguing Culture: Legacies of Colonialism in Museum Doc-umentation* (Vancouver, BC: UBC Press, 2020), chapter 2.

24. Hope A. Olson, *The Power to Name: Locating the Limits of Subject Repre-sentation in Libraries* (Dordrecht, s.l.: Springer Netherlands, 2002). https://doi.org/10.1007/978-94-017-3435-6; Hope A. Olson, "The Ubiquitous Hierarchy: An Army to Overcome the Threat of a Mob," *Library Trends* 52, no. 3 (2004).

Regarding the link between racism and anthropological-evolutionary theories in classification systems, see for example: Melissa Adler, "Classification Along the Color Line: Excavating Racism in the Stacks," *Journal of Critical Library and Information Studies* 1, no. 1 (2017), https://doi.org/10.24242/jclis.v1i1.17.

Gomes and Maria G. d. C. Frota are right in claiming that many knowledge systems, including the GND, are based on a "single voice, that is, a single discourse, usually the scientific-academic one."[25] One reason for this is the use of literary warrant and its focus on the published volume and common language usage on a conceptual basis. Thus, knowledge organization systems privilege Global North knowledge sources over other worldviews and perspectives. This overreliance on Eurocentric interpretations leads to varying degrees of thematic coverage. Another issue is that for a long time the assignment of terms was done according to the so-called "reference book principle." General encyclopedias and—in the ethnological field—outdated reference works had a higher status than other sources. This, together with the need to establish a preferred form of attribution, means that the scope of the authority files is closely interwoven with the worldview and knowledge structuring of the Global North.[26]

Regarding ethical naming practices, several authors stress the importance of cooperative approaches and a broadening perspective shift complementary to the "literary and philosophical warrant" and its strong focus on a Western-centered scholarly publishing system. These approaches aim to incorporate divergent values and foci into the systems that find little space in existing approaches. This includes, for example, a consideration

25. Pablo Gomes and Maria G. d. C. Frota, "Knowledge Organization from a Social Perspective: Thesauri and the Commitment to Cultural Diversity," *Knowledge Organization* 46, no. 8 (2019): 640, https://doi.org/10.5771/0943-7444-2019-8-639.

26. With regard to Indigenous contexts, Duarte and Belarde-Lewis describe four approaches that result in the marginalization of different knowledge systems: „(1) misnaming, or using Western-centric terms to describe Indigenous phenomena; (2) using parts to describe a more holistic phenomena, or the reduction, removal, and de-linking of a piece of a knowledge system from a greater ontology; (3) emphasis on modern nationalist periodization, inclusive of the notion that history as it is written by the colonizers cannot be changed; and (4) emphasis on prohibiting changes to practices that would upset the efficiency of the existing standardized schema." Marisa E. Duarte and Miranda Belarde-Lewis, "Imagining: Creating Spaces for Indigenous Ontologies," *Cataloging & Classification Quarterly* 53, 5–6 (2015): 683–84, https://doi.org/10.10 80/01639374.2015.1018396.

of what is relevant in different (cultural) communities and takes up specific knowledge ontologies. An expansion of literary warrant in a new concept of "cultural warrant"[27] or "epistemic warrant, allowing for different ways of knowing and searching"[28] could, for example, more fully integrate the needs of users based on a more multi-layered source material (e.g., newspapers and magazines, social movement announcements, interviews, or non-written resources). This could enable a closer and more needs-based interaction of users with the corresponding information system.[29]

Other suggestions range from the enrichment of controlled vocabularies based on individually contributed user terms[30] to the complete new development of controlled vocabularies.[31] For example, Naomi R. Caldwell argues for the need for dialogue and cooperation with Indigenous authorities in order to understand what names these groups prefer for themselves, objects, or places,[32] versus which names and labels are imposed on them by others, in order to enrich existing data from different

27. Gomes and Frota, "Knowledge Organization from a Social Perspective: Thesauri and the Commitment to Cultural Diversity," 642.

28. Erin Elzi and Katherine M. Crowe, "This Is the Oppressor's Language yet I Need It to Talk to You: Native American Name Authorities at the University of Denver," in *Ethical Questions in Name Authority Control*, ed. Jane Sandberg (Sacramento, CA: Library Juice Press, 2019), 89.

29. The "choice of the warrant for the basis of system is also an ethical issue," because "a knowledge organization system that is appropriate for the elements of one culture may not recognize elements that are highly important for some other culture, and such exclusions pose problems because we need to integrate knowledge across cultural, geographic, and linguistic boundaries." Daniel Martínez-Ávila and John M. Budd, "Epistemic Warrant for Categorizational Activities and the Development of Controlled Vocabularies," *Journal of Documentation* 73, no. 4 (2017): 704–5, https://doi.org/10.1108/JD-10-2016-0129.

30. Olson, *The Power to Name*.

31. Melissa Adler, "The Case for Taxonomic Reparations," *Knowledge Organization* 43, no. 8 (2016): 635, https://doi.org/10.5771/0943-7444-2016-8-630.

32. A project dedicated to collaborative editing of geographic names is "Stories from the land: Indigenous Place Names in Canada," which created an interactive map of place names based on various Indigenous languages and consultation with its representatives (https://open.canada.ca/data/en/dataset/0a309f2c-4f11-4ddb-bce1-e7ba6f-8c20cf).

perspectives.[33] Debates and approaches from the museum landscape can also be referenced from a library perspective. In this way, experiences regarding the intensive interaction with communities of origin and questions of cultural ownership can be productively investigated. In this context, it is important to reflect on the extent to which the system can be opened up (removal of technical hurdles, further access options) so that different groups of people can influence the content as well as the structure, and their perspectives can be taken into account.

The use of linked data can be productive on different levels in the course of merging different controlled vocabularies: it is thereby possible to involve people in the process of vocabulary enrichment who are not part of the core library community. This provides an alternative to centralized work on authority files, where proposals for additions or changes sometimes have to go through a lengthy process. At the same time, the inclusion of different perspectives allows for greater plurality, e.g., in self-naming, which Ruth Kitchin Tillman points out as an advantage: "one of the greatest possibilities for ethical work in name authority which exists within linked data is multiplicity of representation, this engagement with other communities. Anyone can say anything about anything and express it in similar ways for their own use or for distribution."[34]

Juliet Hardesty and Allison Nolan (as part of the LGBTQ Cultural Center and the Indiana University Bloomington Herman B. Wells Library) present a practical approach to this problem:

33. Thus, she proposes: "Seek ongoing consultation with local authorized indigenous representatives and gatekeepers. [...] Work with community representatives to consider cataloging terminology. [...] Develop institution and community-based agreements of cooperation. [...] Arrange for reciprocal visits to build strong long-term relationships. [...] When in doubt ask questions." Naomi R. Caldwell, "Ethical Questions in Name Authority Control: An Indigenous Global Perspective of Policy, Procedures and Best Practice," in *Ethical Questions in Name Authority Control*, ed. Jane Sandberg (Sacramento, CA: Library Juice Press, 2019), 391.

34. Ruth K. Tillman, "Barriers to Ethical Name Modeling in Current Linked Data Encoding Practices," in *Ethical Questions in Name Authority Control*, ed. Jane Sandberg (Sacramento, CA: Library Juice Press, 2019), 248.

they use a controlled and contemporary community vocabulary (Homosaurus, an international linked data vocabulary of Lesbian, Gay, Bisexual, Transgender, and Queer terms[35]) and link it to an authority file (LCSH). This is possible because both vocabularies are expressed as linked data.[36] Their goal is "to incorporate the terminology from the marginalized community as an overlay or replacement for outdated or absent terms from more widely used vocabularies."[37] In the course of this work, the established links should increase the findability of material and make the search process more inclusive through increased representation and coverage of needs.

Obstacles and Difficulties of Implementation in Practice

The innovative approaches described above are met with various obstacles in my everyday work, with regard both to the enrichment of the GND with ethnological terms and to participation in the Network for Sustainable Research Structures in Colonial Contexts. These issues include historicity of terms, different foreign and self-designations, and who is holding spokesperson positions for certain issues. Not only are many terminologies disputed in the respective heterogeneous communities, but also in the scientific community. This necessitates discussions and decisions that will not be satisfactory for everyone involved. It's important to ask whether changing terminology without preserving a record

---

35. Can be found at: https://homosaurus.org

36. "This project uses skos:exactMatch relationships defined by the Homosaurus to enable researchers to use Homosaurus terms to search a library catalog and retrieve relevant results based on the connected LCSH terms that are already in the catalog record. [...] If the Homosaurus term does not match exactly to the LCSH term, a keyword search is conducted using the Homosaurus term to retrieve library catalog results where the Homosaurus term appears in any indexed field in the catalog record." Juliet Hardesty and Allison Nolan, "Mitigating Bias in Metadata," *Information Technology and Libraries* 40, no. 3 (2021): 2, https://doi.org/10.6017/ital.v40i3.13053.

37. Hardesty and Nolan, "Mitigating Bias in Metadata," 1.

of the original would obscure a Eurocentric or colonial ideology inherent to the original terminology, or if preserving it could hinder discoverability and even cause offense?[38] Furthermore, outdated terms may be necessary for some use cases.

Ethical consideration regarding the extent of material accessibility is also important. To what extent does the need for broadest possible access limit the obligation to absolutely precise naming?[39] For practical implementation, this could mean that (problematic) terms could be retained as synonyms in order to remain usable in a commented form as access vocabulary for research. Within the GND, for example, the record for the group name "Khoikhoin" (http://d-nb.info/gnd/4025936-5) can be found. Here, the problematic term "Hottentotten" has been retained as a synonym, but with a brief explanation that it has a pejorative connotation. In this way, search entry points and knowledge traces have been preserved, while at least a brief contextualization or historical explanation has occurred.

On a quantitative level, there is also the problem that the sheer volume of terms makes a comprehensive detailed check difficult, since sufficient resources are seldom permanently available for this purpose. Collaborative work on the GND represents, at least in part, an attempt at a solution that is intended to enable consistent revision and maintenance of the authority file database. There is a tension between a system that aims at a comprehensive description of the world under Western conditions and more specific/local knowledge systems. A central question in this context is who can be the contact persons for an open and collaborative development of solutions when it comes to comprehensive systems that do not have a local or more narrow focus. In part, this

---

38. For a more in-depth presentation of the facts, see Hannah Turner, *Cataloguing Culture: Legacies of Colonialism in Museum Documentation* (Vancouver: UBC Press, 2020), 159.

39. For example, in workshops of the Network for Sustainable Research Structures in Colonial Contexts, researchers from the Global South pointed out that knowledge about the existence of holdings and making them accessible is central.

distinguishes the two projects (the revision and supplementation of the GND and the participation in the Thesauri Working Group of the Network for Sustainable Research Structures in Colonial Contexts) in terms of scope and different points of contact from others that tend to target a more localized and directly approachable community.[40]

A key step is to conduct a comprehensive and regularly updated assessment. The work on the controlled vocabulary in the course of the Network for Sustainable Research Structures in Colonial Contexts should help to create access. What is available in German institutions on the subject of colonialism will be made transparent. This material will be brought together centrally and, building on this, further cooperation will be established.

The primary goal regarding the Thesauri Working Group is to get an overview of already existing controlled vocabularies by means of research and in-depth interviews and, at the same time, to inquire as to what extent these are available for further processing. The approach of Hardesty and Nolan described above cannot be easily transferred to this project because most of the vocabularies used here, beyond the GND, are not available in a

---

40. As an example, I would like to refer to projects that have explicitly included community perspectives and needs in their work. These are based on direct cooperation with Indigenous communities living on site, a frame of reference that cannot be adapted in the same way for the German-speaking context. The following projects are mentionable: the Brian Deer Classification System for First-Nation-Groups in British Columbia (Alissa Cherry and Keshav Mukunda, "A Case Study in Indigenous Classification: Revisiting and Reviving the Brian Deer Scheme," *Cataloging & Classification Quarterly* 53, 5-6 (2015), https://doi.org/10.1080/01639374.2015.1008717), the Maori Subject Headings (https://natlib.govt.nz/librarians/nga-upoko-tukutuk) or the Mashantucket Pequot Thesaurus of American Indian Terminology (Sandra Littletree and Cheryl A. Metoyer, "Knowledge Organization from an Indigenous Perspective: The Mashantucket Pequot Thesaurus of American Indian Terminology Project," *Cataloging & Classification Quarterly* 53, 5–6 (2015), https://doi.org/10.1080/01639374.2015.1010113). At the same time, there are adaptations that the Library of Congress Subject Headings are working on with reference to Indigenous issues for the Canadian archival context within a dialogic process (Christine Bone and Brett Lougheed, "Library of Congress Subject Headings Related to Indigenous Peoples: Changing LCSH for Use in a Canadian Archival Context," *Cataloging & Classification Quarterly* 56, no. 1 (2018), https://doi.org/10.1080/01639374.2017.1382641).

form that can be directly linked (e.g. as PDF or Word documents). In addition, there are no comprehensive German-language vocabulary lists or thesauri in the field of colonial contexts to date; the few that do exist are sometimes incomplete and it is unclear how appropriate and up-to-date they still are. This makes a merging and editorial revision necessary.[41]

After collecting and reviewing the vocabularies that can be used in the field of colonial contexts, these will first be subjected to a test run using the example of so-called ethnonyms, i.e., ethnic group names, in the program xTree[42], software that enables the administration and collective editing of vocabularies. This procedure is intended to determine the extent to which it is possible to connect and harmonize vocabularies. For this purpose, the group names already available in the GND are to be imported into xTree and in turn intellectually compared with other collected vocabularies. Possible empty spaces are to be filled in this way and problematic terminology, such as foreign-applied vs. self-applied names (i.e., group names that have been assigned by strangers vs. group names developed by groups themselves), is to be subjected to deeper examination and critical reflection. At the same time, questions of correct spelling and preferred group-naming play a role.[43]

41. Hardesty and Nolan also note this problem: "One of the largest obstacles to connecting marginalized communities to reliable, representative controlled vocabularies is the lack of controlled vocabularies that are readily available as linked data. Unless an individual or organization has made the effort to establish connections between a community's vocabulary and LCSH, the representative vocabularies stand alone and remain difficult to discover or use." Hardesty and Nolan, "Mitigating Bias in Metadata," 10.

42. For more information see: http://xtree-public.digicult-verbund.de/vocnet/?action=start&lang=de.

Vocabulary access is available via JSON interface and the vocabularies are accessible as RDF/XML, among others.

43. One project that has already carried out, the merging of inventories from various institutions in the Global North with regard to Kenyan cultural objects into one database, is the International Inventories Programme (https://www.inventoriesprogramme.org). There is some mention of problems that have been encountered in dealing with ethnic designations: "More problematic was the presence of spelling errors

Collective editing makes it possible to draw on a significantly higher level of knowledge from (international) experts than if only individual persons edit the thesaurus. At the same time, xTree offers the possibility to lower barriers to cooperative editing. Rules and regulations, which form the framework for the processing of authority files, recede somewhat into the background and, at the same time, members with more expertise in rules and regulations can provide support. In addition, the procedure enables international cooperation so that, in the best case, direct consultation can be sought with the communities of

Screenshot from xTree. For more information see:

http://xtree-public.digicult-verbund.de/vocnet/

(Maasai? Massai? Masai?) and anthropological and misattribution errors (generally around ethnicities introduced by anthropologists; for instance, the continued use of derogatory terms such as 'Kavirondo' or 'Kitosh' to refer to the Luhya and Luo people of Kenya)." International Inventories Programme, "Invisible Inventories: A Collective Outlook," https://www.inventoriesprogramme.org/publications/2021/5/8/invisible-inventories-a-collective-outlook, 5.

origin concerned. This procedure represents an attempt to realize collaborative work in an equitable and fair way, even in the case of very complex projects with many prerequisites.

The results of this process will then in turn be imported back into the GND so that they can be made available to a wider circle of people in the future and can be applied in various indexing and data networking contexts. These data can thus also contribute to the indexing of "peripheral" literature[44] and enable better visibility and discoverability, as called for by Nora Schmidt, thereby serving to help decolonize access to scientific literature.

Many of the controlled vocabularies are not very sustainable, since they are often available or processed in a decentralized, project-related manner or for a limited period. A later reimport into the GND could counteract this problem of the lack of sustainability. Working collaboratively on these collected vocabularies makes it possible to reconcile resources and datasets across institutional boundaries, although the reconciliation must always take place on a case-by-case basis and consider the differences and limitations in the ways that each institution understands a resource, as well as each institution's capacity.

In the next step, the developed vocabulary will be used by different holding institutions to index resources collected from colonial contexts. These will be gathered at DDB and will be made more accessible to a broader audience through the future implementation of this vocabulary. So far, the imported resources only include the information submitted by the data-providing institutions in the form of their metadata; there is no enrichment with subject headings yet.

In this context, the nexus between colonialism and its problematic language will be an issue. It will then be a question of the

---

44. This refers to literature that is sometimes on the margins of publication from the perspective of the Global North. Nora Schmidt, "Überlegungen für die Dekolonialisierung wissenschaftlicher Bibliotheken in Europa," *Young Information Scientist* no. 6 (2021): 10, https://doi.org/10.25365/YIS-2021-6-1.

extent to which problematic historical terms are displayed publicly. This may include, for example, how individual populations, places, or objects have been historically named or classified. On the one hand, these terms can be discriminatory or problematic, but on the other hand, they can also be necessary for historical research or general findability. What needs to be clarified is to what extent Eurocentric concepts are reproduced in the process, how to respond to multilingualism in the material's communities of origin, and how to ensure improved accessibility of the material.

In addition, another problem specific to linked data is the complexity of linking concepts of one ontology to another: for example, how relationships concerning authorship are defined and mapped in different systems. In this context, ethical questions regarding authorship and cultural property are relevant and need clarification. For example, who is considered the author or rights holder of resources (researcher/collector or communities of origin) and to what extent must the communities of origin or several other entities also be named instead of a single person as one author.[45] An additional question that must be answered on a case-by-case basis is that, on the one hand, the research participants should perhaps be listed as co-authors for reasons of scientific ethics, but this may not make sense for reasons of personal protection. What prevails? How can it be shown that others were significantly involved in the research but do not disclose their names?

---

45. Molly Torsen and Jane Anderson, *Intellectual Property and the Safeguarding of Traditional Cultures: Legal Issues and Practical Options for Museums, Libraries and Archives* (Geneva: World Intellectual Property Organization, 2012) https://doi.org/10.34667/TIND.28634, 12–14; Jane Anderson and Kimberly Christen, "Decolonizing Attribution: Traditions of Exclusion," *Journal of Radical Librarianship* 5 (2019), 131-136.

For an overview regarding various recommendations for action in this area, see: Devon Murphy, "Guidelines on Working with Indigenous Partners and Information," https://www.getty.edu/research/tools/vocabularies/murphy_indigenous_information.pdf.

Conclusion, Open Questions and Outlook

When it comes to indexing and linking material, the advantages of authority files cannot be ignored, despite the problems
described above. An authority file structure, such as the GND,
is not easy to replace due to its extensive data coverage as well
as its firm anchoring in the library (and, hopefully, also museum
and archival) space. While the creation of a totally new authority
database and controlled vocabulary would be ideal, considerations of labor, time, and money prevent such an undertaking.
The GND can serve as a basis for bringing different perspectives
into conversation with one another and making the results accessible to a larger number of users in a low-threshold manner. The
cooperative editing structure and multi-institutional integration,
as well as their permanent maintenance and modification possibilities in the form of term enrichment, enable a high degree
of sustainability. This sustainability is often not achieved with
project-based vocabularies, especially after the end of the project.
Thus, it is possible to avoid insular solutions. Furthermore, in
the case of specialized vocabularies, it can be problematic that
they are only known to a small circle of people. The GND can
be a central reference point for project networking, for example
with regard to further linked data applications. Also, it enables
more extensive indexing, for example, via mass processing in
digitization projects. Through future intensified exchange with
Wikidata in the form of permanent, institutionalized alignment
or backlinking with the GND, the advantages of the standardized vocabulary of the GND can also benefit this project. GND
use can thus contribute to the comprehensive preservation, networking and accessibility of knowledge.

However, numerous questions have not yet been conclusively
discussed, meaning that in many cases the extent to which the
ethical-theoretical problems raised above can be dealt with in
practice still needs to be explored. For example, professionals in

the Global North working with linked data must be cautious of universalistic approaches to authority files, especially when they enter into dialogue with non-Eurocentric knowledge systems.[46] The question here is to what extent systems that reproduce a view of the Global North can be brought into contact with systems that propose a different world order. It is necessary to develop thoughtful approaches on how to deal with the fact that different ontology systems are not completely compatible or can even contradict each other. At the same time, it would be useful to explore to what extent the potential of having multiple views of a resource can be used productively.[47] Linked data offers the possibility of annotation to establish divergent perspectives as well as a higher level of contextualization through interaction with, for example, communities of origin.[48] In addition, knowledge structures can be created such that they are oriented around group-specific perspectives. With the opening of the GND and the potential of linked data, a higher degree of flexibility and better access to collections is possible than has been the case so far in conventional library systems.

At the same time, the ethical issues raised here and elsewhere in this volume should be permanently integrated into debates and questions about data linkage (and everything that it entails). Linked data and linking data should not only be considered from a technical point of view but also from an ethical point of view.

---

46. These systems, which are sometimes to be newly created, may then also be based on different principles than the currently hegemonic systems. In this context, Littletree et al. list seven components for Indigenous Knowledge Organization Systems: "Indigenous authority, Indigenous diversity, wholism and interrelatedness, Indigenous continuity, Aboriginal user warrant, designer responsibility, and institutional responsibility." (Sandra Littletree, Miranda Belarde-Lewis, and Marisa Duarte, "Centering Relationality: A Conceptual Model to Advance Indigenous Knowledge Organization Practices," *Knowledge Organization* 47, no. 5 (2020): 415, https://doi.org/10.5771/0943-7444-2020-5-410).

47. Wikidata offers, for example, the possibility to identify controversial terms and definitions within the data structure and to store contrasting information.

48. Jodie Dowd and Jenny Wood, "Indigenous Knowledge Systems and Linked Data," https://read.alia.org.au/indigenous-knowledge-systems-and-linked-data, 9.

Ethical and political considerations and consequences should be repeatedly invoked, even if there is unlikely to be a satisfactory one-size-fits-all solution. Language is dynamic, so revision processes can never be fully complete and not every change can be identified and implemented in a timely manner. Nevertheless, it should be explored how iterative processes can become part of the maintenance of (authority) datasets.

Questions regarding adequate research and access vocabularies will become increasingly important with the wider dissemination of material through linked data networks. A lack of representation (e.g., of topics or identities) can lead to problems of use, especially if interested parties cannot interact with the systems because their perspectives and concepts/vocabularies have not been included.[49] It must be ensured that the knowledge systems have the greatest possible openness and that interfaces are used that can enable low-threshold participation by all users. At the same time, the advantages that controlled vocabularies possess should not be abandoned. Multivocality or multiperspectivity and a certain degree of normative control should not be negotiated as opposites but should be productively mediated in order to ensure the greatest possible global discoverability and accessibility.

---

49. Gomes and Frota, "Knowledge Organization from a Social Perspective: Thesauri and the Commitment to Cultural Diversity," 641.

Non-Binary Gender Representation in Wikidata

DANIELE METILLI & CHIARA PAOLINI

Introduction

In the era of big data, new ethical questions have arisen from the creation of large knowledge bases, whose data is produced, consumed, and shared by millions of users, both humans and machines. These knowledge bases often contain biographical information about people, including sensitive data such as gender, sex, ethnicity, or sexual orientation. Implicit biases in such data can generate unfairness[1] and lead to discriminatory applications that impact marginalized communities.[2]

This is particularly true for the trans and non-binary communities, who experience discrimination on the basis of gender identity. Digital projects have struggled to cope with the wider

---

1. Michael Veale and Reuben Binns, "Fairer Machine Learning in the Real World: Mitigating Discrimination Without Collecting Sensitive Data," *Big Data & Society* 4, no. 2 (2017): 1–17; Ninareh Mehrabi, Fred Morstatter, Nripsuta Saxena, Kristina Lerman, and Aram Galstyan, "A Survey on Bias and Fairness in Machine Learning." *ACM Computing Surveys (CSUR)* 54, no. 6 (2021): 1–35.

2. Joy Buolamwini and Timnit Gebru, "Gender Shades: Intersectional Accuracy Disparities in Commercial Gender Classification," in *Proceedings of the 2018 ACM Conference on Fairness, Accountability and Transparency*, ACM, 2018, 77–91; Emily M. Bender, Timnit Gebru, Angelina McMillan-Major, and Shmargaret Shmitchell, "On the Dangers of Stochastic Parrots: Can Language Models Be Too Big?" in *Proceedings of the 2021 ACM Conference on Fairness, Accountability, and Transparency*, ACM, 2018, 610–23.

societal acceptance of the fact that gender is not binary,[3] and in many cases they have perpetuated—or even amplified—the misgendering and erasure of trans and non-binary people that has occurred in society throughout history.[4]

In this chapter we present a preliminary quantitative analysis of non-binary gender identities in a large-scale knowledge base: Wikidata.[5] Wikidata is a collaborative project that allows the editing of knowledge—and even the data model itself—by a broad community of users.[6] The present research constitutes the first step of our project, Wikidata Gender Diversity (WiGeDi),[7] which aims to investigate the issue of how gender identities are represented[8] in the knowledge base.

This study aims to contribute to the growing area of data ethics by offering, for the first time, an empirical exploration of the representation of non-binary gender identities in a large knowledge base, and by providing fresh insights and data to gender studies scholars interested in more qualitative approaches to research.

Since every edit and every user discussion throughout the history of Wikidata is archived in the project itself and made publicly accessible, this study allows us to have a unique and comprehensive overview of *how* non-binary identities have been represented in Wikidata, *what* exactly has been represented, and

---

3. Suzanne J. Kessler and Wendy McKenna, *Gender: An Ethnomethodological Approach* (Chicago:University of Chicago Press, 1985).

4. Os Keyes, "The Misgendering Machines: Trans/HCI Implications of Automatic Gender Recognition." *Proceedings of the 2018 ACM Conference on Human-Computer Interaction* 2 (2018): 1–22.

5. Denny Vrandečić and Markus Krötzsch, "Wikidata: A Free Collaborative Knowledgebase," *Communications of the ACM* 57, no. 10 (2017): 78–85.

6. Alessandro Piscopo, Chris Phethean, and Elena Simperl, "What Makes a Good Collaborative Knowledge Graph: Group Composition and Quality in Wikidata," in *Proceedings of the 2017 International Conference on Social Informatics*, (Springer, 2017), 305-22.

7. Wikidata Gender Diversity will be hosted on https://wigedi.com.

8. Whenever we use the terms "represent" or "representation" throughout the chapter, we are referring to the concept of "knowledge representation" (Davis, Shrobe & Szolovits, 1993).

why the users have made certain choices. We performed our analysis from three different—and complementary—perspectives:

1. the modeling question, looking at how the Wikidata ontology has evolved to support non-binary representation, e.g., by updating the properties that directly or indirectly express gender; we aim to analyze the Wikidata ontology to identify representational issues and potential areas of improvement;

2. the data question, computing statistics about non-binary gender representation in the knowledge base, and analyzing it from a quantitative point of view; also, by comparing non-binary people described in Wikidata to the general population(s) of non-binary people in society;

3. the community question, looking at how the Wikidata community has handled the evolution towards a more inclusive non-binary representation, by analyzing user discussions about the topic in a quantitative way; indeed, gender representation is often intrinsically connected to language.

We believe that only by answering all three questions it will be possible to obtain a comprehensive overview of non-binary gender representation in Wikidata. Previous studies on the topic, such as Klein et al. and Konieczny and Klein,[9] have mostly focused on the gender gap in the data, without looking in detail at the model or at the community's interactions and decision processes. Furthermore, to the best of our knowledge, no published research has yet specifically been centered on the modeling of non-binary identities in Wikidata.

---

9. Maximilian Klein, Harsh Gupta, Vivek Rai, Piotr Konieczny, and Haiyi Zhu, "Monitoring the Gender Gap with Wikidata Human Gender Indicators," in *Proceedings of the 12th International Symposium on Open Collaboration*, ACM, 2016, 1–9; Piotr Konieczny, and Maximilian Klein, "Gender Gap Through Time and Space: A Journey Through Wikipedia Biographies via the Wikidata Human Gender Indicator," *New Media & Society* 20, no. 12 (2018): 4608–33.

Based on the research questions listed above, we discuss the theoretical background (Section 2, *Background*) and the state of the art of studies about gender in Wikidata and other knowledge bases (Section 3, *State of the Art*). Then, we present an overview of the current Wikidata model of gender, and a timeline of its historical evolution (Section 4, *The Model*); a set of statistics about gender representation in Wikidata, and non-binary identities in particular (Section 5, *The Data*); a corpus of user discussions about gender called *WiGeTa-En*, and a preliminary analysis of it based on computational linguistics techniques (Section 6, *The Community*). Finally, we conclude with a discussion of the current status of non-binary representation in Wikidata.

Background

We begin our study from the fact that gender is not binary. The binary view that has been prevalent in most of the world until the current century is in fact quite recent[10] and not universal.[11] In this traditional view, gender consisted of a binary classification that allowed only two slots, "man" and "woman," corresponding to two sexes, "male" and "female." Sex was assigned to each person at birth by a doctor based on the person's external anatomy, without regard for genetics, hormonal factors, or identity.

Since the 1970s, the view that gender is a social construct has become prevalent in the scientific community.[12] Gender studies scholars distinguish between *sex assigned at birth* (e.g., female), *gender identity* (e.g., woman), and *gender expression* (e.g., androgynous).[13] Another term that has recently been proposed

---

10. Leah DeVun, *The Shape of Sex: Nonbinary Gender from Genesis to the Renaissance* (New York: Columbia University Press, 2021).

11. Gilbert Herdt, *Third Sex, Third Gender: Beyond Sexual Dimorphism in Culture and History* (Princeton, NJ: Princeton University Press, 2020),.

12. Judith Butler, *Gender Trouble: Feminism and the Subversion of Identity*. (Routledge, 1990).

13. Julia Serano, *Whipping Girl: A Transsexual Woman on Sexism and the Scapegoating of Femininity* (UK: Hachette, 2016).

is *gender modality*, to describe the correspondence between sex assigned at birth and gender identity (e.g., cisgender).[14] A person's gender identity may or may not correspond to the sex assigned at birth, and a person's gender expression may not reflect the gender roles associated with their gender identity by society.

A wide spectrum of identities exists outside the traditional binary view of gender. We hereby provide a few definitions for the reader's convenience. However, it should be noted that the reality of these identities is much more complex and varied than these broad definitions may suggest.

First of all, the term *transgender* (or *trans*) indicates any person whose gender identity is different from the one assigned to them at birth.[15] *Trans women* are women who are assigned male at birth, while *trans men* are men who are assigned female at birth. On the contrary, the term *cisgender* (or *cis*) describes people who identify with the same gender that is assigned to them at birth.

Non-binary people have a gender identity that falls outside the gender binary. A non-binary person may or may not necessarily identify as trans; therefore, we prefer to talk about *trans and gender-diverse* identities to refer to these communities in an inclusive way.

Intersex people are people whose sex is not classifiable in a binary way. The term has traditionally referred to sexual characteristics; however, it is also used for self-identification.[16]

In recent decades, the LGBTQIA+[17] movements have worked to reclaim as valid the identities of people who do not fit into their assigned gender.[18] This work has resulted in a wider societal

14. Florence Ashley, "'Trans' Is My Gender Modality: A Modest Terminological Proposal" *Trans Bodies, Trans Selves* (2021).

15. Serano, *Whipping Girl.*

16. Jens M. Scherpe, Anatol Dutta, and Tobias Helms, *The Legal Status of Intersex Persons* (Intersentia, 2018).

17. Lesbian, Gay, Bisexual, Trans, Queer, Intersex, Asexual, and other sexual orientations and gender identities.

18. Lisa M. Stulberg, *LGBTQ Social Movements* (John Wiley & Sons, 2018).

acceptance and some limited legal recognition, but significant erasure and discrimination persist.[19]

It is important to note that knowledge bases can directly or indirectly contribute to erasure of trans and gender-diverse people. As discussed in Sandberg,[20] the people who are tasked with modeling and cataloging biographical data have important ethical responsibilities that should not be overlooked. This is also true for Wikidata, where the user community holds a collective responsibility over the data.

Given the complex and interlocked nature of gender identity, sex assigned at birth, and gender expression, we cannot study each of these concepts in an isolated way, but rather we need to consider them holistically when looking at gender modeling in Wikidata.

State of the Art

To date, there have not been many studies about gender in Wikidata. The first scholars to approach the subject were Klein et al. and Konieczny and Klein,[21] who carried out an in-depth analysis of the Wikidata gender gap. The authors applied several gender gap indexes to the data contained in the knowledge base, showing that women are under-represented compared to men and that, in general, Wikidata appears to be affected by the same gender disparities that exist in society at large. The most recent project by

19. Michelle Dietert and Dianne Dentice, "Gender Identity Issues and Workplace Discrimination: The Transgender Experience," *Journal of Workplace Rights* 14, no. 1 (2009): 121–140.

20. Jane Sandberg, *Ethical Questions in Name Authority Control* (Sacramento, CA: Litwin Books, 2009).

21. Maximilian Klein, Harsh Gupta, Vivek Rai, Piotr Konieczny, and Haiyi Zhu, "Monitoring the Gender Gap with Wikidata Human Gender Indicators," in *Proceedings of the 12th International Symposium on Open Collaboration* (ACM, 2016), 1-9; Piotr Konieczny and Maximilian Klein, "Gender Gap Through Time and Space: A Journey Through Wikipedia Biographies via the Wikidata Human Gender Indicator," *New Media & Society* 20, no. 12 (2018): 4608–33.

the authors is Humaniki,[22] a tool showing the gender gap among all Wikimedia projects.

Hollink, Van Aggelen, and Van Ossenbruggen[23] measured gender differences in a subset of Wikidata entries. Zhang and Terveen[24] recently conducted a case study about the Wikidata gender content gap. The Wikidata Community Survey 2021[25] has looked at gender metrics in the community of Wikidata editors which show that the Wikidata community is overwhelmingly male (75%), while female users make up just 16% and non-binary users 2.9%.[26] The remaining users (6%) opted not to answer the question.[27]

There have been many studies about the gender gap in Wikipedia, which is a sister project to Wikidata.

Antin et al.[28] were the first to study gender differences in Wikipedia editing, while Reagle and Rhue[29] looked at gender bias in the content of the encyclopedia. Wagner et al.[30] analyzed how men and women are portrayed in Wikipedia. Johnson et

---

22. https://whgi.wmflabs.org.

23. Laura Hollink, Astrid Van Aggelen, and Jacco Van Ossenbruggen, "Using the Web of Data to Study Gender Differences in Online Knowledge Sources: The Case of the European Parliament," in *Proceedings of the 10th ACM Conference on Web Science* (ACM, 2018):381–85.

24. Charles Chuankai Zhang and Loren Terveen, "Quantifying the Gap: A Case Study of Wikidata Gender Disparities," in *17th International Symposium on Open Collaboration* (2021): 1–12.

25. https://commons.wikimedia.org/wiki/File:Wikidata_Community_Survey_2021.pdf.

26. The specific question that was asked was "What is your Gender?", and the possible answers were "Woman", "Man", "Non-binary", "Prefer not to disclose", and "Prefer to self-describe" (see page 15 of the Wikidata Community Survey).

27. See page 23 of the Wikidata Community Survey.

28. Judd Antin, Raymond Yee, Coye Cheshire, and Oded Nov, "Gender Differences in Wikipedia Editing," in Proceedings of the 7th International Symposium on Wikis and Open Collaboration (2011): 11–14.

29. Joseph Reagle and Lauren Rhue, "Gender Bias in Wikipedia and Britannica," *International Journal of Communication* 5 (2011): 21.

30. Claudia Wagner, David Garcia, Mohsen Jadidi, and Markus Strohmaier, "It's a Man's Wikipedia? Assessing Gender Inequality in an Online Encyclopedia," in *Ninth International AAAI Conference on Web and Social Media* (2015).

al.[31] looked at gender differences among the readers of the encyclopedia. Field, Park, and Tsvetkov[32] analyzed social biases in Wikipedia biographies, while Tripodi[33] investigated the frequent deletion of biographies about women.

More recently, Redi et al.[34] have created a taxonomy of knowledge gaps found in Wikimedia projects. Miquel-Ribé & Laniado[35] have developed the Wikipedia Diversity Observatory, a project that tracks the content gaps that are present in Wikipedia, making it easier to remedy them. Miquel-Ribé, Kaltenbrunner & Keefer[36] have looked specifically at LGBT+ content, comparing gaps among different language editions of Wikipedia.

While some of the previous studies about gender in Wikimedia projects acknowledged the existence of marginalized gender identities, they did not investigate specifically how their identities are represented, or how this representation has evolved over time. Our project differs from the previous ones because it is the first to center trans, non-binary, and other gender-diverse identities. Furthermore, we adopt a holistic view of the topic that does not merely focus on statistical data, but also looks at modeling, community processes, and contextual events to build a comprehensive overview of gender diversity in Wikidata.

31. Isaac Johnson, Florian Lemmerich, Diego Sáez-Trumper, Robert West, Markus Strohmaier, and Leila Zia, "Global Gender Differences in Wikipedia Readership." *arXiv Preprint arXiv:2007.10403*,

32. Anjalie Field, Chan Young Park, and Yulia Tsvetkov, "Controlled Analyses of Social Biases in Wikipedia Bios." *arXiv Preprint arXiv:2101.00078*, 2020.

33. Francesca Tripodi, "Ms. Categorized: Gender, Notability, and Inequality on Wikipedia." *New Media & Society* (2021), 14614448211023772.

34. M. Redi, M. Gerlach, I. Johnson, J. Morgan, & L. Zia, "A Taxonomy of Knowledge Gaps for Wikimedia Projects" (second draft), 2020, arXiv preprint arXiv:2008.12314.

35. M. Miquel-Ribé and D. Laniado, "The Wikipedia Diversity Observatory: Helping Communities to Bridge Content Gaps Through Interactive Interfaces," *Journal of Internet Services and Applications* 12, no. 1 (2021), 1-25.

36. M. Miquel-Ribé, A. Kaltenbrunner, and J.M. Keefer, "Bridging LGBT+ content Gaps Across Wikipedia Language Editions," *International Journal of Information, Diversity, & Inclusion (IJIDI)* 5, no. 4 (2021): 90-131.

The Model

In this section we describe the Wikidata modeling of gender and its evolution through time. Due to the open and collaborative nature of Wikidata, the model is fluid and constantly changing.[37]

The Wikidata model defines two basic types of entities: *items* and *properties*. Each Wikidata page describes a single item through one or more *labels* (multilingual strings of text representing the name of the item), one or more *aliases* (alternative names), one or more *descriptions* (multilingual strings of text), and one or more *statements*.

Each Wikidata statement expresses a fact that is known about the item, and is composed of a property, a value, and, optionally, one or more qualifiers and one or more references. For example, the Wikidata item *Q173399 Elliot Page* is connected by the property *P27 country of citizenship* to the value *Q16 Canada*.[38]

Since the term "item" is not widely used in the field of data modeling and may create confusion, in the following we will use the more general term "entity" to refer to Wikidata items.

Ontological Representation of Gender

In this section, we will describe the ontological representation of gender that has been adopted by Wikidata.[39]

In Wikidata, gender is modeled using the property *P21 sex or gender*, connecting a person (an entity that is an instance of

---

37. Alessandro Piscopo, Chris Phethean, and Elena Simperl, "What Makes a Good Collaborative Knowledge Graph: Group Composition and Quality in Wikidata," in *Proceedings of the 2017 International Conference on Social Informatics*, (Springer, 2017): 305–22.

38. For more details about the data model, see https://www.mediawiki.org/wiki/Wikibase/DataModel/Primer.

39. This is based on an analysis conducted in December 2021. To avoid reporting outdated information, we plan to publish an overview of the model that is frequently updated, in an automated way, on the website of our project (https://wigedi.com).

Q5 human) to one or more entities representing sex or gender.[40] Some of these entities are explicitly allowed as values of the property, while others are not. This distinction is evaluated through community discussions, and it is implemented through property constraints.[41] However, these constraints do not prevent the users from setting any value of their choice and are simply used to check for possible errors *after* the sex or gender has already been set.

Since its creation in 2013, the *P21* property has conflated the concepts of *sex* and *gender*, and this ambiguous nature of the property has led to many discussions and controversies (see Section 6, *The Community*). However, no significant changes to the definition of *P21* have been made in the last eight years since the creation of the property.

In the following, we will look at the possible values of *P21* and at their taxonomy. At this stage, we focus only on the labels of each entity without looking at its description. The reason for this is that the label of a Wikidata entity is often stable and consistent across different languages, while the description may change significantly over time and across languages. Therefore, listing the current English description of each entity would be quite misleading.

The allowed values for *P21* include:

1. instances of Q48264 gender identity. At present, there are 59 instances of gender identity, of which 23 are currently in use, and 3 more are reported as allowed on the property's discussion page. These are reported in Table 1.
2. instances of Q290 sex. At present, there are 24 instances of sex, of which 8 are currently in use, and 1 more is reported as allowed on the property's discussion page.

---

40. P21 can also applied to fictional human or other entities. It should be noted that each entity, including humans, is allowed to have multiple values of P21.

41. https://www.wikidata.org/wiki/Help:Property_constraints_portal.

These are reported in Table 2.
3. 8 other values from the set reported in Table 3, of which
7 are currently in use. These are values that are neither
instances of Q48264 gender identity nor instances of
Q290 sex, and their classification is highly varied (see
below).
4. the unknown value.

In total, 31 entities are currently used as values of *P21*, and 40
entities are explicitly allowed as values of the property according
to the constraints listed on *P21*'s discussion page. One entity is
currently in use but not allowed.[42]

Fig. 1 shows the current class taxonomy of the gender entities
reported in Table 1, including only those that are presently used
as values of *P21*.

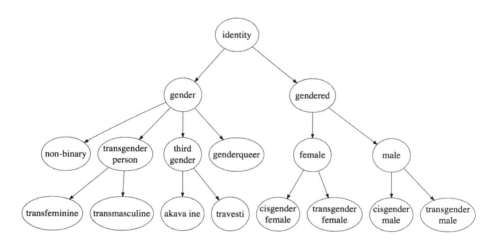

Figure 1: The taxonomy of gender in Wikidata

---

42. The entity is hermaphrodite, which is widely considered a derogatory term
when applied to humans.

Table 1: Gender values of P21

Wikidata ID	English Label	Allowed Value	Usage
Q108876763	abinary	No	–
Q505371	agender	Yes	27
Q104838508	alyha	No	–
Q97595519	androgyne	No	–
Q97577404	aporagender	No	–
Q859614	bigender	Yes	6
Q107144810	binabinaaine	No	–
Q56388896	calabai	No	–
Q65212675	calalai	No	–
Q15145779	cisgender female	Yes	21
Q107785560	cisgender gay male	No	–
Q15145778	cisgender male	Yes	12
Q1093205	cisgender person	No	–
Q93954933	demiboy	Yes	2
Q63715923	demigender	No	–
Q93955709	demigirl	Yes	–
Q1399232	fa'afafine	Yes	4
Q107427210	fakafifine	No	–
Q350374	fakaleitī	Yes	–
Q6581072	female	Yes	1825280
Q11491595	gender identity disorder	No	–
Q56314793	gender incongruence	No	–
Q106647285	gender modality	No	–
Q99485732	gendered	No	–
Q106781857	genderfaun	No	–
Q18116794	genderfluid	Yes	43
Q12964198	genderqueer	Yes	40
Q660882	hijra	Yes	1
Q11713472	intergender	No	–
Q104717073	intersex person	No	–
Q106990131	isogender person	No	–
Q746411	kathoey	Yes	2
Q6581097	male	Yes	5741522
Q82028886	maverique	No	–
Q24886035	mudoko dako	No	–
Q3277905	māhū	Yes	6
Q1289754	neutrois	Yes	2
Q48270	non-binary	Yes	510
Q69990794	non-binary human	No	–
Q48796147	nádleehi	No	–
Q7130936	pangender	Yes	2
Q64606208	polygender	No	–
Q3404005	questioning	No	–
Q106647045	sekhet	No	–
Q27679684	transfeminine	Yes	8
Q1052281	transgender female	Yes	1125
Q2449503	transgender male	Yes	295
Q189125	transgender person	Yes	29
Q27679766	transmasculine	Yes	8
Q107502361	transneutral	No	–
Q17148251	travesti	Yes	14
Q7841680	trigender	No	–
Q301702	two-spirit	Yes	17
Q108266757	vakasalewalewa	No	–
Q104834145	waria	No	–
Q8025501	winkte	No	–
Q96000630	x-gender	Yes	–
Q108854353	xenogender	No	–
Q8053770	yinyang ren	No	–

Table 2: Sex values of P21

Wikidata ID	English Label	Allowed Value	Usage
Q4700377	akava'ine	Yes	1
Q59592239	altersex	No	–
Q4849481	bakla	No	–
Q2904759	bissu	No	–
Q106610856	endosex	No	–
Q6581072	female	Yes	1825282
Q43445	female organism	Yes	4530
Q1054122	futanari	No	–
Q106647285	gender modality	No	–
Q430711	gynandromorph	No	–
Q303479	hermaphrodite	No	1
Q1097630	intersex	Yes	133
Q28873047	intersex organism	Yes	–
Q1062222	khanith	No	–
Q25035965	koekchuch	No	–
Q6538491	lhamana	No	–
Q6581097	male	Yes	5741522
Q44148	male organism	Yes	8927
Q30689479	meti	No	–
Q24886035	mudoko dako	No	–
Q3333006	mukhannathun	No	–
Q3177577	muxe	Yes	1
Q20577996	sex reassignment	No	–

Table 3: Other values of P21

Wikidata ID	English Label	Allowed Value	Usage	Instance of
Q207959	androgyny	Yes	10	gendered expression/identity
Q179294	eunuch	Yes	251	social status/job/physiological condition/occupation
Q64017034	cogenitor	Yes	1	fictional sex
Q52261234	neutral sex	Yes	13	no class
Q16674976	hermaphroditism	Yes	7	reproductive system
Q48279	third gender	Yes	2	subclass of sex; subclass of gender
Q56315990	assigned female at birth	Yes	1	assigned gender
Q25388691	assigned male at birth	Yes	0	assigned gender

As shown in the figure, the top gender classes are *gender* ("range of physical, mental, and behavioral characteristics distinguishing between masculinity and femininity") and *gendered* ("state of having gender identity"). The class *gender* has subclasses *non-binary*, *genderqueer*, *third gender* and *transgender person*, while the class *gendered* has subclasses *male* and *female*.

The class *female* has subclasses *cisgender female* and *transgender female*, while the class *male* has subclasses *cisgender male* and *transgender male*. The class *transgender person* has subclasses *transfeminine* and *transmasculine* (which are not widely used as values). The class *third gender* has subclass *travesti* (a Latin American gender identity often considered a third gender). The class *non-binary* is the superclass of most of the remaining identities.

The current Wikidata gender taxonomy is unusual and, to the best of our knowledge, not based on any model of gender that is described in the literature. It is unclear why the distinction between *gender* and *gendered* exists. This distinction appears to have been added in 2020 to replace a previous sex-based classification of *female* and *male* (e.g., *female* was a subclass of *female organism*) with a gender-based one but, supposing that this was the intention, it would have been more consistent to simply make *female* and *male* subclasses of *gender*.[43]

Let's now look more in detail at the subclasses of *non-binary* that are reported in Fig. 2. The class *genderqueer* is not a subclass of *non-binary* but, rather, is connected to it through the property *P460 said to be the same as*, indicating that this class is "said to be the same as that item, but it's uncertain or disputed." The subclasses of *non-binary* are: *agender*, *bigender*, *demigender*, *fa'afafine*, *genderfluid*, *hijra*, *kathoey*, *māhū*, *neutrois*, *pangender*, and *two-spirit*. We report statistics about the usage of these non-binary identities in Section 5, *The Data*.

---

43. Even though, as we said in the Background section, it is more common to use the terms woman and man to refer to binary genders and female and male when referring to sex assigned at birth.

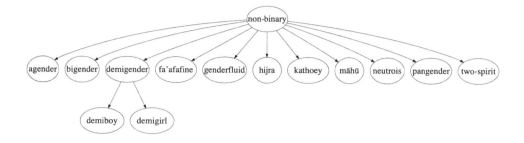

Figure 2: The taxonomy of non-binary gender in Wikidata

The current Wikidata model of non-binary identities is very simple, having only one main class and several subclasses, with no further levels except for *demigender*, which is a superclass of *demiboy* and *demigirl*. This simple taxonomy is consistent (meaning that there are no obvious contradictions); it can be considered accurate only insofar as *non-binary* is recognized as an umbrella term by every person who is described in Wikidata and identifies as one of the identities listed as subclasses of *non-binary*. Unfortunately, it would be very difficult to verify whether this is true or not.[44]

Fig. 3 shows the class taxonomy of the sex entities reported in Table 2, excluding *male* and *female*, which are currently not connected to the sex-based class tree.

As shown in Fig. 3, the current classification of sex contains *female human* and *male human* classes; however, these are not allowed as values of *P21*. The classes *female organism* and *male organism* are used for animals, while the class *intersex* is used for both humans and animals. The class *hermaphrodite* (a term generally considered offensive when applied to people) is a subclass of *intersex*.[45]

---

44. It is interesting to note that according to Wikidata's verifiability policy (https://www.wikidata.org/wiki/Wikidata:Verifiability), every statement that is collected in the knowledge base should be properly sourced; however, very often the structural subclass of relations that make up the model are not sourced at all.

45. At present, this value is used to express the gender of a single entity (a snail).

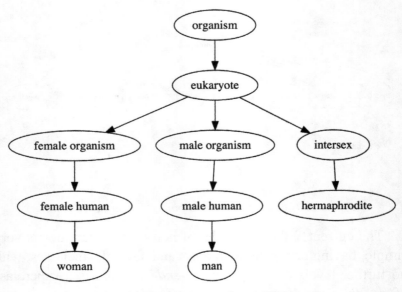

Figure 3: The taxonomy of sex in Wikidata

The remaining values of *P21*, which we reported in Table 3, have highly varied classifications that fall outside of the main ones reported in Fig. 2 and Fig. 3. Providing a detailed description of each is beyond the scope of this chapter; however, we will list them briefly for the reader's convenience. The entity *androgyny* is an instance of *gendered expression* and *identity* but, at the same time, it is also a subclass of *sexual diversity*. The entity *eunuch* is an instance of *social status, job, physiological condition* and *occupation*, but it is also a subclass of *man*[46] and *castrated creature*. The entity *cogenitor* is an instance of *fictional sex*. The entity *neutral sex* had no class assigned at the time of data collection. The entity *hermaphroditism* is an instance of *reproductive system* and a subclass of *sexual reproduction*. The entity *third gender* is a subclass (not an instance) of both *sex* and *gender*. Finally, the entities *assigned female at birth* and *assigned male at birth* are instances of *assigned gender* but also, strangely, subclasses of *assigned gender* and subclasses of *female* and *male* (respectively).

---

46. Confusingly, this entity Q8441 man is not an allowed value for P21.

Gendered Properties

Apart from *P21*, gender is also expressed through other properties, albeit in a more implicit way. In particular, the properties *P25 mother* and *P22 father* express gendered family relations.[47] For a brief historical overview of gendered family properties, see section *Gendered Properties for Family Relations* below.

In addition, gendered properties exist for the representation of athletes and sports competitions, which are often divided by gender (for example, the many properties linking athletes to their descriptions in external databases). At this stage, we are not aware of other non-familial properties that have been divided by gender.

A related issue is that of the property labels, which, in several languages, are affected by the lack of gender-neutral terms. For example, *sibling* in Italian can only be rendered as *fratello o sorella* (brother or sister). We plan to investigate property labels in a future study.

A Timeline of Wikidata Gender Modeling

This section reports a timeline of the main events related to the modeling of gender in Wikidata.

The Beginning

Wikidata opened to the public on October 25, 2012. In the initial stage of the project, the users focused on importing data from the existing Wikipedia. The items Q44148 male and Q43445 female were imported on November 13, 2012. On the same day, a user created the item Q48270 genderqueer, which would later be renamed "non-binary." The concept of non-binary identities was thus present in Wikidata since a very early date.

---

47. A property P8810 parent (unspecified) has recently been created to express a generic parent-child relationship, but it is not meant to replace mother and father.

On November 28, 2012, the item *Q189125 (transgender)*, later renamed *transgender person*, was imported from Wikipedia. The item's description received immediate transphobic vandalism from an anonymous user, which went unremarked upon for a whole year. Similarly, the items *Q1052281 (trans woman)* and *Q2449503 (trans man)* received incorrect English descriptions (e.g., "a person born male but identifying as female" for trans woman) that were not fixed for more than a year.

The first mention of "gender" in the Project Chat, the main English-language discussion page, was made on December 6, 2013. The users discussed the representation of gender and how to source it properly. In this initial stage of the project, there were often tensions between users who favored *completeness* (i.e., Wikidata should grow as fast as possible) versus those who favored *accuracy*. (i.e., every Wikidata statement should be properly sourced).

Looking specifically at gender, some users in the early Wikidata community did not understand the complexity of the gender modeling issue at all ("A sex property needs only male/female options. Demanding reference for that [makes] it look funny"), but there were a few who acknowledged the existence of non-binary people ("There are people [whose] sex can't readily be described as male or female").[48]

Creation of P21

The history of *P21* began on February 2, 2013, when a proposal was made in the Property Proposal section of Wikidata to create a property to represent human gender. After a short discussion, shown in Fig. 4,[49] the property was created on February 4, 2013.

---

48. https://www.wikidata.org/wiki/Wikidata:Project_chat/Archive/2013/02#Reference.

49. The names of the Wikidata users participating in the discussion have been redacted.

Gender / Geschlecht / Genre (sexe)

Status: ■ Done

→ Property:P21

- **Description**: Male, female, intersex
- **Datatype**: ItemValue
- **Links**:
- **Comments**: It may be a good idea to restrict the range of possible values when this will be possible. ▨▨▨ 15:29, 2 February 2013 (UTC) [reply]
    + 1 with ▨ : We must have only 2 possibilities : male / female. Other choices would be very difficult to source them. ▨▨▨ 17:45, 2 February 2013 (UTC) [reply]
        We need three: Male, female, and intersex. (Sexual preferences are private and can change.) ▨▨▨ 18:21, 2 February 2013 (UTC) [reply]
            We need four: Male, female, intersex and unknown/not defined. Some names are for both genders and of some people we have no knowledge neither of their names nor of their gender. This applies for the unknown but distinguishable artists of ancient pieces of arts. de:Notname en:Anonymous masters-- ▨▨▨ 00:08, 3 February 2013 (UTC) [reply]
                In German there is a whole category for unknown gender: de:Kategorie:Geschlecht unbekannt. ▨▨▨ 02:14, 3 February 2013 (UTC) [reply]
                    So, tree item values (Male, female, intersex) and the unknown special value (accessible by clicking to the icon at the left of the input, example ⌕). ▨▨▨ 07:25, 3 February 2013 (UTC) [reply]

Figure 4: The discussion about the creation of P21

Initially, the property was called *P21 gender*, and the only allowed values were *male*, *female*, *intersex*, and *unknown*. However, on the day of its creation, the labels for the property that were set in various languages (Italian, Portuguese, Czech) referred to *sex*, not gender. This created an initial confusion that was not resolved until December 2013, when, after a long discussion, Wikidata users decided to conflate the concept of sex with the concept of gender and change the property labels in all languages to *sex or gender*.[50]

However, the conflation of the two concepts generated additional ambiguities; for example, with regard to the representation of transgender people (see later section on *Representing Trans Identity*), because in many cases, the sex assigned at birth and the gender identity of a person are different.

The Rise of Bots

On February 6, 2013, shortly after the creation of *P21*, a user requested permission to use a bot to add some statements, including gender statements, to Wikidata items, based on information from

---

50. https://www.wikidata.org/wiki/Property_talk:P21/Archive_1#Transgender_/_Cisgender_changes.

Wikipedia categories: "A good example is en:Category:Women physicists. We can safely assume that all members of that category are female."[51] The proposal was approved on February 17, and the gender data started being populated automatically.

From this point onward, the automatic addition of gender data to people became routine. In the first two years of the project, at least seven bots,[52] each developed by a different user, added gender to Wikidata from various sources. Through these means, millions of entities representing people were assigned a gender. In June 2015, it was announced that gender data completeness had reached 93.8%.[53]

The main sources used by the bots were as follows:

1. Wikipedia categories, i.e., the gendered categories found in some Wikipedia language editions (for example, the German Wikipedia category Mann for men, or the English Wikipedia category Women Physicists).

2. External databases, such as VIAF (Virtual International Authority File) and GND (Gemeinsame Normdatei, the German Integrated Authority File).

3. Personal names, as listed in the Wikidata label of the entity or in the title of the corresponding Wikipedia article(s) (e.g., all people named Alice would be marked as women).

4. Personal pronouns, by counting the occurrences of each pronoun in the corresponding Wikipedia article(s), the reasoning being that the most frequent pronoun would be correlated to the gender.[54]

---

51. https://www.wikidata.org/wiki/Wikidata:Requests_for_permissions/Bot/Lego-bot_.

52. The names of the bots are: Legobot, Dexbot, Sk!dbot, JAnDbot, VIAFbot, Sa-moaBot, and Reinheitsgebot. Three of these are still active today, but they are performing different tasks unrelated to gender.

53. https://www.wikidata.org/wiki/Property_talk:P21/Archive_1#Pie_chart.

54. This was initially proposed on June 10, 2013, in the following discussion: https://www.wikidata.org/wiki/Wikidata:Requests_for_permissions/Bot/SamoaBot_33.

Unfortunately, the extraction of gender data from the latter two sources was highly problematic. While Wikipedia categories and external databases likely received at least some overview from human users, the extraction of gender data from personal names relies on the mistaken assumption that a personal name can be applied only to men or only to women. This is not true in general, as even with the most gendered names there are often exceptions, but furthermore, some names are applied to different genders in different languages.

The creation of gender data from personal pronouns, which luckily was performed on a more limited scale, is also flawed, as it relies on the incorrect notion that *he/him* pronouns are applied only to men, and *she/her* only to women. In fact, personal pronouns can be wholly independent of both sex assigned at birth and gender identity.

The systematic process of gender data population through bots introduced significant errors in Wikidata, which then had to be manually corrected by users through the effort of projects focused on gender diversity, such as Wikiproject LGBT[55] and Art+Feminism.[56] However, given the wide scale of gender-related bot activity, it is likely that a significant number of errors are still present in the knowledge base.[57]

Gendered Properties for Family Relations

The second big issue that the Wikidata community had to solve was the use of gendered properties; for example, *mother/father*, *brother/sister*, *uncle/aunt*, etc. This is an issue because it makes it impossible to include non-binary people in family relations. Users began questioning this model from the early days of the project, but it took a long time to bring meaningful change.

---

55. https://www.wikidata.org/wiki/Wikidata:WikiProject_LGBT.

56. https://artandfeminism.org

57. It should be noted that some (more limited) semi-automatic additions of gender data are still being performed today through newer tools, such as PetScan and Quick-Statements. These are more difficult to track, but we intend to do so as future work.

The properties *uncle/aunt* were replaced with *relative* in 2013.[58] The properties *brother/sister* were replaced with *sibling* in 2017, and the same was done for *stepfather/stepmother*, replaced with *stepparent*. The replacement of *brother/sister* took extensive discussions and faced significant opposition from a subset of the Wikidata community, especially due to linguistic issues (several languages lack a word for *sibling*).

The replacement of *mother/father* with *parent* was proposed several times throughout the years (in 2013, 2015 and 2016) but unfortunately, the proposal repeatedly failed to reach the wide consensus required for its approval. As of March 30, 2022, the gendered properties *mother* and *father* still remain.

Representing Trans Identities

Once the gender data was populated, the discussion shifted to the representation of trans identities. This first became an issue in the Wikidata community in August 2013 when the American activist and whistleblower Chelsea Manning publicly announced her trans identity.[59]

Before that time, trans men and women had been quietly added to the knowledge base, sometimes using the *transgender male/female* values for P21, other times simply using *male/female*. The required changes in Chelsea Manning's name and gender identity faced significant opposition, leading to edit wars (i.e., disputes where opposing editors continually change the statements without significant discussion), deadnaming (i.e.,

---

58. This may appear to result in a loss of information but, in fact, the model that was adopted involves the use of a qualifier kinship to subject to list the specific familial relation.

59. The issue was raised in a brief discussion on the Wikidata item's talk page (https://www.wikidata.org/wiki/Talk:Q298423) while the item itself was in the middle of an edit war. (https://www.wikidata.org/w/index.php?title=Q298423&offset=20130901000000&limit=100&tagfilter=&action=history).

when users referred to a trans person by a name they used prior to transitioning), and transphobic comments.

Several early Wikidata items about trans people faced the same issues, after which the community ultimately started labeling trans men and women more consistently as *transgender male/female*. However, in 2014, the classification of these two gender identities was changed in a highly problematic way: *transgender male* was no longer a subclass of *male*, and *transgender female* was no longer a subclass of *female*, meaning that a user querying Wikidata for all women, for example, would not receive any transgender woman as output. Trans men and women were effectively made invisible. This issue was solved only after two years, in 2016, when the correct classification was restored.

Discussion

Unfortunately, due to space limitations we are not able to provide a complete timeline of the evolution of the modeling of gender in Wikidata and of how the model was populated by the users. However, from the abridged timeline reported above, we can already gather the following important facts:

1. the Wikidata gender model has evolved over time;
2. such evolution has been the product of extensive user discussions;
3. such evolution has been influenced by historical events, and in particular by changes in societal acceptance of gender diversity (as evidenced by user discussions);
4. the actual production of gender data has been influenced by inaccurate assumptions about gender held by the users who were participating in the project.

We plan to report a more detailed timeline as an outcome of the first phase of our project, publish the full timeline on the project website, and discuss our findings in a future publication.

The Data

In this section, we report statistical data about non-binary people described in Wikidata.[60] As explained in the Introduction, we have decided to focus this quantitative analysis on people whose gender is explicitly reported as *non-binary* (or any of its sub-classes) in Wikidata, based on data collected in April 2022. We plan to perform a wider, more extensive study of gender diversity at a later stage of our project.

Gender Identity Distribution

First of all, as a general point of reference, we will look at the distribution of the values of *P21 sex or gender* among humans represented in Wikidata. This distribution is reported in Fig. 5.

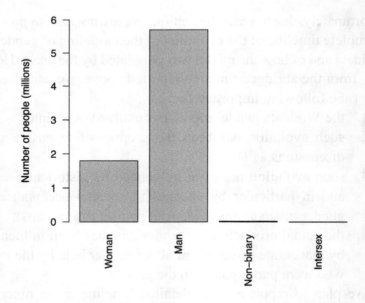

Figure 5: Distribution of sex and gender in Wikidata

---

60. Disclosure: The first author of this paper is represented in this dataset.

Wikidata contains approximately 1.8 million entities representing women and 5.7 million entities representing men. In Fig. 5, we have included both trans and cis women in the *woman* category, and both trans and cis men in the *man* category.[61] The number of trans women is 1089 (about 61 per 100,000 women), while the number of trans men is 282 (about 5 per 100,000 men).

The most glaring fact that emerges from the chart is the very large gender gap between men and women. The number of men in Wikidata currently outnumber women by almost 5-fold. The other significant result is that the percentage of non-binary people represented in Wikidata is extremely low (585, or about 8 per 100,000), as is the percentage of intersex people (132, or about 2 per 100,000).

These values indicate a severe underrepresentation of gender-diverse identities, given that the percentage of non-binary people is estimated to be about 360 per 100,000,[62] while the prevalence of intersex people is at least 18 per 100,000.[63] The number of trans people is also significantly lower than their actual prevalence in society, which is at least 355 per 100,000.[64]

The underrepresentation that we notice is likely influenced by the fact that the retroactive assignment of a non-binary identity to historical people is very difficult to do, and often impossible

---

61. It should be noted that Wikidata uses female and male labels instead of woman and man, but given the conflation of sex and gender in the model, it is impossible to know whether any specific entity has been classified based on sex assigned at birth or based on gender identity.

62. BDM Wilson and IH Meyer, "Nonbinary LGBTQ Adults in the United States." (Los Angeles, CA: UCLA, Williams Institute, 2021)/

63. The number of intersex people in Wikidata is difficult to compare to statistics about intersex people in society due to the fact that the term intersex can refer both to sexual characteristics and to gender identity, and it is impossible to know which definition has been adopted by each Wikidata user who marked an entity as intersex. However, the large gap that we have identified suggests an actual lack of representation of intersex people in Wikidata; Leonard Sax, "How Common Is Intersex? A Response to Anne Fausto-Sterling," *Journal of Sex Research* 39, no. 3 (2002): 174–78.

64. Lindsay Collin, Sari L Reisner, Vin Tangpricha, and Michael Goodman, "Prevalence of Transgender Depends on the 'Case' Definition: A Systematic Review," *The Journal of Sexual Medicine* 13, no. 4 (2016): 613–26.

to verify with absolute certainty. Indeed, as we will see in the later section, *Non-binary Identities Over Time,* the overwhelming majority of non-binary people in Wikidata were born in the 20th century.

Non-Binary Identity Distribution

The distribution of gender identities among non-binary people is shown in Fig. 6. Unlike in the data reported in Table 1, we include only real humans, excluding all fictional characters and other entities that may have a gender.[65]

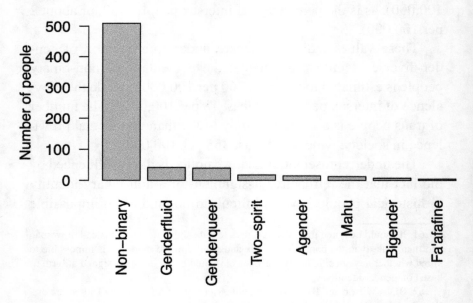

Figure 6: Distribution of non-binary gender identities in Wikidata

Among the 585 non-binary people described in Wikidata, the most represented gender identity is simply *non-binary* (509

---

65. Fictional characters with gender are less than 1 per thousand people with gender. At present, 5 fictional characters are listed as non-binary, 2 as intersex, 1 as trans, and 4 have one of the values of P21 reported in Table 3.

people), followed by *genderfluid* (41 people), *genderqueer* (39 people), *two-spirit* (17 people), *agender* (14 people), *māhū* (12 people), *bigender* (7 people), and *fa'afafine* (4 people).[66]

In the following sections, we will analyze the distribution of non-binary people based on time, space, and other characteristics. These statistics provide a broad overview of which non-binary people are currently described in the knowledge base.

Non-Binary Identities Over Time

First of all, the distribution of non-binary people based on their birth date is reported in Fig. 7.

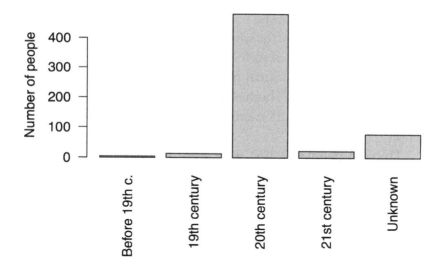

Figure 7. Distribution of non-binary gender identities over time

Fig. 8 reports instead the density of birth years of non-binary people, starting from 1603, which is the first available birth year for a non-binary person in Wikidata.

---

66. The total is greater than 585 due to the presence of people with multiple non-binary identities.

Density of Birth Years

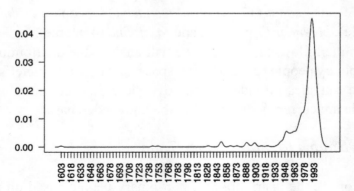

Figure 8. Density of birth years of non-binary people

The oldest person to be considered non-binary in Wikidata is Xu Deng, a Chinese doctor who lived around the year 200.[67] Interestingly, this person is described only in the Chinese and Swedish Wikipedias. Other historical people recognized as non-binary in Wikidata are Thomas/Thomasine Hall (17th century), Theodora de Verdion (18th century), and the Public Universal Friend (18th century).

Thirteen people (2.2%) were born in the 19th century. The vast majority of the people, i.e., 484 (80.4%) were born in the 20th century. 22 people (3.6%) were born in the 21st century. 79 people (13.1%) lack a date of birth or death.

Non-Binary Identities by Country and Language

Looking now at the distribution of non-binary identities by country (Wikidata property *P27 country of citizenship*), we have plotted the distribution on a world map in Fig. 9.[68]

---

67. This person is not represented in Fig. 8 due to the lack of a birth date. Only an approximate death date of "200s" is reported in Wikidata.

68. We have decided to report birth countries instead of citizenship due to incompleteness of the citizenship data; however, the picture that emerges by plotting citizenship is very similar.

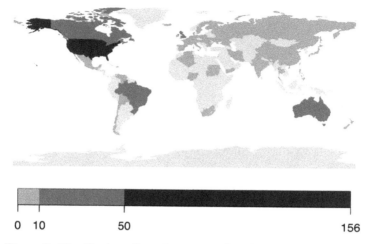

Figure 9: Distribution of non-binary gender identities by country

As shown in the figure, non-binary people represented in Wikidata are distributed throughout the whole world. Most non-binary people represented in Wikidata, however, were born in the United States (156 people), followed by the United Kingdom (30), Canada (27), Australia (13) and Brazil (11). All other countries have fewer than 10 people.

This high prevalence in the Global North is, perhaps, not too surprising given the current legal recognition of non-binary identities, but it is interesting to note how frequently non-binary people from countries outside of the Anglosphere are under-represented in Wikidata. The whole European Union has 56 non-binary people; i.e., about a third of those in the United States and not even twice those in the United Kingdom.[69]

This fact is confirmed by looking at the language(s) spoken by each person. While the data provided by Wikidata is quite

_____

69. It should be noted that the high prevalence of American, British, and Canadian people does not reflect the general statistics about citizenship in Wikidata (https://www.wikidata.org/wiki/Wikidata:WikiProject_Q5/numbers/country_of_citizenship), where the United States is indeed 1st, but the United Kingdom is 5th, and Canada is only 10th. Moreover, people from countries such as France, Germany, or Japan are very highly represented in Wikidata, but the percentage of non-binary people from these countries is extremely small.

incomplete, English is the first language by a factor of 10, as shown in Fig. 10.

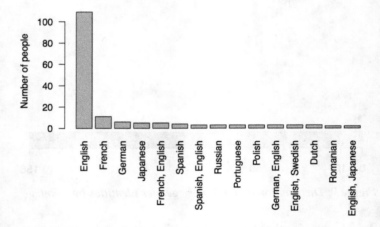

Figure 10: Distribution of non-binary gender identities by language

Non-Binary Identities by Occupation

Finally, we will look at non-binary people by occupation. We believe that this perspective is interesting, because it allows us to compare the distribution of occupations among different gender identities and identify possible gaps in the data (i.e., people who are completely missing from Wikidata, or occupations where non-binary people have been misclassified). The distribution of the 15 most common occupations is reported in Fig. 11.

The most common occupation for non-binary people in Wikidata is *actor* (98 people), followed by *writer* (90 people), *singer* (58 people), and *artist* (37 people).[70] The occupation *LGBTI rights activist* is also common (35 people), as is the more general *activist* (34 people).

---

70. Some occupations, e.g., "actor" and "film actor" may appear duplicated, but this is the way they are listed in Wikidata, and we decided not to alter them.

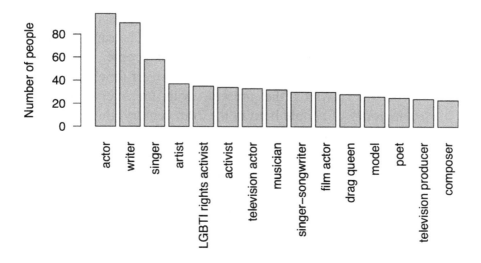

Figure 11: Distribution of non-binary gender identities by occupation.

It is interesting to note that the distribution of occupations for non-binary people is much different from that of men and women. Among men and women, the top occupations include researcher (due to the import of large publication datasets into Wikidata), politician, various subclasses of athlete, and teacher.

In some cases, this under-representation of non-binary people in specific occupations is probably a reflection of societal barriers (e.g., politicians, athletes), but in other cases (e.g., researchers), it may instead be due to incorrect assignment of gender. We plan to conduct a more detailed analysis of these disparities and report it in a future publication.

Discussion

The initial quantitative analysis reported above allows us to have a broad overview about the non-binary people that are described in the Wikidata knowledge base. Our main findings are as follows:

- the number of non-binary people who are described as such in Wikidata is very small, which suggests that they may be significantly under-represented. The same is true for binary trans people and for intersex people.

- the distribution of non-binary people over time is highly skewed towards the present, with an overwhelming majority of people born in the 20th century; this is probably due to the fact that, in the past, fewer people identified as non-binary but, also, that assigning a non-binary identity to a historical figure is often difficult to justify. We intend to explore this topic further in a future study.

- the distribution of non-binary people over space is highly skewed towards the Global North and, in particular, the Anglosphere, despite the fact that Wikidata is a highly multilingual project. In our assessment, this may be due to one or more of the following factors: (i) non-binary may actually be over-represented in such countries (but this explanation seems simplistic); (ii) non-binary people from these countries may declare more openly their gender identity, thus increasing the chance that this information ends up in Wikidata; (iii) Wikidata users who edit from the Anglosphere may be more eager to represent the identity of gender-diverse people.

- the distribution of non-binary people by occupation suggests that most of them work either in the creative arts or as gender rights activists. Some professions that are common among men and women are significantly under-represented in non-binary people, which may be explained by one or more of the following factors: (i) an actual difference in society; e.g., there are few non-binary politicians and non-binary sportspeople due to gatekeeping that excludes them; (ii) non-binary people who hold such occupations may declare less openly their gender identity, thus preventing it from ending up in Wikidata; (iii) Wikidata users who focus on editing certain occupations may be more eager to represent the identity of gender-diverse people.

The Community

This section describes our work on the Wikidata community—more specifically, looking at user discussions. The main goal is to analyze how the narrative around gender-related topics has changed during Wikidata's nine years of existence. For this purpose, we created a specialized corpus of Wikidata discussions related to gender, composed of 613 Wikidata English discussions from October 2012 till September 2021, and performed an unsupervised topic analysis on this corpus.

We have chosen this unconventional approach for studying the community because it is very difficult to elicit gender identity data from the Wikidata community of users—namely, Wikidata does not require users to declare any identity features, such as nationality, age, and of course gender identity, at the time of registration.[71] Therefore, we can only study what the users do on Wikidata—that is, engaging in discussions and editing the knowledge base—and not who the users are.

Corpus-based studies are currently very popular in linguistics, and we believe that building a corpus, and corpus analysis, could allow us to keep track of the narrative about gender identities in the Wikidata community, see how the narrative has changed over time, study the impact of LGBTIQ+ movements and how they have brought awareness in Wikidata discussions, and detect cases of hate speech, sexism, misgendering, etc.

---

71. Wikidata also allows users to participate without registering at all. In this case, they will be identified by their IP address.

The WiGeTa-En Corpus

Wikidata Gender Talks – English (*WiGeTa-En*) is a specialized corpus of Wikidata discussions related to gender. The corpus was collected semi-automatically, first using scraping techniques to collect all the discussions containing relevant keywords as an automatic filter, and subsequently through a manual annotation of the relevant discussions for the corpus.

In particular, we analyzed a total of 2,511 Wikidata discussion pages. These pages were automatically extracted using the Wikidata API by searching for a list of 79 relevant keywords, which included gender identities such as "non-binary" or "woman"; sex-related terms such as "male", "female", "AMAB" (assigned male at birth), "AFAB" (assigned female at birth); relevant entity IDs such as Q1052281 (transgender female) and Q1097630 (intersex); general terms that may refer to gender-diverse people such as "LGBT", "LGBTQ", "LGBTQIA+", etc.

The extracted pages contained a total of 232,688 discussions. In most cases, however, only a few of the many discussions found on each page were actually about gender. We thus wrote a parser to automatically split the discussions and load them into a database, then filtered these discussions to identify the relevant ones. Through this process, 226,225 discussions were automatically removed because they contained no relevant keywords, 2,569 were excluded because they were not real discussions,[72] and 2,065 were removed because they were not in English. The remaining 1,829 discussions were checked manually by four human annotators through a purpose-built web interface and were classified as follows: 604 relevant, 1,225 not relevant.[73] We classified as relevant all discussions that have gender and its representation as their main topic. We also included those discussions that indirectly

---

72. These were, for example, many requests for deletion of Wikidata entities that were created by a single user and did not contain any proper discussion.

73. In case of doubt, the annotators followed a consensus-based approach.

refer to the topic of gender identity[74] (with some exceptions; e.g., when they are primarily about non-human gender). The relevant discussions were cleaned from punctuation and non-useful or redundant metadata, then stored in JSON and plain text format.

The discussions collected in *WiGeTa-En* ranged from October 25, 2012, the starting date of the Wikidata project, to September 18, 2021, and they were saved into a database along with their metadata. The corpus contains several metadata related to each discussion: a randomly-assigned *id*, the *start_date* and *end_date* of each discussion, the *users* involved in the discussion, the *wikidata_location* in which the discussion was stored or could be found and, finally, *discussion_title* and *text_discussion*. For further details about the corpus, see Metilli and Paolini (2021).[75]

WiGeTa-En was automatically compiled on Sketch Engine[76] counting 471,890 tokens, 325,956 words, 9786 sentences and 9 documents.

Inside WiGeTa-En: Topic Modeling with LDA

The topic analysis of *WiGeTa-En* was carried out using the unsupervised *Latent Dirichlet Allocation* technique.[77] LDA, which aims to automatically identify and describe latent topics within a collection of text documents, is one of the most frequently used bag-of-words (BOW) probabilistic models for topic modeling.[78] Topics should be understood as a summary of the meaningful

---

74. For example, there are some discussions in which the main topic is personal names, but there are some references to misconceptions about gender-neutral names.

75. Daniele Metilli and Chiara Paolini, "Non-Binary Gender Identities in Wikidata," WikidataCon, October 30, 2021, https://pretalx.com/wdcon21/talk/7TRCWD/.

76. Adam Kilgarriff, Vít Baisa, Jan Bušta, Miloš Jakubíček, Vojtěch Kovář, Jan Michelfeit, Pavel Rychlý, and Vít Suchomel, "The Sketch Engine: Ten Years On," *Lexicography* 1, no. 1 (2014): 7–36.

77. David M. Blei, Andrew Y. Ng, and Michael I. Jordan, "Latent Dirichlet Allocation," *Journal of Machine Learning Research* 3 (2003): 993–1022.

78. David M. Blei, "Probabilistic topic models," *Communications of the ACM* 55, no. 4 (2012):77–84.

contents of a collection of documents in which each topic is formed by the most frequent words that characterize that specific content. Latency is an intrinsic characteristic of topics—they do not emerge explicitly but are considered to be hidden, inferred content variables.

The ultimate goal of LDA is to reconstruct a compelling, coherent story from textual data in order to shape and substantiate hypotheses. For an in-depth review of this technique, see Maier et al.[79] The technique has already been applied to discussion analysis[80] to discover relationships between topics, as well as to identify their trends over time and gain insight into target communities. LDA is not able to identify what the discussions are about (beyond a simple set of terms) but, rather, requires interpretation through contextual data.[81]

In our study, LDA allows us to identify clusters of discussions that center around specific topics. We expect the main areas of discussion, identified in our qualitative analysis of the timeline of gender modeling in Wikidata (see section, *A Timeline of Wikidata Gender Modeling*), to be represented in the quantitative data. However, it is also possible for other clusters to emerge, perhaps related to topics that we have not yet considered. Furthermore, LDA allows us to track the emergence of topics over time.

We applied LDA as follows: first, we represented the topics for the entire *WiGeTa-En* corpus; then, for each year represented in the corpus, we created a subset of discussions and performed the topic analysis in order to extrapolate a coherent development of the narrative regarding gender. For the sake of brevity, we will

79. Daniel Maier, Annie Waldherr, Peter Miltner, Gregor Wiedemann, Andreas Niekler, Alexa Keinert, Barbara Pfetsch, et al., "Applying LDA Topic Modeling in Communication Research: Toward a Valid and Reliable Methodology," *Communication Methods and Measures* 12, nos. 2-3 (2018): 93–118.

80. Anton Barua, Stephen W Thomas, and Ahmed E Hassan, "What Are Developers Talking about? An Analysis of Topics and Trends in Stack Overflow," *Empirical Software Engineering* 19, no. 3 (2014): 619–54.

81. As such, LDA results may be biased and should be subjected to scrutiny.

not elaborate on the implementation details of the algorithm, which will be made available in the project's GitHub repository.[82]

Results

In this section, we report the results of the topic modeling based on LDA. Fig. 12 shows the results of the topic modeling for the whole corpus, i.e., all discussions from 2012 to 2021. The figure contains nine charts, each reporting the ten most coherent and frequent words that characterize a specific topic, ranked by their weight; that is, scores generated dynamically based on the weighted distribution of words to reduce the influence of high frequency words and improve the role of keywords. The charts are ordered by the score of the most salient term in the topic, but each chart should be considered independently.

In the figure, we can see that our corpus of discussions clusters around the following topics:[83]

1. *Gender identities*, featuring terms such as "gender", "sex", "transgender", "male", "female", "intersex", and "identity". This is the main cluster of discussion about the topic of gender identity and its relation to sex. It should be noted that the term "non-binary" does not appear with high frequency in this chart,[84] nor does it appear in any of the following charts.

2. *Personal names*, featuring terms such as "names", "female", "male", "gender", "unisex". This cluster of discussions is related to the assignment of gender based on personal names (see the section, *The Rise of Bots*).

3. *Grammatical gender*, containing terms such as "male", "female", "label", "masculine", "feminine", and "occupation". This relates to gendered labels; i.e., entity labels

---

82. https://github.com/Daniele/non-binary-matters.

83. It should be noted that the names of the topics have been assigned by us, and reflect our own interpretation of the topic modeling results.

84. It is actually in position 24; thus, not displayed in the figure.

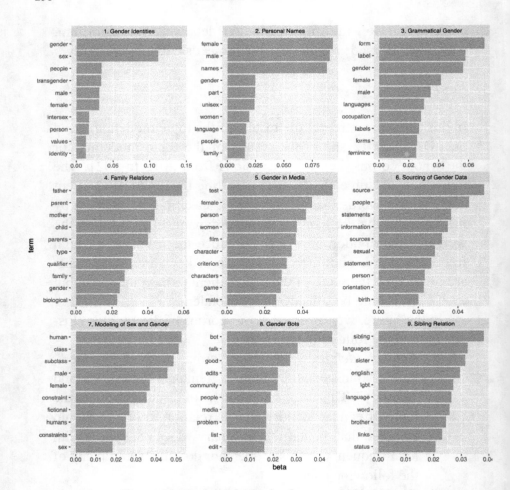

Figure 12: Topic modeling for the years 2012–2021

that have different forms according to the person's gender. We plan to study this topic in more detail in the future.

4. *Family relations*, featuring terms such as "father", "parent", "mother". This cluster of discussions is related to the existence of gendered properties that are not well suited for representing non-binary people (see the section, *Gendered Properties for Family Relations*).

5. *Gender in media*, a cluster of discussions about criteria for gender inclusion in media, such as the Bechdel test.[85] These are not particularly relevant to gender modeling, but it would be interesting to see if these discussions have also evaluated gender diversity.

6. *Sourcing of gender data*, this cluster contains terms such as "source", "statement", "reference", and the discussions featured in it are about the way gender data is sourced. It is interesting to note that these discussions often mentioned sexual orientation as a point of reference (unlike gender, data on sexual orientation has been considered much more carefully by the Wikidata community, and it has not been added indiscriminately to every biographical entity).

7. *Modeling of sex and gender*; this cluster of discussions relates to the modeling of sex and gender, including their taxonomies, and to the application of constraints to the P21 property (see the section, *Ontological Representation of Gender*).

8. *Gender bots*, featuring terms such as "bots" and "edit", but also "problem". These discussions are related to the use of bots to add gender data to the knowledge base and the problems it caused (see the section, *The Rise of Bots*).

9. *Sibling relation*, a specific cluster of discussions about one of the most contentious issues in the modeling of family relations on Wikidata—i.e., whether the *sibling* property should be gendered or not (see the section *Gendered Properties for Family Relations*).

Beside the overall topic modeling, we also performed a year-based topic modeling to assess the topics of discussions for each year. This fine-grained analysis is necessary to understand

---

85. Alison Bechdel, *The Essential Dykes to Watch Out For* (New York: Houghton Mifflin, 2008).

the shades and implications of the main topics discovered in the overall analysis—namely, the sub-topics tackled and related to the main discussions. For the sake of brevity here, we will focus just on the topics that refer to the lemma *nonbinary*. As shown in fig. 13, the LDA analysis shows that this term appears with a high ranking in only two topic clusters, one in 2018 and one in 2019. However, the frequency is still low when compared to the other terms featured in the cluster.

In 2018, the term *nonbinary* appears in the topic cluster *Gender identities*, while in 2019 it appears in *Grammatical gender*, but in both cases, in a low position compared to other terms. As a point of comparison, we also show that the emergence of a *Trans identities* topic for the year 2019 reflects a significantly increased interest and debate on the representation of trans people's identities.

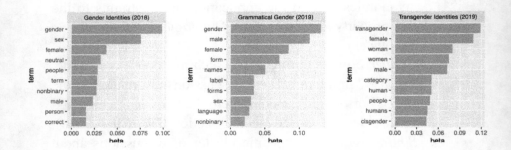

Figure 13: Partial results of topic modeling for the years 2018 (left) and 2019 (right)

Discussion

The overall topic modeling on the corpus (Fig. 12) sheds light on how gender identities are generally discussed by the users who make up the Wikidata community. In most discussion clusters, including those about personal names (topic 2), labeling (topic

3), gender in media (topic 5), and modeling of sex and gender (topic 7), we observe a prevalence of binary terms and a corresponding lack of terms referring to diverse gender identities.

The main cluster of discussions about gender identity (topic 1) features the terms "transgender" and "intersex", but not "non-binary" or any other term referring specifically to a non-binary identity. However, in discussions about family relations (topics 4 and 9), we see prominent usage of gender-neutral terms such as *parent* and *sibling*, in addition to the corresponding binary terms, reflecting the extensive discussions about the topic reported in the section *Gendered Properties for Family Relations*.

Surprisingly, no mention of non-binary identities was found in the overall topic modeling. The low scores of terms referring to non-binary identities show that these identities have been marginalized in the discussions collected in the corpus, providing further support for the findings presented in sections 4 and 5 related to the underrepresentation of non-binary gender identities in Wikidata. In addition, while some of the discussion clusters are related to topics that were already under our scrutiny, there are a few (3, 5, 6) that warrant further analysis. We intend to publish a more complete topic modeling study, with a more in-depth analysis, in a future publication.

The year-based topic modeling (Fig. 13) provides additional insights regarding whether and when discussions on non-binarity have started to be significant and frequent in the Wikidata community. Strikingly, non-binary identities are rarely discussed by the Wikidata users—the lemma *nonbinary* appears only twice in the top positions of the clusters throughout the years and in both cases shows low frequency compared to the other terms. This result suggests that the narrative around non-binary identities has not yet reached the attention it deserves among Wikidata users.

It is interesting to compare this result to the cluster of discussions related to transgender identities that emerges in 2019 (Fig. 13, right), where the term "transgender" is far more central in the discussions, likely due to the tireless work of LGBTQIA+ movements in favor of trans rights being reported by the media, and also to the cases of famous people coming out as transgender.

Conclusions and Future Work

In this chapter, we have reported a preliminary quantitative analysis of non-binary gender identities in the Wikidata knowledge base. This work has been performed as a first step towards the realization of our project, Wikidata Gender Diversity (WiGeDi), aimed at investigating the issue of gender diversity in Wikidata.

Non-binary gender identities are significantly marginalized in society, and this societal discrimination is often reflected in the way these identities are represented in knowledge bases. The data that are contained in a knowledge base are subject to implicit biases that reflect how the data are sourced, modeled, and published. When these biases are not addressed, they can amplify the discrimination of marginalized communities in society.

Our work aims to contribute to the growing field of data ethics by offering a quantitative exploration of the representation of non-binary identities in a large knowledge base, giving fresh insights to gender studies scholars interested in more qualitative approaches to research.

We have investigated non-binary identities from three different—and complementary—perspectives: first, we have looked at the Wikidata ontology model to understand how it currently represents gender identities and how it has evolved to the representation of non-binary identities. Then, we have reported detailed statistics about the current extent of non-binary representation in the knowledge base, also looking at the distribution of non-binary identities according to several factors (time, country, language, occupation). Finally, we have performed a Latent Dirichlet Allocation topic modeling analysis on the Wikidata community discussions collected in the *WiGeTa-En* corpus.

Taken together, these results suggest that the Wikidata knowledge base is still not fully inclusive of non-binary identities. While some important steps towards recognition of these identities have been made during the years, important issues are yet unresolved. First, the Wikidata gender model is still imperfect and in need of further improvements. Moreover, the representation of non-binary people in the knowledge base is still low when compared to the prevalence of these identities in society, and highly skewed towards the Global North and contemporary times. Finally, the topic modeling analysis suggests that non-binary identities are still significantly marginalized in discussions about gender on Wikidata.

The study that we have presented in this chapter is just a first step in our Wikidata Gender Diversity project. Considerably more work needs to be done to computationally and statistically study gender diversity in Wikidata in a more complete way, analyzing the evolution of the knowledge base over time and the role of the community in shaping the current (and future) modeling of gender. It is also highly likely that significant changes will take place in the future to reflect the evolving views of the community and of society as a whole.

As future work, we plan to extend our linguistic analysis (e.g., by including other community languages), publish a complete timeline about gender modeling in Wikidata, and widen our field of study to include other marginalized identities. We hope that our project will help bring awareness about gender-diverse identities in the Wikidata community and beyond.

Acknowledgements

The authors would like to thank Marta Fioravanti and Beatrice Melis for their invaluable help and support in the design of the project, the annotation of the corpus, and their thoughtful suggestions about this chapter; Elisa Metilli for her crucial proofreading;

Michael Mandiberg for sharing research ideas and providing input on our work; and last but not least, the editors and reviewers for their invaluable advice and recommendations, which allowed us to significantly improve the chapter.

The Minnesota Hip-Hop Collection and Wikidata: Practical and Ethical Challenges for Linked Data Creators

KRISTI BERGLAND, CHRISTINE DEZELAR-
TIEDMAN & PATRICK HARRINGTON

Introduction

The Minnesota Hip-Hop Collection is an archive of audio recordings, published materials, and other print and physical ephemera
documenting hip-hop in Minnesota, housed in the Archie Givens,
Sr. Collection of African American Literature at the University of
Minnesota Libraries (UM).[1] The audio recordings from the collection were chosen as the focus of one of the projects for UM's
participation in the PCC Wikidata Pilot based on their potential
for identifying and exploring relationships and linkages between
Minnesota-based hip-hop artists, producers, and labels, and as
a means to increase representation and highlight the activity of
Black Minnesota-based musicians in a distributed database. Since
its emergence in the 1970s, hip-hop has had a sizable impact on
American and world culture. This impact is reflected in the now
well-established presence of hip-hop studies within the academy,
and as a result, within libraries and archives. While the same
principles and practices of metadata description and access apply
to materials related to hip-hop as they would to any other cultural

---

1. Givens Collection of African American Literature, accessed October 6, 2021,
https://www.lib.umn.edu/collections/special/givens.

materials, special consideration and care must be taken when a majority white institution takes custody of these resources. The promise of linked data and its potential to widely disseminate information, as well as enable unexpected connections, can also expose individuals to risk and harm.

Staffing and organizational changes at our institution, as well as the COVID-19 pandemic, impacted our ability to fully realize the project as originally envisioned. In addition, as we began working with the materials, we realized that we had made some inaccurate assumptions about the demographics of the artists represented in the collection and about our ability to glean adequate identifying information about them from the resources we had on hand, that made meeting our intended goals with the project difficult to achieve. However, these challenges gave us the opportunity to step back and interrogate our cultural assumptions and the drawbacks of selecting collections for metadata projects without having full knowledge of their contents in advance.

This chapter uses our early exploration of metadata best practices for describing hip-hop creators as a jumping-off point to dive into ethical issues of representation and access, and identify ways in which we need to be better prepared to undertake future projects. We begin with a description of our Wikidata project as we envisioned it, our rationale for selecting it, and our methodology for creating or updating Wikidata items for hip-hop creators represented in the Minnesota Hip-Hop Collection. We include a brief discussion of issues regarding race and cultural appropriation in hip-hop, particularly as related to the Minnesota hip-hop scene. We next identify organizational and environmental challenges that led us to suspend further work on the project, followed by a discussion of practical and ethical issues of using Wikidata to describe hip-hop creators. We conclude with proposed further steps for us to more effectively and ethically undertake projects of this type.

Case Study: Minnesota Hip-Hop Collection

Background on the Collection and Institution

The Archie Givens, Sr. Collection of African American Literature is one of sixteen collections under the umbrella of Archives and Special Collections (ASC) at UM and contains over 10,000 books, periodicals, archival collections, and other resources by or about African Americans. The Givens Collection is also the host of Umbra Search, a tool that searches digitized materials about African American history from over 1000 institutions.[2] The collection was founded in 1985 with the support of the Givens family and a council of leaders from the Twin Cities African American community. In 1986, it was named in honor of Archie Givens, Sr., an African American businessman and entrepreneur. The Givens Collection continues to work in partnership with the Givens Foundation for African American Literature, which was originally established in order to purchase the private book collection that was the seed of what became the Givens Collection.[3] The Foundation was founded by Archie Givens, Jr. (the son of Archie Givens, Sr.) and others, and he continues to serve on its Board of Directors.[4]

Like many other archives and special collections divisions in large academic libraries, UM's ASC Department holds a variety of collections and archives revolving around specialized subject areas and disciplines. Curatorial oversight over the various collections, and where those subunits fall organizationally within ASC, has fluctuated over time. At the time the Minnesota Hip-Hop Collection was acquired, the Givens Collection was under the curatorial direction of Cecily Marcus, who also oversaw

---

2. Umbra Search, African American History, https://umbrasearch.org/.

3. Givens Collections, accessed May 18, 2022, https://www.lib.umn.edu/collections/special/givens/history.

4. Givens Foundation for African American Literature, accessed May 18, 2022, http://www.givens.org/board-of-directors.

the Performing Arts Archives and the Upper Midwest Literary Archives. There is a fair amount of commonality and synergy between these three collections, and sometimes the decision on where to place a collection is a matter of negotiation between the donor and the curator. For example, when UM acquired the archives of the Penumbra Theatre Company, the largest African American theater in the United States, which is based in Saint Paul, it could have just as logically been added to the Performing Arts Archives, along with the records of other prominent Twin Cities arts organizations such as the Minnesota Orchestra and the Guthrie Theater.[5] But Penumbra artistic director Lou Bellamy felt very strongly that it should be placed in the Givens Collection, within the context of African American artistic output. Similar considerations may have been a factor in the decision to include the Minnesota Hip-Hop Collection in Givens, although it also fell within the scope of the Performing Arts Archives, and in fact, as will be discussed later in the chapter, does not consist of materials created exclusively by Black artists.

Donor Justin Schell collected materials in the Minnesota Hip-Hop Collection in his doctoral research on the performance and culture of hip-hop in Minnesota.[6] The resources in the collection originate from 1996-2014 and consist of commercial recordings on compact disc, audio cassette, and LP vinyl records, as well as digital audio and video clips, print books, pamphlets, flyers, brochures, posters, stickers, magnets, and other ephemera. Footage for the donor's film, *We Rock Long Distance*,[7] which tells global stories through hip-hop, is also included.

Given that the collection emerged from the work of a particular scholar, its scope is limited to a particular period of time. Nevertheless, it does contain a large breadth of many well-known

---

5. Penumbra Theatre Company Records, accessed May 18, 2022, https://archives.lib.umn.edu/repositories/5/resources/331.

6. Justin Schell, "We Rock Long Distance" (Ph.D. diss., University of Minnesota, 2013), accessed October 7, 2021, https://hdl.handle.net/11299/151349.

7. We Rock Long Distance, accessed October 6, 2021, https://www.werocklongdistance.com/.

artists from Minnesota such as Atmosphere, Brother Ali, and the collective, Doomtree. The collection also includes many recordings from Rhymesayers Entertainment, a Minneapolis label founded in 1995 that initially released primarily local artists but has seen its catalog grow to include well-known artists from elsewhere such as Aesop Rock and the late MF Doom.[8]

Because Schell's research covered both the local and global aspects of hip-hop in Minnesota, it also contains many recordings of artists from elsewhere. Schell's research depended on his ability to develop and maintain close relationships with people producing, distributing, or listening to hip-hop, both in Minnesota and abroad. Schell's collection of research material was given to the Givens collection at the completion of his doctoral research, and no additional material has been purchased for the collection since his donation. One of the challenges faced in developing metadata for this collection is that we had only the items donated to use as a basis for creating metadata, and there was no arrangement for future consultations with Schell (who has since left the state) after the donation. This dynamic, though not uncommon in special collections, proved a hindrance as the pilot project was undertaken long after the donation was made, complicating efforts to build upon the relationships Schell had developed over the course of his research.

Hip-Hop, Race, and Cultural Appropriation

Emerging in the 1970s from African American and Caribbean communities in New York City, hip-hop is widely considered to be a Black art form. As it has gained mainstream popularity in the ensuing decades, hip-hop music has been created and performed by artists from a wide variety of races, cultures, and ethnicities, both in the United States and throughout the world.[9] White artists

8. Rhymesayers Entertainment, "Who We Are", accessed December 9, 2021, https://rhymesayers.com/pages/who-we-are.

9. Rory PQ, "Hip Hop History: From the Streets to the Mainstream", ICON Music Blog, November 13, 2019, updated November 25, 2019, https://iconcollective.edu/

who have achieved widespread success within the genre include the Beastie Boys and Eminem in the 1980s and 1990s, continuing on to performers such as Machine Gun Kelly today. Whenever white artists achieve mainstream success in an art form created by a historically marginalized group, often achieving greater financial benefits and acceptance than Black artists (the same pattern has occurred with jazz, blues, and rock music), the issue of cultural appropriation is raised. Historically, white artists have capitalized on the creativity of Black creators to bring new forms to primarily white audiences. While these audiences may, in part, be attracted to the outsider/outlaw aspects of the genre, having them performed by white artists makes them more "palatable to American general audiences."[10] In all forms of art, there is an element of cultural exchange, and where this crosses the line into cultural appropriation is complex and nuanced, and may vary according to context. Among creators themselves, opinions may vary over what constitutes appropriation and what constitutes evolution. Within the culture of hip-hop, "authenticity" is a core value that reflects the genre's origins coming out of street culture. Although white, Eminem was raised in a rough area of Detroit, makes references to his own background and stories in his songs, acknowledges his white privilege, and does not use the n-word in his music. This has earned him respect among some Black hip-hop artists that is not necessarily extended to other white rappers who are viewed as appropriating Black culture in their music and performances.[11]

The evolution of hip-hop in Minnesota, and the Twin Cities of Minneapolis and Saint Paul particularly, in some ways reflects a similar pattern to the development of hip-hop in the United States

hip-hop-history. "Hip Hop: A Culture of Vision and Voice," Kennedy Center Education Digital Learning, viewed June 9, 2022, https://www.kennedy-center.org/education/resources-for-educators/classroom-resources/media-and-interactives/media/hip-hop/hip-hop-a-culture-of-vision-and-voice.

10. Cyan D'Angou, "Out of Line: On Hip Hop and Cultural Appropriation," Medium June 22, 2020. Accessed June 9, 2022, https://medium.com/@cyandanjou/out-of-line-on-hip-hop-and-cultural-appropriation-1c060e6801e9.

11. Ibid.

overall. It can be traced to DJ parties in the early 1980s, and many of the earliest Minnesota-based hip-hop performers were African American.[12] However, as hip-hop entered the mainstream, many of the most prominent Minnesota-based artists emerging in the early 2000s, including Atmosphere, Eyedea and Abilities, and Dessa, represent a variety of mixed races and ethnicities, not necessarily Black. The rapper Brother Ali presents an interesting case regarding issues of race and identity. Born with albinism, there was speculation early in his career regarding his race. After confirming that he is white, Ali has stated that he felt more accepted by Black classmates than white growing up, and felt that he could relate to Black peers more than white classmates, as he had experienced being judged by his skin color.[13]

When selecting the Minnesota Hip-Hop Collection for the PCC Wikidata Pilot, the catalogers at UM made assumptions regarding the racial identity of the artists who would be reflected in the collection. The collection was chosen specifically to highlight Black creators, but as the catalogers began working with the materials, they encountered more non-Black representation than they had expected. This is in part a reflection of our lack of in-depth understanding and awareness of Minnesota hip-hop history and culture before taking on the project, as well as not fully understanding the scope of Schell's research interest, which had a global dimension, inclusive of multiple cultures.

PCC Wikidata Pilot

The PCC Wikidata Pilot[14] was a project sponsored by the Program for Cooperative Cataloging (PCC), a library collaborative

---

12. Peter S. Scholtes, "One Nation, Invisible", City Pages August 18, 2004, retrieved from the Internet Archive, https://web.archive.org/web/20071201115502/http://www.citypages.com/databank/25/1237/article12383.asp.

13. "Brother Ali delivers 'The Undisputed Truth', Today blog, July 13, 2007, https://www.today.com/popculture/brother-ali-delivers-undisputed-truth-1C9430141.

14. Wikidata:WikiProject: PCC Wikidata Pilot, accessed October 6, 2021, https://www.wikidata.org/wiki/Wikidata:WikiProject_PCC_Wikidata_Pilot.

that supports and promotes the creation of shared cataloging standards, as well as bibliographic and authority records. The Pilot's primary goal was to experiment with Wikidata as a linked data hub for identifiers and to serve as a platform for cultural heritage institutions to contribute authority records with fewer barriers than the more traditional, established approach of authority creation through the PCC's Name Authority Cooperative Program (NACO). Nearly 70 institutions around the world participated in the project, which began in August 2020 and concluded in December 2021.

For the University of Minnesota's contribution to the project, we focused on two subsets of the Givens Collection. One aspect of our project involved identifying authors of books held in the Givens Collection that were not already in Wikidata, and creating Wikidata items for those authors. For authors already in Wikidata, we enhanced the items with additional information, such as birth and death dates, places of birth or residence, affiliations, and major works. The second component of our Wikidata Project focused on the Minnesota Hip-Hop Collection. The compact disc audio recordings subset of the collection was chosen as it provided an opportunity to identify and explore relationships and linkages between Minnesota-based hip-hop artists, producers, and labels, and to increase representation and highlight the activity of non-white Minnesota-based musicians in a distributed database. During the early stage of the Pilot, we developed an initial set of input standards and best practices for each sub-project. As we created and edited items, we encountered practical and ethical issues which were discussed at meetings of the UM project group (which consisted of two of the authors of this chapter and two other individuals). Based on these discussions, we made adjustments to our local practices. These issues are described in the section below.

Metadata Approach for PCC Wikidata Project

Scope and Process

Acknowledging that many different types of entities and identities are important to accurately describe the interconnected and highly collaborative relationships that exist between hip-hop performers, producers, recording engineers, instrumentalists, and others, we needed to scope our approach to make the project manageable for the staff time we had available. We chose to focus on performers (individuals and groups) and, understanding that creating and enhancing Wikidata records is an ongoing process, we also decided to create descriptions resulting from only a modest amount of research rather than taking an exhaustive approach, given our lack of capacity to do more during the time frame of the project.

Our process for creating Wikidata items began with searching for performer names in Wikidata. The CDs of the collection are arranged in trays in alphabetical order by artist. We compiled a list of performers and started working our way through the list in order. If a performer was already represented in Wikidata, we enhanced the existing item with other details as available, as we did with the Givens Collection book author entries. For performers not already in Wikidata for whom we were able to find biographical information, we used the Author template[15] in the Wikidata Cradle tool to start a Wikidata item and create labels. Then we described the performer using the Wikidata properties appropriate to the individual and the information at hand,[16] as well

---

15. Cradle author template, accessed December 11, 2021, https://cradle.toolforge.org/#/subject/author.

16. Commonly used statement types for performers include: aliases, description, instance of, work period (start), country of origin, given name, family name, pseudonym, date of birth, place of birth, date of death, place of death, genre, image, logo image, dissolved, abolished or demolished date, ethnic group, discography, location of

as any identifiers found.[17] We then created a Wikidata item for a notable work from our holdings and added a link to it in the item for the artist. We also created an authority record in the Library of Congress authority file for the performer if one did not already exist, and linked that to the Wikidata item as well as to the UM system's catalog record for the CD. In an effort to balance the need to invest time researching the artists against the knowledge that some Wikidata contributors are requesting removal of entries that they feel are "non-notable," we did not create Wikidata items where adequate identifying or disambiguating information was lacking. In many cases, artists have continued to perform and record, providing additional data sources beyond the Minnesota Hip-Hop Collection's 2014 collection scope boundary.

Challenges Encountered When Describing Hip-Hop Creators and Collections in Wikidata

In trying to promote enhanced access to contributors from the local hip-hop community over an historic time frame, we encountered a variety of ethical considerations and practical challenges.

From the start, our pilot project has been an exercise in making peace with ambiguity, and prioritizing creating records only in cases where we have enough evidence to conclusively identify an entity. One useful tool for keeping confusion to a minimum is the "different from" property (P1889), which states with confidence what something is not.

---

formation, influenced by, record label, official website, has works in the collection, notable work. Our profile for Works includes statements of instance of (album), follows, performer, record label, and publication date, as well as any identifiers (most commonly Discogs master ID, Metacritic ID, MusicBrainz release group ID). At this point, we have limited our input to one associated Work from the Minnesota Hip-Hop Collection.

17. Identifiers used include: VIAF ID, Library of Congress authority ID, AllMusic artist ID, Apple Music artist ID (American edition), AZLyrics.com artist ID, Bandcamp ID, Deezer artist ID, Discogs artist ID, Facebook ID, Google Play Music artist ID (former scheme), IMDb ID, Instagram username, Last.fm ID, MusicBrainz artist ID, and Spotify artist ID.

One specific challenge that we encountered was determining whether the named performer is an individual or a group, revealing layers of complexity in establishing performer identities that we did not anticipate. This complexity affected how much we were able to accomplish and limited the level of staff who were able to work on the project. Making assumptions and arbitrarily deciding whether an identity was an individual or group could cause confusion or misinformation later down the linked data chain. There was also a degree of fluidity between performers recording as individuals, as groups, and as featured performers, sometimes listed as both rapper and DJ, and sometimes using different personas in different combinations. Artist names as projections of their stage personas can lead to some very unsatisfying database searches. For example, initial web searches for "Beyond" or "Cheap Cologne" return either far too many results with no effective way to limit them, or too many of the wrong sorts of hits, even when additional qualifiers are used. Basic web and database searches of "Beyond" with added keywords "Minneapolis" and "hip hop" provided more information, which in turn led to results in Discogs, which led back to "Sab the Artist" (Q7395768).[18] In the case of Cheap Cologne, it is difficult to determine conclusively if Cheap Cologne refers to an individual or group. The back of the CD refers to a number of performers/collaborators/roles contrasted by the implied singular in the website "iamcheapcologne.com" (Figure 1). The Internet Archive[19] proved useful in resurrecting the contents of this now defunct website, but language used throughout the website implies both singular and plural (Figures 2 and 3), as well as introducing another persona, Marilyn Handsome.

18. Parenthetical Q numbers throughout the chapter refer to the Wikidata item number for the entity or concept being discussed, see https://www.wikidata.org/wiki/Help:Items.

19. Internet Archive, accessed October 11, 2021, https://archive.org/.

Figure 1: Back cover image of Something Random by Cheap Cologne

Cheap Cologne has produced and recorded tracks with The Lordz Of Brooklyn featuring Busta Rhymes, Slug, I Self Devine & Musab from Rhymesayers, Pigeon John, Z-Man, Slim Kid Tre (Pharcyde) DJ Quest, The Shapeshifters, and DJ T-Rock to name a few.

Figure 2: Snippet of Cheap Cologne biography page, August 13, 2015

Welcome
Mon, 07-Jul-2008 11:44 AM
By System Admin

ALL CD'S $9.99 INCLUDES FREE SHIPPING!

COMPLETE ALBUM DIGITAL DOWNLOADS FOR ONLY $4.99!

I recently completed The Marilyn Handsome Project.
It consists all Cheap Cologne production and DJ work, 2 main MC's:
Awol One from The Shapeshifters and Capaciti from Saturday Morning
Soundtrack, but also features guests Carnage from Hecatomb, Sleep
from Old Dominion, Z-Man from Hieroglyphics and ???????
Expect a winter release and tour to follow.

More info:
www.myspace.com/marilynhandsome

Figure 3: Snippet of Cheap Cologne home page, October 28, 2008

Another challenge was a lack of disambiguating information when identifying the varying and continually evolving genres and subgenres of hip-hop music. While it is possible to include statements on items for creators that identify specific genres or sub-genres of hip-hop, the information in the Wikidata items describing the sub-genres is often not detailed enough for a cataloger lacking in-depth subject knowledge to connect to the item in hand. For example, the Wikidata item for "bounce music" (Q4949812) describes it as an "energetic style of New Orleans hip hop" but unless the CD in hand identifies the music included as being of the bounce genre, the cataloger wouldn't have adequate knowledge to achieve that type of specificity. We sought to find a balance between not wanting to assert authority when metadata creators don't have in-depth subject knowledge, and not using terms that are general to the point of being ineffective, and even "othering."[20] As an interim solution, we decided to use broader items, such as "hip hop music" (Q11401), until we are able to collaborate with others more knowledgeable on local musicians and hip-hop subgenres.

Another set of challenges involves the knowledge that creating metadata in a shared, global environment results in a loss of control over the data. In some cases, Wikidata's property constraints are in opposition to our local policies and values. For example, Wikidata property constraints for human (Q5) recommends adding a value for the sex or gender property (P21). Given that gender information should be private unless an individual chooses to disclose it, and that we do not feel it is appropriate for catalogers to make assumptions about gender, we (following a growing body of literature[21]) questioned the need for including this information in Wikidata and chose not to include the gender

---

20. Beth Iseminger, Nancy Lorimer, Casey Mullin & Hermine Vermeij, "Faceted Vocabularies for Music: A New Era of Discovery" *Notes* 73, no. 3 (March 2017): 409-431.

21. Jennifer M. Martin, "Records, Responsibility, and Power: An Overview of Cataloging Ethics," *Cataloging & Classification Quarterly* 59:2/3 (2021): 281-304.

property for living persons, although it means ignoring alert flags when creating an item without it. Potentially, other Wikidata users may add the gender property to Wikidata items we create (though we have no direct knowledge of that being done on any of our items to date). But omitting gender allows us to be in alignment with PCC guidance for authority work, which advises catalogers to omit gender when creating or updating NACO records and to remove the field when encountered in existing records.[22]

Despite a rather low barrier of entry to create items in Wikidata (discussed in depth in the section on cataloging standards and workflows), we were aware that not all Wikidata editors share the same values of openness and participation as the PCC Wikidata Pilot participants. Although we are not aware of any of our Wikidata items being removed due to lack of notability, we do know that this was an ongoing problem for some other project participants. This was another factor that led us to limit our scope to entities where we had clear identifying and/or disambiguating information.

Pausing UM's Wikidata Pilot

Due to multiple staff vacancies and organizational changes at UM during the PCC Wikidata Pilot, we were not able to devote as much attention to the project as originally planned. Between November 2020 and January 2021, multiple staff in the cataloging department retired or resigned, shrinking our numbers by one-third. One of the project members was appointed as interim director of the department, while others involved in the project had to focus on reducing cataloging backlogs that had accumulated during the COVID-19 pandemic, a situation that was exacerbated due to a lack of staff. In addition, due to the practical issues identified

---

22. PCC Ad Hoc Task Group on Recording Gender in Personal Name Authority Records, "Revised Report on Recording Gender in Personal Name Authority Records", April 7, 2022.

above, we realized that it would be difficult for us to achieve our stated goals in a substantial and meaningful way during the timeline of the project. The Minnesota Hip-Hop Collection materials were partly chosen as a convenient sample to explore Wikidata, as they were materials we had on hand. What we lacked was the fuller context about the history and materials in the collection, which would have helped us more realistically scope the project. While pausing the work was primarily driven by pandemic considerations, we also realized the limitations of our knowledge of the complexities of hip-hop as a genre and of specifics of the local hip-hop scene. We realized that we needed to engage with local hip-hop experts for clarification and additional expertise. At the same time, both in daily, internal conversations among library staff and especially in public social media discussions following the murder of George Floyd, we saw increasing pushback from Black, Indigenous, People of Color (BIPOC) thought leaders, artists, and activists who criticized white individuals and institutions for relying too heavily on community members to do the "emotional labor" of explaining BIPOC perspectives and experiences in real time, instead of conducting research via available printed and multimedia resources. As a result, we put the PCC Wikidata Pilot work on the back burner. A deeper dive into some of the ethical issues encountered, and which should be considered when working with a collection of this nature, are more fully explored in the following sections.

Practical and Ethical Issues Related to Identity Management for Hip-Hop Creators

As described above, several challenges were encountered when creating Wikidata items for hip-hop artists in the Minnesota Hip-Hop Collection. Many of these issues have both practical and ethical dimensions. This section explores these issues in further depth, identifying areas where they have policy implications, not only for hip-hop materials, but for resources created by other historically marginalized communities as well.

Capacity and Institutional Resources

As we learned in the course of the Wikidata Pilot, we underestimated the resources that would be needed in order to meet the goals of the project as we originally envisioned them. Some of the reasons for this (the COVID-19 pandemic, staff retirements) were outside of our control. We were, essentially, a group of catalogers deciding among ourselves that we wanted to contribute to a project that sounded interesting and would be a learning experience. A more formalized proposal, including shared expectations on staffing efforts needed and deliverables, might have helped us acquire institutional support in the form of funding for additional staff or coverage for some of the regular job duties of project staff so that they could devote more time to the project.

Due to the lack of formal institutional support, we had to make compromises regarding the degree to which we could do extensive research or outreach to help us identify artists encountered in the collection. Some of these artists may never have achieved prominence or been recorded again outside of what had been included in the collection, so information about them would be unlikely to be found in reference sources even if we had the time to expend extra effort to track them down. Though compromises were made for practical reasons, it also must be remembered that the iterative nature of Wikidata means that other contributors are able to add information even if our original items lack rich detail. Starting with something is often better than nothing.

Wikidata and the LC Name Authority File

In our project workflow, we made links between existing Library of Congress Name Authority File (LCNAF) records and Wikidata items, and when a record was lacking in the LCNAF we created one. While this can be considered duplicative work, it was a sensible approach for us. Having items in hand in which the creators were identified, we were well positioned to provide verifiable information to assist with interoperability between various authority systems. Although Wikidata arguably provides greater visibility to creators than the LCNAF for those using open web searches, the LCNAF is also part of the greater microcosm of linked data via LC's id.loc.gov service, and providing links between the same identity in different databases helps enable better machine interoperability. Additionally, if we had chosen to create only Wikidata items, and not corresponding LCNAF records, it could have been argued that we were further marginalizing the creators by not considering them worthy of inclusion in the established database. While the linking between systems was done manually for our project, there are methods for automating the generation of authority records from one source to another, which we would plan to explore when and if Wikidata work becomes a regular part of our daily workflow.

While there are many similarities between the types of data that can be included in LCNAF records and Wikidata items (such as place and date of birth and death, field of study or creative output), there are some significant differences in accepted practice and culture. The closed nature of the NACO program, and thus the LCNAF, means that only approved catalogers (primarily working in libraries) are able to create and edit records. Wikidata is much more open (to almost anyone), and while there are mechanisms to correct inaccurate or harmful information, that system is more reactive than proactive. When it comes to ethical issues, such as the aforementioned omission of gender in LCNAF records, catalogers may choose to align their principles between the two platforms even if the omission of gender is, technically, a violation of Wikidata's content guidelines.

Pseudonyms, Personas, and Multiple Identities

Creating and maintaining accurate authority files for artists performing under multiple identities is time-consuming and difficult work, but creators of authority records face this issue when dealing with other material held by libraries, such as the frequently ambiguous and overlapping identities used by publishers of pulp and penny dreadful literature in the late 19th and early 20th century. PCC has issued a FAQ document outlining the different approaches for creating and managing multiple pseudonyms.[23] With some exceptions, discussed below, many aspects of hip-hop that may at first glance pose novel challenges for linked data are in fact covered (at least in some respects) by existing policy and established practice. Consulting reference sources and experts when knowledge or awareness is lacking is part of authority work. This is one reason that appropriately staffing the project with people who have an adequate skill set and job classification to undertake this type of research is important. It would not be appropriate or ethical, for example, to task a low-wage student worker with performing the full range of tasks expected of a degree-holding librarian doing authority work.

One concrete example relevant to linked data work for hip-hop collections is how and when pseudonyms are traced. Though an artist might release all their work under one pseudonym, they

---

23. "FAQ – LC/PCC practice for creating NARs for persons who use pseudonyms" (Washington, DC: Library of Congress and Program for Cooperative Cataloging, 2015), https://www.loc.gov/catdir/cpso/pseud.pdf.

may adopt different personas within a song or album but never release a physical or digital manifestation under this persona. Existing authority practice is still heavily dependent on tracing and recording information from particular manifestations, even though these other names and identities may be well-known to interested users. For example, rapper Gucci Mane is established in the Library of Congress Name Authority file as "Gucci Mane, 1980-" and only his given name Radric Davis is included as a see-from tracing.[24] By contrast, his Wikidata entry offers a number of other names well-known to those familiar with his music, but which may or may not appear on any physical or digital manifestations: Guwop, Gucci Mane La Flare, Mr. Zone 6, Wizop (Figure 4). Even if linked data creators can trace these for artists less renowned than Gucci Mane through familiarity with the collection, the authority record standards themselves enforce a division between these names that may not be clear or useful to users of the collection.

Figure 4: Portion of Wikidata item for Gucci Mane, June 8, 2022

---

24. The Library of Congress, "Gucci Mane, 1980- - LC Linked Data Service: Authorities and Vocabularies | Library of Congress", accessed December 10, 2021, https://id.loc.gov/authorities/names/no2007029593.html.

Genres and Subgenres in Hip-Hop

As mentioned above, project staff encountered challenges in identifying genres and subgenres of hip-hop music for inclusion in Wikidata items for artists. In some cases, the genres were not well-defined in Wikidata, and not all staff working on the project had enough in-depth knowledge of hip-hop to enable them to correctly identify the genres associated with the artists for whom they were creating or enhancing items. However, in a hypothetical later phase of the project where hip-hop expertise was more accessible, Wikidata shows promise and potential for in-depth expression of genres and subgenres. A presentation at the Music OCLC Users Group on microgenres by Leonard Martin looks at how to record information about a variety of musical subgenres including "chopped and screwed" music, which is most closely associated with the work of Houston-based artist DJ Screw. The University of Houston Hip Hop Collection has over 300 of DJ Screw's official recordings in their collection, and Martin's presentation outlines the way that works in this genre are typically recorded in MARC records. Martin emphasizes the role libraries can play as "active participants in understanding and describing the context in which they and their institutions function in documenting and preserving these small cultures."[25] Though maintaining linked data about these kinds of genres presents challenges in terms of maintaining a dataset meant to describe a musical and artistic genre that has always been, and will continue to be, evolving, success in representing these changes in genre in linked data could yield novel insights into the relationship between subgenres within hip-hop, or between hip-hop and other musical genres, that might not otherwise be visible.

Compared with the stringent and time-consuming process for proposing and approving new terms for thesauri maintained by

---

25. Leonard Martin, "Microgenres: Memory, Community, and Preserving the Present", presentation given February 2021, https://hdl.handle.net/10657/7694.

the Library of Congress (LC),[26] Wikidata offers more flexibility. In order to propose a new subject or genre term to the Library of Congress, one must provide multiple references to published sources using the term, and demonstrate that the term is in common and accepted usage. Once the proposal is submitted, it goes through a public comment period and must ultimately be approved by a committee of staff at LC before it can be used in catalog records as a valid term. It is typical for this process to take several months to complete.

By contrast, new or emerging genres can be created as Wikidata items as instances of a genre or music genre by anyone, and then added as statements to Wikidata items representing artists or works. For example, "chopped and screwed" (Q2261628) was added to Wikidata as an instance of a music genre in 2013 (Figure 5). Once this descriptor became available, anyone creating or editing an item for an artist or work related to the genre could add it as a statement (Figure 6). This openness and flexibility allows for much more rapid inclusion of new genres and subgenres into metadata description. If information is found to be inaccurate or incomplete, it can be corrected or enhanced by the Wikidata community later on. In fact, "chopped and screwed" was not included on DJ Screw's Wikidata item (Q743478) until this example was being prepared for inclusion in this chapter, despite his status as inventor of the genre. The lack of widely adopted and understood best practices within Wikidata can lead to these types of inconsistencies and omissions, which can be frustrating to catalogers accustomed to a more rule-bound traditional cataloging that features standards shared across projects and institutions. There are benefits and drawbacks to each approach; metadata creators increasingly need to wrestle with the balance (and sometimes conflict) between hierarchical, authoritative data structures, and those that are collectively created in an open community.

---

26. SACO - Subject Authority Cooperative Program, accessed December 9, 2021, https://www.loc.gov/aba/pcc/saco/index.html.

Figure 5: Wikidata item for chopped and screwed (Q2261628)

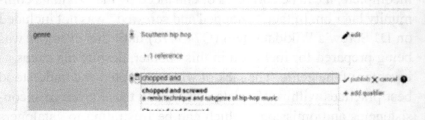

Figure 6: Snippets of Wikidata item for DJ Screw (Q743478)

By creating and maintaining accurate and effective linked data for local hip-hop, libraries not only enhance access to the hip-hop material within their collection but also contribute to a distributed body of knowledge about artists and works that may become relevant in another context. George Floyd appeared under the name Big Floyd on multiple recordings of the Screwed

Up Click and Presidential Playas within the milieu of DJ Screw in Houston. As news of his death spread around the world, a Wikidata entry for him was created three days after he was killed, on May 28, 2020; information about his music was added later that same day.[27] His work as a hip-hop artist was not reflected in a Library of Congress Name Authority record until June 19, 2020, about four weeks after his death.[28]

Wikipedia, Wikidata and "Notability"

As shown above, while Wikidata's flexibility can arguably make it better suited to hip-hop description than traditional RDA and MARC-based cataloging, the platform also comes with its own ethical issues and risks. Wikidata is intended to be an open and broadly accessible platform for humans and machines to collectively create a knowledge base that can be used by web services including, but not limited to, Wikipedia, Google, Facebook, and others. This openness creates a number of tensions: between metadata practitioners, who are accustomed to greater rigor in the creation of content standards and taxonomies, versus the more open, bottom-up nature of open source collaboration; and between individuals and communities with a social justice orientation versus bad actors and gatekeepers who can be skeptical of efforts to increase representation within the knowledge base, or who engage in outright sabotage against descriptions of individuals from traditionally excluded communities.

Wikipedia, which bills itself as "the free encyclopedia,"[29] has had well-documented problems with bias and lack of diversity,

27. "Revision History of 'George Floyd' (Q95677819) - Wikidata," accessed December 10, 2021, https://www.wikidata.org/w/index.php?title=Q95677819&action=history.

28. Library of Congress, "Floyd, George, 1973-2020 - LC Linked Data Service: Authorities and Vocabularies," accessed December 10, 2021, https://id.loc.gov/authorities/names/no2020074637.html.

29. Wikipedia, accessed December 9, 2021, https://www.wikipedia.org/.

both in its coverage and in the editors who create and control the content.[30] Wiki edit-a-thons have been used as one solution to increase representation in the database by focusing on creating articles about women, people of color, and other marginalized identities and topics.[31] Unfortunately, this has led to further targeting by some Wikipedia editors who call into question the "notability" of non-male, non-white, non-cisgender, and non-heterosexual individuals in a variety of fields, where they have been deliberately prevented from achieving the prominence and prestige of those who fit the traditional norm. A glaring example of this is physicist Donna Strickland, whose Wikipedia entry was removed because her work wasn't considered "significant" enough by editors to warrant inclusion, until she was awarded the Nobel Prize in 2018.[32]

Wikidata's goal to be a universal infobase for projects beyond Wikipedia means that its requirements for an item to be included are far less stringent than those of Wikipedia. In order to warrant inclusion, a Wikidata item need only link to another entity within the Wikiverse, must represent a "clearly identifiable conceptual or material entity," and/or fulfill a structural need (such as providing an end point for a statement on another item).[33] This greater openness, while intentionally vague, has helped lead to the broad use of Wikidata for identity management projects in the GLAM

30. S.C. Stuart, "Wikipedia Has a Diversity Problem, But These Librarians Want to Help", PCMag, January 16, 2019, https://www.pcmag.com/news/wikipedia-has-a-diversity-problem-but-these-librarians-want-to-help. Schlomit Aharoni Lir, "Strangers in a seemingly open-to-all website: the gender bias in Wikipedia," *Equity, Diversity and Inclusion* 40, no. 7 (2021): 801-818.

31. Sabrina Clark, "Wikipedia Hip-Hop Edit-a-thon addresses lack of diversity in content and editors", Q City Metro, February 5, 2020, https://qcitymetro.com/2020/02/05/hip-hop-edit-a-thon-addresses-lack-of-diversity-in-wikipedia-content-editors/.

32.. Corinne Purtill & Zoë Schlanger, "Wikidata rejected an entry on a Nobel Prize winner because she wasn't famous enough," Quartz, October 2, 2018, https://qz.com/1410909/wikipedia-had-rejected-nobel-prize-winner-donna-strickland-because-she-wasnt-famous-enough/

33. "Wikidata: Notability," accessed December 8, 2021, https://www.wikidata.org/wiki/Wikidata:Notability.

(Galleries, Libraries, Archives, and Museums) space over the last several years. Unfortunately, some members of the Wiki community continue to apply overly-stringent criteria to what they consider noteworthy enough for inclusion in Wikidata, and some participants in the PCC Wikidata Project (though not UM to date) have had items repeatedly flagged for removal, despite the entries meeting the criteria as stated by Wikidata.

Web-scale aggregators such as Wikidata provide the opportunity to disseminate information about library resources and content creators in a more accessible manner than the largely siloed traditional library catalog. However, this greater accessibility comes with the risk of exposing information about individuals to a broader audience, which includes computers consuming the data. Errors as well as sensitive information can be broadly disseminated, with the possibility of causing harm. Individuals from marginalized communities are at greater risk for being targeted for harassment or sabotage than are those from majority identities. When catalogers have less control over the eventual uses of the metadata they are creating, they must take extra precautions that what they are putting out in the world is accurate and respectful to the people being described. They should be open to honoring take-down requests by individuals if requested. While ongoing maintenance is always an aspect of metadata work, contributing metadata to network-level resources such as Wikidata specifically requires special care to resist sabotage and to justify the presence in the database of the entity being described. The metadata creator must also be open and willing to challenge their assumptions and change traditional practices as they gain more knowledge and cultural competence.

Conclusion and Strategies for Future Work

In selecting the Minnesota Hip-Hop Collection for the PCC Wikidata Pilot, University of Minnesota catalogers made some inaccurate assumptions regarding the overall demographics of the collection and its creators. In a desire to highlight Black creators in the wake of George Floyd's murder, we failed to fully assess the collection and its suitability and practicality for meeting our intended goals. We were partly hamstrung by our lack of access to the artists represented, the donor, and the curator who had acquired the collection, who might have been able to provide more information and context. We were further hindered by impacts of the COVID-19 pandemic, which limited our access to staffing and materials, and shifted our priorities.

In some cases, acquiring greater cultural awareness is necessary. If developing relationships with content creators or cultural representatives is not practical or possible, catalogers should consult with experts and seek out resources to help better understand the context under which the materials they are describing were created. In the case of the Minnesota Hip-Hop Collection, the forced postponement of further work on the project allowed us the opportunity to interrogate our practices and approaches to the work, to explore the ethical issues, and to identify ways we can do better, either for a future iteration of this project, or with other collections of this nature. Both the donor and the curator who acquired the collection have left the University, breaking some of the connections that may have existed with the content creators. In addition, our metadata librarians are physically and organizationally separated from the archivists and curators who acquire collections, and we do not have a formal mechanism for requesting information from content creators that might assist us with creating metadata. It is more difficult to build relationships retrospectively, particularly if the metadata librarians are several degrees removed from the initial acquisition and ongoing maintenance and use of the collection in question (and it would be inappropriate for us to do this outreach without the involvement of the curator). The University of Minnesota's collections, including its Archives and Special Collections, contain a vast array of materials created by historically marginalized communities, including the Givens Collection, The Jean-Nikolaus Tretter Collection in Gay, Lesbian, Bisexual and Transgender Studies, and the Immigration History Research Center Archives. These collections, and others across our library system, offer the potential for numerous projects that we could undertake to highlight or uncover the contributions of individuals and cultures outside the dominant white heteronormative world. Our experience with the Minnesota Hip-Hop Collection has shown us that our efforts must be undertaken with more forethought, planning, and collaboration.

For future iterations of the Minnesota Hip-Hop project (or similar projects), we might consider working with the curator to engage with content creators and community members who might have specialized knowledge about the collection before embarking on metadata work. This engagement could include edit-a-thons, where domain experts are invited to create and enhance Wikidata items related to the collection, or presentations to community groups, where feedback on the existing metadata is solicited. Ideally, relationships should be built in from the time the collection is acquired, and it would be beneficial for us to enhance our ongoing dialogue with curators so that they have increased awareness about what type of information would be helpful to us. For collections that have advisory boards (such as the Tretter Collection)[34] catalogers could be invited to a board meeting to discuss metadata issues from the perspective of users and community members. We would need to coordinate these interactions with curators or collection managers who have existing relationships with communities or individuals. We do not want to burden BIPOC or other marginalized communities with additional labor in social justice work, but we do want to partner with them in situations where they have willingness and

---

34. Tretter collection website, viewed December 13, 2021, https://www.lib.umn.edu/collections/special/tretter.

interest in these types of interactions, and where the relationship is seen as mutually beneficial.

Despite our misreading of the nature of the Minnesota Hip-Hop Collection, there is still potential value in describing the creators in Wikidata as a representation of the evolution of the Minnesota hip-hop scene. Future iterations of the Wikidata enhancement process could include additional associated entities (producers, recording engineers, etc.), deep-dive research into the individual performers and groups, individual track title descriptions, and/or incorporation of the recording studios and record labels represented in the collection, all of which would ideally include the involvement of the local community. In addition, we would want to define appropriate levels of staffing, both in terms of job classification and amount of time expected to dedicate to the project, and gain support and common understanding with all stakeholders regarding expected outcomes. A useful next step, when we have the opportunity to return to this project, might be an informational interview with the donor. We are interested in addressing our knowledge gaps through community engagement, and we recognize that we need to build relationships and trust with community members before we can respectfully engage in such collaboration.

Our participation in the PCC Wikidata Pilot, to the extent that we were able to contribute, was a valuable learning experience in several ways. On the positive side, catalogers at our institution gained hands-on experience working in Wikidata. We were able to discuss ethical issues (such as whether or not to include gender information) and explore methodologies for integrating Wikidata into our authority workflow. In order to be as accurate as possible and respect the communities involved, additional planning and research is required. In some cases, testing the proposed workflow with a sample of items from the collection may be advisable before developing a full project plan. As the PCC project was itself a pilot, it could be argued that our early efforts, whether or not they were fully successful, met the intended goals of learning how to use Wikidata and experimenting with workflows.

However, when it comes to increasing cultural knowledge and community engagement, we may want to move toward a model of closer collaboration with collection managers and curators when embarking on these types of projects. Because of our organizational structure and relatively siloed workplace culture, it may take some time to evolve our practice into this new model, and would require the willing participation of our colleagues in other departments. Formalizing cataloging projects can feel burdensome and inefficient, and isn't appropriate or necessary for every project, but thoughtful care and planning are especially important when resources related to historically underrepresented communities are involved.

Part III: People & Communities

Ethical Considerations in the Development of Responsible Linked Open Data Infrastructure

SUSAN BROWN, ERIN CANNING,
KIM MARTIN, & SARAH ROGER

Introduction

The Linked Infrastructure for Networked Cultural Scholarship (LINCS)—a Canada Foundation for Innovation Cyberinfrastructure project—is converting humanities datasets into organized, interconnected, machine-processable resources for Canadian cultural research.[1] LINCS is infrastructure-in-progress, composed of related but not integrated software, platform, and service components, computational resources, and human experts, which, together, provide resources to researchers for the creation, refinement, and dissemination of linked open cultural data. In its initial stages, the project focus is on replatforming data, producing linked open data by transforming or processing existing datasets. Its open repository will publish linked datasets created by researchers with diverse disciplinary approaches and epistemological frameworks.

1. "Linked Infrastructure for Networked Cultural Scholarship," accessed December 10, 2021, https://lincsproject.ca/. Special thanks to Samel Peacock for assistance with research towards this paper, and to Kelly Hughes for help preparing the manuscript. Funding for this work is provided by the Canada Foundation for Innovation, the Canada Research Chairs program, and the Social Sciences and Humanities Research Council of Canada.

The current chapter offers our initial reflections on the ethics of building infrastructure for linked open data. After introducing the LINCS project, the datasets, and the notion of "replatforming" to describe our work, we present three major areas for consideration. First are the ethics of how the LINCS team collaborates with researchers, in terms of translating the nuances of their data, the prioritization of dataset processing, and the ethical questions raised by linking certain datasets. Next, we discuss the ethical considerations associated with the ontologies and vocabularies used to replatform research data as linked open data. Finally, we discuss the data agreements designed to promote ethical choices with respect to ethics clearance, credit, and licensing.

LINCS Datasets

LINCS datasets vary considerably in size and format, and range from metadata on art or publications, to prosopographical information from diverse historical periods, manuscript variants, second-wave feminist magazine advertisements, literary influences, and features of texts; all represent complex, domain-specific relationships driven by research questions. This makes LINCS unusual in relation to humanities linked data projects, which tend to work with a specific dataset or domain, as well as in relation to GLAM, where initiatives most frequently focus on object metadata, whether to publish a single institution's holdings, to drive a user interface, for metadata management, or metadata aggregation to increase findability.[2] In contrast, LINCS creates

---

2. To provide a small selection of examples, the Georgia O'Keeffe Museum exemplifies the increasingly common use of linked data to publish data from a single institution, in this case using the Linked Art data model. This model, along with the International Image Interoperability Framework (IIIF), is also behind the Getty Research Collection Viewer. IIIF also drives image viewers for numerous cultural heritage collection websites, such as the Digital Bodleian. The use of linked data for metadata management is a key component of the LUX: Yale Collections Discovery platform. The Islandora 8 framework manages object metadata internally using linked data, as well as generating JSON-LD for node, media, and taxonomy terms for the

linked data by transforming or processing researcher-collected (and, eventually, selective institutional) data content in addition to object metadata as a basis for ongoing research. LINCS also handles data formats from the entire range of source material: from highly structured spreadsheets, through semi-structured XML, to natural language. A small subset of LINCS data is born linked, that is to say, created using spreadsheets with linked data structures in mind from the outset, and some of it is automatically generated as Web Annotations when researchers encode named entities using an XML editor. However, most LINCS data is derived from existing datasets whose content is either fully or partially translated into linked open data depending on researcher priorities and resources on both sides.

Infrastructure and Ethics

LINCS is a relatively well-resourced, albeit time-limited, humanities infrastructure development project dedicated both to making data reusable and providing systems for storing and accessing data, with professional staff amounting to approximately 10 FTEs plus additional paid student labour. The team provides substantial support for the complex extraction and transformation process, which varies for each dataset, and provides access to the datasets

interface. "Georgia O'Keeffe Museum," Georgia O'Keeffe Museum, accessed January 8, 2022, https://www.okeeffemuseum.org/; "Linked Art," accessed January 8, 2022, https://linked.art/; Lynn Rother, "The History of Art Is Linked but the Data Is Not: Georgia O'Keeffe, Provenance and Scholarship - from Panel 'Linked Art: Networking Digital Collections and Scholarship,'" accessed January 8, 2022, https://hcommons.org/deposits/item/hc:32069/; Getty Research Institute, "Research Collections Viewer," Getty, accessed January 12, 2022, https://www.getty.edu/research/collections/about; Bodleian Libraries, "About," Digital Bodleian, accessed January 12, 2022, https://digital.bodleian.ox.ac.uk/about/; Robert Sanderson, "LUX: Illuminating the Collections of Yale's Museums, Libraries and Archives via Linked Open Usable Data," https://www.slideshare.net/azaroth42/lux-illuminating-the-collections-of-yales-museums-libraries-and-archies-via-linked-open-usable-data; "Metadata - Islandora 8," accessed January 8, 2022, https://islandora.github.io/documentation/user-documentation/metadata/; "RDF Generation - Islandora 8," accessed January 8, 2022, https://islandora.github.io/documentation/islandora/rdf-mapping/.

as named graphs within a larger interlinked dataset hosted by project infrastructure. In the case of derivative datasets, the focus of our chapter, responsibility for the source data, such as XML documents, remains with the researcher.[3]

The LINCS platform disseminates LOD extracted from existing research outputs previously covered by the ethics policies of universities and funders. However, converting existing datasets and publishing associated metadata as linked open data generates greater findability and deeper connectivity to other research than would have been considered during researchers' initial ethics clearance, or when deciding whether an ethics review was required. Tara Robertson has compellingly presented harms associated with digitization generally, using the example of lesbian pornography,[4] and the nature of linked data compounds the risks of publishing content in ways that make it accessible in contexts that were not originally anticipated. Robertson's example is the potential harm involved in a shift from having a person's image or name published in a low-circulation print magazine associated with a specific subculture and geographical region, as opposed to digitizing that content and making it searchable across the internet. Similarly, interlinking data with related entities, resources, and assertions on the Web is different than, for instance, indexing it and disseminating it via download from an institutional repository, since the data becomes more discoverable, accessible, and susceptible to processing by machines. Publishing research content as linked open data makes it easier

---

3. Although all members of the LINCS team bear ethical obligations collectively and individually, the present authors (whose roles in the project can be found in their biographical statements) found themselves debating ethical considerations with which the project team needs to grapple. As far as pronouns here are concerned, "we" indicates the four authors of this piece unless connected to "the LINCS team," in which case we mean all or a substantially larger subset of the team's staff. "LINCS" by itself refers to the socio-technical infrastructure the project is building, whereas the "LINCS project" refers to the process of creating that infrastructure.

4. Tara Robertson, "Digitization: Just Because You Can, Doesn't Mean You Should," Tara Robertson Consulting (blog), March 21, 2016, https://tararobertson.ca/2016/oob/.

to search for people and to triangulate information about them by drawing on other datasets. While this provides benefits, it also introduces new potential for harm.[5] Catherine D'Ignazio and Lauren Klein note that, despite admirable aims, the open data movement has in effect worked against the ethical urgency of providing context for data.[6] Linked open data, like open data generally, is hard to do well.

We therefore recognize that LINCS as an infrastructure introduces risks as well as providing benefits. Infrastructure is not neutral, and we join others who reject the argument that information platforms have no responsibilities regarding the data they make available. As Jack M. Balkin argues, "digital infrastructure owners . . . must take up a new set of social obligations to preserve the global public good of a free Internet and a healthy and vibrant global public sphere."[7] This stance is inherent in the project's founding values: LINCS is rooted in intersectional feminism and collaborative communities of practice in terms of the expertise, experience, and research areas of the team leads and many of its researchers, as well as in its commitment to advancing the visibility and utility of research associated with underrepresented and marginalized groups.[8] LINCS aims to contribute to the "diversity stack"—infrastructure that attends to diversity and

---

5. Ruth Kitchin Tillman, "Barriers to Ethical Name Modeling in Current Linked Data Encoding Practices," in *Ethical Questions in Name Authority Control* (Sacramento, CA: Library Juice Press, 2019), 241–57.

6. Catherine D'Ignazio and Lauren F. Klein, *Data Feminism* (Cambridge, MA: MIT Press, 2020), 155.

7. Jack M. Balkin, "Free Speech in the Algorithmic Society: Big Data, Private Governance, and New School Speech Regulation," *UC Davis Law Review* 51 (2017), 1210; Marika Cifor et al., "Feminist Data Manifest-No," Feminist Data Manifest-No, accessed November 27, 2020, https://www.manifestno.com; Tiffany Li, "Beyond Intermediary Liability: The Future of Information Platforms," Information Society Project (Yale Law School, February 13, 2018), https://scholarship.law.bu.edu/faculty_scholarship/819.

8. Kimberlé W. Crenshaw, *On Intersectionality: Essential Writings* (New York City: New Press, 2017). D'Ignazio and Klein, *Data Feminism*; Etienne Wenger, *Communities of Practice: Learning, Meaning, and Identity* (Cambridge, UK: Cambridge University Press, 1999). See lincsproject.ca/docs/about-lincs/research.

difference, and uses linked data in non-hegemonic ways.[9] This very aim, however, means that some LINCS data describes and represents vulnerable populations, intensifying the possibilities for harm of members of groups that have been subject to misrepresentation and injustice.

We here lay out ethical considerations associated with "replatforming," by which we mean, generally, recirculating existing data through a new platform that provides different affordances and, specifically in this case, as linked open data. The ability of members of a three-year infrastructure implementation project to grapple with the myriad ethical nuances of linked open data is limited by time and resources. However, the LINCS project benefits from occupying an oblique relationship both to institutions as digital resource holders and to researchers as digital resource users and creators. This situates LINCS differently in the space of what Jarrett Martin Drake has termed "archival dynamics" to probe the complex ways in which archival institutions and processes are entangled with social inequities,[10] and positions the project to help researchers think through the ethical implications of linking data. Cognisant of the harm inflicted on Indigenous and other groups by extractive attitudes to knowledge gathering,[11] we aim to ground LINCS in a relational conceptualization of data that complexifies but also enriches.

Replatforming

One might assume that a project working primarily with derivative or secondary data like LINCS would involve few ethical

9. Alan Liu, "Toward a Diversity Stack: Digital Humanities and Diversity as Technical Problem," *PMLA/Publications of the Modern Language Association of America* 135, no. 1 (January 2020): 130–51, https://doi.org/10.1632/pmla.2020.135.1.130.

10. Jarrett Drake, "Blood at the Root," *Journal of Contemporary Archival Studies* 8, no. 1 (April 16, 2021), https://elischolar.library.yale.edu/jcas/vol8/iss1/6.

11. Deborah McGregor, "Coming Full Circle: Indigenous Knowledge, Environment, and Our Future," *American Indian Quarterly* 28, no. 3/4 (2004): 397; Jane Anderson and Kimberly Christen, "Decolonizing Attribution: Traditions of Exclusion," *Journal of Radical Librarianship* 5 (2019).

considerations, but the "replatforming" of data in ways that amplify or make it more accessible raises as many ethical questions as the contrary action of "deplatforming" or removing access to online platforms.[12] We use the term replatforming to refer to several aspects of providing a platform on which data is disseminated anew and, in the case of LINCS, in newly structured ways. Replatforming points to the data's prior life on other platforms; the affordances that platforms can provide for redressing historical under- or misrepresentation by amplifying or reframing data; and the need for critical analysis of the implications of providing a new platform for existing data.[13] In the case of LINCS, these implications are closely related to the processes and structures whereby existing data is replatformed as linked open data.

Linked open data is centrally concerned with identifiable information about people, places, organizations, events, or other things, as well as their properties or relationships. To the extent that public identifiers are its core strategy for data linking, such linking has ethical consequences, as is increasingly recognized in Canadian research ethics policies and in ongoing developments in privacy legislation, such as the introduction of Canadian Consumer Privacy Protection Act (replacing the Personal Information Protection and Electronic Documents Act) and Europe's General Data Protection Regulation.[14] Although many LINCS datasets do

---

12. This sense of replatforming is distinct from that used by Innes and Innes to designate workarounds for being deplatformed from social media. LINCS tools can be used to derive, reconcile, or link data that will not be hosted by the project, and will also enable the authoring of new linked data, but our focus here is the data being replatformed. Shagun Jhaver, et al., "Evaluating the Effectiveness of Deplatforming as a Moderation Strategy on Twitter," *Proceedings of the ACM on Human-Computer Interaction* 5, no. CSCW2 (October 18, 2021): 381:1-30, https://doi.org/10.1145/3479525; H. Innes and M. Innes, "De-Platforming Disinformation: Conspiracy Theories and Their Control," *Information, Communication & Society* 2021 (October 28, 2021): 1–19, https://doi.org/10.1080/1369118X.2021.1994631.

13. Susan Brown, "Replatforming," in *Critical Infrastructure Studies and Digital Humanities*, ed. Alan Liu, Urszula Pawlicka-Deger, and James Smithies (Minneapolis: University of Minnesota Press, forthcoming).

14. "Bill C-11: An Act to Enact the Consumer Privacy Protection Act and the Personal Information and Data Protection Tribunal Act and To Make Related and Con-

not involve direct human participation in research, some, such as oral histories, do. Additionally, some datasets draw on records of individuals that were published prior to the era of networked information: neither the information gatherers nor the subjects of that information would have expected those records to be linked to data about that person from a separate context. For example, the Canadian Writing Research Collaboratory (CWRC) will be able to produce LINCS data automatically from metadata and content, requiring careful consultation with researchers about whether or not to generate data from any particular CWRC dataset.[15] Finally, many cultural datasets in LINCS refer to people such as artists and writers who are long dead. However, there remain ethical considerations regarding the categories embedded in the ontologies and vocabularies mobilized to represent historical figures in LINCS data, since they may perpetuate epistemic injustice, particularly hermeneutical injustice, as articulated by Miranda Fricker to describe situations in which the language available does not adequately represent someone's experience.[16] Replatforming encapsulates a kind of action, like remediation, while also flagging through its echo of deplatforming the high ethical stakes involved.

Working with Researchers

The mission of LINCS is to create linked *open* data wherever possible to allow people to reuse data, find connections, follow paths, and stumble upon new research questions. LINCS cannot control the use of the data by others once it is published,[17] but

---

sequential Amendments To Other Acts," https://www.justice.gc.ca/eng/csj-sjc/pl/charte-charte/c11.html.

15. Canadian Writing Research Collaboratory, http://cwrc.ca.

16. Miranda Fricker, *Epistemic Injustice: Power and the Ethics of Knowing* (Oxford, UK: Oxford University Press, 2007).

17. David J. Hand, "Aspects of Data Ethics in a Changing World: Where Are We Now?" *Big Data* 6, no. 3 (2018), https://doi.org/10.1089/big.2018.0083.

can try to lay the groundwork for an ethical future. Indeed, the Canadian national ethics policy for research involving human subjects points to linking as a crucial consideration, giving it a section unto itself within the chapter on privacy and confidentiality, and noting that "data linking can be a powerful research tool."[18] So powerful is data linking that data identifying participants in research studies should be kept confidential, safeguarded, and de-identified or anonymized prior to publication in order to prevent re-identification of individual research participants.[19] Moreover, the usual exemption of secondary data usage from ethics review holds only "so long as the process of data linkage or recording or dissemination of results does not generate identifiable information."[20] This results in quite an ethical dilemma, as one of the goals of linked data is to connect datasets via easily locatable identifiers.

When inviting researchers to contribute their data to LINCS, we thought hard about what topics we wanted to cover, how data on these topics might relate, and who would be interested in considering these problems alongside the LINCS team. At the proposal stage, forty-six researchers joined the LINCS project, with thirty-five datasets among them.[21] A number of ethical concerns arise when working with a project with so many moving parts. We here raise three concerns and showcase small changes made as a result of ethical considerations that arose in working with researchers: the development of the areas of inquiry (AoI), the prioritization of datasets for ingestion, and considerations around connecting these datasets both to each other and to the larger web of linked data.

---

18. Canadian Institutes of Health Research, Tri-Council Policy Statement: Ethical Conduct for Research Involving Humans, 2018, http://publications.gc.ca/collections/collection_2019/irsc-cihr/RR4-2-2019-eng.pdf.

19. Canadian Institutes of Health Research, 172.

20. Canadian Institutes of Health Research, 16, 17.

21. For a list of researchers and their respective projects, please see https://lincsproject.ca/docs/about-lincs/people/collaborators.

Areas of Inquiry

When LINCS was proposed, the project's grant application focussed on seven AoIs: groups of scholars who would collaborate on specific problems that arise when creating linked data from material on a specific subject. Throughout the grant-writing process, all researchers were consulted about organizing inquiry into the following AoIs: *Literary and Performance History, London and the British Empire, Prosopography, Material and Textual Cultures, Canadian Publishing, Knowledge Systems,* and *Alternative Epistemologies.*[22] After securing the grant—and realizing that many researchers' interests involved more than one AoI—the LINCS team created a survey where researchers could declare multiple interests. In the process of creating this survey, the Research Board[23] noted concerns with using the term *alternative* to bring together all forms of non-hegemonic epistemology. Researchers with datasets categorized as alternative had included those on Indigenous worldviews, environmental activism, and queer identities. The only thing that connected these datasets was their apparent deviation from "the norm."

The LINCS team recognizes that we face an ethical conundrum in replatforming data associated with difference and diversity: when a researcher, a project team, or an AoI works to build nuance into the data, they are faced with the power of existing information infrastructures.[24] These, more often than not, center a white, cisgender, male "normative" view of the world.[25] The Research Board ended up removing the term "alternative"

---

22. For more on the LINCS areas of inquiry, see lincsproject.ca/docs/about-lincs/research.

23. The founding LINCS Research Board of Stacy Allison-Cassin, Jon Bath, and Janelle Jenstad is chaired by Kim Martin.

24. Irfan Ullah et al., "An Overview of the Current State of Linked and Open Data in Cataloging," *Information Technology and Libraries* 37, no. 4 (December 17, 2018): 47–80, https://doi.org/10.6017/ital.v37i4.10432; Rinke Hoekstra et al., "An Ecosystem for Linked Humanities Data," in *Lecture Notes in Computer Science* 9989, 425–40.

25. Hope A. Olson, "The Power to Name: Representation in Library Catalogs," *Signs* 26, no. 3 (2001): 639–68.

altogether, breaking the *Alternative Epistemologies* AoI into two: *Indigenous Knowledges* and *Resistant Epistemologies*. When we surveyed LINCS researchers, notably more interest was shown in participating in the latter group than the former, indicating to us that we need to do more work to support and nurture a community related to Indigenous knowledges, starting by looking for similar work being done elsewhere. These small steps towards creating the conditions for situated voices to be heard are needed to foster the scholarly dialogue required for thinking past hegemonic categories in order to represent nuance and diversity on the web.[26]

Dataset Prioritization

The LINCS team also has important decisions to make about the order in which researchers' datasets get converted to linked data. A number of evaluation criteria are taken into consideration: the readiness of the dataset, the capacity of the research team to work with LINCS, the level of researcher engagement, and how the dataset connects to others that have already entered the LINCS pipeline. Technical considerations are also a factor: for example, the relative ease of starting with structured rather than less-structured data formats has meant that the former were mobilized while we built and tested tools for the latter.

From the outset, LINCS aimed to prioritize voices that are underrepresented on the web. Alongside long-standing projects such as Map of Early Modern London and Orlando, we worked while building the grant to include newer, less- (or un-)funded projects, such as those focusing on feminist magazine networks, the francophone press in Canada, or the reading habits of Canadians. Researcher capacity and engagement ebb and flow from

---

26. Donna Haraway, "Situated Knowledges: The Science Question in Feminism and the Privilege of Partial Perspective," *Feminist Studies* 14, no. 3 (1988): 575-599, https://doi.org/10.2307/3178066; Susan Brown, "Categorically Provisional," *PMLA/Publications of the Modern Language Association of America* 135, no. 1 (2020): 165–74.

semester to semester as teaching and service duties, job hunting, and life changes factor into the time each researcher can spend working with LINCS. This creates shifting tensions among criteria that were already difficult to weigh against each other and were then exacerbated by the pandemic.

The problem of time itself is an ethical one: researchers with successful grants (read: projects with substantial datasets) are often tenured and have either more time themselves or more money to hire a research team to help them with scholarly labour. This means that less established researchers in LINCS risk being deprioritized because they are unable to meet to discuss mappings or their research questions, attend LINCS workshops, or engage with LINCS tools meaningfully. This busyness, of course, is more likely to be the case for researchers who are women—who generally take on more service roles than men—and more so again for faculty whose identities see them take on the demanding work of diversity, equity, accessibility, and inclusion.[27]

In considering what material LINCS should be adding to the Semantic Web, we factored in two sets of connections: those between the data and what exists outside of LINCS—for data from the Orlando Project, for example, there are many other women's writing projects for which connections could prove fortuitous—and within LINCS itself (the very reason the AoIs were created was to see what resulted when researchers connected their projects on these topics). Such connections, however, need to be carefully balanced against the needs and desires of voices that are missing from the Semantic Web as it stands.

Given the above, how then can LINCS take a more ethical approach to dataset prioritization and meet the researchers where

---

27. Joya Misra et al., "The Ivory Ceiling of Service Work," *Academe* 97, no. 1 (January–February 2011), 22-26. https://www.aaup.org/article/ivory-ceiling-service-work; Muninder K. Ahluwalia et al., "Mitigating the 'Powder Keg': The Experiences of Faculty of Color Teaching Multicultural Competence," *Teaching of Psychology* 46, no. 3 (July 2019): 187–96, https://doi.org/10.1177/0098628319848864; Sara Ahmed, *On Being Included: Racism and Diversity in Institutional Life* (Durham, NC: Duke University Press, 2012).

they are? Our approach is to meet with each research group, as they are able, for a dataset intake interview, where we ask about their goals as researchers, the importance of the data conversion to their own work, and whether the project they originally committed to is still a priority for them.[28] At that point, the LINCS technical team assesses existing capacity and readiness to support the project through the workflow and identifies ways to assist them. We also offer microgrants to help support the data-conversion process for researchers who require additional funding. These grants can be used to hire a student to help with reconciliation, data clean-up, and conversion. The LINCS team trains the researcher and research assistants, working with them until they are set up to complete the conversion process on their own. The first round of microgrants including related support from LINCS saw five datasets move closer to conversion. In the first round, we managed to balance some established projects with others, one of which was not among our initial datasets, but for which the LINCS team felt that the topic, a bibliography of queer history, should be prioritized.

Impacts of Linking

The dynamic nature of the Semantic Web, with its foundation on the open-world assumption, means that we cannot control what is said about, or connected to, LINCS datasets once they are published. We remain wary of and critically alert to what these links can surface. We posit that the most interesting research questions will be those resulting from interconnected datasets, but also that many challenges and larger moral conundrums will be encountered when linking this data.

Linked data is valued because it allows multiple perspectives to be attached to a single data point.[29] We recognize that we have

---

28. Kim Martin et al., "LINCS Research Dataset Intake Questionnaire," https://doi.org/10.5281/zenodo.6048520.

29. Tillman, "Barriers to Ethical Name Modeling."

additional ethical responsibilities when replatforming data that is personal and sensitive, and for which consent to (re)platform may not have been properly secured. For instance, the data of the Lesbian and Gay Liberation Project directed by Constance Crompton and Michelle Schwartz draws on a range of published content related to activism and community engagement by individuals, some of whom are still living, that entails some of the same risks as those about digitization articulated by Robertson.[30] Linking could also surface unwanted, or potentially dangerous, information by connecting the deadnames of transgender persons to their current names and web presences,[31] through resurfacing data about social media movements such as #GamerGate or #MeToo, or creating unhappy results if the name of an oral history participant is linked to a dating app profile or a stale social media account. Worse still, bad actors might harvest personal data for misuse.[32] In this regard, we follow the lead of the *Feminist Data Manifest-No*, which commits to "embracing agency and working with intentionality" for data about people.[33] The team is therefore ensuring that its pending feedback mechanisms can be used to flag problematic data for review, anonymization, and takedown where appropriate. The writing of this chapter brought home the need to be vigilant in tracking how effectively our agreements with users, drafted at the application stage and since revised, communicate their ethical responsibilities. Those agreements are living documents that will continue to change as the project mobilizes more data and as new considerations arise, and documentation and training materials will also need to highlight ethical matters. We are proceeding carefully, because once information is interlinked, excising portions becomes complicated.

---

30. Robertson, "Digitization."

31. Tillman, 252.

32. David J. Hand, "Aspects of Data Ethics in a Changing World: Where Are We Now?"

33. Cifor et al., "Feminist Data Manifest-No."

Mobilizing Data as Linked Open Data

In the context of LINCS, replatforming involves not just making it easier to discover data about people, places, and things, but also a restructuring of source data to be deployed as linked open data. The transformation of source data into linked data can bring new meaning to the data, as infrastructures contribute to the meaning of the information they describe.[34] Linked data brings meaning to data in two ways: through the ontology that defines types of entities and relationships between them, and through vocabularies that define what the entities are and mean. In the practical context of linked data, ontologies say what can be connected together in what ways through the assertion of classes and properties, and vocabularies declare instances of these classes: they define exactly who, where, or what is being referenced. Shared reference to the same vocabulary term allows data creators to identify the same entity as identified by other projects or creators.

Employing ontologies and vocabularies requires both precision about the relationships being represented and disambiguation of entities; this degree of specificity may not exist in the source dataset. In mobilizing existing datasets as linked open data, data creators and publishers must therefore think carefully about which ontologies and vocabularies to adopt, since they have the potential to introduce new meaning to the data through the relationships and definitions that they carry with them.

---

34. Geoffrey C. Bowker and Susan Leigh Star, *Sorting Things Out: Classification and Its Consequences* (Cambridge, MA: MIT Press, 1999); D'Ignazio and Klein, *Data Feminism*; Miriam Posner, "What's Next: The Radical, Unrealized Potential of Digital Humanities," in *Debates in the Digital Humanities 2016*, ed. Matthew K. Gold and Lauren Klein (Minneapolis: University of Minnesota Press, 2016), 32–41, https://dhdebates.gc.cuny.edu/read/untitled/section/a22aca14-0eb0-4cc6-a622-6fee9428a357#ch03; Erin Canning, et al., "The Power to Structure: Making Meaning from Metadata through Ontologies," *KULA: Knowledge Creation, Dissemination, and Preservation Studies* 6, no. 3 (2022):1-15. https://doi.org/10.18357/kula.169.

Selecting Ontologies: Policy- and Decision-Making

LINCS takes an approach to linked data development—namely, the adoption of ontologies and vocabularies for the transformation and representation of source data—that reflects the project's founding values. The first step of this work was to develop a policy that describes how LINCS project values can be put into practice when considering how to mobilize data as linked open data, in order to govern the project's approach to ontology selection and implementation.[35] A key part of the LINCS Ontologies Adoption & Development Policy (OADP) is a table of aspirational metrics and the structural problems they address—such as ableism, cissexism, classism, colonialism, heteronormativity, racism, and other forms of discrimination—inspired by a similar table in D'Ignazio and Klein's *Data Feminism*.[36] Creating this table of concerns and goals, as well as creating the policy document as a whole, provided an opportunity to think through approaches to issues that the project is likely to encounter.

The OADP was developed by the LINCS team with input from the LINCS researcher community, as represented by the Ontology Working Group, prior to evaluating ontology solutions. The Ontology Working Group is comprised of the LINCS Project Lead, Technical Chair, Ontology Systems Analyst, and researchers from across LINCS; it is bolstered by additional LINCS staff and domain experts as required. By developing the policy first, potential ontology solutions could be assessed through the lens of the values and criteria articulated in the policy document. The OADP is a living document that continues to be updated in order to reflect ongoing developments in LINCS.

LINCS requires ontology solutions capable of representing difference and diversity in data across the axes introduced by the participating researcher projects, including heterogeneous

---

35. Erin Canning et al, "LINCS Ontologies Adoption & Development Policy," https://doi.org/10.5281/zenodo.6047747.

36. D'Ignazio and Klein, *Data Feminism*, 218–19.

scholarly domains, historical difference, and the positionality of the researchers themselves and the theoretical perspectives foundational to their work. Working across a wide variety of datasets requires solutions flexible enough to accommodate such differences while still bringing data together within a shared information ecosystem by employing common classes and properties across domains, where appropriate. A single ontology would risk flattening the complexity of domain-specific data in an attempt at consistency and cohesion. Instead, LINCS adopted a core ontology to connect datasets, combined with the integration of domain-specific ontologies as required, in order to balance these needs of interoperability and domain specificity.

The OADP helps the project to evaluate possible solutions that meet these practical needs without compromising on project values.[37] Ultimately, LINCS decided to adopt the CIDOC Conceptual Reference Model (CRM) as a core ontology.[38] CIDOC CRM is a robust ontology for cultural heritage data, intended to work as "semantic glue" between diverse datasets within this wider domain and capable of expressing alternative viewpoints about an entity.[39] The CRM supports this range of data, as well as general extensibility, through its structure: the ontology is composed of generic classes and properties that can then be refined through the use of domain-specific vocabularies external to the ontology itself. This way, different vocabularies can be implemented according to the needs of the dataset without needing to adjust the ontology and without compromising on the interoperability afforded by shared use of CRM classes and properties. This solution met the need to support interoperability while adhering to project values articulated in the OADP including representing diversity and difference in the data.

---

37. For more on this see Erin Canning et al., "The Power to Structure: Making Meaning from Metadata through Ontologies."

38. Chryssoula Bekiari et al., "Definition of the CIDOC Conceptual Reference Model v7.1.1" (The CIDOC Conceptual Reference Model Special Interest Group, 2021), https://cidoc-crm.org/sites/default/files/cidoc_crm_v.7.1.1_0.pdf.

39. "CIDOC CRM," accessed January 11, 2022, https://cidoc-crm.org/.

In practice, adopting CIDOC CRM as a core ontology leaves space for domain-specific ontologies or extensions as required by specific datasets when the generic nature of the main CRM ontology is insufficient for addressing domain-specific classes of entities and the relationships between them. To select such ontologies, a literature review and evaluation of ontology options is conducted by the LINCS Ontology Systems Analysts and students working alongside them, and then debated and approved by the Ontology Working Group along with additional domain experts as required.[40] CIDOC CRM extensions exist for many related domains, but the LINCS team nevertheless seeks to consider all available options, weighing project-wide interoperability against the need to represent researcher perspectives as precisely as possible in keeping with project values. The LINCS Ontology Working Group has so far approved ontology extensions for four domains and will soon be debating a fifth.[41]

Because these decisions affect how data is mapped and converted according to these structures, decisions are made collaboratively with researchers through an iterative process of meetings, mappings, and feedback to ensure that researcher perspective is reflected in the ongoing ontology decision-making processes.

---

40. Students who have assisted with this work as of the date of publication include Devon Hayley Farrell, Samuel Peacock, and Thomas Smith.

41. The domains considered and ontology solutions approved are as follows: Annotations and reference statements (approved: Web Annotation Data Model); Prosopographical, relationship, and social role data (approved: CRM property classes); Bibliographic and library data (approved: FRBRoo); Ontologies for Performance, Music, and Intangible Cultural Heritage Data (approved: FRBRoo and further extension DoReMus); Ontologies for Geospatial Data (proposed: CRMgeo). For a discussion of the reconciliation of the Web Annotation Data Model and CIDOC CRM, see Erin Canning et al., "The Power to Structure: Making Meaning from Metadata through Ontologies.

Selecting and Implementing Linked Data Vocabularies

The selection and implementation of linked open data vocabularies is also done in close collaboration with project researchers.
Here, too, the LINCS project seeks to balance specificity and
interoperability, this time at the level of project in addition to
domain: CIDOC CRM allows for interoperability on the level of
structure while letting terminology be chosen by researchers, but
a greater degree of interoperability between datasets in LINCS, as
well as with external resources, is possible with alignment at the
level of vocabulary as well as ontology. Supporting researchers
in adopting linked data vocabularies whose definitions and structures align with their perspectives is crucial to replatforming data
ethically.[42]

Vocabularies provide precise identifiers and can define terms
through descriptions of meaning or their location within a controlled vocabulary structure. After all, linked data vocabularies
are themselves linked data, and ideally a vocabulary's structure
brings further meaning to terms beyond narrative description.
Furthermore, different vocabularies can use the same word for
a term but then define that concept differently. For example, the
term "woman" or "women" is defined differently in four linked
data vocabularies:

1. Getty Art & Architecture Thesaurus: "Refers to female
   human beings from young adulthood through old age."[43]
2. Homosaurus: "Adults who self-identify as women and
   understand their gender in terms of Western conceptions
   of womanness, femaleness, and/or femininity. The term
   has typically been defined as adult female humans, though

---

42. Brown, "Categorically Provisional."
43. "Women (Female Humans)," Getty Art and Architecture Thesaurus, Getty Research Institute, n.d., accessed January 11, 2022, http://vocab.getty.edu/page/
aat/300025943.

not all women identify with the term 'female' depending on the context in which it is used."[44]

3. The CWRC Ontology: "Indicates a subject identification with or labeling as the gender woman; often but not necessarily understood to be sexed female. 'One is not born, but rather becomes, woman.' (Simone de Beauvoir, 1973) Where terms associated with this label are applied to younger individuals, 'girl' is understood to apply for 'woman'."[45]

4. Wikidata: "Female adult human."[46]

Additionally, each vocabulary places the term in a different part of their structure. For Homosaurus and the CWRC Ontology, it is a term within concepts of "gender": it is within the schema of "Gender identity" in Homosaurus and within the schema of "Gender" in the CWRC Ontology. For Wikidata, it is instead a term within the concept of "people": here, it is a subclass of "Adult," "Person," and "Female Human," which is itself a subclass of "Person." Furthermore, Wikidata declares "Woman" is the opposite of (P461) "Man," and cites passage Genesis 2:18 of the Bible as the reference for this assertion.[47] Getty AAT sits between these two approaches to classification—gender or persons—positioning it within the schema of "People by gender or sex." It is key to also understand these groupings and classifications to see how the term is defined and used in the context of a chosen vocabulary. Although these four vocabularies use the same term, their narrative and structural definitions vary, and one of these options may be more appropriate than the others, depending on the intended meaning and wider context.

---

44. "Women," Homosaurus, accessed January 11, 2022, https://homosaurus.org/v3/homoit0001509.

45. "Woman," The CWRC Ontology Specification, Canadian Writing Research Collaboratory, 2022, accessed January 11, 2022, https://sparql.cwrc.ca/ontologies/cwrc.html#woman.

46. "Woman," Wikidata, accessed January 11, 2022, https://www.wikidata.org/wiki/Q467.

47. Gen. 2:18 "Then God said: 'It is not good for the man to be alone. I will make a helper suitable for him.'"

The selection of ontologies and vocabularies shapes the representation of researcher data and so must be grounded in a clear articulation of project values, and undertaken in collaboration with the researcher community and researchers themselves. These relationships permeate project activities and are formalized through data publication agreements.

Developing and Implementing Data Agreements

Replatforming takes place within a larger ecosystem. LINCS is part of a web of data producers, holders, and users, all subject to institutional and jurisdictional obligations. The LINCS Data Publication License (DPL) Agreement delineates the rights and responsibilities of both data contributors and the project.[48] The DPL explains the obligations by which LINCS as a project is bound: those set down by sponsoring universities; by the laws of Canada and the province of Ontario; and by a network of other contracts, legal and goodwill agreements, and funding and partner commitments.[49]

As a legal agreement, the DPL struggles to capture the spirit of collaboration at the project's core. This tension is part of a broader pattern between "institutional requirements [and] researchers' experiences and motivations" across projects that work with research data.[50] In response, the LINCS core team strives to foster mutual understanding. The body of the agreement has two columns: the left one states *principles* in accessible

48. Susan Brown et al., LINCS Data Publication License Agreement, https://doi.org/10.5281/zenodo.6229544.

49. As a CFI-funded project, LINCS is contractually obliged to conform to various regulatory requirements and applicable laws, including the Tri-Council Policy Statements on Ethical Conduct for Research Involving Humans and Privacy and Confidentiality. For more information. See the "Program and Policy Guide" (Canadian Foundation for Innovation, 2019), https://www.innovation.ca/sites/default/files/file_uploads/guide_patch_2019_en.pdf.

50. Urszula Pawlicka-Deger, "Digital Humanities and a New Research Culture: Between Promoting and Practicing Open Research Data," in *Access and Control in Digital Humanities* (London: Routledge, 2021), 40–57.

language, while the right one lists the *provisions* in legalese. In this way, the DPL foregrounds a commitment to linked data that is "more readily available, shareable, searchable, and reusable by other researchers and the larger public" and that "adhere[s] to ethical guidelines about data collection and information sharing," while still making clear the legal relationship between researchers and the project.[51]

The LINCS team did not develop policies *ex nihilo*, but rather built on policies of related projects by which we are inspired.[52] In crediting these agreements, the DPL highlights the larger network of scholarly and GLAM communities and the ways in which LINCS data interconnects with, will be reused as part of, and therefore must also align (where possible) with the terms set by other projects. The DPL was collaboratively developed by the LINCS technical and research teams, with advice from researchers. From this collaboration emerged the project's recommended approach to licensing data, which encourages contributors to acknowledge the work of data creators and data stewards and to facilitate broad reuse of data, but also recognizes that in some cases widespread circulation is inappropriate and access must be respectfully limited.

Credit for Data Creators and Data Stewards

All too often, the labour that underpins the digital humanities is undervalued or disregarded.[53] The DPL invites contributors

---

51. Susan Brown et al., "LINCS Data Contribution License Agreement."

52. The data contribution licensing agreement is built on the Interdisciplinary Project Charter template by Stan Ruecker and Milena Radzikowska, the DANS (Data Archiving and Networked Services) License Agreement Version 3.2, the DARIAH (Digital Research Infrastructure for the Arts and Humanities) Model Deposit License Version 1.0, and the CWRC (Canadian Writing Research Collaboratory) Data Donation License Agreement Version 1.0.

53. Bethany Nowviskie, "Where Credit Is Due: Preconditions for the Evaluation of Collaborative Digital Scholarship," *Profession*, 2011, 169–81; Tarez Samra Graban, et al., "Introduction: Questioning Collaboration, Labor, and Visibility in Digital Humanities Research," *Digital Humanities Quarterly* 13, no. 2 (August 1, 2019).

to publish their data using a Creative Commons Attribution 4.0 (CC-BY) license.[54] CC-BY is an established way to acknowledge those who produce and maintain the data. It enables LINCS to promote an ethical framing of datasets that extends beyond data ownership to recognize those who create, remediate, and sustain them.[55] For LINCS datasets, this means attributing credit in standardized, machine-readable form to those who helped produce the linked dataset in addition to those who created the source data.

The choice of CC-BY is possible because the project is based in—and operating under the laws of—Canada, where metadata compiled for a researcher's own dataset is subject to copyright.[56] The DPL is based on the understanding that all LINCS data, whether object description or data representing content, qualifies as metadata in this context. Canadian copyright may not be enforceable across borders, but control of the data is not the motivation for this provision: the LINCS community both within and beyond Canada additionally benefits from "community norms [which] act as guidelines without the mandate of compliance," and which encourage good faith practices from data users more broadly.[57] Claiming copyright—even if not universally applicable—is a meaningful way to foreground the work of project contributors and to encourage others to subsequently do the same.[58]

---

54. "CC BY 4.0," Creative Commons, n.d., https://creativecommons.org/licenses/by/4.0/.

55. See principle 23 of the "Feminist Data Manifest-No," which calls for a refusal of "data empires [built] on the backs of precarious workers and hidden labour" and asks for a commitment "to working against the exploitation of labour and precarity in all of its forms." Cifor et al., "Feminist Data Manifest-No."

56. CCH Canada Ltd. v. Law Society of Upper Canada (2004) is a landmark, unanimous Supreme Court of Canada judgment that (among other things) established copyright for metadata, https://decisions.scc-csc.ca/scc-csc/scc-csc/en/item/2125/index.do.

57. Krista L. Cox, "Metadata and Copyright: Should Institutions License Their Data about Scholarship?" *Copyright, Fair Use, Scholarly Communication* 59, (2017), http://digitalcommons.unl.edu/scholcom/59.

58. In the European Union databases are subject to sui generis rights, as per Directive 96/9/EC. https://eur-lex.europa.eu/LexUriServ/LexUriServ.do?uri=CELEX-:31996L0009:EN:HTML.

Facilitating Broad Data Use

Notably absent from LINCS's license choice is a non-commercial (NC) restriction, such as in CC-BY-NC.[59] For the GLAM community (which LINCS works to serve), restricting commercial use is problematic: research may be non-commercial, but publications and exhibitions often are not.[60] What counts as non-commercial varies between Europe and North America. Although permitting commercial uses risks the (unlikely) exploitation of LINCS data, it also facilitates more-likely para-commercial uses. Bethany Nowviskie articulates the benefits of allowing commercial use as part of the scholarly and cultural ecosystem:

> Limiting my default scope to non-commercial ventures seems presumptuous and naïve. Current presses and projects I admire are struggling, and if any of my content, bundled in some form that can support its own production by charging a fee, helps humanities publishers to experiment with new ways forward—well, that's precisely why I CC-licensed it in the first place .... any little road bump on the path to permission will virtually assure my content not be republished.[61]

Opening LINCS data to commercial reuse broadens its potential reach, particularly within GLAM communities and for scholarly engagement and knowledge mobilization.

Respectful Limits on Openness

A desire to promote reuse and interoperability informs the project's recommendations for openly licensed data. However, certain datasets will require divergence from the recommended policies.

---

59. "CC BY-NC 4.0."

60. For more information, see Paul Kimpel, "Free Knowledge Thanks to Creative Commons Licenses: Why a Non-Commercial Clause Often Won't Serve Your Needs," 2012, https://upload.wikimedia.org/wikipedia/commons/c/c7/Free_Knowledge_thanks_to_Creative_Commons_Licenses.pdf; and "Non-Commercial Interpretation," Creative Commons Wiki, n.d., https://wiki.creativecommons.org/wiki/NonCommercial_interpretation.

61. Bethany Nowviskie, "Why, Oh Why, CC-BY?" Bethany Nowviskie (blog), 2011, http://nowviskie.org/2011/why-oh-why-cc-by/.

Some data owners will want to relinquish all control, and others will want to restrict their data from broader circulation, either temporarily or permanently. Not all data should be freely available to all people.

Warranting specific attention are datasets associated with Indigenous knowledges. Respectful work with this data requires awareness of the historical and ongoing misuse and appropriation of Indigenous and traditional data, and the many ways in which openness and reuse are unsuitable to some ways of knowing.[62] The LINCS team must therefore be deliberate and listen with care to Indigenous researchers and communities about how such data is structured and replatformed, being vigilant about the downstream implications of choices made.[63]

Consultations with project partners, Indigenous researchers, and researchers working with Indigenous communities and resources, including extensive input from Stacy Allison-Cassin and Sharon Farnel, shaped the DPL's acknowledgement that there is no pan-Indigenous approach for respectfully working with data related to Indigenous peoples and their information, language, people, culture, identity, knowledge, and Traditional Knowledge, whether provided by Indigenous knowledge holders or other contributors.[64] The DPL asserts the project's commitment to the

---

62. For an in-depth discussion, see Kimberly Christen, "Does Information Really Want to Be Free? Indigenous Knowledge Systems and the Question of Openness," *International Journal of Communication* 6 (2012): 2871–93.

63. A suitable data publication license is only one step in the process of working ethically with Indigenous data in a way that is "culturally sensitive, ethically valid and relevant to [Indigenous] communities"; a thoughtful, open approach must imbue the project from conceptualization to data ingestion, from interface development to researcher engagement. For an example of this, see Coppélie Cocq, "Revisiting the Digital Humanities through the Lens of Indigenous Studies—or How to Question the Cultural Blindness of Our Technologies and Practices," *Journal of the Association for Information Science and Technology* 73, no. 2 (2021), 333-34.

64. Dr. Stacy Allison-Cassin is a Citizen of the Métis Nation of Ontario; an Assistant Professor at the School of Information Management at Dalhousie University; and a researcher who works on knowledge organization, metadata, and knowledge equity. Dr. Sharon Farnel is the Head of Metadata Strategies, University of Alberta Library; a researcher working with Indigenous communities to develop accurate, respectful descriptive standards and practices; and a contributor to the First Nations, Métis, and Inuit Indigenous Ontology.

CARE Principles and to principles of self-determination and data sovereignty;[65] to facilitate Indigenous work with Indigenous and traditional data that specifically benefits Indigenous Peoples; and to the rights of Indigenous Peoples to control access to and govern the use of their data.

The DPL is intentionally broad because there is no single correct approach to working with data. Like the OADP, it affirms the team's aspirations to address with care and respect the needs of the individuals and communities with whose data LINCS is entrusted. The project's data agreements are part of an iterative, reflective process that must remain open to modification to meet the specific needs of data contributors and those impacted by the data's replatforming.

Conclusion

Documentation and agreements are key to communicating amongst the LINCS team and researchers the ethical reasoning underlying principles, decisions, and processes. As is typical with digital humanities projects, LINCS governance, ontology and vocabulary, data publication, and other policies[66] are embedded in living documents that will be iterated as new cases arise and conditions change. Because the ethical responsibilities for LINCS data are shared by researchers and the LINCS project team, there will necessarily be ongoing dialogue about linked data-specific ethical considerations and their relationship to matters such as accuracy, data privacy, academic freedom, academic responsibility, and the communities, including Indigenous ones,

---

65. "CARE Principles of Indigenous Data Governance," Global Indigenous Data Alliance, accessed January 11, 2022, https://www.gida-global.org/care.

66. Stan Ruecker and Milena Radzikowska, "The Iterative Design of a Project Charter for Interdisciplinary Research," in *Proceedings of the 7th ACM Conference on Designing Interactive Systems, DIS '08* (New York: Association for Computing Machinery, 2008), 288–94, https://doi.org/10.1145/1394445.1394476; Bethany Nowviskie, "Charter-Ing a Path," Bethany Nowviskie (blog), November 21, 2014, https://nowviskie.org/2014/charter-ing-a-path/.

connected to the data. Not all source data will be open, and some linked data may not be fully shared. Although space constraints here preclude discussion of the ethics of interfaces, these too require transparency. Interfaces can leverage metadata elements, such as the Traditional Knowledge Labels developed by the Local Contexts hub founded by Jane Anderson and Kim Christen,[67] to support culturally sensitive data sharing, support Indigenous data sovereignty, and raise awareness of the ethics of data publication.

Decisions regarding specific LINCS datasets will be recorded and communicated in multiple forms: through an application profile[68] aimed at a technical audience; dataset documentation and agreements aimed at researchers; and openly available dataset metadata. This metadata will combine machine-readable data with narratives to represent conditions of production such as provenance, context, and contributors, including students, as well as other properties of datasets. Policies and practices for LINCS-born contributions will need to be developed in consultation with researchers from that portion of our community of practice as it becomes active: data born within LINCS will at a minimum be linked to the user profiles of creators, and those profiles could be expanded to permit articulation of research principles, preferred vocabularies, and the like.

Going forward, as it reaches maturity, LINCS will increasingly house a broader range of data: researchers' enhancements and refinements of initial datasets; new datasets converted and ingested with less intervention by and support from LINCS team members; datasets related to institutional partners' collections; and born-digital datasets newly created using LINCS interfaces rather than the conversion workflows. The range of use cases and routes towards creating data, let alone the shared responsibilities in a situation in which researchers must take primary

---

67. "Traditional Knowledge Labels," Local Contexts, n.d., https://localcontexts.org/labels/traditional-knowledge-labels/.

68. Rob Atkinson et al., "Profile Guidance," W3C, April 4, 2022, https://w3c.github.io/dxwg/profiles/.

responsibility for ensuring that their research meets ethics standards, makes creating an ethical framework for LINCS complex and multi-faceted. The process has been, and will continue to be, iterative.

The LINCS project and the ongoing work described here contribute to a larger conversation about important matters at the intersection of linked open data infrastructure and ethics. As a community of practice that is not aligned with any single institution, but allied with stakeholders with a range of interests, LINCS is situated to push back against the presumptions of methodological individualism that makes ethics a personal rather than a corporate or collective responsibility, towards what Mark Fisher has articulated as "the idea of a public space that is not reducible to an aggregation of individuals and their interests."[69] Infrastructures such as LINCS can help to advance the continuing conversation among researchers, communities, and institutions about the ethics of linked open data.

---

69. Mark Fisher, *Capitalist Realism: Is There No Alternative?* (Hants, UK: 0 Books, 2009), 77.

Ethical Expressions of Collective Memory: Re/presenting Central Brooklyn Jazz Oral Histories as Linked Data

ZAKIYA COLLIER & SARAH ANN ADAMS

Introduction

> It is hardly surprising that Manhattan's jazz history has overshadowed that of Brooklyn, for the latter borough had nothing like the organized entertainment industry that took root on Broadway or 52nd Street. But just ask those who lived in Brooklyn during those glory days—most notably pianist, composer and bandleader Randy Weston—and you will get an earful: not just about the clubs, though there were many, but about community, about a social network that existed among jazz musicians of which most historians are completely unaware.[70]

There is power in naming and in representation—power to oppress, empower, claim, and reclaim. Too often, traditional archival description fails to account for this power. In projects that aim to uncover and semantically represent both names and relationships from Central Brooklyn jazz history, it is difficult to ignore that power. Linking Lost Jazz Shrines (LLJS) is one such project.

---

70. Jeffrey Taylor, "Across the East River: Searching for Brooklyn's Jazz History," *American Music Review* 38, no. 2 (Spring, 2009): 6–7.

LLJS is a collaborative project between the Weeksville Heritage Center (WHC)[71] and the Semantic Lab at Pratt[72] to create linked open data from the Weeksville Lost Jazz Shrines of Brooklyn (WLJSB) oral history collection,[73] which documents Central Brooklyn's cultural legacy of jazz between the 1930s and the 1960s.[74] LLJS aims to expand the discoverability and accessibility of WLJSB by adding the influential, yet underrepresented Black people, music groups, organizations, and music venues from the oral history collection to the existing network of jazz musicians from the Semantic Lab's Linked Jazz Project.[75]

This chapter opens with a literature review that examines how provenance, hierarchy, and the privileging of published works exclude Black people and culture from archival description and, ultimately, the historical record. The following section is an introduction to LLJS and the two intersecting projects from which this project emerged: the WLJSB oral history collection and Linked Jazz. Then, using LLJS as a case study, the chapter explores the implementation of ethical, inclusive, and culturally relevant name authority creation and ontological data modeling in order to holistically represent a complex jazz community in a semantic digital environment. The chapter concludes with a discussion of the ramifications of the ethical decision-making

71. "WHAT WE DO," Weeksville Heritage Center, accessed January 5, 2022, https://www.weeksvillesociety.org/our-vision-what-we-do.

72. "Semantic Lab," Semantic Lab at Pratt, accessed January 5, 2022, http://semlab.io.

73. Linking Lost Jazz Shrines began in 2019, funded as part of Cohort 1 of Collections as Data: Part to Whole (https://collectionsasdata.github.io/part2whole/cohortone/). Additional funding was secured in February 2021 through the Metropolitan New York Library Council (METRO) Equity in Action grant (https://metro.org/grants/equity-in-action/recipients).

74. Weeksville Heritage Center, "The Weeksville Lost Jazz Shrines of Brooklyn Collection (WLJSB)," finding aid, 2015, http://bit.ly/FindingAidWLJSB. WLJSB finding aid prepared by Alexsandra Mitchell (2012) and Deidre Dinniga (2013), Research Interns. Edited by Ardra Whitney (2012) and Joyce LeeAnn Joseph (2012-13), Project Archivists. Revised by Megan Goins-Diouf, Resource Center Manager & Reference Archivist in 2014-15.

75. "Linked Jazz," Linked Jazz, accessed January 5, 2022, https://linkedjazz.org/.

processes implemented throughout this project, and future considerations for the project team.

As project collaborators, the authors acknowledge the privilege and power in the ability to create linked data for this project: to name, shift narratives, and easily assert and represent multiple perspectives and truths as they are expressed in WLJSB. Although the project is decentralized in the sense that "proposals don't have to make their way through months or years of review or contend with entrenched practice,"[76] there are primarily only two people—the authors—interpreting the text of the oral histories and identifying key entities and relationships. Moreover, we are not jazz historians, Central Brooklyn jazz community members, WLJSB interviewers, or WLJSB interviewees, and only one of us identifies as Black. Following Tonia Sutherland's powerful declaration that "it matters who does this work,"[77] we intentionally worked to foreground ethics and care, maintaining awareness of our positionality as outsiders, discarding the notion of neutrality and objectivity, and relying on the strength of collaboration to ensure ethical linked data creation.

Literature Review

Scholarship and professional guidelines in the archival and library science profession increasingly critique the myth of neutrality, the impact of whiteness on the profession, our practices—and consequently—our collections, the prioritization of narratives that reinforce white supremacy, and the numerous absences and erasures of the histories of communities of color in mainstream archives and libraries.[78] These critiques have resulted in initiatives

---

76. Ruth Kitchin Tillman, "Barriers to Ethical Name Modeling in Current Linked Data Encoding Practices," in *Ethical Questions in Name Authority Control*, ed. Jane Sandberg, 243–59 (Sacramento, CA: Library Juice Press, 2019), 243.

77. Sutherland, "It Matters Who Does This Work," *Journal of Critical Digital Librarianship* 1, no. 1, (Fall 2021): 5-14, https://digitalcommons.lsu.edu/jcdl/vol1/iss1/2/.

78. See for example: Tonia Sutherland. "Archival Amnesty: In Search of Black

to diversify the profession, efforts to expand collections through collaboration with communities and community archives, implementations of ethics of care or empathy in archival practice, and the creation of diversity statements in core values and codes of ethics for professional organizations. Additional outcomes of these critiques include new best practices for redescription and reclassification, and the prioritization of digitization projects that center historically excluded and intentionally marginalized communities.[79]

American Transitional and Restorative Justice." *Journal of Critical Library and Information Studies* 2 (2017); Michelle Caswell, "Owning Critical Archival Studies: A Plea," Archival Education and Research Institute, July 2016; "'Graveyards of Exclusion:' Archives, Prisons, and the Bounds of Belonging," Sustainable Futures (blog), March 24, 2019. https://medium.com/community-archives/graveyards-of-exclusion-archives-prisons-and-the-bounds-of-belonging-c40c85ff1663; Michelle Caswell, Ricardo Punzalan, and T-Kay Sangwand, "Critical Archival Studies: An Introduction." *Journal of Critical Library and Information Studies* 1, no. 2 (June 27, 2018): 1–8; Bergis Jules, "Confronting Our Failure of Care Around the Legacies of Marginalized People in the Archives," OnArchivy (blog), November 11, 2016. https://medium.com/on-archivy/confronting-our-failure-of-care-around-the-legacies-of-marginalized-people-in-the-archives-dc4180397280; Anthony W. Dunbar, "Introducing Critical Race Theory to Archival Discourse: Getting the Conversation Started," *Archival Science* 6, no. 1 (2006): 109–129; April Hathcock, "White Librarianship in Blackface: Diversity Initiatives in LIS," In the Library with the Lead Pipe, October 2015, http://www.inthelibrarywiththeleadpipe.org/2015/lis-diversity.

79. See for example: Michelle L. Caswell and Marika Cifor. "From Human Rights to Feminist Ethics: Radical Empathy in Archives," *Archivaria* 81 (2016): 23-43. https://muse.jhu.edu/article/687705; Dorothy Berry, "Centering The Margins in Digital Project Planning," Special Issue, *Journal of Critical Digital Librarianship* 1, no. 1 (Fall 2021): 15-22; Tonia Sutherland, "Redescription as Restorative Justice," November 19, 2020, Louisiana Library as Data Online Speaker Series, YouTube, 1:02:56, https://louisianadigitallibrary.org/LDLasData/speaker-series; Lae'l Hughes-Watkins, "Moving Toward a Reparative Archive: A Roadmap for a Holistic Approach to Disrupting Homogenous Histories in Academic Repositories and Creating Inclusive Spaces for Marginalized Voices," *Journal of Contemporary Archival Studies* 5, no. 6 (2018): 1–17, Jarrett M. Drake, "RadTech Meets RadArch: Towards A New Principle for Archives and Archival Description," OnArchivy (blog), April 6, 2016. https://medium.com/on-archivy/radtech-meets-radarch-towards-a-new-principle-for-archives-and-archival-description-568f133e4325; Archives for Black Lives in Philadelphia Working Group, "Archives for Black Lives in Philadelphia Anti-Racist Description Resources," Archives for Black Lives in Philadelphia, (October 2019), https://archivesforblacklives.files.wordpress.com/2020/11/ardr_202010.pdf, Emily Drabinski, "Queering the Catalog: Queer Theory and the Politics of Correction," *The Library Quarterly: Information,*

Despite these increasing efforts to address and redress the impacts of whiteness in the profession, Archives for Black Lives in Philadelphia (A4BLiP), an association of Philadelphia area archivists focused on combating racism in archives, has noted that name authorities are still rarely addressed as an issue of equity and inclusion in archival work. In a chapter underscoring the power of names and name authorities in archival description, Antracoli and Rawdon of A4BLiP write, "the lack of name description and name authority work for Black people represented in archival collections hampers research access, creates false silences by obscuring the names—and by extension, the existences—of Black people, and ultimately leads to the ongoing erasure and dehumanization of Black lives in our society's cultural memory and conscience."[80]

As highlighted by Antracoli and Rawdon, archival principles, standards, and systems themselves erase Black people from archival description.[81] In particular, they discuss the archival

---

Community, Policy 83, no. 2 (2013): 94–111. https://doi.org/10.1086/669547; Michelle Caswell, Marika Cifor, and Mario H. Ramirez, "'To Suddenly Discover Yourself Existing': Uncovering the Impact of Community Archives," *The American Archivist* 79, no. 1 (June 1, 2016): 56–81. https://doi.org/10.17723/0360-9081.79.1.56; Stacie M. Williams and Jarrett M. Drake, "Power to the People: Documenting Police Violence in Cleveland," *Journal of Critical Library and Information Studies* 1, no. 2 (2017):1-27.

80. Alexis A. Antracoli and Katy Rawdon, "What's in a Name? Archives for Black Lives in Philadelphia and the Impact of Names and Name Authorities in Archival Description," in *Ethical Questions in Name Authority Control*, ed. Jane Sandberg (Sacramento, CA: Library Juice Press, 2019), 308.

81. The authors name several factors contributing to the lack of name authority control in archival description and the exclusion of Black names from 'the record,' which can have grave and necropolitical consequences. (See: Bergis Jules, "Confronting Our Failure of Care Around the Legacies of Marginalized People in the Archives," OnArchivy (blog), Medium, November 11, 2016, https://medium.com/on-archivy/confronting-our-failure-of-care-around-the-legacies-of-marginalized-people-in-the-archives-dc4180397280 and Achille Mbembe, *Necropolitics* (Durham, NC: Duke University Press, 2019). "Insufficient name information in archival collections; lack of established names in national authority databases for those found within a collection; lack of training or ability among archivists to establish name authority records; and the privileging of certain creators and subjects by processing archivists because of archival practice or their own personal biases" (Antracoli and Rawdon, "What's in a Name?," 308.), amongst other factors, obscures the reality of Black experiences, bolsters the violence of erasure, and centers whiteness.

principle of provenance, which "dictates that records of different origins (provenance) be kept separate to preserve their context."[82] Antracoli and Rawdon illuminate Jarrett Drake's critique of provenance, remarking, "the provenance and context of records supplies much of their meaning, however, the concept of records-source-as-creator—who gets to be a collection creator/collector/main entry—determines whose names are deemed most important."[83] As it relates to Black life in archival records and description, Drake himself asks, "to the disenfranchised, marginalized, and colonized, what is the idea of provenance? For one who legally cannot own her body, what does it mean to own records?"[84] When Black people and other groups who've borne the brunt of colonization are often not the authors of their own "official" records, the privileging of collection creators and collectors is, de facto, a privileging of normative whiteness. Even when included in archival records, Black people may not be included in the description of those records, or may only be included non-prominently further down in a finding aid. This hampers access, as archival description is hierarchical in nature, with those deemed important commonly appearing first or exclusively.[85]

Beyond privileging the names of collection creators and collectors, name authority systems such as the Library of Congress Name Authority File (LCNAF) prioritize authors and subjects of published works, which is inherently influenced by the biases of the publishing industry and those who have the means to produce published works.[86] The primary U.S. archival description stan-

82. Dictionary of Archives Terminology, s.v. "provenance," accessed January 15, 2022, https://dictionary.archivists.org/entry/provenance.html.

83. Antracoli and Rawdon, "What's in a Name?", 316.

84. Jarrett Drake, "RadTech Meets RadArch: Towards A New Principle for Archives and Archival Description," OnArchivy (blog), Medium, April 6, 2016, https://medium.com/on-archivy/radtech-meets-radarch-towards-a-new-principle-for-archives-and-archival-description-568f133e4325.

85. Antracoli and Rawdon, "What's in a Name?", 316.

86. See, for example, Molly Higgins and Rachel Keiko Stark, "Mitigating Implicit Bias," *American Libraries Magazine*, January 4, 2021, https://americanlibrariesmagazine.org/2021/01/04/mitigating-implicit-bias/ on the ways biases in the publishing industry affect libraries.

dard, Describing Archives: A Content Standard (DACS), includes a section on archival authority records, which "identifies and describes a personal, family, or corporate entity associated with a body of archival materials; documents relationships between records creators, the records created by them, and/or other resources about them; and may control the creation and use of access points in archival descriptions."[87] While many record and collection creators may also be the authors or subjects of published works, that is not always the case. Exclusion from name authority systems decreases the visibility and discoverability of certain communities and their experiences in archival records.

Antracoli and Rawdon go on to list A4BLiP's collaboratively developed best practices for naming and the use of name authorities as it relates to Black people, including, but not limited to: approaching naming as an affirmation of humanity, revisiting legacy description to provide better name access, acknowledging the limits of provenance, and providing better archival description for oppressed or marginalized collection subjects.[88] Naming is an affirmation of humanity as well as a rejection of the narratives that erase or invisibilize the participation, contributions, and lived experiences of Black people. Yusef Omowale, Director of the Southern California Library for Social Studies and Research, writes, "We must refuse the rules of inclusion, and vocabularies of recognition and legitimacy that are meant to contain our histories. We should not echo articulations that we do not already exist in the archive. We are not marginal or other to the archive, but integral to it. We may be silenced or made invisible, but we have always been present."[89] Naming Black people—in spite of archival description's insistence on provenance, hierarchy, and/

---

87. Describing Archives: A Content Standard - DACS 2019.0.3 (Chicago: Society of American Archivists, 2020), 85.

88. Antracoli and Rawdon, "What's in a Name?", 327-328.

89. Yusef Omowale, "We Already Are," Sustainable Futures (blog), Medium, September 3, 2018, https://medium.com/community-archives/we-already-are-52438b863e31.

or published status—is key to refusing the rules that uphold the structures in a world where Black people were, as Audre Lorde writes, "never meant to survive."[90]

Project Description and Context

Weeksville Lost Jazz Shrines of Brooklyn Collection (WLJSB)

Linking Lost Jazz Shrines is foregrounded by its two project predecessors: the WLJSB oral history collection and Linked Jazz. The WLJSB oral history collection emerged from a 2008 Weeksville Heritage Center (WHC) research proposal to document Central Brooklyn's cultural legacy of jazz between the 1930s and 1960s. WHC is a Central Brooklyn-based historic site and cultural center that preserves, documents, and activates the history of Weeksville—one of the largest free Black communities in pre-Civil War America—and its historic Hunterfly Road Houses.[91] The goal of the place-based WLJSB oral history collection was to extend and localize An Arts Center 651's earlier *Lost Jazz Shrines* project by recording the music venues—the "lost jazz shrines"—in Central Brooklyn that served as hubs for the cultural legacy of jazz.[92] WLJSB documented Central Brooklyn's underrepresented yet unique and rich African-American jazz culture

---

90. Audre Lorde, *The Black Unicorn: Poems by Audre Lorde* (New York: W.W. Norton & Company, Inc., 1978), 31-32.

91. Weeksville Heritage Center, "WHAT WE DO."

92. David Earl Jackson, Mikki Shepard, and An Arts Center 651, *Lost Jazz Shrines* (Brooklyn, N.Y.: 651, An Arts Center, 1998). In 1998, as an effort of 651 Arts, Mikki Shepard created the "Lost Jazz Shrines" Project, a coalition of performing arts centers around the country partnering to research and showcase strong jazz histories and talents of "forgotten" places, which culminated in a book co-authored by Mikki Shepard and David Earl Jackson. The book commemorates great venues that were important to the development of jazz around the country. Unique cities that were a part of the development of jazz included: Newark, Kansas City, San Antonio, Cleveland, Indianapolis, Philadelphia, Washington DC, and Brooklyn. Building on the legacy of Mikki Shepard's "Lost Jazz Shrines" Project, Weeksville's Lost Jazz Shrines of Brooklyn Oral History Project collaborated with advisors and community members to collect oral histories, identify historically Black jazz venues and their former sites in the built landscape, and conduct preliminary archival searches for valuable Brooklyn jazz-related materials—from early interviews to photographs to musical recordings.

through exploring the "key musicians, institutions, organizations, venues, and supporters" of Brooklyn's historic jazz scene.[93] As described by Jennifer Scott, WHC Research Director at the time:

> WHC's objective is to create a Brooklyn jazz history and culture archive at Weeksville by documenting "lost" jazz music venues in the local area. Some of these are still standing, although have ceased to operate as performance spaces, and others no longer physically exist. The collection maps out not only the physical locations of these "lost shrines" but also their cultural histories: What happened at these places? Who performed there? Who frequented them? What did they mean to people? How did Brooklyn residents experience them? What do they remember most about them? Who did these places bring together? What was their relationship with other local (e.g., Harlem), regional and national jazz scenes and various jazz communities? How did these communities interact? How did they differ? How was the Central Brooklyn area referenced in the jazz music created in New York? What was the impact of jazz in Brooklyn on the area, New York City, and beyond? How is Brooklyn remembered through jazz? To what extent were women involved in this history? How did Brooklyn jazz build and sustain the local community?[94]

The WLJSB collection consists of 29 oral history interviews collected between 2007-2011 of instrumentalists, vocalists, community members, music venue proprietors, magazine publishers, photographers, and additional figures of the Central Brooklyn jazz scene at the time. Twelve of the oral histories currently appear as item records on WHC's 5th of July Omeka Classic site.[95] Each Omeka item includes one or more audio clips, metadata fields for eight of the core Dublin Core elements, and metadata fields for six WLJSB-specific elements (interviewer, location, duration, collection, tags, and citation).[96]

---

93. Weeksville Heritage Center, "The Weeksville Lost Jazz Shrines of Brooklyn Collection (WLJSB)."

94. Jennifer Scott, "Weeksville Lost Jazz Shrines of Brooklyn: Project Overview," Weeksville Heritage Center, (2008).

95. "Lost Jazz Shrines," 5th of July Resource Center for Self-Determination & Freedom, Weeksville Heritage Center, accessed January 12, 2022, https://5thofjuly.org/oralhistory/lostjazzshrines.

96. Ibid. Within this Omeka Classic presentation of WLJSB, "tags" function as subjects that might be found in a catalog record or finding aid.

Linked Jazz

The second project underpinning LLJS is Linked Jazz, a research project started in 2014 that continues to operate under the Semantic Lab at Pratt, "investigating the application of Linked Open Data tools and methodologies to cultural heritage materials, focusing on the personal and professional lives of jazz artists."[97] The source material for Linked Jazz is over 50 transcribed oral histories from digital jazz archives,[98] and the project resulted in RDF data of more than 2,000 people in the jazz community and their relationships to one another.[99] Throughout the project life-cycle, the Linked Jazz applied ontology expanded, incoporating six pre-existing predicates and minting seven new predicates of its own.[100] The resultant RDF data was originally available through a SPARQL endpoint, but the legacy data of the project is currently accessible on the Linked Jazz website[101] and can be explored through the Linked Jazz Network Visualization.[102] When the Semantic Lab at Pratt was founded in May 2018, the legacy Linked Jazz dataset was migrated to the Semantic Lab's instance of Wikibase.[103] In addition to supporting other linked data

97. "Revealing the Relationships of the Jazz Community," Linked Jazz, accessed January 10, 2022, https://linkedjazz.org/.

98. "Data Sources," Linked Jazz, accessed January 10, 2022, https://linkedjazz.org/?page_id=899.

99. Linked Jazz, "Get all people in triple format," accessed January 12, 2022, https://linkedjazz.org/api/people/all/nt.

100. Semantic Lab at Pratt, Linked Jazz Applied Ontology (1.0), (2020), https://doi.org/10.5281/zenodo.3687248. The existing predicates incorporated into the Linked Jazz applied ontology consisted of rel:hasMet, rel:acquaintanceOf, rel:closeFriendOf, rel:influencedBy, mo:collaborated with, and rel:mentorOf. The newly minted predicates for the Linked Jazz applied ontology consisted of lj:playedTogether, li:touredWith, lj:inBandWith, lj:bandLeaderOf, bandMemberOf, lj:knowsOf, and lj:influencedBy.

101. "Legacy Data Access," Linked Jazz, accessed January 10, 2022, https://linkedjazz.org/?page_id=905.

102. "Network," Linked Jazz, accessed January 10, 2022, https://linkedjazz.org/network/.

103. Most commonly known as the underlying infrastructure that supports Wikidata, Wikibase is a suite of knowledge base software for managing linked open data. ("Wikibase/FAQ" MediaWiki, accessed January 2, 2022, https://www.mediawiki.org/

sub-projects,[104] the Semantic Lab is also developing tools such as Sélavy, a document-to-data tool that allows for the creation of linked data from documents,[105] which will be the mechanism that facilitates the creation of LLJS linked data and its ingestion into the Semantic Lab's Wikibase.

Linking Lost Jazz Shrines (LLJS)

LLJS endeavors to make the WLJSB collection and the relationships contained therein more discoverable and accessible to both Brooklyn community members and jazz researchers alike, using the precious pieces of Black cultural heritage held in the collection as eclectic and authoritative sources on the relationships and built environment of Brooklyn's "geographies of jazz."[106] Linked Jazz provided LLJS a methodological project model and a shared core ontology, WLJSB provided LLJS a collection of rich Brooklyn-specific data within the same jazz domain as Linked Jazz, and the Semantic Lab's Wikibase provides LLJS the technological infrastructure to support name authority creation and, ultimately, hold the linked open data that will be generated by this project.

Identifying and describing this web of richly interconnected relationships between people, places, institutions, and organizations acknowledges the value of oral history in communities where

---

wiki/Wikibase/FAQ.)The SPARQL query available at https://tinyurl.com/y4wvwvk4 can be used to see all person records associated with the Linked Jazz Oral History Network that were migrated from the Linked Jazz triple store to the Semantic Lab at Pratt's Wikibase instance. The homepage for the SemLab's Wikibase is https://base.semlab.io.

104. Please see: https://semlab.io/projects/.

105. The alpha version of Sélavy is available at http://159.89.242.202:3000/. A video demo of an earlier version of the tool is available at https://semlab.io/howto/selavy_alpha. Both Sélavy and Pomodoro are being developed by Semantic Lab at Pratt co-director Matt Miller. A user can load a document, clean up and 'block' the document into chunks of text, send the text for (NER) Named Entity Recognition, reconcile the NER outputs with existing Wikibase and/or Wikidata items, create linked data triples, and then export those triples into Wikibase. The integrated Pomodoro OCR tool can help extract text from more complicated documents.

106. Lenard D. Moore, *The Geography of Jazz: Poems* (Durham, N.C.: Blair, 2020).

the connections are complex, overlapping, and improvisational.[107] This mode of linked data work contributes to the externalization and interplay of individual memory, a process which can produce new public knowledge that was once "logically created, but never retrieved, brought together, and interpreted."[108] Considering the value and prevalent use of orality and oral records for Black diasporic people,[109] this externalization and re/production of knowledge is especially significant for an oral history collection documenting a Black community. Given the exclusion of Black histories from mainstream archival institutions, oral history-based projects like LLJS fill in the gaps pervasive throughout written historical records.[110]

---

107. See: Fred Moten, "come on, get it! with Thom Donovan, Malik Gaines, Ethan Philbrick, Wikipedia and the Online Etymology Dictionary," *The New Inquiry*, February 19, 2018, https://thenewinquiry.com/come_on_get_it/ quoted in David S. Wallace, "Fred Moten's Radical Critique of the Present," The New Yorker, April 30, 2018, https://www.newyorker.com/culture/persons-of-interest/fred-motens-radical-critique-of-the-present. In "come on, get it!" Moten writes, "Improvisation is how we make no way out of a way. Improvisation is how we make nothing out of something." Here we call on both this reference and the improvisational quality of jazz music to describe the jazz community's complexity. See also. Fred Moten, *In the Break: The Aesthetics of the Black Radical Tradition* (Minneapolis: University of Minnesota Press, 2003).

108. Don R. Swanson, "Undiscovered Public Knowledge," *The Library Quarterly* 56, no. 2, (1986): 103-118, quoted in Amalia S. Levi and Douglas W. Oard, "From Personal Narratives to Collective Memory: Spinning a Web from Oral History," (presentation, XVII International Oral History Association Conference, Buenos Aires, Argentina, September 2012): 2, https://terpconnect.umd.edu/~oard/pdf/ioha12.pdf.

109. See for example: Masegonyana Keakopa, "The Role of the Archivist in the Collection and Preservation of Oral Traditions." *South African Archives Journal* 40, (June 1998); Tonia Sutherland, "Where There's A Will: On Heir Property, African American Land Stories, and the Value of Oral Records in American Archives." In *Defining a Discipline: Archival Research and Practice in the 21st Century – Essays in Honor of Richard J. Cox*, Jeannette Bastian and Elizabeth Yakel, eds. (Chicago: Society of American Archivists, 2020): 238-255; and Deborah Turner, "Conceptualizing Oral Documents*,"* *Information Research* 12, 4 (2007), http://InformationR.net/ir/12-4/colis/colis32.html; Amalia S. Levi and Douglas W. Oard, "From Personal Narratives to Collective Memory: Spinning a Web from Oral History," (presentation, XVII International Oral History Association Conference, Buenos Aires, Argentina, September 2012): 2, https://terpconnect.umd.edu/~oard/pdf/ioha12.pdf.

110. Masegonyana Keakopa, "The Role of the Archivist in the Collection and Preservation of Oral Traditions," *South African Archives Journal* 40, (June 1998).

Of great significance to LLJS is the precedent set by Linked Jazz—the creation of linked data from "scratch": using rather than repurposing existing metadata about a resource (e.g., DACS fields and values from a finding aid). Instead, Linked Jazz used the *content* of the resources themselves (in this case, oral history transcripts) as the dataset source.[111] During the implementation of Linked Jazz, team members identified a list of candidate classes to incorporate into the ontology. The list included the classes of "Music Group" and "Venue," the latter of which became the scaffolding for incorporating the titular "lost jazz shrines" into the LLJS dataset. The class "Organization" was originally intended to represent commercial businesses like record labels and record stores. However, it became quickly apparent that it was imperative to include non-commercial community organizations—formal and informal alike—to enable holistic representation of the varied components of the social and cultural network that supported the jazz culture of Central Brooklyn between the 1930s and 1960s.

Beyond identifying named entities in the oral history collection, LLJS describes connections within this community in ways that have not been implemented through any current ontological models. The once-dominant object-oriented "bibliographic paradigm" of linked data in the cultural heritage field is increasingly being set aside in favor of event-centric models like the CIDOC Conceptual Reference Model (CIDOC-CRM) and the Europeana Data Model (EDM).[112] In contrast to both object-centric and event-centric modes of representation, LLJS is, instead, concerned with places (venues) and agents, either in the form of individual people or groups of people (music groups, community

---

111. M. Cristina Pattuelli, Alexandra Provo, and Hilary Thorsen, "Ontology Building for Linked Open Data: A Pragmatic Perspective," *Journal of Library Metadata* 15, no. 3–4 (October 2, 2015): 269, https://doi.org/10.1080/19386389.2015.1099979.

112. M. Cristina Pattuelli, Matt Miller, and Sarah Ann Adams, "Ontology Shift: Cultural Heritage Ontologies in the Time of Linked Open Data," in *Ontologies for Linked Data in the Humanities Workshop* (Digital Humanities 2019 (DH2019), Utrecht, The Netherlands, 2019), https://cwrc.ca/islandora/object/islandora%3A34f1ac71-c799-4f24-a9a1-0732e3920e52.

organizations, etc.).[113] Unconventional, but still falling within the scope of the experimental ethos of the Semantic Lab, this modeling tactic enables LLJS to operate within a "person-centred theory of archival care."[114]

Case Study

Patrick Ngulube stresses that "every aspect of oral history work has an ethical dimension" and "it is important that archivists identify and become aware of ethical issues most pertinent to them."[115] As the present edited volume might suggest, there are also ethical dimensions in every aspect of linked data. Our professional societies, employers, and specific areas of librarianship and archival

---

113. Aside from a handful of references to the April 1965 recordings of Freddie Hubbard, James Spaulding, Harold Mabern, Larry Ridley, Pete La Roca, Big Black (Daniel Ray), and Lee Morgan performing at Club La Marchal issued as "The Night of the Cookers," the WLSJB oral history collection does not generally contain information about specific events, performances or otherwise. These kinds of events would customarily be the class of entity through which a person or a music group, for example, would be linked to a music venue through a performance action. In lieu of supporting the use of blank nodes for events to denote "the existence of some unnamed resource" (Aidan Hogan, Marcelo Arenas, Alejandro Mallea, and Axel Polleres, "Everything You Always Wanted to Know about Blank Nodes," *Journal of Web Semantics*, Semantic Web Challenge 27–28 [August-October 2014]: 42. https://doi.org/10.1016/j.websem.2014.06.004), the LLJS project describes and manages WLJSB content by establishing properties that can directly link people and music groups directly to the "Lost Jazz Shrines" music venues. Where specific events like "The Night of the Cookers" do exist, future iterations of LLJS work will incorporate those events in keeping with the events that are included in two other current Semantic Lab at Pratt projects: the International Sweethearts of Rhythm Project and E.A.T. + LOD. An example of one such event is the Semantic Lab Wikibase item "International Sweethearts of Rhythm Performance at McElroy's Ballroom, September 14, 1944," which has a URI of http://base.semlab.io/entity/Q23402.

114. Jennifer Douglas, Mya Ballin, and Sadaf Ahmadbeigi, "Call for Papers: Defining and Enacting Person-Centred Archival Theory and Praxis," *Archivaria* (June 18, 2021), https://archivaria.ca/index.php/archivaria/announcement/view/45.

115. Patrick Ngulube, "Professional Ethics in Building Collections from Oral Traces of the Past in Zimbabwe," *Information Development* 32, no 5, (December 6, 2015), https://doi.org/10.1177/0266666915620707.

work are guided by codes of ethics, and there is a specific need for ethics around the ability for "anyone to say anything about any topic,"[116] a uniquely shared characteristic between oral history and linked data.

This edited volume gathers evidence that it is possible to "acknowledge and mitigate the damage caused by existing systems [and] to create a place and space of justice for the minoritized."[117] In a linked data context, these considerations can be categorized as work that is ethical due to its additive and expansive nature, and work that is ethical due to its conservatism—or even avoidance—in the generation of linked data. In relation to "additive" ethics, Ruth K. Tillman observes that "linked data [both] undermines and expands ideas of authority, as anyone could create records describing individuals and publish them."[118] In contrast, Tillman additionally acknowledges that linked data assumes "inherent incompleteness."[119] This speaks to the open-world assumption,[120] encouraging linked data creators to use restraint when making semantic statements. Through this case study, the authors will describe Linking Lost Jazz Shrines with respect to these two ethical working modes: additive and consertive linked data creation.

---

116. Tillman, "Barriers to Ethical Name Modeling," 243.

117. Rory Litwin, "Call for Chapter Proposals: Ethics in Linked Data," Litwin Books & Library Juice Press, January 11, 2021, https://litwinbooks.com/call-for-chapter-proposals-ethics-in-linked-data/.

118. Tillman, "Barriers to Ethical Name Modeling," 243-44.

119. Tillman, 244.

120. M. A. Matienzo, "To Hell With Good Intentions: Linked Data, Community, and the Power to Name," (keynote presentation, Library Information Technology Association Forum, Minneapolis, MN, November 14, 2015), https://matienzo.org/2016/to-hell-with-good-intentions/. Matienzo writes: "The open world assumption states that the truth value of a statement may be true irrespective of whether or not it is known to be true. As such, it emphasizes the fact that no single person or agent has comprehensive knowledge, and accordingly, we are limited about what we can infer from that knowledge to which we have access." In this respect, linked data creators have the ethical duty to be specific with the statements they create based on the knowledge they have, using inference with caution and avoiding assumptions.

Entity Selection and Creation: The Power of Naming

The standard hierarchical nature of archival description enables only prominent entities to be included in a collection's finding aid: collector, creator, and/or notable subjects. The creation of a finding aid is the result of interpreting a collection and distilling the breadth of its content into one digestible document, a process that limits the number and kind of entities included in the finding aid. This limitation depends on whether an entity is deemed "notable" enough to be selected—from a collection's competing entities—for inclusion in the finding aid. In contrast, LLJS establishes an alternative method of archival collection documentation and expression molded not by the austerity inherent in hierarchical "top-down" description that both generalizes and obscures, nor by prioritizing names that are already present, for example, in LCNAF. LLJS' intervention is an expansive and maximalist approach to entity selection, supported by the ability to create authorities within Wikibase and informed directly by textual representation of the collection itself.

Aside from interviewees, the original creation of Wikibase URIs for LLJS was limited to musicians, music groups, and music venues. As our work continued, however, we observed how these initial parameters were creating "false silences" in the presentation of the WLJSB dataset.[121] The exclusion of certain names obscured the fullness of the network of people, places, and organizations that energized and sustained the Central Brooklyn jazz community. Encountering "Club Jest Us" was a turning point in the project where we decided to be more intentional and inclusive with entity selection and subsequent authority creation.

Below is an excerpt from the Larry Ridley and Harold Mabern transcript describing "Club Jest Us":

---

121. Antracoli and Rawdon, "What's in a Name?", 308.

Larry Ridley: [Club La Marchal] was a club that wasn't really noted for presenting a lot of jazz. But how that came about was several of the musicians that were living in Brooklyn, like Bobby Timmons' wife Stella [Estella Timmons], and Freddie Hubbard's wife at the time Brenda, and Cedar Walton's wife [Ida Walton], they had a club—and Charles Davis' wife [Lori Samet Davis], I think she was involved as well—they had formed a club called the Club Jest Us. They were musicians' wives who wanted to do something to promote their husband's careers and so they rented the Club La Marchal in order to present this evening, which ended up being called "The Night of the Cookers" and that recording.[122]

As music writer Brandon Stosuy observes, music is "ultimately deeply about people—those who make it, the real communities around it. Weird how easily that's forgotten."[123] Based on our original parameters, the informal community organization of "Club Jest Us" would have been excluded from the LLJS dataset because it was not a music group, nor was it a commercial organization like a record store or label. Additionally, the four individual members of the club—Estella Timmons, Brenda Hubbard, Ida Walton, and Lori Samet Davis—would also not have been included because they were not themselves musicians, despite having organized the April 1965 performances at Club La Marchal that resulted in the "remarkable aural document" that is "The Night of the Cookers," hailed as "undoubtedly the most famous jazz album recorded in Brooklyn."[124]

The change in project scope to include non-musical and/or non-commercial organizations enabled the incorporation of notable community organizations: the Central Brooklyn Jazz

122. "Larry Ridley and Harold Mabern," oral history interview by Willard Jenkins, Weeksville Lost Jazz Shrines of Brooklyn oral history collection (WLJSB), 5th of July Resource Center for Self-Determination and Freedom, Weeksville Heritage Center, New York, NY., April 5, 2010, transcript.

123. Brandon Stosuy (@brandonstosuy), "I love music, and it's ultimately deeply about people— those who make it, the real communities around it. weird how easily that's forgotten," tweet, November 7, 2021, https://twitter.com/brandonstosuy/status/1457180388770648070.

124. Taylor, "Across the East River: Searching for Brooklyn's Jazz History," 6.

Consortium (CBJC), The East,[125] African American Teachers Association, and the Brooklyn chapter of the Black Panther Party, to name a few. Continuing with the example of "Club Jest Us," and in relation to individuals rather than organizations, we also decided to expand our initial parameters to non-musicians and community members. Bringing these "less notable" individuals into the fold of the data uncovered various non-performance-based roles that were integral to the endurance of the jazz community, but also highlighted the reality that many of these unnamed support roles were often held by women. Particularly in relation to the jazz and gender work undertaken by the Semantic Lab,[126] the inclusion of non-musician persons in the scope of LLJS not only supported the specific project mission to re/present a holistic view of the Brooklyn jazz community, but it also put LLJS in line and in conversation with the research intentions of other ongoing Semantic Lab subprojects.

A great deal of the intermediary work that occurs in the life cycle of a linked data project can bring about deeper understandings of the project itself.[127] For example, LLJS is currently utilizing Google Sheets to plan out the linked data statements that will eventually be produced using Sélavy. With this preparatory data, we can count the frequency that entities occur in the WLJSB

125. For more information on The East see, Tayo Giwa and Cynthia Gordy Giwa, The Sun Rises in the East, directed by Tayo Giwa (2022; Brooklyn, NY), https://www.sunrisesintheeast.com. The East was "a pan-African cultural organization founded in 1969 by teens and young adults in Bedford-Stuyvesant, Brooklyn. Led by educator and activist Jitu Weusi, ... [t]he organization hosted world-famous jazz musicians and poets at its highly sought-after performance venue, and it served as an epicenter for political contemporaries such as the Black Panther Party, the Young Lords and the Congress of Afrikan People, as well as comrades across Africa and the Caribbean.

126. M. Cristina Pattuelli, Karen Hwang, and Matthew Miller, "Accidental Discovery, Intentional Inquiry: Leveraging Linked Data to Uncover the Women of Jazz," *Digital Scholarship in the Humanities* 32, Issue 4 (October 10, 2016): 918–924, https://doi.org/10.1093/llc/fqw047. See also the 'Women and Jazz' and 'International Sweethearts of Rhythm Project' information at https://semlab.io/projects/.

127. Jonathan Lill, "An Institutional View of Art Communities: The Possibilities of Linked Exhibition Histories" (presentation, New York Archives Week Symposium, New York, N.Y., October 19, 2017), http://jonathanlill.com/presentations/.

collection as a whole. The entities with the highest counts of occurrences—e.g., Randy Weston (350), Max Roach (227), and Jitu Weusi (224)—are all expected, since they are named entities present in the WLJSB finding aid. Inspection of entities named less than a handful of times, however, highlights the kinds of unique and hidden named-entities that would be completely obscured by hierarchical archival descriptions' tendency to "[privilege] majority representation."[128] Excluding churches and museums, there are thirty-seven music venues, whether formal or informal, that were mentioned only once among the twenty-nine oral history transcripts.[129] While some linked data practitioners may not see the usefulness of including such seemingly negligible locations in a research project dataset, we asked ourselves: what are the ramifications of not including such entities? In the words of Mitchell Whitelaw discussing the heterogeneous long tail of metadata present in digital projects, these "outliers" and "oddities" are not superfluous or errant, but are precious kernels of information because they are rare.[130] If a digital life by way of URI creation is not established for these locations for a linked

---

128. Dorothy Berry, "Digitizing and Enhancing Description Across Collections to Make African American Materials More Discoverable on Umbra Search African American History," The Design for Diversity Learning Toolkit (blog), Northeastern University Library, August 2, 2018, https://des4div.library.northeastern.edu/digitizing-and-enhancing-description-across-collections-to-make-african-american-materials-more-discoverable-on-umbra-search-african-american-history/.

129. For the interview transcripts that have been processed, the music venues mentioned only once across the WLJSB oral history collection are: Ali's Alley, The Beehive, The Billie Holiday Theatre, Bottle & Cork, Browning's Hide Away, Browns, Carver Theatre, City Lights, Club 845, Club Baron, Community Center 35, Connie's, Dickie's Monterey, Dizzy's Club, Elks Club, Environ, Farmer John's, Gaslight, Hancock Hall, The Hole (Eastern Parkway and Nostrand location), Lennox Lounge, Lucky Spot, Metropole Cafe, Michelle's, The New World, Parlor Jazz, Pookie's, Raintrees, The Regent, Sankofa, Savoy Ballroom, Shadow Gardens, St. Nick's Pub, The Uptown Lounge, Unnamed music venue (aka The Bucket of Blood), Unnamed music venue (Eastern Parkway, top of hill), and Unnamed music venue (Fulton Street/Bedford Avenue)

130. Mitchell Whitelaw, "Generous Interfaces for Digital Cultural Collections," *Digital Humanities Quarterly* 009, no. 1 (May 21, 2015), http://www.digitalhumanities.org/dhq/vol/9/1/000205/000205.html.

data project about the "lost jazz shrines" of Brooklyn, what scenario would warrant more of a mandate to establish authority records for these venues?

In addition to a maximalist approach to named entity selection, LLJS also establishes a radically low threshold of notability for determining who or what "gets" an authority record in the Wikibase. For a project about jazz, we are—perhaps surprisingly—not currently interested in creative works, but are rather guided by a "person-centred theory of archival care."[131] This framework provides a mandate for broad generation of Wikibase authorities, based not on whether a person is a creator or subject of a published work,[132] but rather based on a person's presence in and among the jazz community, even if only as an attendee of a performance. In this mode of URI creation, the ethical decision is one of dislodgement from the LCNAF bibliographic paradigm which privileges the creation of entities based on their work, labor, or output. In the LLJS paradigm, all forms of participation in Central Brooklyn's jazz culture are deemed valuable. While there would be no jazz community without the musicians, there would also be no jazz community without venue proprietors,[133] announc-

---

131. Douglas, Ballin, and Ahmadbeigi, "Defining and Enacting Person-Centred Archival Theory and Praxis."

132. Antracoli and Rawdon, "What's in a Name?", 323. Antracoli and Rawdon write, "There are several issues at work within archival description and name authority work that serve to privilege the naming of the white creators, collectors, and subjects over the naming of Black people represented in archival collections. One is the privileging of published authors and subjects of published works in the LCNAF."

133. For example: "Richard (Dickie) Habersham-Bey" oral history interview by Willard Jenkins, Weeksville Lost Jazz Shrines of Brooklyn oral history collection (WL-JSB), 5th of July Resource Center for Self-Determination and Freedom, Weeksville Heritage Center, New York, NY., June 15, 2010, transcript: Willard Jenkins: ... Did you have other places at the time? Richard Habersham-Bey:...I had four other bars at the time, all in Brooklyn – Dickie's Monterey; The New World on Flatbush Avenue; The Uptown Lounge on Sterling Street..."

ers,[134] record store workers,[135] photographers,[136] or an audience to attend and promote performances by word-of-mouth.[137]

The original WLSJB finding aid only contained 49 unique key terms and contributor names that served as access points to the collection.[138] At the time of this publication, 898 LLJS entities have been added to the Semantic Lab's Wikibase,[139] with more entities to be added as the remaining transcripts are processed. Ethically wielding the power of naming through Wikibase URI creation, LLJS eschews the limitations of traditional archival description and URI entity establishment to affirm Black life and underscore the role of collective participatory efforts in sustaining this jazz community.

---

134. For example: ibid: "Willard Jenkins: Did you have MCs at The Blue Coronet? Richard Habersham-Bey: Yeah, we had Irvin C. Watson… he was from Brooklyn, he was a friend. And Jimmy Morton…"

135. For example: "Joe Long," oral history interview by Willard Jenkins, Weeksville Lost Jazz Shrines of Brooklyn oral history collection (WLJSB), 5th of July Resource Center for Self-Determination and Freedom, Weeksville Heritage Center, New York, NY., 2011, transcript: "Willard Jenkins: So, did you have other people who worked for you who went on to have their own record stores? Joe Long: Yep, a couple of them. Not only record stores. I've had them that learned the business that went on to be producers. Matter of fact, Biggie [Notorious B.I.G.] I started."

136. For example: "Jimmy Morton," oral history interview by Willard Jenkins and Jennifer Scott, Weeksville Lost Jazz Shrines of Brooklyn oral history collection (WLJSB), 5th of July Resource Center for Self-Determination and Freedom, Weeksville Heritage Center, New York, NY., April 5, 2010, transcript: "Willard Jenkins: We're looking at one of your photos; please tell us about this photo. Jimmy Morton: This was taken at Tony's [Grand Dean] (in Brooklyn), and it's Max Roach, Miles Davis, Gigi Gryce, Charles Mingus."

137. For example: "Randy Weston and Donald Sangster" oral history interview by Willard Jenkins, Weeksville Lost Jazz Shrines of Brooklyn oral history collection (WLJSB), 5th of July Resource Center for Self-Determination and Freedom, Weeksville Heritage Center, New York, NY., March 16, 2010, transcript: "Willard Jenkins: If you wanted to go out and hear somebody, how would you find out who was playing where?… Randy Weston: Word of mouth. Donald Sangster: Word of mouth… You had to be hip… You had to be in that circle…"

138. Weeksville Heritage Center, "The Weeksville Lost Jazz Shrines of Brooklyn Collection (WLJSB)."

139. As of January 15th 2021, these 898 entities can be found by running the Semantic Lab at Pratt Wikibase query available at https://tinyurl.com/yxdb6p87.

Avoiding Assumptions: The Authority of One's Own Experiences

As an archival document type, oral history interviews are valued for their ability to preserve histories directly from the narratives of those who've experienced them, but information science has traditionally prioritized tangible modes of recordkeeping.[140] Guided by Douglas, Ballin, and Ahmadbeigi's definition of person-centred theory of archival care, LLJS not only foregrounds the oral history transcripts as documents but also gives prominence to the people of the project—the interviewees and those they mention. Understanding naming as both "an act of affirming humanity"[141] and an act of establishing those named in the transcripts as authorities (on Central Brooklyn jazz history) in their own right, throughout the creation of the LLJS linked data, we made it our duty to put ourselves in the background in order to foreground and prioritize the people—previously named and unnamed—identified in the transcripts.

After identifying named-entities from the oral history transcripts, and acknowledging them as integral components to this particular telling of Central Brooklyn jazz history, the project then required reading the natural language transcripts and deciding which triple statements would faithfully represent the relationships narrated within. For example, in an interview by Willard Jenkins with visual artist, filmmaker, and hip hop artist Fab Five Freddy, the natural language statement "I'm saying all that to say that I also realized later in life that my dad [Fred Braithwaite, Sr.] was a big part of Max [Roach]'s consciousness and awareness at that time"[142] can be represented by the following triple

---

140. Deborah Turner, "Conceptualizing Oral Documents," *Information Research* 12, 4 (2007), http://InformationR.net/ir/12-4/colis/colis32.html.

141. Antracoli and Rawdon, "What's in a Name?", 327.

142. "Fab Five Freddy," oral history interview by Willard Jenkins and Jennifer Scott, Weeksville Lost Jazz Shrines of Brooklyn oral history collection (WLJSB), 5th of July Resource Center for Self-Determination and Freedom, Weeksville Heritage Center, New York, NY., October 8, 2010, transcript.

statements, of which the first two include additional qualifying information:

<Fred Braithwaite, Sr.> <relative of> <Fab Five Freddy> <is relation> <father>.
<Fab Five Freddy> <relative of> <Fred Braithwaite, Sr.> <is relation> <son>.
<Max Roach> <influenced by> <Fred Braithwaite, Sr.>.
<Fab Five Freddy> <knows of> <Max Roach>.

In certain instances, it could have been possible to create triple statements based on information inferred from the text. However, since the LLJS project collaborators are not a part of the Central Brooklyn jazz history, are not scholars of Brooklyn jazz, and were not involved in the initial interviewing process, we made the decision to only create triple statements about information explicitly stated in the interview text, keeping to the essence of the oral histories as they were presented to us and respecting the agency and authority of the interview participants. In one such example, jazz pianist Randy Weston describes his interactions with another jazz pianist, Thelonious Monk:

Randy Weston: …I remember bringing Monk here because I used to pick up Monk and bring him to Brooklyn and we'd just hang out and go to different places and look for pianos.
Maxine Gordon: When he lived on 63?
Randy Weston: Yeah, yeah.
Maxine Gordon: Uh-huh, uh-huh. And then you had the car?
Randy Weston: Yeah, I had my dad's car and I'd pick him up. Yeah, and we'd just hang out, you know. This is one of the spots I'd take him.
Maxine Gordon: Oh great. Oh, that's great. Okay. Where else did you take him?
Randy Weston: Oh, a lot of places. My father [Frank Edward Weston]'s place, my home; we would just hang out, you know, go to guy's houses that had pianos at two or three o'clock in the morning and wake them up.[143]

---

143. "Randy Weston," oral history interview by Jennifer Scott, Maxine Gordon, and Jitu Weusi, Weeksville Lost Jazz Shrines of Brooklyn oral history collection (WL-JSB), 5th of July Resource Center for Self-Determination and Freedom, Weeksville

Several options for predicates were available from our ontology to describe this relationship between Randy Weston and Thelonious Monk. Our first inclination was to state that Randy Weston was a "friend of" (P34) Thelonious Monk, and vice versa. However, upon second examination of the transcript, we recognized this would be creating a triple statement based on assumption and inference, as Randy Weston did not explicitly name Thelonious Monk as a friend. Despite their familiarity with one another and the frequency of their interactions, we could only verifiably conclude that they were acquaintances. Therefore, we represented that relationship by stating that Randy Weston was an "acquaintance of" (P32) Thelonious Monk, and vice versa. Through this revision, we recognized Randy Weston as an agent who could have identified "Monk" as a friend and could very well consider him as such, but did not choose to do so in this instance. In naming Weston as the authority of his own experiences and following the ways he chooses to describe himself,[144] we elected to avoid this inference that could later be accessed, used, or quoted beyond our control.

Conclusion

Discussion: Reverberations of Ethical Linked Data Generation

The considerations surrounding the power of naming and honoring the authority of the WLJSB oral history interviewees have afforded LLJS the opportunity to begin to ethically re/present

---

Heritage Center, New York, NY., October 22, 2008, transcript.

144. Antracoli and Rawdon, "What's in a Name?", 328: "Use terminology that Black people use to describe themselves, while recognizing that the Black community is not a monolith, and different people will have different and sometimes conflicting preferences."

Central Brooklyn's jazz community in a linked data environment.[145] LLJS explicitly identifies named entities and defines relationships between them, creating a web of knowledge and collective memory about a particular jazz-centered time and place for a specific Black community.

We hope that LLJS can serve as a resource in and of itself for learning new knowledge about Central Brooklyn jazz between the 1930s and 1960s.[146] Upon the availability of Sélavy, linked data triples will be loaded into the Wikibase and users can explore the LLJS project data therein, either through targeted SPARQL querying or through serendipitous exploration. LLJS also intentionally points to external resources, fulfilling the fourth rule of linked data by including "links to other URIs so that [users] can discover more things."[147] This work is done through the identification or creation of Wikidata items for each applicable LLJS Wikibase item. Of the current 898 LLJS items, 545 existed in Wikidata prior to the start of LLJS; items have been created for 135 entities thus far and more than 201 entities are slated to be added. Once a Wikidata item is identified or created, the Wikidata identifier is added back to the LLJS Wikbase item. Once all of the transcripts have been fully processed and their semantic triples loaded into the Wikibase, our vision is that a user could traverse from the WHC Omeka S site, to the Semantic Lab Wikibase, and then through to Wikidata to access the collaborative knowledge captured there. In this sense, the existence of LLJS enables the opportunity for inter-platform serendipitous exploration.

Lastly, aside from meeting the needs of both targeted inquiry and serendipitous exploration, the creation of Wikidata items in support of LLJS invites the generation of new public

145. Arthur A. Schomburg, "The Negro Digs Up His Past," Survey.
146. Tim Berners-Lee, "Linked Data," W3, July 27, 2006, https://www.w3.org/DesignIssues/LinkedData.html: "When someone looks up a URI, provide useful information, using the standards (RDF*, SPARQL)."
147. Berners-Lee, "Linked Data."

knowledge in the public square of Wikidata. The Sun Ra Arkestra (Q65548769) and Kaitlyn Greenidge (Q65554909)[148] are two examples of LLJS entities that were created as minimally described Wikidata items but have since seen a proliferation of claims, qualifiers, and references, made either by individual users or bots. This is a quantifiable way we can see the reverberations of LLJS reinfusing knowledge about "lost jazz shrines" and a vibrant cultural community into the public discourse.

Future Considerations: Equity as a Process

In managing all parts of the project from entity identification to triple-making, it was imperative for us to set intentions and maintain project scope. We identified the intention of LLJS as one of equity, as opposed to objectivity or neutrality.[149] As such, we approached our work using the tenets of "slow librarianship" as a means to remain grounded in the guiding working principles for the project. Meredith Farkas frames slow librarianship as "anti-racist, responsive, values-driven, focused on relationship-building, equitable, reflective, collaborative, and a process."[150] LLJS implemented this framework by allowing ample time for contemplative, reflective, and reflexive collaboration, which involved multiple quality assurance steps of reviewing each other's decisions, asking questions, making suggestions,

---

148. Sun Ra Arkestra Wikidata entry: https://www.wikidata.org/entity/Q65548769. Kaitlyn Greenidge Wikidata entry: https://www.wikidata.org/entity/Q65554909. The 'View history' tab of each item (https://www.wikidata.org/w/index.php?title=Q65548769&action=history and https://www.wikidata.org/w/index.php?title=Q65554909&action=history) displays each change that has been made since each items' creation.

149. Matienzo, "To Hell With Good Intentions: Linked Data, Community, and the Power to Name." Matienzo writes "Moreover, naming is fundamentally unavoidable in knowledge representation. As such, we need to make a decision whether we choose to name with an intention of justice, or with the pretense of neutrality and objectivity."

150. Meredith Gorran Farkas, "What Is Slow Librarianship?", Information Wants To Be Free, last modified October 18, 2021, https://meredith.wolfwater.com/wordpress/2021/10/18/what-is-slow-librarianship/.

and discussing and implementing solutions, where possible.

Concerns often related to whether or not a specific name, name representation, or triple statement aligned with the equity intentions of the project. Additional concerns arose around the needs of intended users, and/or if current ontological models already offered ways to express relationships represented in the oral histories. Oftentimes, solutions were not readily available at the moment of questioning, especially when the question at hand brought up completely new considerations. In such cases, we read and re-read the oral history transcripts, requested input from the Semantic Lab and other linked data practitioners, and conducted additional research. Even so, there were instances where we were not able to reach a decision. Rather than making a hasty choice for the sake of it, we permitted ourselves to have ongoing conversations, unresolved questions, and "back burner" lists, letting the project guide our processes as we visited and revisited conversations. Forcing decision-making may not be in the best interest of the project if it only serves the ends of productivity rather than the intention of equity.

To that end, there are several aspects of the project we plan to address moving forward. The possibilities of linked data can prompt both excitement and apprehension. Linked data's decentralized nature affords the ability to make many decisions locally, resulting in the need for data stewardship and care to be a priority in every project decision. Co-author and project collaborator, Zakiya Collier, in a 2020 interview, defines care in this context as "being 'full of thought' about all the particulars of a thing we're preserving."[151] For LLJS, care, as defined, was intentionally built into the project workflows in a number of ways including but not limited to slow and intentional linked data creation and centering interview participants' authority.

---

151. Megan Williams and Zakiya Collier, "Archiving with Care: A Conversation with Zakiya Collier," Metropolitan Archivist, Fall Issue: Invisible City, (October 30, 2020), https://medium.com/metropolitan-archivist/archiving-with-care-a-conversation-with-zakiya-collier-fedd81a0d0d6.

In working on a project involving both a marginalized community and linked data, we recognize our responsibility to avoid replicating the violences of the Web, metadata, name authorities, and linked data.[152] At present, decisions about linked data creation are centralized within the LLJS project team and the two institutional collaborators, Weeksville Heritage Center and the Semantic Lab at Pratt. While the project has engaged with the Central Brooklyn jazz community and some of the oral history participants through programming held in the summer of 2020,[153] we have not yet developed a plan to engage the community with the data the project will produce. We recognize that the full success of LLJS depends on three things: the development of Sélavy to realize the technical project goals, the data literacy of users who visit the Semantic Lab's Wikibase instance to query and explore the LLJS data, and comunity access to these tools and knowledge in order for people to—in the words of Tim Sherratt—"take what they're given and build something new—to challenge, to criticise, to offer alternatives."[154] Moreover, since this project creates linked data about older jazz communities, it

152. Matienzo, "To Hell With Good Intentions: Linked Data, Community, and the Power to Name." Matienzo writes, "I think those of us who work at the intersection of libraries and technology are directly responsible for the implementation choices that we make, and by merely opting into linked data in this manner we are tracking in a Web that is built by corporations who are opting out of this responsibility. That lack of inaction is a conscious choice that allows for searching the Web to remain fundamentally undemocratic as described by Safiya Umoja Noble."

153. "Updates." Linking Lost Jazz Shrines, Accessed January 10, 2022, https://sites.google.com/weeksvillesociety.org/linking-lost-jazz-shrines/updates.

154. Tim Sherrat, "Small Stories in A Big Data World," (presentation, National Digital Forum, Wellington, New Zealand, November 12, 2012), http://discontents.com.au/words/conference-papers/small-stories-in-a-big-data-world.html quoted in M.A. Matienzo, "To Hell With Good Intentions: Linked Data, Community, and the Power to Name." Worth quoting at length, Matienzo cites Tim Sherratt's presentation "Small Stories in A Big Data World": "But to really have access, for something to be truly open, people also have to have the power to create. To take what they're given and build something new—to challenge, to criticise, to offer alternatives. That means allowing people the space to have ideas, giving them the confidence to experiment, providing useful tools and the knowledge to use them."

is imperative that we continue to be thoughtful about how we activate this dataset for an intergenerational audience. These considerations for Linking Lost Jazz Shrines' continued relationship with the Central Brooklyn jazz community serve to remind us that LLJS is only a simplified and distilled re/presentation of the real, lived experiences of the people who created and sustained this rich jazz community and history.

The Oklahoma Native Artists Project: Oral History to Linked Open Data

MEGAN MACKEN, MADISON CHARTIER, SARAH MILLIGAN, & JULIE PEARSON-LITTLE THUNDER

Introduction

Linked open data, particularly Wikidata, offers a compelling solution for improving discoverability of library collections representing marginalized groups. The potential of linked open data to uncover previously obscured relationships between entities, however, calls for a thoughtful examination of its possible repercussions on living individuals and their communities. In practice, is it possible for libraries to embrace the increased visibility that linked open data promises while respecting the priorities, privacy, and self-representation of living individuals? Oklahoma State University (OSU) Library wrestled with this question while developing linked open data for Indigenous artists featured in the Oklahoma Native Artists oral history series (ONA series).[1] OSU

1.Oklahoma State University Libraries, "Oklahoma Native Art," Oklahoma Oral History Research Program, accessed April 4, 2022, https://oknativeart.library.okstate.edu/. This chapter uses the terms "Native" and "Indigenous" interchangeably to reflect the current scholarly discourse in Oklahoma and the nation at large. Members of Native communities in Oklahoma use a wide range of naming practices for themselves that are generationally inflected. Academic usage is subject to its own historicity. When the above referenced oral histories were recorded, "Native artists" was the favored term in Oklahoma scholarly discourse—hence the collection's title. Since 2010, scholars have advocated moving back and forth between Native, Indigenous, Native American, Indian, etc., so as to further destabilize and subvert the concept of "Native" as a

Library presents this chapter as a case study for other GLAM institutions interested in creating linked open data for collections whose subjects are living people. First, the original oral history project is introduced in the context of the history of the state of Oklahoma and the current environment of Oklahoma State University. A discussion of the Oral History Association's Principles and Best Practices for Oral History and the CARE Principles for Indigenous Data Governance and their application to linked open data specifically describing oral history interviews follows.[2] These ethical guidelines help maintain the respectful approach of the original project without inviting oversimplification. Next, we describe preparatory steps for deriving linked open data from oral histories for the Wikidata platform, such as cultivating professional and cultural competencies, identifying problematic properties, and wrangling data. Finally, we share our process for communicating with the artists and documenting their decisions to participate in the production of linked open data about themselves or to decline a public profile. Through our local framework for organizing this effort in the library and communicating as an institution with individual members of Indigenous communities, we demonstrate how a thoughtful approach to linked open data creation can de-center data output and instead center the Indigenous living people we are describing.[3]

monolithic descriptor. For more information about this, please see, National Museum of the American Indian, "Native Knowledge 360°—The Impact of Words and Tips for Using Appropriate Terminology: Am I Using the Right Word?", accessed April 4, 2022, https://americanindian.si.edu/nk360/informational/impact-words-tips. Daniel Francis, The Imaginary Indian: The Image of the Indian in Canadian Culture (Arsenal Pulp Press, 2012); Robert F. Berkhofer, The White Man's Indian: Images of the American Indian, from Columbus to the Present (Vintage Books, 1979).

2. "OHA Principles and Best Practices," Oral History Association, accessed December 11, 2021, https://www.oralhistory.org/principles-and-best-practices-revised-2018/. "CARE Principles of Indigenous Data Governance," Global Indigenous Data Alliance, accessed December 11, 2021, https://www.gida-global.org/care. See Stephanie Carroll Rainie, Desi Rodriguez-Lonebear, and Andrew Martinez, "Policy Brief: Indigenous Data Sovereignty in the United States" for more (Tucson: Native Nations Institute, University of Arizona, 2017).

3. As such, our efforts for this linked open data project, which began in 2020, and this case study chapter, are not directed toward the output of linked open data, which is

Oklahoma Native Artists (ONA) Oral History Series

Since 2010, author Julie Pearson-Little Thunder from the OSU Library's Oklahoma Oral History Research Program has interviewed 141 people for the ONA series. Interviewees include enrolled citizens of Tribal Nations and artists of self-identified Indigenous ancestry, as well as festival and exhibition organizers, gallery owners, and collectors. ONA artists work in a range of media from painting to fashion design; installation art to bow-making. In the interviews, they answer questions about their family and tribal backgrounds, schooling, business strategies, shows and awards, creative process, subject matter, and techniques. The purpose of this oral history series is to document and share with the public the history and culture of Native artists with an Oklahoma connection. Together these firsthand accounts offer a unique record of the artists' cultural achievements and economic contributions to the state of Oklahoma, as well as a richer encounter with their art.

The History of Oklahoma and the Indian Arts and Crafts Act

The ONA series also demonstrates the resonating impact of historical events and legislation upon Native identity and culture. The convoluted history of the state of Oklahoma turns on a series of federal land seizures. Treaties between the United States government and Tribal Nations concerning land in present Oklahoma were first signed in 1818.[4] By the 1830s, the Indian Removal

---

progressing slowly as we await artists' responses. Instead, our focus lies in building a sustainable foundation for future projects: maintaining existing relationships with the artists; building bibliographic and exhibition data to populate additional references for future linked open data records; and, most importantly, carefully considering platforms in order to produce linked open data that most benefits the individual artists and their communities and best facilitates their data sovereignty.

4. Oklahoma State University Libraries, "Oklahoma - Tribal Treaties Database," accessed March 31, 2022, https://treaties.okstate.edu/treaties-by-state/oklahoma.

and Trade Acts established Indian Territory, the name generally used to describe Oklahoma prior to its 1907 statehood, as a reservation for Nations forcibly displaced from the southeastern United States.[5] During the second half of the nineteenth century, Indian Territory functioned as a holding zone for diverse Indigenous peoples uprooted from the Northeast, Midwest, and West as a result of American wars of expansion, or so-called "Indian Wars." Beginning in 1862 with the first Morrill Act, land-grant universities also profited from the sale of stolen lands gifted to them by the federal government, and Oklahoma State University, a land-grant institution, was founded under the Morrill Act in 1890.[6] Finally, the allotment process of the 1887 Dawes Act, which linked tribal membership and privatized land holding, was purposely crafted by the U.S. Congress to open Indian Territory to non-Native settlers and to induce statehood in 1907.[7] As a result of forcible removal and broken treaties, today the state of Oklahoma is home to thirty-nine Sovereign Nations from across North

5. Oklahoma Historical Society, "Indian Territory | The Encyclopedia of Oklahoma History and Culture," accessed April 4, 2022, https://www.okhistory.org/publications/enc/entry.php?entry=IN018.

6. Robert Lee et al., "Land-Grab Universities: A High Country News Investigation," High Country News, March 30, 2020, https://www.landgrabu.org/. "How They Did It: Exposing How U.S. Universities Profited From Indigenous Land," Pulitzer Center, accessed March 31, 2022, https://pulitzercenter.org/stories/how-they-did-it-exposing-how-us-universities-profited-indigenous-land. "Land-Grant University FAQ," Association of Public & Land-Grant Universities, accessed April 4, 2022, https://www.aplu.org/about-us/history-of-aplu/what-is-a-land-grant-university/. Oklahoma State University, "OSU Timeline," accessed March 31, 2022, http://timeline.okstate.edu/.

7. Cholakocee Werito, Oklahoma History Booklet 2019: From Trails to Truths (Oklahoma City Public Schools, 2019), https://www.okcps.org/cms/lib/OK01913268/Centricity/Domain/130/OK%20History%20Booklet%202019%20From%20Trails%20to%20Truths.pdf; Citizen Potawatomi Nation Cultural Heritage Center, "Oklahoma Statehood," accessed April 4, 2022, https://www.potawatomiheritage.com/encyclopedia/oklahoma-statehood/. "Only the Native Americans who accepted the division of tribal lands were allowed to become US citizens. This ended in the government stripping over 90 million acres of tribal land from Native Americans, then selling that land to non-native US citizens." "The Dawes Act (U.S. National Park Service)." Accessed March 31, 2022. https://www.nps.gov/articles/000/dawes-act.htm.

America.[8] This fraught history has added layers of complexity for Native Americans in Oklahoma who do not live on their ancestral lands and may identify with more than one Sovereign Nation. Furthermore, as artists, they are subject to the 1990 federal Indian Arts and Crafts Act, as well as 1974 Oklahoma state legislation, regulating who may call themselves a Native artist and market their work as such: "Under the Act, an Indian is defined as a member of any federally or officially State recognized tribe of the United States, or an individual certified as an Indian artisan by an Indian tribe."[9] Later in the chapter we will discuss the difficulty of representing this unique history, with its complex identities and tribal affiliations, on the Wikidata platform.

Native Peoples Representation at Oklahoma State University (OSU), a Land-Grant University

Oklahoma State University is uniquely positioned to create linked open data for Indigenous campus collections. Although founded as a land-grant university, Oklahoma State is second in the nation for Native Americans who graduate with a bachelor's

---

8. "Oklahoma - Tribal Treaties Database," accessed March 31, 2022, https://treaties.okstate.edu/treaties-by-state/oklahoma. Oklahoma Historical Society, "Tribal Nations in Oklahoma," accessed April 4, 2022, https://www.okhistory.org/research/tribalnations.

9. "The Indian Arts and Crafts Act (Act) of 1990 (P.L. 101-644) is a truth-in-advertising law that prohibits misrepresentation in the marketing of Indian art and craft products within the United States. It is illegal to offer or display for sale, or sell, any art or craft product in a manner that falsely suggests it is Indian produced, an Indian product, or the product of a particular Indian or Indian tribe or Indian arts and crafts organization, resident within the United States." U.S. Department of the Interior, "Indian Arts and Crafts Act of 1990," Indian Arts and Crafts Board, October 22, 2015, https://www.doi.gov/iacb/indian-arts-and-crafts-act-1990. For a simple introduction to the act see, U.S. Department of the Interior, "The Indian Arts and Crafts Act of 1990," Indian Arts and Crafts Board, October 19, 2015, https://www.doi.gov/iacb/act. "American Indian Arts and Crafts Sales Act of 1974," Okla. Stat. tit. 78 § 71 (1974), http://www.oklegislature.gov/osstatuestitle.aspx.

degree.[10] According to the U.S. Department of Education, OSU has the most Native American undergraduates in Oklahoma, and the twelfth highest enrollment of Native American undergraduates in the US.[11] On campus, the Center for Sovereign Nations was founded at OSU in 2015 to promote awareness, respect and practice of tribal sovereignty, and Native American student success.[12] The center aims to increase the quantity and quality of partnerships between OSU and the thirty-nine federally recognized tribal nations in Oklahoma.[13] The Native American Student Association and the Native American Faculty & Staff Association support Native American students, faculty, and staff as well. In addition to the ONA oral history series, the OSU Museum of Art and OSU Library house many collections of Indigenous art and historical documentation, including the Charles Little Collection, featuring Native artists' paintings from the 1930s to the present; the Maxine and Jack Zarrow Collection of Native art; and the Angie Debo Collection, detailing 20th-century Native American history in Oklahoma.[14] The Tribal Treaties Database, produced

10. "Oklahoma State University Leads the Nation in Native American Graduates," Indian Country Today, September 13, 2018, https://indiancountrytoday.com/archive/oklahoma-state-university-leads-the-nation-in-native-american-graduates. "Diverse TOP 100 Degree Producers," accessed December 13, 2021, https://top100.diverseeducation.com/ALL_SCHOOLS_2019-2020/?search_degree=Bachelor&search_race=Native+American&search_major=All+Disciplines+Combined&search_school=&search_rank=&search_state=&search=search#anchor. "Native American Student Resources - Oklahoma State University," March 26, 2019, https://diversity.okstate.edu/student-resources/native-american-student-resources.html.

11. "Title III and Title V Institutions Designated Eligible for the Waiver of the Non-Federal Share Matching Requirements," Eligibility Designations and Applications for Waiver of Eligibility Requirements (US Department of Education (ED), December 9, 2021), https://www2.ed.gov/about/offices/list/ope/idues/eligibility.html#el-inst.

12. "Center for Sovereign Nations - Oklahoma State University," accessed December 11, 2021, https://sovnationcenter.okstate.edu/index.html.

13. For a description of the recognition process see, "Office of Federal Acknowledgment (OFA) | Indian Affairs." Accessed March 31, 2022. https://www.bia.gov/as-ia/ofa.

14. Oklahoma State University Museum of Art, "The Charles Little Collection," January 29, 2021, https://museum.okstate.edu/art/collections/little-collection.html. Oklahoma State University Library, "The Maxine & Jack Zarrow Collection," accessed December 13, 2021, https://zarrow.library.okstate.edu/. Oklahoma State University

in partnership with the U.S. Departments of Agriculture and the Interior, provides access to agreements between tribal nations and the United States (1778-1886) as published in the 1904 work "Indian Affairs: Laws and Treaties" (Volume II) compiled and edited by Charles J. Kappler.[15]

Impetus for Creating Linked Open Data for the ONA Oral History Series

By creating linked open data for the ONA oral history series beginning with Wikidata, the OSU Library aims to offer Native artists more visibility online; to provide a new vantage point for interacting with unstructured oral history interview transcripts; to further support both grassroots and academic research on Indigenous history and culture; to engage students in the scholarly conversation about Indigenous culture; and to draw connections between siloed collections.

Although this unique oral history series is cataloged, transcribed, and made publicly available online, much of the exhibition history contained in these oral history interviews—such as Native artists' representation in museums, regional art fairs, or international exhibitions—would be much more accessible and extensible as structured data. Linked open data offers promise not only for interlinking Native artists with their work in library and museum collections, and thus increasing awareness of Native art, but also for activating these artists' archives for research and inclusion in contemporary art discourse.

We also hope that surfacing these collections as linked data will provide new opportunities for Native American students in particular to engage with Indigenous history and culture as part

Archives, "The Angie Debo Collection," accessed December 11, 2021, https://info.library.okstate.edu/c.php?g=151950&p=997579.

15. "Indian Affairs: Laws and Treaties" (Oklahoma State University Library), accessed December 11, 2021, https://library.okstate.edu/search-and-find/collections/digital-collections/indian-affairs-laws-and-treaties/.

of their university experience and will reveal potential pathways for participating in that scholarly conversation themselves.[16] A recent History of American Art course project offers one example of student research engagement with metadata. The students scoured the student newspaper archives to compile metadata about campus artists and exhibitions, and in the process, they discovered over 400 exhibitions, many of which had been forgotten. Their project indicated that more local history remains to be documented and that metadata generation can facilitate student learning about that history. The course instructor, Professor Louise Siddons, observed at the end of the project:

> The students' research revealed that, from at least the 1970s through today, Oklahoma State has consistently exhibited Native American art. What was interesting to me about the shows that the students discovered is that many of them were curated by Native American artists. Today in museums, we talk a lot about the importance of self-representation, hiring Native curators to work with collections and communities and related issues of cultural preservation and repatriation. Thanks to this project, we have new insight into the deep history of Native art exhibitions at Oklahoma State.[17]

Linked open data could highlight connections between the Native art exhibition metadata produced in this course project, for example, and recordings of the artists' ONA oral history interviews. Links could be made between contemporary Native artists' professional profiles, representations of their work, exhibition venues, related publications, the recorded interviews, and also to other OSU Native American collections. Future course research projects could be built on this linked open data as well.

---

16. Nancy Marie Mithlo discusses "insider research" (Linda Tuhiwai Smith's term) in the context of barriers to research and entry into museum fields for Native American students. She also clearly illustrates the tension between settler institutions like Oklahoma State and the burden of inclusion for Native Americans. Nancy Marie Mithlo, "'Red Man's Burden': The Politics of Inclusion in Museum Settings," American Indian Quarterly 28, no. 3/4 (2004): 743—63.

17. OkStateLibrary, Discovering Digital Humanities, Episode 3: Dr. Louise Siddons, 2021, https://www.youtube.com/watch?v=-kyLYF9_WtI.

Principles and Best Practices for Oral History and Linked Open Data

Oral history interviews provide an abundance of context that linked open data can only hint at through references and relationships between entities. This context is particularly important for Native artists whose presentation of identity necessarily switches depending on their audience, whether that audience be institutions, such as libraries and museums, the public they encounter at fairs, festivals, and other engagements, or their own communities. The situational positionality of contemporary Native artists is essential context for providing accurate documentation of these artists and their art. They are self-aware of occupying a liminal space in which they hold a responsibility to be both outward facing towards the public and inward facing towards the community, creating bridges of understanding through their art.[18] These nuances, expressed visually in their work and often centered verbally in their oral histories, risk further erosion of meaning in the process of translation from oral history into standardized data about the artist and their artwork.[19] As their information is repurposed across mediums, reduced to a few words belonging to someone else—a metadata creator, an anonymous Wikidata editor, the Library of Congress Subject Headings—significant

---

18. For more information about liminality or a "third space" in post-colonial theory, see Homi K. Bhabha, *The Location of Culture*, 2nd ed. (London: Routledge, 2004), https://doi.org/10.4324/9780203820551.

19. Nancy Marie Mithlo discusses the complexity of Native American artist identity and the terminology used to describe it in terms of sovereignty, beginning with artists who have "no word for art" in their language: "From one perspective, the 'no word for art' descriptor indicates an Indigenous rejection of how Native arts are perceived in non-Native contexts such as museums, cultural centers, galleries, and scholarly texts— contexts that imbue fine arts with the Western values of individualism, commercialism, objectivism, and competition, as framed by an elitist point of reference. A rejection of the term 'art' is then a rejection of Western culture as capitalist, patriarchal, and, ultimately, shallow, one that does not value the central principles of Indigenous identity, such as land, language, family, and spirituality." Nancy Marie Mithlo, "No Word for Art in Our Language? Old Questions, New Paradigms," *Wicazo Sa Review* 27, no. 1 (2012): 111—26, https://doi.org/10.5749/wicazosareview.27.1.0111.

details of the Native artists' lives that inform their work could be lost or mischaracterized.[20] More so, the public, reductionist nature of linked open data, especially Wikidata, may even exacerbate issues of representation, particularly concerning tribal affiliation and sovereignty, preferred language and nomenclature, and fluidity in preferred identity. In contrast, an oral historian may respectfully address these topics in conversation with an artist or avoid them entirely in response to the artist's wishes.[21]

The Oral History Association's (OHA) Principles and Best Practices documents for oral history projects offer some insight into respectful generation of linked open data.[22] They endeavor to safeguard the well-being of narrators (oral history interviewees)—especially those from vulnerable communities like tribal nations—throughout the oral history process, from interview to preservation, use, and access. The Principles and Best Practices reinforce the responsibility of the oral history creator to engage with the narrators: "The interview process must be transparent, with ongoing participation, consent, and engagement

---

20. There is an inherent tension between data sovereignty and the inclusion that linked open data (LOD), particularly Wikidata, promises. While this is not fully resolved in oral history, interviewees do have a literal platform for their own voices, unlike most LOD, unless that data is created by the artists themselves. Ash-Milby and Phillips ask, "On whose terms should inclusion take place? What does sovereignty look like in terms of institutional practice?", and later conclude, "'Inclusion,' in other words, whether it takes the form of an autonomously governed museum within a larger system, or a separate gallery within a single institution, will remain the marked element as long as neocolonial power relations continue." Kathleen Ash-Milby and Ruth B. Phillips, "Inclusivity or Sovereignty? Native American Arts in the Gallery and the Museum since 1992," *Art Journal* 76, no. 2 (2017): 10—38.

21. This chapter doesn't permit a full exploration of metadata as it relates to art reproduction (Walter Benjamin) or a hot/cool media (Marshall McLuhan), but these suggestions may illuminate the disparity between the work of art of an Indigenous artist, and a metadata record created by a representative of a land-grant institution, and the oral history interview somewhere in the third space between the two. For a thorough examination of the limitations of data structures in Wikidata, see Stacy Allison-Cassin, "Asserting Métis Nationhood: An Examination of Indigenous Nationhood, Sovereignty and Linked Data Through a Wikidata Case Study" in this book.

22. "OHA Principles and Best Practices," Oral History Association, accessed December 11, 2021, https://www.oralhistory.org/principles-and-best-practices-revised-2018/.

among all parties from the first encounter between interviewer and narrator to the creation of end products."[23] At Oklahoma State, creating linked open data for the ONA oral history series is one of the end products of the interview process.

The OHA Principles and Best Practices emphasize participation, thoughtfulness, and transparency, particularly because there is always an existing power differential between interviewer and narrator. Oral history and linked open data creators may approach the project as members of the dominant culture or on behalf of educational institutions historically complicit in the systematic erasure of Indigenous culture. They may even employ some of the same bureaucratic tools—forms, signed documents, written pledges to behave honorably or ethically—that Indigenous people may recognize as devices used to inflict damage on and maintain colonial power over their communities.[24] The Global Indigenous Data Alliance also offers guidance for addressing the implications of power and context in data sharing in its CARE Principles for Indigenous Data Governance. In the section below, we walk through the process established at OSU for working with Native artists to create linked open data profiles on Wikidata based on information gleaned from their oral histories, indicating along the way where procedures relate to the OHA Principles and Best Practices and CARE Principles.

Linked Open Data for Oklahoma Native Artists

A work in progress, the initial development of linked open data for the ONA oral history series has been shaped by local factors,

---

23. Guiding Principle 6 in "OHA Core Principles," Oral History Association, accessed December 11, 2021, https://www.oralhistory.org/oha-core-principles/.

24. Rachel Parsons, "Anthropology Association Apologizes to Native Americans for the Field's Legacy of Harm," *Scientific American*, accessed March 31, 2022, https://www.scientificamerican.com/article/anthropology-association-apologizes-to-native-americans-for-the-fields-legacy-of-harm/. "Native American Graves Protection and Repatriation Act (U.S. National Park Service)." Accessed March 31, 2022. https://www.nps.gov/subjects/nagpra/index.htm.

including an established oral history program, varying techno-logical capabilities of project participants, as well as the global circumstances of the COVID-19 pandemic. From these unique conditions, we have derived general takeaways, which we share in this section, for compiling and wrangling data, communicating with narrators about the project and Wikidata, and developing a consensual and ethical approach to creating linked open data for living people, Native artists in particular.

Data Sources and Data Sharing

The OSU Library initiated the project in 2020 to create linked open data in Wikidata, a platform that permits artists and their communities to manage their own profiles if they choose. As we were preparing the data, however, it became clear that we would have to alter our existing metadata to fit Wikidata and that those changes may not accurately represent the identities of the artists as they would choose to be represented. Creating the data itself would have been relatively straightforward for the ONA oral history series—the metadata is reliable, sourced directly from the interviewed artists, and already standardized for digital col-lections, using controlled vocabularies. In the context of CARE and OHA Principles and Best Practices, however, other Wikidata properties such as gender, nationality, and language raised ques-tions that we could answer only with additional input from the artists themselves.

While Wikidata includes properties for ethnicity or nation-ality, the unique history of Oklahoma demands a more nuanced approach.[25] The OSU Oklahoma Oral History Research Program records tribal affiliation for each artist in the ONA series. While tribal affiliation may have a high degree of correspondence to

---

25. The Wikidata property ids are P172 for ethnic group and P27 for country of citizenship.

tribal citizenship in other states, that is not necessarily the case in Oklahoma. Here, a Native artist may have multiple tribal affiliations they wish to acknowledge as part of their identity, even though their tribal enrollment and citizenship will be with a single tribal nation. The category of tribal affiliation may also be used with artists of Native ancestry whose families are not listed on their respective tribal rolls.[26] One example might be that of an artist of Cherokee heritage. The terms "heritage," "ancestry," or "descendancy" may be recorded under tribal affiliation, to point to the fact that these artists are not, for example, Cherokee citizens. These nuances are also important from a legal standpoint in view of the 1974 and 1990 Indian Arts and Crafts Acts referenced above, which requires verifiable citizenship or documented support of a tribal nation.[27]

Similarly, the categories of ethnicity and/or nationality in Wikidata do not adequately cover citizens of tribal nations. The term may even undercut a tribal nation's sovereignty when the only country of citizenship listed for an artist is the United States. To use the Cherokee example again, an enrolled Cherokee artist has dual citizenship—as a citizen of the Cherokee Nation and as a citizen of the United States. Because accurate representation is not just legally, but ethically important, these sometimes unclear details demand equally significant attention. For example, although a Native artist's gender or connection to a particular language may be shared in their oral history, this information was not

---

26. For more information about issues around tribal enrollment and blood quantum see "Tribal Enrollment Process," July 1, 2015. https://www.doi.gov/tribes/enrollment; Kat Chow, "So What Exactly Is 'Blood Quantum'?", NPR, February 9, 2018, sec. The Code Switch Podcast, https://www.npr.org/sections/codeswitch/2018/02/09/583987261/so-what-exactly-is-blood-quantum. "Developing Stories - Native Photographers in the Field." Accessed April 1, 2022. https://americanindian.si.edu/developingstories/irvine.html. Cecily Hilleary, "Some Native Americans Fear Blood Quantum Is Formula for 'Paper Genocide,'" VOA, accessed April 1, 2022, https://www.voanews.com/a/usa_some-native-americans-fear-blood-quantum-formula-paper-genocide/6208615.html.

27. For a discussion of the impact of these acts on Oklahoma Native artists, see Julie Pearson-Little Thunder, *A Life Made with Artists: Doris Littrell and the Oklahoma Indian Art Scene*, (Oklahoma City, OK: The RoadRunner Press, 2016).

explicitly documented in the oral history metadata. The complex history of forced repression of Native languages and an individual artist's present relationship to this cultural trauma can also inadvertently be reproduced in an unqualified "language" property.[28] Entering a best guess for the fluid, multifaceted nature of public and personal identity in public databases like Wikidata would risk unnecessary harm for the Native artists who have trusted OSU Library's Oklahoma Oral History Research Program with their individual stories. Instead, curating the data with intention and care—in this case by reaching out to interviewees—reduces or possibly eliminates those harms.

More research was necessary before we could contact these artists, and the information we compiled in advance supported the communication process in several ways. First, the Native artists' personal information, recorded in a structured form, could be repurposed as linked open data, along with the Oklahoma Native Artists collection metadata, to support future research on Oklahoma Native artists. This information could then also enhance the notability of Native artists in Wikipedia and contribute to the relationship-building and knowledge sharing processes between the library and the artists.[29] Compiling information about the artists in advance of our conversations with them would permit greater reciprocity and transparency on the part of the library. We could share the available information with the artists, seek corrections, and get their explicit permission (or refusal) to create linked open data from that particular information. The artists

28. In Wikidata, Languages Spoken, Written or Signed (P1412) is described as "language(s) that a person or a people speaks, writes or signs, including the native language(s)" and may be qualified by proficiency, the "measurement of linguistic ability." "Languages Spoken, Written or Signed," Wikidata, accessed December 11, 2021, https://www.wikidata.org/wiki/Property:P1412.

29. In 2015, the OSU Library supported a student internship position to generate new Wikipedia articles focusing on publicly under-recognized individuals represented in the OSU archives, primarily women and artists from the Oklahoma Native Artists Project. This project, begun by Anna DeKoning, was resumed during a shift to remote work in 2020 by Claire Patton, another Library intern and undergraduate history major.

could also conceptualize information missing from their profiles, especially exhibitions and awards used to establish notability, which we could gather from their CVs if they chose to share those as well. The more data we obtain and verify with an artist, the less likely that automatic processes or anonymous editors would apply unverified information to their Wikidata entry. This transparency reassured the artists that they could reach out to the library for assistance if they had questions or issues with what was happening with their data. While our power in this area is limited because this information can still be changed by other editors, this approach provides awareness for the artists that they have some degree of agency in shaping their information and recourse in making future changes to it.[30]

Library staff worked together to compile the supplemental artist information from various sources. During the 2020-21 academic year, a student intern was tasked with scouring transcripts of the oral histories, looking through digital archives, particularly community newspapers, and exploring exhibition catalogs for art exhibitions, museum-owned works, and biographical information.[31] Afterward, OSU Library staff used OpenRefine,

---

30. As an example, in 2020, an artist asked the OSU Library to remove their Wikipedia entry. The OSU Library submitted the request for deletion on the Wikipedia platform and the article was removed. While all requests for changes may not go as smoothly as this did, artists have generally expressed appreciation that library staff are available to help them—through technical assistance or training—shape their representation on these platforms.

31. This research continues in 2022. The growing list of resources has included Julie Pearson-Little Thunder, "Bibliography — Oklahoma Native Art," accessed December 13, 2021, https://oknativeart.library.okstate.edu/index.php/resources/bibliography/. "Oklahoma Digital Newspaper Program," The Gateway to Oklahoma History, accessed December 13, 2021, https://gateway.okhistory.org/explore/collections/ODNP/; "Kansas Historical Open Content," Newspapers.com, accessed December 13, 2021, https://kansashistoricalopencontent.newspapers.com/; "American Indian Newspapers — Uncovering Two Centuries of Important North American Indigenous Journalism," accessed December 13, 2021, https://www.amdigital.co.uk/about/news/item/american-indian-newspapers; "Indigenous Peoples of North America," accessed December 13, 2021, https://www.gale.com/intl/preview/c/indigenous-peoples-north-america. Lawrence Abbott, "Contemporary Native Art: A Bibliography," American Indian Quarterly 18, no. 3 (1994): 383–403. Lawrence Abbott, "Contemporary Native Art II: A

a tool for data cleaning and reconciliation, to collect identifiers for Native artists from the Library of Congress Name Authority File (LCNAF), the Getty Research Institute's Union List of Artist Names (ULAN), and the Virtual International Authority File (VIAF). Native artist roles (such as beadworker or painter), nationalities, and birthdates were also harvested from the ULAN for matching artists.[32] OpenRefine was also used to reconcile these artists with existing Wikidata information.

Data Wrangling

The process of multiple library staff compiling data from many different sources resulted in further reconciliation work to create a shareable, cohesive data set. Since it is difficult to reference a large data table while talking with artists over the phone, we created individual tables for each artist's data that could be shared with the artist verbally or by email. To do this, the digital scholarship librarian manipulated the OpenRefine data in R (a programming language) to remove duplicates and to join the various data with Oklahoma Native Artists metadata and the intern's research. Since our intention was to share the data with the artists for approval, create linked open data, and correct any inaccuracies discovered along the way, it was necessary to keep track of the source of the data along with any changes, which could then be communicated to the Getty or Library of Congress as needed. Finally, the data wrangling process provided an opportunity for organizing the project itself. Artists were grouped to facilitate communication—prioritized from artists with well-established public profiles and/or a high degree of digital literacy to those accustomed to working in more local settings and/or who had

Bibliography," *American Indian Quarterly* 22, no. 1/2 (1998): 98–103.

32. Because OSU Library's Oklahoma Oral History Research Program has a general policy to use an interviewee's preferred name for all public-facing mentions, regardless of its legal status, we confirmed those names with artists and did not transfer an artist's non-Anglo name from other sources into Wikidata.

fewer digital skills and little interest in the Internet.[33] A checklist to record communication was also created at this stage.[34]

Developing Cultural and Technical Competencies

Team members for this project included two oral historians, a metadata librarian, an art/digital scholarship librarian, and an undergraduate history major intern. This project was an opportunity for staff to learn from each other and to develop a working understanding of issues around documentation of Native artists. Some staff had extensive experience in oral history ethics—one of the authors co-chaired the task force to develop the current OHA Principles and Best Practices—or lived experience as a member of the Oklahoma Native artists' community. Others had experience working with metadata, historical research, expert finder systems, or art information, but no personal or academic background in Native American studies. A list of resources initially compiled for the student intern proved useful for identifying problematic subject terms, applying appropriate terminology, and writing about Indigenous peoples.[35]

The global pandemic created unprecedented access to linked open data initiatives and to research presentations by Indigenous scholars, since most meetings shifted to free, online platforms. Although OSU is not currently a member of the Program for Cooperative Cataloging (PCC), staff participated in regular

---

33. With these considerations, we divided the list of artists into the following groups: Artists already in Wikidata; Artists with ULAN/VIAF IDs; Artists with artwork in permanent collections; Artists with Wikipedia articles; Artists with websites on the Oklahoma Native Artists Project site; Artists without Wikipedia articles or websites.

34. View a version of the checklist file here: https://osf.io/3ghyn/?view_only=-9c1a04b0b6274e1a861f3c793290dd23

35. View the resource list here: https://osf.io/3ghyn/?view_only=9c1a04b0b6274e-1a861f3c793290dd23. For a full discussion of library subject headings for Native American people see Michael Q Dudley, "A Library Matter of Genocide: The Library of Congress and the Historiography of the Native American Holocaust," *International Indigenous Policy Journal* 8, no. 2 (March 10, 2017), https://doi.org/10.18584/iipj.2017.8.2.9.

meetings of the PCC Wikidata group.[36] Attendance at meetings of Linked Data for Production (LD4), the ARLIS/NA Wikidata group, and WikiEdu's Wikidata Institute, provided a foundation in working with Wikidata.[37] Two "Digital Humanities at Guelph" workshops offered a comprehensive overview of more theoretical aspects of linked open data: Infrastructure for Linked Open Data and Ontologies for Diversity.[38] Non-oral history staff participated in the basic oral history workshops offered to the public by OSU Library's Oklahoma Oral History Research Program.[39] Virtual presentations by Dr. Sandy Littletree, Dr. Dwanna McKay, and Dr. Kim TallBear, as well as speakers hosted by the OSU Center for Sovereign Nations, provided insight from Indigenous scholars on data and information sovereignty.[40]

In addition to attendance at presentations and workshops, several active learning opportunities engaged staff in examining their own biases. *The Ethical Toolkit for Engineering/ Design Practice from the Markkula Center for Applied Ethics*

36. "PCC Wikidata Pilot - Wikidata." Accessed April 1, 2022. https://www.wikidata.org/wiki/Wikidata:WikiProject_PCC_Wikidata_Pilot.

37. "LD4 Community Site." Accessed April 1, 2022. https://sites.google.com/stanford.edu/ld4-community-site/home. "ARLIS/NA Wikidata Group - Google Groups." Accessed April 1, 2022. https://groups.google.com/g/arlis-wikidata?pli=1. Wiki Education. "Courses," February 17, 2022. https://wikiedu.org/learn/.

38. Digital Humanities at The University of Guelph. "2021 Summer Workshops | College of Arts." University of Guelph. Accessed April 1, 2022. https://www.uoguelph.ca/arts/dhguelph/summer2021.

39. "Oral History Resources." Oklahoma State University Library. Accessed April 1, 2022. https://library.okstate.edu/oralhistory/oral-history-resources.

40. Sandy Littletree, "Co-Creating Knowledge in LIS Research: An Indigenous Researcher's Approach," https://www.ala.org/rt/lrrt-past-webinars. Dwanna McKay, "Resistance, Resilience, & Reclamation: Exploring Academic Success Among Native/ Indigenous Students," https://www.youtube.com/watch?v=LDehX6OCl1o.

Kim TallBear, "Standing With and Speaking as Faith," Institute for Research Design in Librarianship (IRDL) Speaker Series, January 27, 2021, https://digitalcommons.lmu.edu/irdl-speakerseries/1. OSU Center for Sovereign Nations, "Sovereignty Speaks - Oklahoma State University." Accessed April 1, 2022. https://sovnationcenter.okstate.edu/csn-2020/sov-speaks.html.

offers practical exercises for ensuring ethical project outcomes.[41] The sixth tool, "Remembering the Ethical Benefits of Creative Work," was especially relevant for our project because it helped align our intention—to create linked open data for the benefit of Native artists, their communities, and researchers of Native art—with ethical practice.[42] Presenting our work while it was in progress has also been an invaluable part of our learning process. Preparing presentations helped articulate our goals for the linked open data project, and feedback and questions from various audiences provided both guidance and reinforcement for our approach. Writing this chapter while the linked open data project was still in progress helped articulate and document our rationale for taking a slower, more ethical approach to creating linked open data and the workflow we established to carry out that plan.

Communication with Artists

According to the Oral History Association, "Oral history refers to both the interview process and the products that result....Once completed, an interview, if it is placed in an archive, can be used beyond its initial purpose with the permission of both the interviewer and the narrator."[43] Because adding linked open data about the interviews to Wikidata would take Native artists' information

---

41. Santa Clara University, "An Ethical Toolkit for Engineering/Design Practice," accessed December 11, 2021, https://www.scu.edu/ethics-in-technology-practice/ethical-toolkit/.

42. Megan Macken and Madison Chartier, "Representation and Data Collection: The Ethics of Using Linked Open Data for Oklahoma Native Artists," https://connect.ala.org/core/viewdocument/core-ig-virtual-week-metadata-ig-se?CommunityKey=a38252d1-29e5-42e7-8b5d-a43a19f99aea&tab=librarydocuments. In this presentation, the authors respond to questions from tool five: "Why are we doing this, and for what good ends? Will society/the world/our customers really be better off with this tech than without it? Or are we trying to generate inauthentic needs or manufactured desires, simply to justify a new thing to sell? Has the ethical benefit of this technology remained at the center of our work and thinking? What are we willing to sacrifice to do this right?"

43. Oral History Association, "OHA Core Principles: 9."

from the relatively local sphere of the library website to a prominent public place such as a Google knowledge panel, it is not
necessarily covered by the explicit permission we have already
secured from the artists to share their oral history interviews on
the library website.[44] Not only is linked open data more prominent than the oral history interviews, it is also easier to share
and repurpose, and could highlight relationships or connections
that the artists do not wish to broadcast or have changed their
mind about years later.[45] Linked open data can be challenging
to understand even for librarians who work with metadata, and
it is generally not a familiar topic for many people outside of
libraries. Assuming cultural and power differences between
librarians at OSU and the artists, and differing levels of familiarity with technology, clear communication is vital to ensure that
the artists understand the linked open data project and its benefits
and risks before consenting to have the library create linked open
data about them. Once we had envisioned various scenarios and
were familiar with the available artist data, we devised a process and workflow for communicating with individual artists as
detailed below.

Library Liaison to the Native Artist Community

An oral historian on staff at the OSU Library and a member of
the Oklahoma Native artists community, Dr. Julie Pearson-Little
Thunder conducted the original oral history interviews with the
artists. She now serves as liaison to the Native artists for this
linked open data project and plays a key role in securing their

---

44. Oral History Association, "OHA Core Principles: 2 and 9."

45. For an overview of the discussion around revision of oral history data in the
digital era, see Elinor Mazé, "Deconstruction without Destruction: Creating Metadata
for Oral History in a Digital World," in *Oral History and Digital Humanities: Voice,
Access, and Engagement*, ed. Douglas A. Boyd and Mary A. Larson (New York: Pal-
grave Macmillan, 2014), http://ebookcentral.proquest.com/lib/oks-ebooks/detail.ac-
tion?docID=1953056.

permission.[46] In working through consent for linked open data, Dr. Pearson-Little Thunder contacts artists by phone to talk through the project and discuss the data we have compiled. She asks whether they would like to have a Wikidata profile created or edited for them and relays any desired data changes or related Wikipedia entry to the metadata librarian, who then updates the data in the project spreadsheet. If an artist does not want us to create a Wikidata profile, then we ask if they would be comfortable being part of an OSU-curated linked open data profile on a platform hosted at OSU—the main difference being that OSU could more readily secure the integrity of the artist's personal information. If they agree to either scenario, we also ask them to provide the library with a copy of their CV, so we can include exhibition and award data. Artists may also request assistance in removing a Wikipedia page or Wikidata profile, which may not permanently keep their data from appearing, but does empower the artists to take control of personal data.[47] Afterward, Dr. Pearson-Little Thunder sends an email to document the conversation, which is then saved locally for project recordkeeping. Those artists who decline, or who request assistance in removing an existing profile, are documented internally but are not sent a follow-up email. Throughout the process, the digital scholarship librarian records contacts made and consent received on the communication checklist. This communication process is necessarily time consuming and, at the time of writing, only a small portion of the 141 artists had been contacted. The response so far has been positive with few requests to change our existing data. Artists are generally interested in learning about the platform

---

46. While Dr. Pearson-Little Thunder has been an essential contributor, the sustainability of this project and others like it is not dependent on a single researcher. The OSU Library's Oral History Research Program is available to offer guidance to other GLAM institutions who are interested in conducting work with similar communities or have questions about the ethical guidelines presented here.

47. One artist did request assistance in removing a Wikipedia article that the library had created on the artist's behalf several years ago. This process was equally as important in terms of individual agency as the creation of public data profiles.

for themselves, sometimes with the help of their younger family members. Wikidata will be created in bulk after more discussions with artists have taken place.[48]

Supporting Documentation

To support the communication process, we created two Frequently Asked Questions (FAQ) documents, which were informed by CARE and OHA guidelines.[49] These FAQs address the usefulness of Wikidata for researchers, the possibility of greater representation for Native artists as a group, and publicity for the individual artist. They also inform artists of the potential proliferation and modifications of the data and offer training and support for both individual and community involvement in editing Wikipedia and Wikidata. The information from the FAQs informed phone conversations with the artists, and the documents could be shared with the artists if they wish to see them. The FAQs also confirm our ongoing commitment to facilitate changes to the data in the future. This measure is one step toward providing Native artists the "authority to control" their data, as outlined in the Indigenous Data Governance CARE Principles A1 through A3. The FAQs and our open offer to provide Wiki training support CARE R2 are a "reciprocal responsibility to enhance data literacy." Although we created follow-up letter templates to share with the artists after the phone conversation, these letters proved too formal. Dr. Pearson-Little Thunder has opted instead to follow up the phone conversations with personal emails that reiterate her understanding of their phone conversation. These emails are archived, in a process similar to our oral history consent forms, as documentation of an artist's agreement to have a linked open data profile created or edited for them. The thoughtful, yet informal

---

48. For an example data see: https://osf.io/qxkng/?view_only=9c1a04b0b6274e-1a861f3c793290dd23.

49. View the FAQ documents here: https://osf.io/3ghyn/?view_only=9c1a04b-0b6274e1a861f3c793290dd23.

nature of this process underscores the personal connection between the individual artists and the OSU Library, facilitated by Dr. Pearson-Little Thunder, and the importance of preserving that relationship (CARE R1).[50]

Conclusion

The OSU Library has not approached this linked open data project as an isolated exercise in dealing with the intricacies of a particular platform or standard. Rather, we view the project as a way to curate linked open data for underrepresented, living people in the context of oral history practice and to center the individuals who have agreed to share their histories with the OSU Library. We do this with an awareness of the inherent tension present in the concept of inclusivity.[51] According to the OHA Principles and Best Practices, "The value of oral history lies largely in the way it helps to place people's experiences within a larger social and historical context."[52] The Oklahoma Native Artists oral histories not only offer a biographical and career overview of these artists' lives, but also situate them within a community cultural context, as well as a national and global art scene. In so doing, they constitute the history of Oklahoma Native art itself. Because these lives are often not thoroughly documented elsewhere, the value of linked open data for the Oklahoma Native Artists oral histories also lies in its promise of contextualization, even if in the abbreviated form of metadata. As with history, linked open data networks are predetermined by narratives of the powerful or, in the case of Wikipedia or Wikidata, the notable. Developing

---

50. "R1: For Positive Relationships. Indigenous data use is unviable unless linked to relationships built on respect, reciprocity, trust, and mutual understanding, as defined by the Indigenous Peoples to whom those data relate. Those working with Indigenous data are responsible for ensuring that the creation, interpretation, and use of those data uphold, or are respectful of, the dignity of Indigenous nations and communities." CARE Principles of Indigenous Data Governance.

51. Mithlo, "Red Man's Burden."

52. Oral History Association, "OHA Core Principles: 3."

linked open data for artists from typically marginalized cultures positions the artists in the larger web of data, where their presence in art collections and exhibitions and their connection to other contemporary artists and museums is made explicit.

While other linked open data projects may share data as a starting point, our approach places greater emphasis on preparation than data production. As Bell, et al., have argued in favor of a cybernetic approach, "By de-centralising the data as the unit of analysis, and identifying and analysing the system that data are a part of, we open up greater opportunities for deeper insight and understanding, as well as greater possibilities to disrupt the status quo and drive positive change."[53] Thoughtful advance planning allows greater flexibility during an oral history interview. Similarly, careful planning can contribute to a fluid communication process for a linked open data project on living people. Prior to contacting the artists, we addressed questions about our own goals, the nature of the data that exists or needs to be collected, potentially sensitive or problematic data, and the impact of linked open data on the individual artist and their community. Working through these questions from the outset simplified the communication process, resulting in fewer follow ups to address artists'

---

53. Bell, Genevieve, Maia Gould, Brenda Martin, Amy McLennan, and Ellen O'Brien. "Do More Data Equal More Truth? Toward a Cybernetic Approach to Data." *Australian Journal of Social Issues* 56, no. 2 (2021): 213—22. https://doi.org/10.1002/ajs4.168. Bell et al.'s cybernetic approach offers another compelling framework for decentering data in favor of living people and the systems they are part of, "Cybernetic praxis could appreciate a different kind of diversity: that of voices, and points of view. Making room for such diverse conversations requires up-front commitment, considerable attention and a capacity to tolerate the conflicts that inevitably arise when persistently different viewpoints are articulated. Central to this is creating space for productive discomfort, or even systemic incommensurability…. It yields opportunities for additional data collection, but also problematises how collection might proceed and the impact on the communities it is collected from and the environment which houses it. By de-centralising the data as the unit of analysis, and identifying and analysing the system that data are a part of, we open up greater opportunities for deeper insight and understanding, as well as greater possibilities to disrupt the status quo and drive positive change."

concerns. Reducing confusion and ambiguity freed up the dialogue and made it possible to listen to the concerns, questions, and opinions of the artists about whether they find linked open data beneficial at all. Poorly planned projects may not only encumber communication, they may also obscure information that needs to be shared with artists, unintentionally exclude them from the process, and thus undermine ethical goals.

As with oral history, the afterlife of linked open data representing living people is necessarily dynamic and cybernetic. We anticipate changing our responses and processes in tandem with the artists as the technology, preferences, and relationships evolve over time. Although we may encounter negative, unanticipated outcomes that require us to retool our process, this would be difficult to ascertain without the existing partnership of the artists. Ideally, library platforms for linked open data will develop into something less akin to historical recordkeeping of church registers and census records, and more like community-controlled systems that Native communities use to determine the shape of the data that represents them.[54] Until then, by framing linked open data as an end product of oral histories that is informed by the ethical considerations of both oral history and Indigenous data governance, this project has offered one path forward for working with living people to create linked open data that reflects their self-representation.

---

54. Examples of community-controlled systems include Traditional Knowledge Labels and Mukurtu: Local Contexts, "Traditional Knowledge Labels," accessed December 11, 2021, https://localcontexts.org/labels/traditional-knowledge-labels/. "Mukurtu CMS: A Safe Keeping Place," accessed December 11, 2021, https://mukurtu.org/about/.

"All We Want Are the Facts, Ma'am": Negotiating User Needs and Creator Privacy in Name Authority Records

HANNA BERTOLDI, PEGGY GRIESINGER,
& MIKALA NARLOCK

Introduction

In the *Dragnet* franchise, a police detective character named Joe Friday is associated with the catchphrase, "All we want are the facts, ma'am."[1] Although the exact wording of this phrase changes over the different remakes of the series, the spirit of it remains the same: only the facts are important for solving police cases, and women must have this explained to them. By facts, Friday doesn't mean that female witnesses are untruthful; he means that, by virtue of being women, they cannot help but embellish their personal statements with emotion and subjectivity. Friday lived in a fictional Los Angeles where patriarchal, status quo "logic" was valued above other forms of reasoning and knowledge, but, ironically, he could not see the emotional, illogical fallacy of his own highly subjective views about women.

Library and museum catalogers, who are disproportionately women,[2] might be reminded of Friday's catchphrase when following widely accepted best practices for creating authority

---

1. Commonly quoted as "Just the facts, ma'am."
2. American Library Association, "Diversity Counts 2009-2010 Update," last modified September 18, 2012, http://www.ala.org/aboutala/offices/diversity/diversity-counts/2009-2010update.

records for authors or artists. As a product of the standards and systems used to record authority data, biographical metadata is presented as objective fact. However, the library and museum cataloging professions are slowly coming to the realization that recording the world involves some degree of uncertainty, and, perhaps more importantly, bias. Rather than trying to achieve objectivity, the process of recording facts is a matter of perspective beholden to a white, patriarchal worldview. As library and museum catalogers become increasingly aware of the ways that personal and systemic biases can influence their work,[3] online catalogs and related technologies haven't been changed to accommodate these new approaches.

This chapter will use the University of Notre Dame's Marble (Museum, Archives, Rare Books, and Library Exploration platform) project[4] as a useful framework for exploring some ethical cataloging concerns associated with biographical metadata as they relate to linked data in libraries, archives, and museums (LAM). During the development of this platform, extensive user testing revealed frequent requests for additional information about content creators. While a linked data solution *could* be deployed to enhance personal information about creators, the team questioned the ethical implications of such an approach. This chapter is the result of their analysis. First, the authors will provide an overview of how linked data infrastructure is leveraged by Marble to meet user needs within resource limitations. Next, the authors will describe the methods used for product testing

---

3. CalPoly Robert E. Kennedy Library, "Gaps and Silences in the Archives: Critical Use of Archives and Primary Sources," Accessed March 3, 2022, https://guides. lib.calpoly.edu/archives/critical; Alexis Antracoli, Annalise Berdini, Kelly Bolding, Faith Charlton, Amanda Ferrara, Valencia Johnson, and Katy Rawdon, "Archives for Black Lives: Anti-Racist Descriptions," *Philadelphia, USA: Archives for Black Lives in Philadelphia (A4BLiP)*. October 2019. https://archivesforblacklives.files.wordpress. com/2019/10/ardr_final.pdf; Dorothy Berry, "Umbra Search African American History: Aggregating African American Digital Archives," *items*, December 14, 2016, https://items.ssrc.org/parameters/umbra-search-african-american-history-aggregating-african-american-digital-archives/.

4. https://marble.nd.edu.

and development. After presenting a review of current literature, the authors will then use the framework of the slow movement,[5] or the effort to slow down aspects of our society, to explore how time is an important factor for creating more ethical metadata. Finally, the team concludes by considering potential future solutions for the tension between user needs and ethical cataloging of creator metadata. While time is not an unlimited resource of LAM, the authors argue that focusing cataloging efforts on local holdings and working with living creators to create ethical metadata will benefit the community as a whole.

Overview of Marble

In 2017, the University of Notre Dame received a grant from The Andrew W. Mellon Foundation to support the development of an application that would provide unified access to rare and unique digitized materials on campus.[6] The Marble platform, which the authors collaborated on between January 2019 and June 2021, consolidates cultural heritage materials from the Snite Museum of Art (SMA) and Hesburgh Libraries, which includes both the Rare Books & Special Collections (RBSC) department and the University of Notre Dame Archives (UA), into an online collections platform. The resulting discovery system harvests metadata directly from disparate source systems and displays unified fields based on a custom metadata map.[7] This harvest model allows grant partners to use their respective best practices to catalog in their source system and updates metadata on the Marble site as partners change local records.

---

5. Carl Honoré, *In Praise of Slow: How a Worldwide Movement Is Challenging the Cult of Speed.* (London: Orion, 2004).

6. Diane Walker and Charles Loving, "The Hesburgh Libraries and Snite Museum of Art, University of Notre Dame: Proposal for a Unified Preservation and Exhibition Platform," October 31, 2018, https://osf.io/dmt47/.

7. Hesburgh Libraries uses the MARC 21 Format for Bibliographic Data and EAD XML. Snite uses EmbARK XML that loosely follows VRA Core. The final format of the metadata on the Marble site is JSON.

A crucial piece of that metadata is subject terms or keywords because these terms are what allow users to thematically search collection items across SMA, RBSC, and UA holdings, a key objective of the grant. To make this possible, the team made keywords and subject terms a required element of the metadata crosswalk for inclusion in Marble,[8] despite the fact that the Libraries and the Museum were using different controlled vocabularies based on best practices for their respective collections: Library of Congress Subject Headings (LCSH) or Getty (Iconography Authority and Art & Architecture Thesaurus®). After testing different ideas to combine the vocabularies, the team ultimately decided to make use of the pre-existing linked open data capabilities of the vocabularies that each institution was already using. The team decided to mine the LCSH and Getty hierarchies by either downloading the expanded subject authority records directly (LCSH in JSON) or utilizing publicly available application programming interfaces (Getty using the Getty Web Services APIs). Since controlled vocabularies have broader, narrower, and variant terms, these terms facilitate searching for thematic and topical keywords by augmenting the individual terms chosen during local cataloging.[9] Term expansion relies on harvesting a unique identifier (*i.e.*, URI) from the source system, which is then used to expand subject content from LCSH and Getty. The augmentation does not change the subject analysis in the source system, but, rather, creates better results when a user searches online. With a greater number of terms associated with each record because of this augmentation process, the user can find connections among campus collections through a simple keyword search.

The use of linked data vocabularies to enrich local metadata was a solution that fulfilled user needs and worked within the

---

8. As of February 24, 2022, keywords are no longer required metadata for the Snite's records.

9. Hanna Bertoldi, Peggy Griesinger, Jon Hartzler and Steve Mattison. "Thematic Metadata Solutions Report." February 4, 2022. https://osf.io/dv6tg/.

capacity and time constraints of the grant team. By leveraging the power of controlled vocabularies, users can thematically search across cultural heritage collections on campus. The other advantage of using controlled vocabularies is that it eliminates the time and labor needed to regenerate information that is already available.[10] While it should be acknowledged that these vocabularies are not without bias and harmful terminology, the hope is that when these issues are iteratively remedied,[11] changes will be applied to Marble without manual intervention because the keywords from LCSH and Getty are linked to the authoritative sources. Utilizing linked open data infrastructure through controlled vocabularies is a lightweight way of using linked data to develop greater consistency and findability within an online catalog. While the team ultimately did not leverage a robust implementation of linked open data (e.g., RDF), due in part to the high technical burden of establishing and maintaining this complex infrastructure, the Marble project provided a valuable opportunity to explore the ethical considerations of linked data and name authority records.

User-Centered Design

The use of linked data infrastructure for subject searching was driven by the campus users' need to serendipitously discover digitized objects from multiple campus units. From the outset of the grant, user-centered design[12] was a driving force. This

---

10. Amber Billey, "Just Because We Can, Doesn't Mean We Should: An Argument for Simplicity and Data Privacy with Name Authority Work in the Linked Data Environment," *Journal of Library Metadata* 19, nos. 1-2 (2019): 12, https://doi.org/10.10 80/19386389.2019.1589684; Hope A. Olson, "The Power to Name: Representation in Library Catalogs," *Signs: Journal of Women in Culture and Society* 26, no. 3 (2001): 640, https://doi.org/10.1086/495624.

11. Emily Drabinski, "Queering the Catalog: Queer Theory and the Politics of Correction," *The Library Quarterly: Information, Community, Policy* 83, no. 2 (2013): 103, https://doi.org/10.1086/669547; Olson, "The Power to Name," 646.

12. Reveall, "A Guide to User-Centered Design: Principles, Methods, and Processes," Last modified 2022. https://www.reveall.co/guides/user-centered-design.

is an approach to software engineering that places target users and key demographics at the center of development. The result of this practice is that the platform is built in collaboration with end-users, not just for them.[13] To fulfill this design goal, campus users—students, faculty, and staff—and internal stakeholders—library and museum faculty and staff—tested the product in numerous iterations.[14] Both campus and internal users regularly said that they wanted more cataloging information about individual items, such as more robust descriptions, more complete item-level description (especially in archival finding aids), more personal information about creators, and easier ways of finding depictions of, and works by, identity groups outside of the socially dominant cultures.

The feedback that the Marble team received from user experience testing centered around identifying objects and creators of particular races, ethnicities, genders, and sexual orientations.[15] Marble site users wanted to find the socially perceived "others" in Notre Dame's catalogs from the perspective of a heteronormative, white, phallocentric worldview.[16] Historical practices in library

13. Elena Gonzales, *Exhibitions for Social Justice*. (London: Routledge, 2019), 147-8.

14. E.g., see: Abigail Shelton, "If you give a college student a donut: Flash UX for academic museums," March 3, 2021, https://osf.io/mh3jz; Mikala Narlock and Abigail Shelton, "You're a (testing) wizard, Harry: LibWizard and virtual user testing," Academic Libraries of Indiana (ALI) Assessment Committee 2021, online presentation, https://doi.org/10.7274/r0-g4en-6780; Mikala Narlock and Abigail Shelton, "It's just different: Pivoting from in-person to virtual user testing," Academic Libraries of Indiana (ALI) Assessment Committee 2021, online presentation, https://doi.org/10.7274/r0-arcx-h349; Mikala Narlock and Abigail Shelton, "The same but different: Collaborating on user interface expectations for a campus art museum, library, and archives," Designing 4 Digital 2021, online presentation, https://doi.org/10.7274/r0-s4gx-p050.

15. One could imagine that other identity affiliations such as religious beliefs, national origins, or disability status would also be of interest.

16. Francis E. Kendall, "Understanding White Privilege," 2002, http://www.goldenbridgesschool.org/uploads/1/9/5/4/19541249/understanding_white_privilege_-_kendall_edited.pdf; George W. Stocking, *Objects and Others: Essays on Museums and Material Culture* (Madison, WI.: University of Wisconsin Press, 1985), 4; Anita Coleman, "Using the Anti-Racism Digital Library and Thesaurus to Understand Information Access, Authority, Value and Privilege," *Theological Librarianship* 13, no. 1 (2020): 4, https://doi.org/10.31046/tl.v13i1.560.

and museum cataloging already reflect this biased viewpoint. Authority records of artists in the SMA's catalog contain racial and ethnic information from the perspective that whiteness is the standard.[17] Pablo Picasso, for example, is cataloged as a Spanish painter; his authority record does not identify his race because his whiteness is considered unexceptional.[18] As a white artist, he is cataloged by his nationality (Spanish) instead of by his race. Similar critiques have been pointed out with LCSH,[19] where the identity of the reader is assumed to be "white, Christian...male, and heterosexual."[20] Subject headings primarily express race or gender when the term is "outside of the norm, especially in terms of subject/object relations,"[21] as evidenced by the fact that it is more common to apply non-white racial identities and treat white as the default,[22] even though "Whites" was added as a LCSH in 1986.[23] The inconsistency by which identity information is recorded (i.e., only when it is exceptional) is relevant when trying to build an online collection that will return results for a user search on race, e.g. African American artists. Authority records for people would need to include race, ethnicity, nationality,

---

17. Elena Fernandez-Sacco, "Framing 'The Indian': The Visual Culture of Conquest in the Museums of Pierre Eugene Du Simitiere and Charles Willson Peale, 1779-96," *Social Identities* 8, no. 4 (2002): 571–618, https://doi.org/10.1080/13504630220 00068389; Susan Cahan, *Mounting Frustration: The Art Museum in the Age of Black Power* (Durham, NC: Duke University Press, 2016), 266.

18. Ellen Fernandez-Sacco, "Check Your Baggage: Resisting Whiteness in Art History," *Art Journal* 60, no. 4 (2001): 59, https://doi.org/10.1080/00043249.2001.10792 096.

19. Sanford Berman, *Prejudices and Antipathies: A Tract on the LC Subject Heads Concerning People* (Metuchen, NJ: Scarecrow Press, 1971); Joan Marshall, "LC Labeling: An Indictment," in *Revolting Librarians*, edited by Celeste West and Elizabeth Katz, 45–49 (San Francisco: Booklegger Press, 1972).

20. Mary M. Huston and Joe L. Williams, "Researcher Response to the Politics of Information," *Research Strategies* 5, no. 2 (Spring 1987): 92.

21. Olson, "The Power to Name," 647.

22. Coleman, "Using the Anti-Racism Digital Library," 5.

23. Library of Congress Subject Headings, "White people," last modified January 19, 2022, https://id.loc.gov/authorities/subjects/sh85146547.html; Elizabeth Hobart, "Antiracism in the Catalog: An Analysis of Records," *College & Research Libraries News* 81, no. 8 (2020): 378–81, https://doi.org/10.5860/crln.81.8.378.

sexual orientation, and gender identity information in all cases when reasonably and ethically possible for searches to be accurate and fair, and not just when it falls outside of the norm—the norm of WEB3CH2A2MS: "white, ethnically European, bourgeois, Christian, cisgender, citizen, heterosexual, able-bodied, allosexual, monogamous, men, settlers."[24]

The technological capabilities of providing users with racial information (and any other identity affiliations that users might be interested in searching) already exist both in theory and in practice. A cataloger could populate additional metadata fields in a content management system manually or use linked open data (LOD) that has this information pre-populated. Moreover, community-driven ontologies (e.g., *Homosaurus*) provide marginalized communities the opportunity to control the terms used by and about them. The Marble team also looked to sources like Wikidata, which aggregate the unique identifiers of LCSH and Getty name authority records, as a way of reconciling the same person in the online search engine across different structured vocabularies. Unlike local cataloging, LOD provides a technical solution to the complexities of identity formation, in particular by allowing multiple identity affiliations.[25] Many collection

---

24. Originally WEBCHAM from Hope Olson's naming of the default and assumed universal center of cataloging and classification systems, expanded by Michelle Caswell to include "cis" and "citizen" at the encouragement of Marika Cifor, and here expanded by Watson to include settler status, relationship, and romantic orientations (Hope A. Olson, "Patriarchal Structures of Subject Access and Subversive Techniques for Change," *Canadian Journal of Information and Library Science* 26, no. 2-3 (2001): 4; Michelle Caswell, "Dusting for Fingerprints: Introducing Feminist Standpoint Appraisal," *Journal of Critical Library and Information Studies* Special Edition "Radical Empathy in Archival Practice" 3 (2019): 7; Brian M. Watson, "Advancing Equitable Cataloging," *NASKO* 8, no. 1 (November 12, 2021): 8, https://doi.org/10.7152/nasko.v8i1.15887; B. M. Watson, email to authors, February 24, 2022).

25. Kelly J. Thompson, "More Than a Name: A Content Analysis of Name Authority Records for Authors Who Self-Identify as Trans," *Library Resources & Technical Services* 60, no. 3 (2016): 140–155, https://doi.org/10.5860/lrts.60n3.140; Ruth Kitchin Tillman, "Barriers to Ethical Name Modeling in Current Linked Data Encoding Practices," in *Ethical Questions in Name Authority Control*, edited by Jane Sandberg, 234–259 (Sacramento, CA: Library Juice Press, 2019).

management systems only allow one value in a field, and since people have multiple axes of identity, choosing one over another may give inaccurate priority to one.[26] The values in LOD are not controlled by the limitations of cataloging databases, so a multiplicity of identities can be expressed in the authority record. At first glance, the infrastructure of LOD seems to provide both a technical and ethical solution to displaying creator identities on online catalogs, as requested by users during extensive product testing. However, the work of creating and managing name authority records for living artists presents different, and equally pressing, ethical concerns.

Name Authority Records

The authors examined how name authority records (NARs) are created by libraries and museums to test how LOD could be used to deliver more information about creators. Libraries in general started using NARs as a means of enforcing consistency in catalogs.[27] These records organized items under one standardized name of an entity.[28] Records only contained as much information as needed to disambiguate one name from the next.[29] The library profession has seen this so-called "name-centered" approach transition to a "person-centered" approach due to the adoption

26. Ivan Karp, "On Civil Society and Social Identity," in *Museums and Communities: The Politics of Public Culture*, edited by Ivan Karp, Christine Mullen Kreamer, and Steven Lavine, 19–33, (Washington, DC: Smithsonian Institution Press, 1992); Hope A. Olson, "Sameness and Difference," *Library Resources & Technical Services* 45, no. 3 (2001): 116, https://doi.org/10.5860/lrts.45n3.115.

27. Thompson, "More Than a Name,"140.

28. Rebecca A. Wiederhold and Gregory F. Reeve, "Authority Control Today: Principles, Practices, and Trends," *Cataloging & Classification Quarterly* 59, no. 2-3 (2021): 129, https://doi.org/10.1080/01639374.2021.1881009.

29. Niu has pointed out that LOD makes disambiguating records much easier because numeric identifiers can be used instead of text strings (Jinfang Niu, "Evolving Landscape in Name Authority Control," *Cataloging & Classification Quarterly* 51, no. 4 (2013): 404–19, https://doi.org/10.1080/01639374.2012.756843). This means that it is no longer necessary to assign personal information to disambiguate records.

of the Resource Description and Access (RDA) standard and creation of vocabularies like the Library of Congress Demographic Group Terms.[30] In an article examining NARs for trans creators, data analyst Kelly Thompson writes that "with the instruction and adoption of the Functional Requirements for Authority Data (FRAD) and Resource Description and Access (RDA), the original scope of a name authority record was broadened from simply that of a carrier of an authorized heading or access point to a description of an entity with the development of an expanded list of attributes that can be included in name authority records."[31] These attributes can be additional forms of the name, key dates, related places, occupation, or gender.[32] The cataloger can include this information to further disambiguate records and name entities[33] and store information about identity.[34]

While traditional library cataloging is evolving NARs from a documented list of authorized name headings to a means of recording characteristics about authors, this practice has been commonplace in the theoretical framework for creating NARs in museum catalogs.[35] A common tombstone format lists an artist's nationality/race/ethnicity/cultural group and life dates, usually immediately above the title of the artwork.[36] The SMA's online

30. Thomas A. Whittaker, "Demographic Characteristics in Personal Name Authority Records and the Ethics of a Person-Centered Approach to Name Authority Control," in *Ethical Questions in Name Authority Control*, edited by Jane Sandberg, 57 (Sacramento, CA: Library Juice Press, 2019); Library of Congress, "Demographic Group Terms PDF Files," last modified September 17, 2021, https://www.loc.gov/aba/publications/FreeLCDGT/freelcdgt.html.

31. Thompson, "More," 140.

32. Wiederhold and Reeve, "Authority," 137.

33. Ibid.

34. Lihong Zhu, "The Future of Authority Control: Issues and Trends in the Linked Data Environment," *Journal of Library Metadata* 19, no. 3-4 (2019): 226, https://doi.org/10.1080/19386389.2019.1688368.

35. Christine Hennessey, "The Status of Name Authority Control in the Cataloging of Original Art Objects," *Art Documentation: Journal of the Art Libraries Society of North America* 5, no. 1 (1986): 3–10, http://www.jstor.org/stable/27947541.

36. Fiona Cameron and Helena Robinson, "Digital Knowledgescapes: Cultural, Theoretical, Practical, and Usage Issues Facing Museum Collection Databases in a

collection displays this kind of basic tombstone information about creators to provide context to objects in time and place. However, as will be discussed below, museum catalogers need to be more specific about how they are storing identity information in their databases. Identifying nationality for white creators while identifying the ethnicity, race, or cultural group of a minority perpetuates othering. This practice of assumed whiteness is a problem in both library and museum cataloging. Although users may not intend to facilitate assumed whiteness, it is important to confront the structures of bias that are present in library and museum catalogs before we are able to address user requests for more complete biographical information.

Ethical Concerns

Professional standards in libraries are moving closer to the style that museums have adopted towards NARs—as a means of organizing identity rather than only disambiguating it, a process that has been facilitated by the technological capabilities of linked open data and its increasing adoption in libraries. But, while cataloging technologies allow catalogers to store identity information in NARs, what are the ethical concerns about classifying artists and authors by additional categories like gender, race, and ethnicity? This question is particularly provocative when considering the kind of biographical information that should or should not be available in online collections for living creators. For LAM professionals, the amount of professional guidance is sparse, although recent progress is promising. Because many LAM institutions have online collections and cataloging information holds so much weight in the public sphere, this lack of instruction is all the more surprising. LAM institutions are trusted by the public

---

Digital Epoch," in *Theorizing Digital Cultural Heritage: A Critical Discourse*, edited by Fiona Cameron and Sarah Kenderdine, 166 (Cambridge, MA: MIT Press, 2007).

and, thus, the public views its records as authority.[37] Technology masks the complex decisions that catalogers make when creating metadata,[38] causing users to assume that these data points are fact, rather than highly simplistic reductions of reality influenced by bias.[39] Online collections only show the end result of intensive research and complex cataloging decisions—the choices institutions make about what biographical information to display and how to categorize it is an ethical concern that demands particular care.[40]

---

37. Lisa Gilbert, "Valuing Critical Inquiry Skills in Museum Literacy," *Social Studies Research & Practice* 11, no. 3 (Fall 2016): 80–95; Elaine Heumann Gurian, "Curator: From Soloist to Impresario," in *Hot Topics, Public Culture, Museums*, edited by Fiona Cameron and Lynda Kelly (Newcastle upon Tyne, UK: Cambridge Scholars, 2010), 96.

38. Drabinski, "Queering," 104; Sheila Bair, "Toward a Code of Ethics for Cataloging," *Technical Services Quarterly* 23, no. 1 (2005): 15, https://doi.org/10.1300/J124v23n01_02; Geoffrey Bowker and Susan Leigh Star, *Sorting Things Out: Classification and Its Consequences* (Cambridge, MA: MIT Press, 1999), 135; Anna M. Ferris, "The Ethics and Integrity of Cataloging," *Journal of Library Administration* 47, no. 3-4 (2008): 179, https://doi.org/10.1080/01930820802186514; Hannah Turner, "The Computerization of Material Culture Catalogues: Objects and Infrastructure in the Smithsonian Institution's Department of Anthropology," *Museum Anthropology* 39, no. 2 (2016): 163–77, https://doi.org/10.1111/muan.12122.

39. Jennifer M. Martin, "Records, Responsibility, and Power: An Overview of Cataloging Ethics," *Cataloging & Classification Quarterly* 59, no. 2-3 (2021): 281, https://doi.org/10.1080/01639374.2020.1871458; Suse Anderson, "Some Provocations on the Digital Future of Museums," in *The Digital Future of Museums: Conversations and Provocations*, edited by Keir Winesmith and Suse Anderson, 13, (Abingdon, Oxon: Routledge, 2020); Olson, "The Power to Name," 640; Meredith Broussard, *Artificial Unintelligence* (Cambridge, MA: MIT Press, 2018), 18; Billey, "Just Because We Can," 3; Fiona Cameron and Sarah Mengler, "Complexity, Transdisciplinarity and Museum Collections Documentation: Emergent Metaphors for a Complex World," *Journal of Material Culture* 14, no. 2 (June 2009): 199, https://doi.org/10.1177/1359183509103061; Hope A. Olson and Rose Schlegl, "Standardization, Objectivity, and User Focus: A Meta-Analysis of Subject Access Critiques," *Cataloging & Classification Quarterly* 32, no. 2 (2001): 77, https://doi.org/10.1300/J104v32n02_06; Amber Billey, Emily Drabinski, and K. R. Roberto, "What's Gender Got to Do with It? A Critique of RDA 9.7," *Cataloging & Classification Quarterly* 52, no. 4 (2014): 414, https://doi.org/10.1080/01639374.2014.882465; Lisa Gitelman, *Always Already New: Media, History and the Data of Culture* (Cambridge, MA: MIT Press, 2006).

40. Thompson, "More Than a Name," 141; Tillman, "Barriers to Ethical Name Modeling," 249.

Although there have been strides made in recent years,[41] the lack of ethical considerations in the guidance about cataloging living people is particularly concerning. A call for greater attention during the creation of NARs for living authors is not totally absent, however.[42] The majority of the literature assesses the controversial inclusion of gender in RDA personal name authority records.[43] Additional criticism has been written about how authors' names, particularly non-European names,[44] are recorded in the bibliographic record, and recording sexual orientation is an option in the field: "Other Designation Associated with Person" (RDA 9.6).[45] The primary concern of these authors is that the people these authority records represent do not have control over their personal information or how they are being represented.[46] In an effort to complete a NAR, a cataloger may include Personally Identifiable Information (PII) that the author does not want publicized. Billey explains that "[r]ecording this information could violate a person's privacy, make their personal

---

41. Amber Billey, Matthew Haugen, John Hostage, Nancy Sack, and Adam L. Schiff, "Report of the PCC Ad Hoc Task Group on Gender in Name Authority Records," *Program for Cooperative Cataloging*, October 4, 2016, https://www.loc.gov/aba/pcc/documents/Gender_375%20field_RecommendationReport.pdf.

42. On April 7, 2022, the Program for Cooperative Cataloging (PCC) released the "Revised Report on Recording Gender in Personal Name Authority Records," which recommends the following: "Do not record the RDA gender element (MARC 375) in personal name authority records. Delete existing 375 fields when editing a record for any other reason." This is a very welcome and much needed change in PCC policy towards gender and will help alleviate some of the issues addressed in this paper for organizations that follow PCC guidelines (PCC Ad Hoc Task Group on Recording Gender in Personal Name Authority Records, "Revised Report on Recording Gender in Personal Name Authority Records," April 7, 2022, https://www.loc.gov/aba/pcc/documents/gender-in-NARs-revised-report.pdf).

43. Tina Gross and Violet B. Fox, "Authority Work as Outreach," in *Ethical Questions in Name Authority Control*, edited by Jane Sandberg, 342-3 (Sacramento, CA: Library Juice Press, 2019); Billey, et al., "What's Gender Got to Do with It?"413; Thompson, "More Than a Name"; Wiederhold and Reeve, "Authority Control Today," 151.

44. Frank Exner, Little Bear, "North American Indian Personal Names in National Bibliographies," in *Radical Cataloging: Essays at the Front*, edited by K. R. Roberto and Sanford Berman, 150–164 (Jefferson, NC: McFarland & Co., 2008).

45. Whittaker, "Demographic Characteristics."

46. Martin, "Records, Responsibility, and Power," 294.

information vulnerable to bad actors, and even possibly put someone in danger."[47] Neither the cataloger nor the author has control over that information once it has been published. While some authority systems allow users to contact them to request a change, this puts an undue burden on the creator to be aware of such options and do the onerous work of arguing their case.[48] Moreover, by collaborating with local creators and communities to ensure that harmful or inaccurate information is excluded from the start, LAM institutions can take responsibility for advocating for creator privacy.

Even though many museums work with living artists by exhibiting or purchasing their artwork, there has been little critical discourse of how living artists should be cataloged by the museum community. The root of this is likely twofold: (i) a lack of community-wide cataloging standards,[49] and (ii) a sentiment that cataloging processes are objective rather than subjective.[50] The former is an issue that *Cataloging Cultural Objects* (CCO) strived to solve, and, by being the only book to outline best practices in data content standards for museums, is thus the "*de facto*

---

47. Billey, "Just Because We Can," 11.

48. A promising development in this area is the recent publication of the Authority Control FAQs for Authors and Creators by the Program for Cooperative Cataloging, which offers a way to ensure authors and creators can give informed consent to the use of their personal information by clearly explaining for a non-librarian audience how name authority records are used and how to request information changes or removal in NACO records. Program for Cooperative Cataloging, "Authority Control FAQs for Authors and Creators," February 12, 2022, https://www.loc.gov/aba/pcc/naco/documents/PCC-SCT-Authority-Control-FAQs-Authors-Creators.pdf.

49. Patricia Harpring, *Introduction to Controlled Vocabularies Terminology for Art, Architecture, and Other Cultural Works* (Los Angeles, CA: Getty Research Institute, (2010), 3; Gabriela Zoller and Katie DeMarsh, "For the Record," *Art Documentation* 32, no. 1 (2013): 61, https://doi.org/10.1086/669989.

50. Eilean Hooper-Greenhill, "The Space of the Museum," *Continuum* 3, no. 1 (1990): 60, https://doi.org/10.1080/10304319009388149; Candace S. Greene, "Material Connections: The Smithsonian Effect in Anthropological Cataloguing," *Museum Anthropology* 39, no. 2 (2016): 148, https://doi.org/10.1111/muan.12121; Hannah Turner, *Cataloguing Culture: Legacies of Colonialism in Museum Documentation* (Vancouver, BC: UBC Press, 2020). Compare: Zoller and DeMarsh, "For the Record," 62.

cataloging standard" for museums.[51] CCO encourages that display biographies contain "the nationality and life dates" of the artist[52] and that NARs include gender, "which refers to the sex of the individual,"[53] both of which can be part of online catalogs. Although gender is an additional element that is not required, conflating gender and sex has the potential for serious harm. The guide also does not address any privacy concerns of living artists, or give clear advice on when to differentiate among "national, geopolitical, cultural, or ethnic origins or affiliation of the person,"[54] attributes combined into the field called "nationality."[55] Without distinguishing these identities in different fields, this information is not machine-readable and search engines will not be able to deliver on user needs that require more care to be given to how these attributes are stored in the metadata.

In the absence of guidance, forward-thinking museums have taken steps locally to allow artists more agency over their NARs. Minneapolis Institute of Art and Philadelphia Museum of Art are two examples of museums that send out a form to ask artists how they would like to be identified in the museum catalog.[56] This effort is critical: recording biographical information about individuals, particularly that which is othering, is potentially problematic and can even be dangerous for living artists.

---

51. Emily Nedell Tuck, "MFAH TMS Style Guide," September 2005, https://emi-lynedelltuck.com/wp-content/uploads/2015/09/MFAH_TMS_Manual.pdf, 1.

52. Patricia Harpring, Ann Baird Whiteside, Linda McRae, Elisa Lanzi, and Murtha Baca, *Cataloging Cultural Objects: A Guide to Describing Cultural Works and Their Images* (Chicago: American Library Association, 2006), 79.

53. Harpring et al., Cataloging, 301.

54. Harpring et al., Cataloging, 296.

55. This definition matches how ULAN defines their Nationality field: "A reference to the nationality, culture, ethnicity, race, religion, sexual identity, or sexual orientation of the person or corporate body." (Getty Research Institute, "Editorial Guidelines: Union List of Artist Names (ULAN)," rev. October 11, 2021, https://www.getty.edu/research/tools/vocabularies/guidelines/index.html#ulan, 3.6).

56. E.g., Frances Lloyd-Baynes, "Documenting Diversity: How Should Museums Identify Art and Artists?" *Medium,* March 27, 2019, https://medium.com/minneapolis-institute-of-art/documenting-diversity-17f55a4118da.

Archivists have been leaders in the library profession at including personal experiences of living individuals and recording them as they wish to be remembered, such as the ongoing descriptive work at the Charles Teenie Harris Archive.[57] Museums and libraries also need to be prepared for when creators do not want identity markers to be connected to their NARs.[58] Both RDA and CCO have suggestions for what fields to include in online NARs, but publishing the information contained in these fields can have negative consequences for the living artists and authors that are being cataloged without their consent, especially historically under-documented individuals.[59] Therefore, efforts like the ones described above should be the norm moving forward so as to best respect creators' agency over their information.

Linked Open Data

The risk of violating the privacy of a living artist or author by including PII during the creation of their NAR is high, especially since library and museum catalogers are encouraged to record this information as part of their duties.[60] Additionally, the sources that catalogers are encouraged to use to create NARs are often opaque about how biographical information concerning living creators was collected. This is a problem that the authors of this

---

57. Dominique Luster, "Professionalism: As Pursuit of Archivist Identity," in *Archival Values: Essays in Honor of Mark A. Greene*, edited by Christine Weideman and Mary A. Caldera, 248–256, (Chicago: Society of American Archivists, 2019); Dominique Luster, "Archives Have the Power to Boost Marginalized Voices," *Archival Outlook* (Nov/Dec 2018): 10.

58. Jarrett M. Drake, "Liberatory Archives: Towards Belonging and Believing (Part 2)," *On Archivy*. October 22, 2016, https://medium.com/on-archivy/liberatory-archives-towards-belonging-and-believing-part-2-6f56c754eb17.

59. Simone Browne, "B®anding Blackness: Biometric Technology and the Surveillance of Blackness," in *Dark Matters: On the Surveillance of Blackness*, 89–129 (Durham, NC: Duke University Press, 2015), https://doi.org/10.1215/9780822375302-004; Antracoli, et al, "Archives for Black Lives."

60. Billey, "Just Because We Can," 9.

article have noticed with the Library of Congress Name Authority File (LCNAF), Getty Union List of Artist Names® (ULAN), and Virtual International Authority File (VIAF), all controlled vocabularies published as LOD. This point became clear to Bertoldi when she was working on an exhibition of photographs by Alen MacWeeney at the SMA, whose NAR in the local catalog recorded his nationality as American based on his entry in ULAN. From personal communication with him, Bertoldi learned that MacWeeney preferred to be identified as Irish and asked ULAN to update their record. His record on ULAN now correctly identifies him as Irish, but there is no reference to the SMA's personal correspondence with him as being the source of this change. If the only way to truly respect a person's wishes is to get their consent,[61] the infrastructure of LOD is not working hard enough to reduce the labor required to ethically create NARs because it is often not recording the source of this information.

Wikidata is another common source that libraries and museums use when creating NARs. Unlike LCNAF, ULAN,[62] and VIAF, Wikidata has issued a policy with regards to how living people should be cataloged: "Instead of striving to provide all possible information about living people we strive to provide only information in whose veracity we have a high confidence and which doesn't violate a person's reasonable expectations of privacy."[63] It is impressive that Wikidata has directly addressed the issue of cataloging PII, but, because Wikidata is an open

61. Thompson, "More Than a Name," 141; Gross and Fox, "Authority Work," 343.

62. ULAN's editorial guidelines mention that "[f]or sensitive or private information, such as religion or sexual orientation, do not include the information except in the following situations: If this information is commonly published in references to the person and if the person wishes for the information to be public" (Getty Research Institute, "Editorial," 3.6). The authors argue that, while this is an important step towards ethically sourcing information, information gathered from personal interactions should be identified as such in the NAR user interface.

63. Wikidata, "Living People," edited on August 29, 2021, https://www.wikidata.org/wiki/Wikidata:Living_people.

public knowledge graph that anyone can edit, enforcement of this policy is up to individual contributors, and its application cannot be consistently guaranteed. Another troubling problem is that the sources cited on Wikidata are the same sources that have transparency issues. Alen MacWeeney's Wikidata record, for example, has numerous sources cited, but these are museum online collections and gallery websites that are subject to the ethical problems that have already been mentioned above. Some of these sources may have contacted Alen MacWeeney personally, but online collections do not make this information apparent. By citing locally created NARs in LOD, we are cutting out the living person from the cataloging process and, thus, perpetuating an unethical cycle.

Removing the living person from the cataloging process is a problem already highlighted by Gross and Fox: "In the process of creating personal name authority records, NACO [Name Authority Cooperative Program] participants usually do not attempt to contact people for whom authorized names are being established, even when the person is known to be alive and contact information is readily available."[64] Sadly, museums that reach out to living artists about their NARs are also the exception rather than the norm. Extensive time and labor are required to contact creators about their NARs—a burden that LOD was intended to help alleviate—but since LOD is built on the same practices used in local cataloging, the process excludes the people that we are trying to catalog in the same way.

Slow Movement

Based on this research, the ethical way to fulfill user needs would be to contact all living creators on the Marble website before publishing PII online. The creation of NARs is already

---

64. Gross and Fox, "Authority Work," 337.

a time-consuming process,[65] so this would require a tremendous amount of additional human effort and funding. The Marble team considered using LOD in the form of structured vocabularies to draw from the collective cataloging efforts of LC and Getty contributors to address this need. Concerned about the ethical implications of this solution, the authors hosted a birds of a feather session at the 2021 LD4 conference to explore the tension between user-centered design and best practices of creating LOD NARs.[66] In the session, they learned anecdotally that there is not a good response rate to the forms sent out to artists by museums. Knowing that museums that have tried contacting artists have received low response rates, is this a waste of time?

The slow movement provides a useful framework to address some of the common issues that hold LAM organizations back from engaging in ethical cataloging—most notably, time. The slow movement is a response to modern society's favoring of efficiency and speed over quality and personal connections. It was popularized by the slow food movement, particularly by the book *Slow Food Nation* by Carlo Petrini,[67] which was a response to fast food chains. The idea of slowing down has been applied to a variety of activities and aspects of culture, including librarianship and museology. Christen and Anderson have written about how the slow archives movement prioritizes relationship building over the pace of processing collections.[68] Slow museum work can take the form of investing time into building relationships with

---

65. Beth Thornton, "The Existential Crisis of a Cataloger," in *Radical Cataloging: Essays at the Front*, edited by K. R. Roberto and Sanford Berman, 13–17 (Jefferson, NC: McFarland & Co., 2008).

66. Hanna Bertoldi, Peggy Griesinger, and Mikala Narlock, "Is User-Centered Design in Conflict with Cataloging Ethics?" *LD4* 2021, Virtual, https://doi.org/10.7274/r0-5q79-rr41.

67. Carlo Petrini, Clara Furlan, and Jonathan Hunt. *Slow Food Nation: Why Our Food Should Be Good, Clean, and Fair* (New York: Rizzoli Ex Libris, 2007), originally published in Italian in 2005 as Buono, Pulito e Giusto by Gli struzzi Einaudi.

68. Kimberly Christen and Jane Anderson, "Toward Slow Archives," *Archival Science* 19, no. 2 (2019): 87–116, https://doi.org/10.1007/s10502-019-09307-x.

Indigenous communities,[69] educational programs that ask visitors to look at artwork for an extended period of time,[70] or engaging with a wider audience to inform decisions about exhibitions.[71] Cataloging processes for creating NARs, including those available as LOD, can benefit from the values of the slow movement to approach with ethical considerations. The demanding workload of cataloging and the lack of resources present in LAM organizations is in conflict with the principles of the slow movement, but such an approach is not without precedent.

An example of slow principles applied to cataloging work is the Oklahoma State University Library's efforts to transform the metadata of oral histories in the Oklahoma Native Artists Project into linked data.[72] To create artist records on Wikidata and ULAN, the team plans to speak to the living interviewees to verify that they want their information shared, record how they prefer to be represented, and explain the implications of data sharing so that any consent given can be as informed as possible. Library staff plan to augment the records with primary and secondary sources, many of which are not easily accessible documents. While planning the project, the team prioritized the

69. Raymond A. Silverman, "Introduction: Museum as Process," in *Museum as Process: Translating Local and Global Knowledges*, edited by Raymond A. Silverman, 12 (London: Routledge, 2015); Margaret M. Bruchac, "Lost and Found: NAGPRA, Scattered Relics, and Restorative Methodologies," *Museum Anthropology* 33, no. 2 (2010): 137–56, https://doi.org/10.1111/j.1548-1379.2010.01092.x.

70. Sherry Farrell Racette, "Pieces Left along the Trail: Material Culture Histories and Indigenous Studies," in *Sources and Methods in Indigenous Studies*, edited by Chris Andersen and Jean M. O'Brien, 227 (London: Rutledge, 2016); Honoré, *In Praise of Slow*, 14.

71. Laura Raicovich, *Culture Strike: Art and Museums in an Age of Protest*, 148 (London: Verso, 2021).

72. Madison Chartier and Megan Macken, "Representation and Data Collection: The Ethics of Using Linked Open Data for Oklahoma Native Artists," *Core Metadata presentation at Interest Group Week, American Library Association*, July 28, 2021, http://www.ala.org/core/continuing-education/interest-group-week; Madison Chartier and Megan Macken, "Oklahoma Native Artists Project: Oral Histories to Linked Open Data," in *Ethics in Linked Data*, edited by Alexandra Provo, Kathleen Burlingame, and Brian M. Watson (Sacramento, CA: Library Juice Press, 2023).

reputation of the Oklahoma Native artists over the speed and volume of linked data created. The slow movement demonstrates that the time required to create ethical NARs should be worth the cost to institutions because it allows greater control over a living person's self-representation. Oklahoma State University is using this intentionally slow process to forge long-lasting relationships with Native artists. Asking how they would like to be represented in an online catalog will not be a one-off request but, instead, a part of a larger dialogue in advocating for their right for representation. The critical components of advocacy rest on relationships, and a more personal interaction in place of a survey dropped in an email inbox may lead to vastly superior results. In other words, museums may continue to have low response rates to their inquiries if they do not do the extensive relationship-building labor, and may cause more distrust with communities that already feel taken advantage of with one-off requests.[73]

Future Solutions

The slow movement is a useful framework to address the tension between user needs and cataloging ethics on the Marble site, since time, a common limitation for libraries and museums, is not a reason to compromise quality.[74] While LOD presents a partial technological solution to offer users more robust biographical information about creators, a deeper look into the systems used to create these NARs shows that cataloging efforts can be othering and even potentially harmful, and there is no way to know whether

73. Raicovich, *Culture Strike*; Vera L. Zolberg, "Art Museums and Living Artists: Contentious Communities," in *Museums and Communities: The Politics of Public Culture*, edited by Ivan Karp, Christine Mullen Kreamer, and Steven D. Lavine, 105–136 (Washington, DC: Smithsonian Institution Press, 1992); Research Data Alliance International Indigenous Data Sovereignty Interest Group, "The CARE Principles for Indigenous Data Governance," *Global Indigenous Data Alliance*, September 2019. https://www.gida-global.org/care.

74. Catherine D'Ignazio and Lauren F. Klein, *Data Feminism*, 147 (Cambridge, MA: MIT Press, 2020).

the sources used were ethically gathered. In applying slow principles to cataloging work, the investment in time has the benefit of creating ethical data and building connections with living creators. The implications of using slow cataloging principles to create ethical NARs are vast because the practice challenges the current structures present in museums and libraries. The following sections address aspects of these structures that require change in order for PII of living creators to be created and used ethically.

Transparency in Information Sourcing

Marble is an example of how standardized vocabularies can be used to augment subject metadata and create connections across LAM collection items. The SMA, RBSC, and UA catalogers benefited from the work done by the Library of Congress, Getty, and their contributors to produce these resources. Marble would benefit from these advantages of LOD NARs as well. The structure of LOD solves some of the ethical conundrums addressed in this chapter, but the authors advocate for improvements to be made, specifically around the need for greater transparency in how NARs are created for living people. If biographical information, gathered with consent from the living creator, can be clearly identified in LOD created both outside and inside LAM institutions, it could save cultural institutions wanting to use that information the labor of creating ethically-sourced personal creator metadata themselves, because they could draw from the efforts of others. Without citing interactions with living people, cultural institutions are not able to work together to build a system of LOD NARs that is founded on creator consent. Libraries, archives, and other memory institutions are uniquely positioned to lead the way in developing this ethically-sourced linked open dataset. These institutions are best poised to connect with their local communities because of their critical holdings and their responsibility to steward and share them globally.

Additionally, online collections need to be better at explaining to their users how their information is created and sourced.[75] The way this information is currently presented leads users to confuse interpretation with fact. This misrepresentation can have devastating repercussions for living people, since the digital space memorializes the choices that catalogers make.[76] To be more ethical in our cataloging work, we should proceed more slowly when recording information, consider the long- and short-term impact of the work that we do, and explain this thoroughly to living creators.

Applying a slow approach to creating NARs for living creators, ethical cataloging means recording information that the person has given permission to share or in the way that they prefer. Working on a local level makes the most sense when cataloging creators that may not already have authority records. Like Oklahoma, museums and libraries can prioritize creating LOD NARs for those living people whose work, culture, and viewpoints are specific and special to their community. This slow approach not only encourages relationship-building, but also operates in service to the communities where these cultural institutions are located, particularly if the institutions have locally-relevant holdings.

---

75. For example, UCLA Library, "Toward Ethical and Inclusive Descriptive Practices in UCLA Library Special Collections," accessed December 1, 2021, https://www.library.ucla.edu/location/library-special-collections/toward-ethical-inclusive-descriptive-practices-ucla-library-special-collections.

76. Gitelman, *Always Already New*; Jennifer Trant, "Curating Collections Knowledge: Museums on the Cyberinfrastructure," in *Museum Informatics: People, Information, and Technology in Museums*, edited by Paul F. Marty and Katherine Burton Jones, 284–5 (New York and Oxon: Routledge, 2008), https://doi.org/10.4324/9780203939147.

Work Culture

The second structure that affects the ethics of NAR creation is the work culture of libraries and museums—i.e., short timelines, huge backlogs, and limited or inconsistent labor. These constraints negatively impact ethical cataloging work because they suppress the environment necessary for "reflexive thinking" about current practices.[77] The Marble project highlighted the problematic effect that term-limited positions, contingent labor, and unskilled workers can have when these types of positions are created for cataloging work. SMA and Hesburgh Libraries relied on employees with different work statuses for cataloging and digital preservation during the grant period.[78] At the SMA, the term-limited Collections Database Coordinator, Bertoldi, was responsible for upholding the standardization of NARs. The Museum had a limited and error-prone dataset because metadata creation was historically done as an auxiliary role by a staff member with additional responsibilities or delegated to student workers. The work that Bertoldi did to normalize legacy data was constrained by a limited timeline, a tightly scoped-grant project, and unclear/competing priorities that did not allow for relationship-building with local, living artists. In contrast, Hesburgh Libraries tasked full-time staff with cataloging and digital preservation matters during the grant period. The Libraries leveraged the expertise of their permanent staff, which allowed greater continuity and encouraged staff buy-in to sustain metadata and preservation work beyond the grant period. The SMA's metadata would have benefited from time allocated to the Collections Database Coordinator position for the ethical cataloging of NARs.

Unfortunately, it is not unusual for contingent labor, especially grant-funded or student interns, to be tasked with cataloging

---

77. Greene, "Material Connections," 149.

78. Hanna Bertoldi, Peggy Griesinger, and Mikala Narlock, "Harmonizing Human Infrastructure: A Case Study of Bringing Preservation Workflows of a Library, Archive, and Museum into Alignment," *iPres Proceedings*, 2021.

work in museums.[79] This differs from libraries, where extensive training and mentorship is required before an individual or institution is allowed to contribute new or updated records to NACO. While this chapter has demonstrated some of the ways that libraries and archives could improve in this area, a library/ archives model that encourages training and mentorship would be beneficial to museums. Libraries and museums both can do better at prioritizing cataloging and resource description positions, which includes sufficient, permanent funds.[80] Since the creation of NARs is sensitive work with far-reaching ramifications, museums need to invest in professional staff who have the experience and time to catalog in a holistic way that includes robust relationship building. That means reducing the number of temporary staff, including students, that are responsible for this important work, and supporting full-time positions devoted to cataloging. Without proper training or the time to create ethical NARs, catalogers may end up categorizing people based on assumptions[81] or create records that will be inaccessible and harmful.[82] Cataloging work should slow down so that trusted relationships can be formed with the artists and authors who the cultural institutions are working to make accessible,[83] prioritizing local holdings and collaborating with other LAM institutions that have overlapping specialties. It is only with an investment in the quality of their data and, by extension, the data creators, that museums will be able to critically evaluate how their metadata is

79. John E. Simmons, "Natural History Collections Management in the United States," *Journal of Biological Curation* 1, no. 3/4 (1993): 6.

80. Hillel Arnold, Dorothy J. Berry, Elizabeth M. Caringola, Angel Diaz, Sarah Hamerman, Erin Hurley, Anna Neatrour, Sandy Rodriguez, Megan Senseney, Ruth Tillman, Amy Wickner, Karly Wildenhaus, and Elliot Williams, "Do Better – Love(,) Us: Guidelines for Developing and Supporting Grant-Funded Positions in Digital Libraries, Archives, and Museums," January 2020, https://dobetterlabor.com.

81. Paul Hitlin and Lee Rainie, "Facebook Algorithms and Personal Data," *Pew Research Center*, January 16, 2019, https://www.pewresearch.org/internet/2019/01/16/facebook-algorithms-and-personal-data/.

82. Bair, "Toward a Code," 20.

83. D'Ignazio and Klein, *Data Feminism*, 135.

created and fulfill the public's expectation that their online collections have reliable information.

Access and Discovery

How museums and libraries manage access to their collections, particularly online, affects how PII is used. Well-made NARs are important access points for users and require professional staff to collect and create the metadata ethically. Access to collection items is mediated through technology, and professionals need to work harder at exposing the labor involved in cataloging these items.[84] We must address the fact that online collections are *not*, by their very nature, democratizing.[85] Rather, thoughtful attention is required to present metadata marking minoritized identities and expose previously hidden objects.

Historically, American art museums have excluded artists who are not "male and caucasian,"[86] and the continuation of this trend can be seen in online collections, which are "imbalanced, often skewing heavily white and male."[87] Similarly, the "omission of color and perpetuation of whiteness in the LIS [library and information science] field" has been documented in

---

84. In designing and building tools for user needs, LAM professionals need to create technology that does not further obscure their labor. For example, services like "Never Been Seen," which prompts users to view that have zero views online ("be the first to see object [title]"), obscure the labor that went into: acquiring, digitizing, describing, and making accessible online the content (not to mention the creation and use of the physical item, which surely had a life before it ended up in a museum).

85. Anderson, "Some Provocations," 13.

86. Chad M. Topaz, Bernhard Klingenberg, Daniel Turek, Brianna Heggeseth, Pamela E Harris, Julie C. Blackwood, C. Ondine Chavoya, Steven Nelson, and Kevin M. Murphy, "Diversity of Artists in Major U.S. Museums," *PloS One* 14, no. 3 (2019): 15, https://doi.org/10.1371/journal.pone.0212852; Maura Reilly, *Curatorial Activism: Towards an Ethics of Curating* (London: Thames & Hudson, 2018).

87. Anderson "Some," 13.

existing literature.[88] Despite the Marble team's good intentions of prioritizing objects created by artists and authors from under-represented groups, the initial batch of objects added online had a disappointing lack of diversity. This is a result of online collections mimicking the strengths and blind spots that already exist in the library or museum collection that they are presenting. At the SMA, the European collection had the best metadata—thorough, up-to-date, and correct. Thus, this collection formed the best sample for testing Marble and made up the initial ingest. Similarly, Hesburgh Libraries prioritized content that was thoroughly described and already digitized, which heavily featured American history and Irish literature and languages.[89] Without intentional work to make objects created by those previously without representation more visible through robust research and ethical cataloging, those objects will still remain invisible online. Furthermore, having ethically-sourced metadata about living artists' minoritized identities will create a better dataset for museums and libraries to promote culturally diverse works and fulfill user needs. There is a balance in providing an appropriate level of

88. Todd Honma, "Trippin' Over the Color Line: The Invisibility of Race in Library and Information Studies," *InterActions: UCLA Journal of Education and Information Studies* 1, no. 2 (2005), http://dx.doi.org/10.5070/D412000540; Freeda Brook, David Ellenwood, and Althea Eannace Lazzaro, "In Pursuit of Antiracist Social Justice: Denaturalizing Whiteness in the Academic Library," *Library Trends* 64, no. 2 (2015): 246–84, https://doi.org/10/f8bv9g; April Hathcock, "White Librarianship in Blackface: Diversity Initiatives in LIS," *In the Library with the Lead Pipe*, October 7, 2015, http://www.inthelibrarywiththeleadpipe.org/2015/lis-diversity; David J. Hudson, "On 'Diversity' as Anti-Racism in Library and Information Studies: A Critique," *Journal of Critical Library and Information Studies* 1, no.1 (2017): 1–36, https://doi.org/10.24242/jclis.v1i1.6; Gina Schlesselman-Tarango, *Topographies of Whiteness: Mapping Whiteness in Library and Information Science* (Sacramento, CA: Library Juice, 2017)..

89. The Snite's European Collection had the most up-to-date metadata due to an active curator who had a unique interest in learning and using the database and frequent requests to use the collection for teaching and research. Materials from Hesburgh Libraries are digitized based on user requests, which in turn increases their use in teaching and research purposes and further drives digitization demands of similar materials.

information—some communities may wish to remain invisible, while others may want to be named. This should be discussed and evaluated alongside communities and not on their behalf.[90]

Conclusion

In this chapter, the authors explored the tension between authorized access points for names and the needs of the user. Users' needs to search robust personal creator metadata surfaced during user testing for the Marble platform, a unified online collections platform at the University of Notre Dame. The team's desire to utilize LOD NARs to fulfill this need triggered concern about the ethics of using PII, especially for living authors and artists, even though it was technologically possible to implement. The authors suggest greater transparency in how LOD NARs are created as well as other systemic changes to library and museum cataloging work. By approaching the problem of ethically-created LOD NARs from the perspective of the slow movement, the authors' recommendations are not quick fixes but, rather, are sustainable solutions requiring extensive commitments of funding and personnel. Changes to transparency in information sourcing, work culture, and access are all long-term strategies to address structures that "tacitly or explicitly uphold systems of dispossession, oppression, and exclusion."[91] All three areas will benefit from LAM institutions working closer with their community to prioritize cataloging collections that are meaningful locally and sharing resources among organizations with similar goals to maximize limited time and funding. As trusted cultural institutions, libraries and museums have a responsibility to involve contemporary creators in the cataloging process and approach the metadata in their online catalogs with the care it deserves.

---

90. D'Ignazio and Klein, Data, 92, 110.
91. Christen and Anderson, "Toward," 112..

Authors' Note

A discussion inspired by this chapter proposal was presented at the LD4 conference, Building Connections Together, on July 22, 2021.[92] Thank you to all who participated.

---

92. Bertoldi et al., "Is User-Centered."

Ethical Explorations Using Wikidata and Wikidata Tools to Expose Underrepresented Special Collection Materials

DARNELLE MELVIN & CORY LAMPERT

Introduction

For the custodians of digital collections, there is demand for better tools to share data between systems, manage workflows, track metrics, assess user needs, and increase visibility of these collections while simultaneously managing potential community concerns regarding privacy and sensitive materials, and protecting sacred places, artifacts and information. Linked data technologies are seen as one tool in a larger strategy to address these needs. One specific linked data approach, which has been gaining momentum in the galleries, libraries, archives, and museums (GLAM) community, is creating and ingesting data from Wikidata, a multilingual, crowdsourced, structured data knowledge base built upon Wikibase and MediaWiki technologies to enhance, augment, and link to digital collections and other web-based applications.[1]

1. Mairelys Lemus-Rojas, and Lydia Pintscher, "Wikidata and Libraries: Facilitating Open Knowledge," in Leveraging Wikipedia: Connecting Communities of Knowledge, ed. Marrilee Proffitt (Chicago: ALA Editions, 2018), 143-158; Eunah Snyder, Lisa Lorenzo, and Lucas Mak, "Linked Open Data for Subject Discovery: Assessing the Alignment Between Library of Congress Vocabularies and Wikidata" (paper pre-

As the archives, special collections, and rare books library communities investigate opportunities to structure collection data as linked open data, questions and tensions have arisen regarding balancing the push to increase access and discovery, and the necessity for ethical creation of linked data. While cultural heritage professionals develop projects in Wikidata, pilot projects reveal uncharted territories where ethical deliberation is both nuanced and necessary. In this chapter, we will introduce linked data contributions from cultural heritage institutions, including a discussion of some ethical concerns and risks of harm in linked data projects. The authors will draw upon specific local use cases, presenting project scope, methods, and lessons learned. As part of the discussion of ethical concerns, the Ethics of Care theoretical framework will be introduced along with some of the implications of applying ethical theory in practice. The chapter will conclude with a call to ignite interest and broader engagement for linked data creation as we work together to enact, empower, and reflect upon responsive approaches to ethical challenges.

Linked Data Contributions from Cultural Heritage Institutions

Background and Contest

Over the past decade, efforts by GLAM institutions to publish and use structured linked data have increased significantly.[2]

sented at International Conference on Dublin Core and Metadata Applications, Seoul, September 2020), 12–20; Fredo Erxleben, Michael Günther, Markus Krötzsch, Julian Mendez, & Denny Vrandečić, "Introducing Wikidata to the Linked Data Web," in The Semantic Web – ISWC 2014, Riva Del Garda, Italy, October 2014, 50–65; "Wikibase-Home," Wikibase, accessed April 25, 2022, https://wikiba.se/; "MediaWiki, Mediawiki," Mediawiki, accessed April 25, 2022, https://www.mediawiki.org/wiki/MediaWiki.

2. Karen Smith-Yoshimura, "Analysis of International Linked Data Survey for Implementers," D-Lib Magazine 22, no. 7/8 (2016), https://doi.org/10.1045/july2016-smith-yoshimura; Karen Smith-Yoshimura, "Analysis of 2018 International Linked Data Survey for Implementers," Code4Lib Journal 42 (2018), https://journal.code4lib.org/articles/13867.

These institutions are taking an in-depth look at how to further increase access to collections, engage with a wider user audience, and enhance education outcomes.[3] GLAM contributions to the linked data ecosystem (often visualized as a cloud) are significant and vary in scope and scale.[4] Participants in the Semantic Web include national libraries and museums,[5] GLAM-centric data aggregators,[6] academic institutions,[7] and information-dependent industries.[8] Some projects aim to reuse and further expose legacy

3. Julia Marden, Carolyn Li-Madeo, Noreen Whysel, and Jeffery Edelstein, "Linked open data for cultural heritage: Evolution of an information technology," (paper presented at International Conference on Design of Communication - SIGDOC '13), Greenville, NC, September 2013, 107–112.

4. Erik Mitchell, "Library Linked Data: Early Activity and Development," *Library Technology Reports* 52, no. 1 (2016): 37; Hilary Thorsen, and M.C. Pattuelli, "Linked open data and the cultural heritage landscape," in *Linked Data for Cultural Heritage*, edited by Ed Jones, and Michele Seikel (Chicago: ALA Editions, 2016): 1–22.

5. Martin Malmsten, "Making a library catalogue part of the Semantic Web," *Data Analysis and Knowledge Discovery* 3, no. 3 (2009): 3-7; "BIBFRAME," LOC, accessed April 25, 2022, https://www.loc.gov/bibframe/; Victor De Boer, Jan Wielemaker, Judith van Gent, Marijke Oosterbroek, Michiel Hildebrand, Isaac Michiel, Jacco van Ossenbruggen, and Guus Schreiber, "Supporting Linked Data Production for Cultural Heritage Institutes: The Amsterdam Museum Case Study" (paper presented at In Extended Semantic Web Conference, Heraklion, Crete, May 2012), 733-747, Berlin, Springer; Barbara Bushman, David Anderson, and Gang Fu. "Transforming the Medical Subject Headings into Linked Data: Creating the Authorized Version of MeSH in RDF," *Journal of Library Metadata* 15, no. 3–4, (2015): 157–176.

6. Carol Jean Godby, The Relationship between BIBFRAME and OCLC's Linked-Data Model of Bibliographic Description: A Working Paper (Dublin, OH: OCLC, 2013); Thomas Hickey, and Jenny Toves, "Managing Ambiguity in VIAF," *D-Lib Magazine* 20, no. 7–8 (2014), doi:10.1045/july2014-hicke; Joan Cobb, "The Journey to Linked Open Data: The Getty Vocabularies," *Journal of Library Metadata* 15, no. 3–4, (2015): 142-156.

7. Philip Schreur, "Linked Data for Production (LD4P)," in Companion Proceedings of The Web Conference, Lyon, France, April 2018, 429–430; MacKenzie Smith, Carol Stahmer, Xiaola Li, and Gloria Gonzalez, BIBFLOW: a roadmap for library linked data transition, University Library, University of California, Davis and Zepheira Inc., 2017; Elise Wong, "LD4L: Linked Data for libraries," *Technical Services Quarterly* 34, no. 3 (2017): 332–333.

8. "The Open Graph protocol," OGP, accessed September 11, 2021, https://ogp.me/; Amit Singhal, "Introducing the Knowledge Graph: Things, Not Strings," Official Google Blog (blog), Google, May 16, 2012, https://blog.google/products/search/introducing-knowledge-graph-things-not/; Ramanathan V. Guha, Dan Brickley, and Steve Macbeth, "Schema. org: evolution of structured data on the web," *Communications*

metadata, which has traditionally been siloed in string-based records, databases, and catalogs.[9] These types of projects transform rich descriptions into RDF-encoded statements, which can be used by the wider community through referencing and reusing universal resource identifiers (URIs) and incorporating non-library data.[10] Other projects investigate methods that differentiate descriptive and contextual information,[11] often requiring mapping robust metadata to general purpose ontologies. The University of Nevada, Las Vegas (UNLV) has aligned its work with these efforts through an initial study group established in 2014 and subsequent pilot projects focused on transforming digital collections metadata into linked data, metadata preparation, evaluation of programmatic implementation of linked data in a digital asset repository, and strategic investments in Wikidata project work.

of the ACM 59, no. 2 (2016): 44–51; Natasha Noy, Yuqing Gao, Anshu Jain, Anant Narayanan, Alan Patterson, and Jamie Taylor, "Industry-scale knowledge graphs: Lessons and challenges," *Communications of the AMC* 62, no. 8 (2019): 36–43; Jesse Weaver, and Paul Tarjan, "Facebook Linked Data via the Graph API," *Semantic Web* 4, no. 3 (2013): 245–250.

9. Jacob Jett, Timothy Cole, Myung-Ja Han, and Caroline Szylowicz, "Linked Open Data (LOD) for library special collections," in 2017 ACM/IEEE Joint Conference on Digital Libraries (JCDL), Ontario, Canada, June 2017, 1-2. Piscataway, New Jersey, IEEE Press; Darnelle Melvin and Seth Shaw, "CONTENTdm to Islandora 8: Remediation & Migration," paper presented at the Islandora Online Virtual Conference. Virtual, August 2020, 6; Theo van Veen, "Wikidata: From "an" Identifier to "the" Identifier," *Information Technology and Libraries* 38, no. 2 (2019): 72–81.

10. Rick Bennett, Eric Childress, Kerre Kammerer, and Diane Vizine-Goetz, "Linking FAST and Wikipedia," in IFLA WLIC 2016, Columbus, OH, August 2016, 1-10.

11. Maliheh Farrokhnia, and Mitra Zarei, "Integrated access to cultural heritage information pieces in Iran over Imam Reza's 4th Zarih (burial chamber) as a sample," *Program* 47, no. 3, (2013): 304-319; Ciro Mattia Gonano, Francesca Tomasi, Francesca Mambelli, Fabio Vitali, and Silvio Peroni, "Zeri e LODE. Extracting the Zeri photo archive to Linked Open Data: formalizing the conceptual model," in International Conference on Design of Communication - SIGDOC '13, Greenville, NC, September 2013, 107-112; Jacob Jett, Timothy Cole, and Myung-Ja Han, "Disambiguating descriptions: Mapping digital special collections metadata into linked open data formats," in *Proceedings of the Association for Information Science and Technology* 53, no. 1 (2016): 1–5; Timothy Cole, Myung-Ja Han, Maria Sarol, Monika Biel, and David Maus, "Using Linked Open Data to Enhance the Discoverability, Functionality and Impact of Emblematica Online," *Library Hi Tech* 35, no. 1, (2017): 159-178.

Wikidata

A number of studies show how GLAM and other informa-
tion-driven organizations are investing resources to create and
integrate Wikidata into information products and services. A
2021 systemic review notes fifty-seven relevant studies within
the time period of 2012-2019.[12] In their joint summit with the
Wikimedia Foundations, the Association of Research Libraries
agrees that linked open data can be used to enhance Wikimedia
related projects and library resources in addition to adding value
to collections by addressing known cultural barriers in library and
archival practice, such as the underrepresentation of people of
color, women, or other marginalized communities.[13] In 2020, the
Program for Cooperative Cataloging (PCC) announced a Wikidata Pilot with the goal to lower the barrier for authority creation
and management.[14] In this pilot, PCC and non-PCC participants
from around the world experimented with ways to incorporate
Wikidata creation in cataloging activities. The pilot aligned with
broader PCC strategic initiatives, such as strategic directions #4,
which states: "Accelerate the movement toward ubiquitous identifier creation and identity management at the network level."[15]
As GLAM and other information aggregators invest in linked
data systems and services, ethical concerns and risk of harm can
negatively impact the community members described in these
public knowledge graphs.

---

12. Marçal Mora-Cantallops, Salvador Sánchez-Alonso, and Elena García-Barrio-
canal, "A Systematic Literature Review on Wikidata," *Data Technologies and Applications* 53, no. 3 (2019): 250–268; Karim Tharani. "Much more than a mere technology:
A systematic review of Wikidata in libraries," *The Journal of Academic Librarianship*
47, no. 2 (2021): 1–8.

13. Association of Research Libraries, "ARL White Paper on Wikidata: Opportunities and Recommendations," Washington, DC: Association for Research Libraries,
April 18, 2019.

14. "PCC Wikidata Pilot - Wikidata," Wikidata, accessed April 25, 2022, https://
www.wikidata.org/wiki/Wikidata:WikiProject_PCC_Wikidata_Pilot.

15. Program for Cooperative Cataloging, PCC Strategic Directions, Washington,
DC: Library of Congress, 2021, 5.

Ethical Concerns and Risks of Harm in Linked Data Projects

Recently, conversation amongst professionals within special collections, rare books, and archival communities has raised awareness of not only the potential opportunities and obstacles organizations may face as they attempt to transform legacy collection data into structured data, but the ethical ramifications of these transformations.[16] In the midst of this growth in production of linked data, we can expect vast new potential for use, including reuse and possibly uncontrolled or unethical use. In the digital world, information can be replicated, tampered with, and transferred far more rapidly than information stored in an archival box. It cannot and should not be assumed that all users will act in good conscience. On this possibility, librarian Ruth Kitchin Tillman writes, "we should also be mindful that everything published as linked data could be harvested and used, whether by those who will examine and question it, or by those putting faith in automated systems and the strength of its perceived authority, and exercise care in its creation and publication."[17] As cultural heritage organizations undertake large-scale digitization projects and efforts to "entify everything" by expressing strings as statements that can be leveraged in knowledge graphs, SPARQL queries, or new forms of computational research, ethical issues associated with the governance of the data are certain to arise. This idea is addressed in Terras et al.:

> Those encouraging creative reuse of large-scale heritage data need to establish robust approval, monitoring and governance processes which should be considered aspects of, rather than

---

16. OCLC Research Archives and Special Collections Linked Data Review Group, Archives and Special Collections Linked Data: Navigating Between Notes and Nodes (Dublin, OH: OCLC Research, 2020).

17. Ruth Kitchin Tillman, "Barriers to Ethical Linked Data Name Authority Modeling," in *Linked Data for Cultural Heritage*, edited by Jane Sanberg, 241–257. (Sacramento, CA: Library Juice Press, 2019).

being separate to, mass digitization programmes. This will allow for confidence in reuse, including unexpected interventions from creatives, and the ability to respond to archival content issues, particularly around the identification of individuals.[18]

Another issue, which can impact data reuse, is bias in record creation as well as its cascading effects on public-knowledge graph construction, data-driven processes, or data-driven services. Studies have shown evidence of bias on Wikidata in multiple forms, including implicit,[19] from people and algorithms,[20] related to gender,[21] social,[22] and numerous studies provide templates for identifying and measuring bias. In a study on how knowledge graph embeddings encode social biases and their impacts on downstream applications, Fisher, Palfrey, and Christo found that algorithms trained on real-world data may pick up undesirable historic or current associations and they demonstrate how differences in the distribution of entities translate into harmful

18. Melissa Terras, Stephen Coleman, Steven Drost, Chris Elsden, Ingi Helgason, Susan Lechelt, Nicola Osborne, Inge Panneels, Briana Pegado, Burkhard Schafer, Michael Smyth, Pip Thornton, and Chris Speed, "The Value of Mass-Digitised Cultural Heritage Content in Creative Contexts," *Big Data & Society* 8, no. 1 (2021): 7.

19. Gianluca Demartini. "Implicit Bias in Crowdsourced Knowledge Graphs," in *Companion Proceedings of the 2019 World Wide Web* Conference, San Francisco USA, May 2019, 624–30.

20. Emma J. Gerritse, Faegheh Hasibi, and Arjen P. de Vries, "Bias in Conversational Search: The Double-Edged Sword of the Personalized Knowledge Graph," in *Proceedings of the 2020 ACM SIGIR on International Conference on Theory of Information Retrieval*, 133–36; Lucie-Aimée Kaffee, and Elena Simperl, "Analysis of Editors' Languages in Wikidata," in Proceedings of the 14th International Symposium on Open Collaboration, Paris France, August 2018, 1–5.

21. Maximilian Klein, Harsh Gupta, Vivek Rai, Piotr Konieczny, and Haiyi Zhu, "Monitoring the Gender Gap with Wikidata Human Gender Indicators," in Proceedings of the 12th International Symposium on Open Collaboration, Berlin, Germany, August 2016, 1–9; Charles Chuankai Zhang, and Loren Terveen, "Quantifying the Gap: A Case Study of Wikidata Gender Disparities," in 17th International Symposium on Open Collaboration (OpenSym 2021), Spain, September 2021, 1-12.

22. Mario Arduini, Lorenzo Noci, Fredrico Pirovano, Ce Zhang, Yash Raj Shrestha, and Bibek Paudel, "Adversarial Learning for Debiasing Knowledge Graph Embeddings," in MLG 2020: 16th International Workshop on Mining and Learning with Graphs - A Workshop at the KDD Conference, San Diego, CA, August 2020, 1–7.

biases related to representation.[23] In their investigation into racial and citizenship representation in Wikidata, researchers found that when measuring racial bias, evidence shows how Wikidata is skewed towards overrepresentation of Europeans. When measuring citizenship representation, evidence further illustrates how the graph is skewed towards Europeans and North Americans.[24]

Case Study

At the University of Nevada, Las Vegas (UNLV) Libraries, linked data investigations began around 2011. As these have grown from pilot, to project, to program, much has been learned about the confluence of competencies (metadata, curatorial, technical, and ethical) required to successfully implement linked data as part of sustained digital collections workflows. Ethical decision-making for linked data was not one of the initial competencies studied in UNLV pilot projects. As the archival and cultural heritage stewardship professions are being called to account for omission and erasure of some community histories, attention is being focused on ethical practices in all aspects of traditionally accepted workflows. The associated acknowledgement of gaps in ethical decision-making professional competencies has become vital to continued success.

Since 2006, the UNLV Libraries have been building collections that document community history. This is usually initiated through the UNLV Oral History Research Center or the work of faculty oral historians who provide a bridge between the community's narrators and the professional practice of archivists, librarians and technologists. There is a robust ethical framework

---

23. Joseph Fisher, Dave Palfrey, Christos Christodoulopoulos, and Arpit Mittal. "Measuring social bias in knowledge graph embeddings." arXiv preprint arXiv:1912.02761 (2019): 1-11.

24. Zaina Shaik, Filip Ilievski, and Fred Morstatter, "Analyzing Race and Country of Citizenship Bias in Wikidata," ArXiv:2108.05412 [Cs], August 11, 2021, http://arxiv.org/abs/2108.05412.

established by oral historian interviewers that has formed a strong foundation for developing community-based and community-created collections in partnership with community members. The process may begin with one interview but often expands to include the sharing of family history, photograph collections, or even organizational records. Over the years, project teams have worked together to develop a model of community documentation with oral history as the center: community advisory boards acting as guides for the project methods, and co-created deliverables such as metadata records, post-custodial digital collections for accession, and online web exhibits with context and interpretation of the community.

One of the first projects was the *Nevada Test Site Oral History Project*[25] (2003-2009), a comprehensive program dedicated to documenting, preserving and disseminating the remembered past of persons affiliated with and affected by the Nevada Test Site during the era of Cold War nuclear testing. This project was followed by *Documenting the African American Experience in Las Vegas*[26] (2011-2016) and the *Southern Nevada Jewish Heritage Project*[27] (2013-2017). In more recent years, projects centering the Latinx community[28] and Asian American Pacific Islander[29] communities in Southern Nevada have also been undertaken. These projects live beyond their initial timelines due to community engagement, and oral histories continue to be added to all of these projects as time passes. Some of these oral history projects have spawned other pedagogical and outreach projects, such as

25. "Nevada Test Site Oral History Project," UNLV, accessed April 25, 2022, http://digital.library.unlv.edu/ntsohp/.

26. "Documenting the African American Experience in Las Vegas," UNLV, accessed April 25, 2022, http://digital.library.unlv.edu/aae.

27. "Southern Nevada Jewish Heritage Project," UNLV, accessed April 25, 2022, http://digital.library.unlv.edu/jewishheritage/about.

28. "Latinx Voices of Southern Nevada," UNLV, accessed April 25, 2022, https://www.library.unlv.edu/latinx.

29. "Reflections: The Las Vegas Asian American & Pacific Islander Oral History Project," UNLV, accessed April 25, 2022, https://www.library.unlv.edu/reflections.

the "We Need to Talk" panel presentations[30] (2020-present) and the "Voices" exhibit,[31] which featured the stories of a number of influential African Americans in the Las Vegas community.

With a strong history of community engagement in the documentation projects and subsequent outreach work, the Special Collections and Archives Digital Collections Department felt that oral history collections would be an ideal resource to leverage linked data projects that are capable of expressing rich relationships between people, organizations, archival collections, and other data points. These collections, specifically, became the basis of significant work in Wikidata. Considering even a relatively small set of project sprints as pilot projects offered a huge opportunity to learn how knowledge in Special Collections and Archives could be represented in a global knowledge graph.

The following short case study shows this evolution in practice and reflects on how ethical questions regarding reuse of data, bias and underrepresentation, and partnerships (internal and external) were considered and how these reflections informed decisions on a larger scale when transitioning archival data into structured data.

Case: PCC Wikidata Pilot: Las Vegas Historic Westside Sprints

Project Description

The Las Vegas Westside is a historic neighborhood that grew in prominence due to segregation laws preventing African Americans from living, entertaining, or conducting business on the strip.

---

30. "We Need to Talk: Conversations on Racism for a More Resilient Las Vegas," UNLV, accessed April 25, 2022, https://www.library.unlv.edu/weneedtotalk.

31. "Voices: an exploration of Black Las Vegas through the resources in UNLV Special Collections and Archives," UNLV, accessed April 25, 2022, https://guides.library.unlv.edu/c.php?g=1163135&p=8491382.

Source data was taken from published transcripts of oral history interviews and manuscript or photographic collection guides, all of which had gift agreements and online access permissions, and were screened for personal or sensitive information before digitization. Donald Ritchie writes that "oral history collects memories and personal commentaries of historical significance through recorded interviews. An oral history interview generally consists of a well-prepared interviewer questioning an interviewee and recording their exchange in audio or video format."[32] The UNLV Oral History Research Center has a long tradition of building community trust and partnerships which document the local and regional history of Las Vegas and Southern Nevada. These first-hand accounts and primary source materials serve as the foundation for our Wikidata efforts and contributions.

The project scope focused on raising awareness around contributions from Las Vegas Westside community members by enhancing existing archival collections and oral histories with semantic data in the form of Wikidata creation and editing; incorporating Archival Resource Keys (ARKs[33]—a type of persistent identifier) into Wikidata reference statements, linking UNLV archival collections and oral histories using the *archives at* (P485) or *oral history at* (P9600) properties[34]; and feeding back Wikidata persistent identifiers (Q-numbers) into agent records in the Special Collections and Archives Portal (SCA Portal).[35] SCA Portal is a discovery system that brings digital objects, archival components and descriptions, agent records, and numerous

32. Donald A. Ritchie, "An Oral History of Our Time," in *Doing Oral History* (Oxford, UK: Oxford University Press, 2014), 1.
33. "ARK Alliance – Home of the Archival Resource Key (ARK)," ARKS, accessed April 25, 2022, https://arks.org/.
34. "archives at - Wikidata," Wikidata, accessed April 25, 2022, https://www.wikidata.org/wiki/Property:P485; "oral history at - Wikidata," Wikidata, accessed April 25, 2022, https://www.wikidata.org/wiki/Property:P9600.
35. "UNLV Special Collections Portal," UNLV, accessed April 25, 2022, http://special.library.unlv.edu/.

special collections databases together in an integrated user view by managing resources as nodes in a graph.

Two Wikidata sprints were organized to highlight notable people, local businesses, and landmarks associated with the historic neighborhood and were documented in the project wiki.[36] Additional enhancements were contributed to the newly created Wikidata items, including: incorporating sitelinks to related Wikimedia projects and content; adding persistent identifiers from existing authority records for people, corporate bodies, and

```
PREFIX wd: <http://www.wikidata.org/entity/>
PREFIX wdt: <http://www.wikidata.org/prop/direct/>
PREFIX wikibase: <http://wikiba.se/ontology#>

SELECT ?item ?itemLabel ?itemDescription ?instanceOfLabel
WHERE
{
 ?item wdt:P31 ?instanceOf ; wdt:P5008 wd:Q100202113 .
 SERVICE wikibase:label { bd:serviceParam wikibase:language "en". }
}ORDER BY ASC (?itemLabel)
```

Figure 1. SPARQL Query to list Wikidata items on the UNLV Wikimedia project focus list Wikidata Query Service (https://w.wiki/56y2)

organizations, if one existed; and adding UNLV to the focus list of Wikimedia project[37] for easy recall of Wikidata items related to the sprints.

Historic Westside Legacy Park Sprint

The Westside Legacy Park is a site dedicated to honoring the African American history of Las Vegas and features a playground,

---

36. "Wikidata:WikiProject PCC Wikidata Pilot - Wikidata," Wikidata, accessed April 25, 2022, https://www.wikidata.org/wiki/Wikidata:WikiProject_PCC_Wikidata_Pilot.

37. "on focus list of Wikimedia project - Wikidata," Wikidata, accessed April 25, 2022, https://www.wikidata.org/wiki/Property:P5008.

open space, and public art; it includes installations where visitors can learn about notable community leaders.[38] In this sprint, Wikidata items were created for the park site, park award, and each community leader who was a part of the first cohort of honorees. ARKs were added to them, linking archival collections and oral histories associated with the honorees.

Prior to the sprint, multiple metadata application profiles for a variety of classes of entities (consisting of core and optional properties used in Wikidata statements) were documented for persons, corporate bodies, and awards.[39] Properties were selected after consulting the Archives Linked Data Interest Group's recommendations for describing people and corporate bodies.[40] Two SPARQL queries were also created to highlight honorees and related collections, and were published on the project wiki for community reuse by others in the various GLAM, linked open data, and Semantic Web communities.[41] These SPARQL queries can be used to explore honorees and related facts about them, and the code can also be repurposed as a template to recall other values in Wikidata qualifier or reference statements.

Westside Businesses Sprint

During the 1940s through 1960s, the Las Vegas Westside had a thriving business district and a local economy that was fueled by various local enterprises. This mapping project highlights former sites of restaurants, nightclubs, casinos, churches, and

---

38. "Historic Westside Legacy Park," Las Vegas Nevada, accessed April 25, 2022, https://www.lasvegasnevada.gov/Residents/Parks-Facilities/Historic-Westside-Legacy-Park.

39. "Best Practices," Wikidata, accessed April 25, 2022, https://www.wikidata.org/wiki/Wikidata:WikiProject_PCC_Wikidata_Pilot/UNLV#Best_Practices.

40. "Wikidata:WikiProject Archives Linked Data Interest Group - Wikidata," Wikidata, accessed April 26, 2022, https://www.wikidata.org/wiki/Wikidata:WikiProject_Archives_Linked_Data_Interest_Group.

41. "Wikidata Query Service:List all Legacy Park honorees," Wikidata, accessed April 26, 2022, https://w.wiki/54Cg.; "Wikidata Query Service:List collections associated with the Legacy Park honorees," Wikidata, accessed April 26, 22, https://w.wiki/54Ch.

other institutions of the Westside during that time period. Using geographic coordinates captured at the former sites, manuscript collections, and oral histories as source data, Wikidata items describing businesses were created to document the location of these historic sites. In this sprint, *Result Views* provided by Wikidata's SPARQL query service were utilized to display query results on an urban map with layers, sortable by business type.[42]

```
PREFIX wd: <http://www.wikidata.org/entity/>
PREFIX wdt: <http://www.wikidata.org/prop/direct/>
PREFIX wikibase: <http://wikiba.se/ontology#>

#defaultView:Map
SELECT ?West_Las_Vegas ?West_Las_VegasLabel ?coordinate_location ?layerLabel
WHERE
{
?West_Las_Vegas wdt:P276 wd:Q7985710 .
OPTIONAL {?West_Las_Vegas wdt:P31 ?instance ; wdt:P625 ?coordinate_location . }
BIND(?instance AS ?layer) .
SERVICE wikibase:label { bd:serviceParam wikibase:language "[AUTO_LANGUAGE],en".
}
}ORDER BY ASC(?layerLabel)
```

Figure 2. SPARQL Query to visualize West Las Vegas businesses on an urban map Wikidata Query Service (https://w.wiki/54gY)

Project Methods:

Throughout the project, a multiphase methodology was employed consisting of five themes, including: (1) planning, (2) documentation, (3) hiring and training, (4) project sprint execution, and (5) documenting lessons learned. These themes did not follow a set linear path, but rather flowed in an iterative manner where decisions, actions, and new insight were the driving forces behind the sprints.

---

42. "Wikidata:SPARQL query service/Wikidata Query Help/Result Views - Wikidata," Wikidata, accessed April 26, 2022, https://www.wikidata.org/wiki/Wikidata:SPARQL_query_service/Wikidata_Query_Help/Result_Views.

Planning

During project planning, project managers met with curators from UNLV's Special Collections and Archives to prioritize high-demand collections that had little-to-no web presence. In these meetings, multiple project ideas were presented and final decisions were made by consensus from meeting participants.

Documentation

During documentation, three activities were the main focus. Decisions were made on how Wikidata items should be modeled, application profiles of selected properties to use in Wikidata statements were created for multiple types of items,[43] and a project wiki and supplemental pages were created for transparency, ongoing training, and reuse.

Hiring and Training

During initial hiring and training, a national search was successfully conducted, after which the project Wikimedian-in-Residence was onboarded and asynchronous training was completed. Training topics covered system access, software installations and configurations, and Wikidata editing basics and best practices. In addition, project goals and deliverables were discussed, and the team began examining Wikidata productivity tools for batch editing[44] and form-based editing.[45]

---

43. "Best Practices," Wikidata, accessed April 25, 2022. https://www.wikidata.org/wiki/Wikidata:WikiProject_PCC_Wikidata_Pilot/UNLV#Best_Practices.

44. "QuickStatements - Meta," Wikimedia, accessed April 25, 2022, https://meta.wikimedia.org/wiki/QuickStatements.

45. "Wikidata:Cradle - Wikidata," Wikidata, accessed April 25, 2022, https://www.wikidata.org/wiki/Wikidata:Cradle.

Project Sprint Execution

During the project sprint, the project team took an Agile[46] soft-ware development approach towards Wikidata creation. This is when development or production is carried out iteratively in short, focused sprints. Agile is highly adaptable and designed to work with cross functional teams. Sprints were run in two-week production cycles, during which manual and batch editing techniques were explored.

Document Lessons Learned

At the conclusion of a Wikidata sprint, the team would reconvene to discuss any lessons learned, new opportunities worth exploring during future sprints, or challenges that were encountered during production. The group discussions often led to further refinements in the production workflows and documentation. These lessons were then chronicled in various sections of the project wiki, including the section on best practices, general help, and SPARQL queries.

Analysis

Ethics of Care

In this chapter, we propose that the Ethics of Care framework should be applied to linked data project planning and assessment in order to ensure that decision making on all aspects of metadata design, from creation through discovery to reuse, is analyzed through an appropriate lens to consider complex relationships and the potential impacts of data in a digital world.

---

46. "What is Agile? | Agile 101 | Agile Alliance," Agile Alliance, accessed April 25, 2022, https://www.agilealliance.org/agile101/.

Arising out of the late twentieth century feminist movement and originated by Carol Gilligan and Nel Noddings, Ethics of Care is an ethical theory positing that moral action centers on interpersonal relationships and care. Specifically, this centering is based on viewing relationships with a priority on care-giving (responsibility for others) over justice (responsibility for self). Ethics of Care later led to the development of other relational theories such as intersectionality and relational identity. As part of an ethical toolkit, this theory is particularly useful as a lens through which to view archives, linked data, and metadata work by considering theoretical foundations such as the idea that people have interdependent relationships and must therefore rely upon each other. The model below (Figure 3) suggests that all roles can benefit from working within an ethical sphere where relationships are prioritized. The Ethics of Care model, along with other ethical frameworks, can form elements of this sphere; naming smaller inner spheres where limitations and challenges may arise. Committing to practical steps early on, such as ethics-focused project planning, allows metadata design and linked data creation decisions and system development to overlap or connect within that framework. There will not always be harmony between linked data philosophies of openness and sharing, guidance of metadata standards, and the limitations of system design, but surfacing the conflicts can be an important outcome of applying the Ethics of Care ideas. The theory is imperfect and has been criticized for its reliance on stereotypical views of gender, but, taken with additional inputs from other research disciplines, it can serve us as "a position from which to begin our moral reasoning, rather than as a tool to use in sorting out particular moral cases or dilemmas."[47]

---

47. Kathryn MacKay, "Feminism and Feminist Ethics," in *Introduction to Philosophy: Ethics*, edited by George Matthews (Montreal: Rebus Community, 2019): 66.

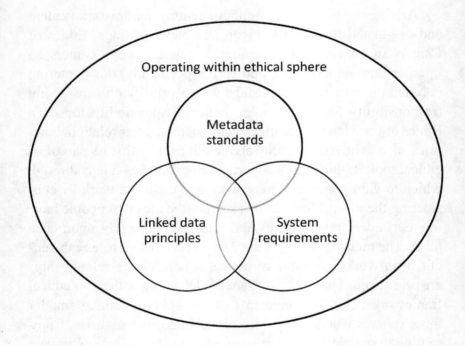

Figure 3. Perspectives informing roles of Linked Data implementers situated within a sphere of ethical considerations, such as those in Ethics of Care model

Interrogating the relationships and power structures in typical relationships (curator/digital services unit, developer/user, or standards governing body/metadata creator) raises interesting questions for our field. Are curators relaying the most important context of a collection to the people describing it online? Should we always defer to developer expertise or the limited system administration options available when faced with multiple, sometimes poor, outcomes for users? How can metadata creators be empowered to resist standards when they do not fit the materials they are describing?

These questions are most critical when we examine the relationships outside of library staffing and think about where archives interface with communities directly, as curators often do in UNLV community documentation projects. Are the traditional roles in archives working to serve communities when we seek to document their history? Ethics of Care states that people in these relationships are affected by and impacted by choices, including those that represent their identities, portray their experience, and represent the knowledge in their documents. The theory asks that we examine specific situations and prefer these over generalized approaches with the goal of reducing harm to those involved. Using tools and practices beyond Ethics of Care, including radical empathy frameworks, ethical assessments, and questioning tradition when developing metadata strategy, new systems, or entification of community history, is essential to the development of linked data projects of the future.[48] Understanding how harm has been systematically built into practice is the beginning of a complex unraveling of assumptions in our institutions.

Temi Odumosu writes in the article "The Crying Child" about a decontextualized photograph of an Afro-Carribean child shared widely outside of its source—a curated Danish archive, later digitized and made available online—resulting in the photo becoming even more disturbingly ubiquitous beyond its use as an iconic image by colonizers "telling their story." Odumosu writes, "The real child...felt pain. But they entered the archive (and come to us now) as a metaphor for displacement, a repeating data-body with no name, no caretakers, no clear gender markers, no explanatory context... Orphaned via the technology of photography into a 'zone of non-being'."[49] In calling on those of us in the digital collections and metadata field to employ an Ethics of Care, he goes on to argue, "But the important issue for us now is where we stand as onlookers in this colonial constellation, as witnesses to a Black child being archived and appropriated."[50]

---

48. "Care Ethics | Internet Encyclopedia of Philosophy," UTM, accessed April 25, 2022, https://iep.utm.edu/care-eth/.

49. Temi Odumosu, "The Crying Child: On Colonial Archives, Digitization, and Ethics of Care in the Cultural Commons," *Current Anthropology* 61, no. 22, 292.

50. Odumosu, "The Crying Child," 293.

The Ethics of Care model, along with other ethical considerations in practice, can offer a potential way forward if used as a foundational component for planning future projects. Tronto outlines four elements: attentiveness, responsibility, competence, and responsiveness.[51] Of these, all are relevant to communities working on linked data projects and improving representation of archival collections, and they can be implemented by all project partners, regardless of role, by using a variety of local methods. In the library technology field, Henry argues that, "it is critical that library technologists see themselves in that role of providing care through advocacy."[52] This statement is validated by the work of Wright, who proposes a framework for the ethical impact assessment of information technology and concludes with the statement that, "the key to a successful ethical impact assessment is finding a way to engage stakeholders effectively."[53] How the GLAM profession chooses to adopt aspects of ethical practice in their work will vary, but, if we agree to take up the challenge, it will involve working to weave ethical considerations into the implementation of linked data throughout every project life-cycle until it becomes a valued aspect of digital archives, library technology, and metadata work.

Addressing the Ethical Issues within the Case Study

The Las Vegas Historic Westside sprints were attempts to increase equitable access to community oral accounts. A few ethical issues around the privacy of living persons, however, warranted special care when publishing Wikidata statements about them. The Wikidata policy regarding living people states, "as we value

51. Joan Tronto, "An Ethics of Care." in *Feminist Theory: A Philosophical Anthology*, edited by Ann E. Cudd and Robin O. Andreasen, 251-263 (Malden, MS: Blackwell Publishing, 2005).

52. Ray Henry, "Library Technologies and the Ethics of Care," *Journal of Academic Librarianship* 42, no. 3 (2016): 285.

53. David Wright, "A framework for the ethical impact assessment of information technology," *Ethics and Information Technology* 13 (2010): 224.

the dignity of living people, the information that we store about them deserves special consideration."[54] This document not only provides guidance on publishing information about living persons, it also provides a mechanism for the removal of private information; maintains a list of properties that may violate one's privacy; and includes total usage of those properties. Seven of the forty-three properties identified on the list were included in our project's metadata application profile associated with persons.

Property Label	Property	Number of Claims
occupation	P106	9,199,128
employer	P108	1,608,919
ethnic group	P172	158,948
place of birth	P19	3,016,714
sex or gender	P21	7,824,130
position held	P39	1,440,790
date of birth	P569	5,559,654

Table 1. *Wikidata properties in use at UNLV University Libraries that have been identified as having the potential to violate Wikidata's privacy policies.*

Even though the selected properties may have potentially posed some risk of policy violations, this information was included in some project items, when source data was available and verifiable. In this case, the information included had already been published in the transcripts and archival collection guides. In addition, the project team determined that the honorees were notable public figures, and there were no privacy concerns associated with the statements being published.

Another ethical issue needing consideration dealt with the recording of *sex or gender* values in Wikidata items using the

---

54. "Wikidata:Living people - Wikidata," Wikidata, accessed April 26, 2022, https://www.wikidata.org/wiki/Wikidata:Living_people.

property P21.[55] A number of linked data projects, both within and outside the Wikidata community, have recorded gender attributes in order to highlight hidden contributions of underrepresented communities.[56] In these communities, consensus has not yet been

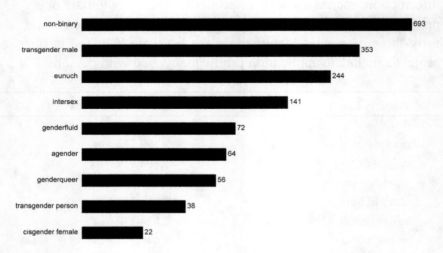

Figure 4. SPARQL results of top 10 non-binary sex or gender values Wikidata Query Service (https://w.wiki/53dR)

reached on how to apply gender, and numerous values are available for use in P21 statements.

Figure 4 lists the top genders by count minus the top four values (male: 5,942,881; female: 1,905,805; male organism: 9,049; and female organism: 4,666) applied to Wikidata items and further illustrates how gender representation is biased towards perceived gender norms. In the Program for Cooperative Cataloging (PCC) community, publishing gender information in name authority

55. "sex or gender – Wikidata," Wikidata, accessed April 26, 2022, https://www.wikidata.org/wiki/Property:P21.

56. M Cristina Pattuelli, Karen Hwang, and Matthew Miller, "Accidental Discovery, Intentional Inquiry: Leveraging Linked Data to Uncover the Women of Jazz," *Digital Scholarship in the Humanities* 32, no. 4 (December 1, 2017): 918-924, https://doi.org/10.1093/llc/fqw047; "Home - Art + Feminism," Art and Feminism, accessed April 26, 2022, https://artandfeminism.org/; "Wikidata:WikiProject Women - Wikidata," Wikidata, accessed April 26, 2022, https://www.wikidata.org/wiki/Wikidata:WikiProject_Women.

records (NARs) has been getting greater scrutiny in recent years due to concerns regarding identity and misrepresentation, privacy, and safety.[57] Within this community, the current practice is to not include gender statements in name authority records (NARs).[58] This recent change in cataloging policy is a shift in practice and reflects the changing nature of name authority work. What constitutes a name authority record has been changing as other types of non-library data are now being incorporated into these records. An excellent example is the practice of including Wikidata URIs in the MARC 024 fields or by including external URIs in their corresponding Wikidata item. Even though there is compelling evidence to support each side of the gender debate on whether to use or not to use sex and gender property statements, gender information was included in some project items. In this case, the information was only included when narrators described themselves in that fashion. Taking this approach protects from possible harm, but also provides opportunities to take on gender underrepresentation in public knowledge graphs.

Communication

In the case presented, communication and decision-making were key to tackling ethical challenges. It was also a foundation for reflecting on projects and creating documentation for practices we sought to continue. In the Wikidata sprints, a conscious choice was made to work with materials in oral history collections that had an established reciprocal communication pattern that featured narrators reviewing questions, answers, and all transcripts

57. Amber Billey, Emily Drabinski, and K. R. Roberto, "What's Gender Got to Do with It? A Critique of RDA 9.7," *Cataloging & Classification Quarterly* 52, no. 4 (May 19, 2014): 412–21; Kelly J. Thompson, "More Than a Name: A Content Analysis of Name Authority Records for Authors Who Self-Identify as Trans," *Library Resources & Technical Services* 60, no. 3 (July 28, 2016): 140–55.

58. PCC Ad Hoc Task Group, Revised Report on Recording Gender in Personal Name Authority Records, April 7, 2022. https://www.loc.gov/aba/pcc/documents/gender-in-NARs-revised-report.pdf.

before publication, and with an established embargo process for narrators who were not ready to publish their work. In addition, Ethics of Care concepts, and modified work with tools such as the Archival Ethics Worksheet in Culbertson and Lanthorne,[59] helped to scale discussions for a larger project and helped with the most important piece of developing an ethical framework: getting people to engage in the process, repeatedly and until it eventually became the norm.

Within this case, expressing commonalities and discussing differences in vocabulary terms/definitions, primary audiences, and project priorities formed a strong basis for the projects' ethical foundations. The better people communicate their perspectives and collaborate on projects, the more ethically-grounded linked data projects will be. During the Wikidata sprints, these conversations not only informed how we decided to model new types of entities, they also provided avenues to explore new types of computational research questions harnessing SPARQL within the Wikidata Query Service.

Wikidata Community

One of the most successful ways to overcome the obstacles in any implementation stage is by developing a community that can provide educational opportunities, facilitation of discussion, and oversight for decisions and governance. The Wikidata community does this well, and its system architecture supports such community activities. Throughout the two Wikidata sprints, we intended to incorporate and sustain learning opportunities, through experimentation and ongoing training, and by creating and sharing documentation. Oversight and shared governance within the Wikidata community takes shape in numerous forms. In our

---

59. Anna Culbertson, and Amanda Lanthorne, "Praxis, Not Practice: The Ethics of Consent and Privacy in 21st Century Archival Stewardship," *Across the Disciplines* 18, no. 1/2, (2021), https://doi.org/10.37514/ATD-J.2021.18.1-2.02.

efforts, governance was maintained through project talk pages, user talk pages of individual editors, and property proposals talk pages. In those pages, these discussions led to community developed best practices, improved workflows, higher data quality, and increased transparency.

Conclusion

As linked data work in the GLAM sector enters a more mature phase of larger-scale projects, deeper collaboration, and sustainable tools and shared methods, assessment of the work becomes critical. Beyond delivering on the promise of access to collections, automated connections, and data interoperability, linked data projects must also be assessed on the ways they develop models for collaboration and how they address the dangers that interconnected data pose for the most vulnerable. Assessment should include ethical considerations at all steps and incorporate communities (like the Wikidata community) as well as the community being documented in the historical record. Building communication channels customized for each project can not only improve the quality of the project data, but build authentic partnerships between all the roles involved in linked data work. Integrating ethical considerations and committing to these in community documentation projects will ensure that the next generation of linked data development embeds principles that benefit data quality alongside those that benefit human rights and respect for communities.

Appendix:
Ethics in Linked Data Checklist

ETHICS IN LINKED DATA AFFINITY GROUP

Introduction & Definitions

This checklist was developed over the course of a year in consultation with several LD4 Affinity Groups (especially the Wikidata and Discovery Affinity Groups), and attendees at multiple LD4 events and conferences. It was circulated to the authors of other chapters in this volume for peer review and additional comments.

The initial inspiration for the formatting of this chapter originated from an article on fast.ai's blog titled "16 Things We Can Do to Make Tech More Ethical" in three separate parts.[60] The article's first recommendation was for a "Checklist for Data Projects," commenting that the book *Ethics and Data Science* argues that, just as checklists have helped doctors make fewer errors, they can also help those working in tech make fewer ethical mistakes. The authors propose a checklist for people who are working on data projects.[61]

---

60. The fast.ai project (tagline: "making neural nets uncool again") is a project by artificial intelligence researchers Jeremy Howard and Rachel Thomas that aims to make "deep learning" (i.e., artificial intelligence machine learning) more accessible by offering free courses, software, and other benefits. Beginning in April of 2019, Thomas authored an article with Rachel Thomas, "16 Things We Can Do to Make Tech More Ethical, Part 1," fast.ai, April 2019, https://www.fast.ai/2019/04/22/ethics-action-1/#-checklist.

61. Ibid.

The Ethics in Linked Data Affinity Group began work on a checklist with the explicit goal of having it included as a chapter within this book.

In the intervening time, several other "Ethics Checklists" originating from the Data Science field have been published, none of which (that the authors are aware of) aimed at considerations around linked data or data in cultural heritage contexts. All of these publications were reviewed in the final version of this document; some questions were adapted, but the vast majority of the recommendations below originate from the time and labor of members in the Ethics in Linked Data Affinity Group listed in the Acknowledgement section.

This checklist is divided into three major areas (**Planning**, **Implementation**, and **Maintenance**) that are meant to represent the lifecycle of a linked data project. The initial area, **Planning**, focuses largely on questions about source data and is aimed at projects in their developing stages, but could also be useful for long-running initiatives that would like to re-examine their foundations. Many of the questions would be useful for project leads/principal investigators to ask during their initial planning stages, and/or to inform discussions with data providers. The second area, **Implementation**, offers more practical questions about what the data or project looks like in action, including how it adheres to broader standards and guidelines. This section also offers questions about the individuals and teams that are responsible for the implementation of the project. The final section, **Maintenance**, offers questions meant to provoke discussion around what day-to-day and ongoing maintenance entails for a specific project, and how a project engages with its audience or users.

These three areas are subdivided into seven subsections:

1. **General**, consisting of broad questions that could not be easily placed in a more thematic subsection and/or questions that could be easily located in multiple subsections.

2. **Accessibility**, consisting of questions around accessibility, in three different senses of that word: 1) can disabled/crip users access our project? 2) Should the data be opened or closed? and 3) Is the data accessible to users who should have access?

3. **Provenance, Sources, & Citations,** consisting of questions connected to a project's source data, its origination/provenance, its veracity, and how it offers credit and citation.

4. **Oppression & Harm**, consisting of questions about the potential harms caused by our data or projects and/or the ways that the data or project documents oppressions.

5. **Inclusion & Diversity**, consisting of questions that consider how our project and/or its data includes (or excludes) diverse communities and opinions.

6. **Identity Management & Privacy**, consisting of questions connected to a project's management of identities or its use of personal data that may violate the privacy of its subjects.

7. **Data Sovereignty & Intellectual Property**, consisting of questions around copyright obligations as well as questions that consider the ownership of data used in a project beyond narrow legal obligations.

The **Planning** area also includes a **Sunsetting** section, which consists of considerations for a project's end of life (loss of funding, loss of interest, archiving, etc.). We have located these considerations in the **Planning** stage due to repeated experiences and stories about how projects seem to simply disappear, how URIs stop resolving, and how others are left to clean up the resulting mess, much of which could be avoided if anticipated early on. Each section concludes with a list of **Additional Resources** for projects to draw from and/or that were consulted in the development of this resource.

The divisions between these areas and subsections are *explicitly* artificial. They are not meant to be firm, as there are several overlapping and some repeated questions. Depending on the project that the checklist is applied to, these boundaries could be limiting. For example, questions about the environmental impacts of a project (in Planning) are applicable to projects beyond the Planning and/or Implementation stages.

Furthermore, not all questions or sections will be relevant to all projects. This checklist (and the checklist alone) is licensed under a CC-BY license. Therefore, we encourage the remixing, editing, and restructuring of this document to make it more applicable, timely, and relevant to specific projects. For example, one author applied it to a review of the CIDOC CRM ontology structure and documentation by selecting a relevant subset of questions from the checklist and adjusting the wording so that the items spoke specifically to the context at hand. Another way this checklist could be applied would be, for example, as an advocacy tool to demonstrate to an institution's leadership the degree to which a project complies with ethical standards or to help address crucial areas that are lacking in consideration and need action.

Finally, we hope that this document will be considered and utilized holistically as well as critically, as there are limitations to the perspectives and experiences of its authors and other contributors. This checklist is not meant to be a one-stop guide; it is not a method that frees you, your project, and/or its source or resultant data from other legal, moral, and ethical obligations. There are no easy answers to these questions, and this checklist does not seek to provide them; instead, the authors of this checklist hope that it can provide a starting point for critical thinking and thoughtful engagement with matters of ethics in the linked data context.

Additional Data Ethics Checklists Consulted

Baxter, Kathy. "How to Build Ethics into AI — Part I." Salesforce Design (blog), April 30, 2018. https://medium.com/salesforce-ux/how-to-build-ethics-into-ai-part-i-bf35494cce9.

———. "How to Build Ethics into AI — Part II." Salesforce Design (blog), April 2, 2018. https://medium.com/salesforce-ux/how-to-build-ethics-into-ai-part-ii-a563f3372447.

Data Science for Social Good Foundation. "An Ethical Checklist for Data Science," September 18, 2015. https://www.dssgfellowship.org/2015/09/18/an-ethical-checklist-for-data-science/.

Deon and Driven Data. "An Ethics Checklist for Data Scientists." Deon, March 7, 2022. https://deon.drivendata.org/.

Design, Inclusive. "How to Recognize Exclusion in AI." Microsoft Design (blog), August 27, 2019. https://medium.com/microsoft-design/how-to-recognize-exclusion-in-ai-ec2d6d89f850.

Hudson, Laura. "Technology Is Biased Too. How Do We Fix It?" FiveThirtyEight (blog), July 20, 2017. https://fivethirtyeight.com/features/technology-is-biased-too-how-do-we-fix-it/.

Knight, Will. "The Dark Secret at the Heart of AI." *MIT Technology Review* 120, no. 3 (April 11, 2017). https://www.technologyreview.com/2017/04/11/5113/the-dark-secret-at-the-heart-of-ai/.

Loukides, Mike, Hilary Mason, and DJ Patil. "Case Studies in Data Ethics." O'Reilly Media, August 7, 2018. https://www.oreilly.com/content/case-studies-in-data-ethics/.

Patil, DJ, Hilary Mason, and Mike Loukides. "Of Oaths and Checklists." O'Reilly Media, July 17, 2018. https://www.oreilly.com/radar/of-oaths-and-checklists/.

Vallor, Shannon, Brian Green, and Irina Raicu. "Ethics in Technology Practice: An Ethical Toolkit for Engineering/Design Practice." The Markkula Center for Applied Ethics at Santa Clara University, 2018. https://www.scu.edu/ethics/.

Planning

General

- Does our project have a statement of ethics and values against which our implementation can be measured?
  - ○ Do these statements align with our Institutional/ Ethics Review Board?
  - ○ Have our ethics and values statements been reviewed by members of the community that we are documenting?
- Why is this information being collected, recorded, controlled, and provided? Whom does it serve and whom does it harm?

Accessibility

- Does our project and its documentation follow Universal Design principles?
- What ontologies and/or vocabularies do we plan to use, and are they open, well-documented, and widely implemented? Are they interoperable with other systems? Are they likely to be continually preserved?
- If no one ontology or vocabulary meets our needs—have we surveyed available ontologies and/or vocabularies for constructs we can adopt, rather than coining a new construct covering the same territory?
- Are we prepared to meet the demands (e.g., time and labor costs) of a potential influx in requests for access to our materials resulting from its increased discoverability?

Provenance, Sources, & Citations

- Do we know the provenance of the data? Who wrote the data and why?

- Where is our data coming from and what assumptions does it bring with it? Have possible sources of bias in the data been considered?
- Do we have questions about the reliability or trustworthiness of the data? How can we address these concerns, or indicate these doubts?
- Can we track metadata transformations back to the original form of the record?
- Regarding source data for triples, are there "preferred" sources? That is, are some source/citation references considered more pertinent? Less pertinent?
- Is the data comprehensive (enough)? Is there information from sources that is not being included or fully described in the data? If not, why?
- If the linked data uses historical terminology, is it properly contextualized? Where more modern terminology is available, have appropriate linkages been made?
- Who/what isn't represented in our source data?

Oppression & Harm

- What data model or ontology does our project use? Are there limits to the model(s) or ontology used and are these limits disclosed? Some questions to consider:
  - Have we ensured that the model does not rely on variables or proxies for variables (e.g., "suburban neighborhoods" for white people, or assumptions that all people receiving a certain type of aid are disabled) that are unfairly discriminatory?
    - For example, historical datasets and census data often made racist, sexist, or ableist assumptions about certain groups, or engaged in outright erasure of individuals or experiences.

- ○ Have we examined our model results for fairness with respect to different affected groups?
- ○ Have we considered the ramifications of optimizing, enhancing, or displaying certain data-points or fields or of not doing so?
- ○ Can we both justify and explain the choices we or others have made in our project's data model or ontology?
- Is historical harm modeled? Do these models accurately reflect the lived experience of marginalized subjects, especially racialized or colonized ones?
- How could this data be used to spread harmful misinformation, hate speech, or propaganda?
- If this data deals with living people, could it be used to harm them? Could this data be used by governments for surveillance?

Inclusion & Diversity

- Does the source data, where it mentions a person or group, use the person or group's preferred terminology? How have we determined that this is the correct terminology? If there is conflicting terminology, have we attempted to document those conflicts?
  Examples:
  - ○ Black vs. African-American
  - ○ Native vs. Aboriginal vs. Indigenous
- Do we have mechanisms or policies to deal with terminology that is accurate in one country / language / context but not in other countries / languages / contexts?
- Who/what isn't represented in our sources?

Identity Management & Privacy

- Have we considered not collecting or publishing personal information that isn't relevant to our project's goals or analysis? (This is especially important for living subjects as personal information, like birthdate and city of birth, can be used for identity theft)
- If the source data uses historical terminology, is it properly contextualized, either in an unstructured note or via structured methods such as additional properties and/or qualifiers?

Examples:

  - ○ Colonial names for places (e.g., **Siam** vs. **Thailand**).
  - ○ **Invert** (from 19th and 20th century sexological term "**sexual inversion**" to refer to what we would understand as homosexuality) vs. **homosexual** (later 20th and 21st century term) vs. **queer** (a newer common umbrella term).

- Does the source data misidentify a person's gender?
  - ○ Is gender a necessary datapoint?
  - ○ Do we know how this gender data was produced?
  - ○ Does it deadname or mispronoun trans individuals?
- Are there procedures in place to ensure that all data related to identities collected initially is accurate and up-to-date?
- Is all sensitive/personal information included absolutely necessary? Does our system allow for the protection of private/personal information?

Examples:

  - ○ Wikidata allows editors to add statements to properties, using the living people protection class property (P8274), which can class it as a property that may violate privacy (Q44601380)

- ○ There are kinds of personal information which indicate the authenticity of an author's account. Should they be included in descriptions of the author, or are they unnecessary?
- Does our project obtain consent when possible? How do we represent data as truly accurate when there is no citation or confirmation?
- Is there a way to obtain consent and/or verify information from individuals?

Examples:

- ○ Assumptions about deceased people: when we go to communities to get consent from living people, can we say that their data will be shared as respectfully after their death as while they are living?
- ○ Protection of the contributions of living people (for example, those who participated in political protests and demonstrations).
- Is the source data up to date?

Examples:

- ○ Ivan E. Coyote's record is based on Canadian CIP data from a publisher, which does not reflect their current wishes.
- ○ Information about an author's birthdate. The author has a current, personal website that does not include a birthdate, while a previous version of the author's website captured in the Internet Archive Wayback Machine does include the birthdate. If using an older source, is the situation one of ephemeral Internet or of conscious removal of information by the author?

Data Sovereignty & Intellectual Property

- Does our project involve Indigenous knowledge and/or data? If so, does our project adhere to the FAIR / CARE and/or OCAP Principles?
- What copyright is used on our project? In our source data? On our data transformations?
- Does the data used in our project satisfy legal, moral, and ethical obligations?
- Are there ways for minoritized groups to retain control over their data? What are these ways?
  Examples derived from OCAP:
  - Do communities have rights to deletion? How have we implemented these rights?
  - Have communities requested access restrictions? How have we implemented these restrictions?
  - Have communities requested corrections? How will we implement these corrections?

Sunsetting

- Will the data from the project be archived or preserved somewhere?
- Will any coined URIs continue to resolve?
- For projects using Wikidata, who will check the new data added for accuracy? Who will check vandalism? Privacy?
- If our project has a web-facing component, are final versions of our webpages preserved in the Internet Archive or another easily-accessible location?
- Do we engage in any verification or vetting for incoming data (i.e., Do we represent data from projects that link to our own)?
- If we (or our institution) can no longer steward the data, have we found someone to take over? Does this contact

person (or group) have up-to-date contact information?

- Do we have an archival plan in place for the project's data and/or findings? Is the plan clearly outlined and can it be easily implemented?
- Has our team thought about the carbon cost for the project? Are there any ways that the environmental cost of the project can be reduced in implementation (i.e., lower quality images, minimal computing, etc.)?
- Does our project have an ongoing and updated plan for the end of funding or wrapping up the project? Where will the data and/or the findings "live on"?
- Is there a plan in place for future users of the data?
- How significant is the environmental cost to maintaining the project indefinitely?

Additional Planning Resources:

British Columbia First Nations' Data Governance Initiative. "BC First Nations Data Governance Initiative." BC First Nations Data Governance Initiative, 2022. https://www.bcfndgi.com.

Carroll, Stephanie Russo, Edit Herczog, Maui Hudson, Keith Russell, and Shelley Stall. "Operationalizing the CARE and FAIR Principles for Indigenous Data Futures." Scientific Data 8, no. 1 (April 16, 2021): 108. https://doi.org/10.1038/s41597-021-00892-0.

DLF AIG Metadata Working Group. "Metadata Assessment Framework and Guidance." DLF Metadata Assessment Working Group, 2022. http://dlfmetadataassessment.github.io/framework.

FNIGC-CGIPN. "First Nations Information Governance Centre." The First Nations Information Governance Centre, 2022. https://fnigc.ca/.

National Disability Authority. "What Is Universal Design." Centre for Excellence in Universal Design, 2020. https://universaldesign.ie/what-is-universal-design/.

Research Data Alliance. "FAIR Data Maturity Model WG Case State-
    ment." FAIR Data Maturity Model WG, September 23, 2018.
    https://www.rd-alliance.org/group/fair-data-maturity-mod-
    el-wg/case-statement/fair-data-maturity-model-wg-case-state-
    ment.

————. "Implementing the CARE Principles: The CARE-Full Pro-
    cess." International Indigenous Data Sovereignty IG, August 4,
    2020. https://www.rd-alliance.org/implementing-care-princi-
    ples-care-full-process.

Fox, Violet B., and Kelly Swickard. "'My Zine Life Is My Private Life':
    Reframing Authority Control from Detective Work to an Ethic
    of Care." In Ethical Questions in Name Authority Control,
    edited by Jane Sandberg, 9–24. Sacramento, CA: Library Juice
    Press, 2019.

Implementation

General

- Who isn't represented on our team but ideally should be?
- What assumptions do we make about the lived experiences, desires, and values of the groups contained within our data? Why have we done this, and with what justification?
- Has our team reflected on the issues of equity, inclusion and diversity, and do they have a policy regarding these issues?
- Are all project members given adequate credit for their work on the project? If yes, have project members consented to having their names, personal data, or other information in the project's credits?
- Have we addressed blind spots or missing perspectives from our team through engagement with relevant stakeholders (e.g., checking assumptions and discussing

implications with affected communities and subject matter experts)?

Accessibility

- Is the data presented (for example, on a human readable web page or knowledge panel) accessible to users with disabilities?
  - ○ Can it be read by screen readers?
  - ○ Does it use accessible colors?
  - ○ Can it be navigated by keyboard only?
  - ○ Do images have alternative text? How reliable is it?
- Is our data internationalization-friendly?
  Examples:
  - ○ If the project or its data is based on or derives from non-English-speaking communities, have we translated the text or labels into relevant languages (to the extent possible)?
  - ○ Do we have an intake method for translations (of labels or text) from other communities (to the extent possible)?
- If we host a web-facing project, how do we monitor uptime? Domain renewal? If our project or data is privately hosted, is our hosting provider likely to remain in business?
- If we transform data in significant ways, are the steps that we took well documented and reproducible by others?
- If we undertake additional analysis on our data, are these steps documented and reproducible by others?
- If openly available, has it been labelled and made accessible via open access? (A large amount of publicly-funded information and research has been paywalled, and a great number of datasets are inaccessible).

Provenance, Sources, & Citations

- Where are we providing citations to data sources? At the knowledge panel level? At the statement/attribute level?
- Is our editing/linked data curation process clearly documented and contextualized? Is it flagged or noted that data comes from a source that is open access/editable by anyone?
- Are our data collection methods, sources, and purpose transparent and clear?
- If we are aware of bias within our data, what steps have we taken to address or mitigate it? Have we examined the data for possible sources of bias and taken steps to mitigate or address issues such as stereotype perpetuation, confirmation bias, imbalanced classes, or omitted confounding variables?
- Do our visualizations, summaries (descriptions, reports, statistics) honestly and accurately reflect the underlying data? What possible misinterpretations could result from them? How could they be abused?

Oppression & Harm

- Do the controlled vocabularies (labels, definitions/scope notes, and other pertinent attributes/properties) in use align with the project's ethics and values?
- Does the implementation reflect diversity of knowledges, backgrounds, and kinds of thought, especially from marginalized communities?
- How does this knowledge diversity come into tension with other ethics and values of the project (if at all)? For example, do some knowledges/opinions or kinds of thought oppress?
- Does the implementation include/center the voices of

those represented in the linked data? If not, is there a plan to center them moving forward?

- Are there other features of, or activities on, our collection, platform, or institution that are working against our efforts?
  Example:
  - Wikidata has several automated bots that assign binary genders to individuals based on their name.

Inclusion & Diversity

- Have we identified who is being included or excluded from our data and discussed the possible impact upon users?
- If the majority of our data represents one group of users, have we disclosed this, or adopted models to check that the (statistical and political) minority are represented in an equal manner?
- Have we developed a response plan with our organization if users are harmed by the results?
- Does our team include and/or consider individuals, communities and/or institutions who will be ultimately affected by the project? How?

Identity Management & Privacy

- Is there a way to turn off, remove, or roll back the data in production if necessary?
- Do we have a method by which people represented in our data may request to have their personal information removed? How do we address the right-to-be-forgotten? This is a legal requirement in some jurisdictions.
- Are data using the individuals' or groups' preferred terminology?

Examples of ways to identify preferred terminology:
- In an academic setting, consult with research institutes or student groups on campus with expertise and/or lived experience.
- Using terms the person themselves uses in interviews, official biographies, etc.

- Are the sources that we are depending on reliable?
Example consideration:
- Much "open" information (i.e., Wikipedia) doesn't cite anything directly or cites IMDB (which also has accuracy and privacy issues).

- Have we considered if it is necessary to use personally identifying information, like birth dates, for living people? Should we ask for consent even when date or place of birth are data available in open sources? Would this consent cover data that hasn't been disclosed publicly so far?

- Do we have the consent of the individuals involved to share and use this information in our project's context, and/or does the information come from a reliable source (as defined by our project or relevant community of practice)?
Example:
- if someone declares their gender or sexuality on one platform, does that mean they've given consent for the information to go everywhere? Also, what happens if a person locks their social media accounts and that is the source of our information?

Data Sovereignty & Intellectual Property

- If the linked data describes sensitive or sacred knowledge, do we have a mechanism to restrict access to all but a defined subset of users?
- If necessary, do we have content warnings or other mechanisms for warning users about data sovereignty or

intellectual property rights? If appropriate, do we use TK labels?

- If our project connects to Indigenous individuals or communities, do we have a method for working with these communities and establishing relationships? Does our team include and/or consider individuals or communities that will be ultimately affected by the project?
- Is the data openly available, when appropriate?
- Does our metadata carry an open license such as Open Data Commons licenses (ODC-BY)? If copyright can be asserted, is it licensed permissively, for example using Creative Commons licenses (CC0; CC-BY)?

Additional Implementation Resources:

ColorSafe.Co. "Color Safe - Accessible Web Color Combinations," 2022. http://colorsafe.co/.

Creative Commons. "About The Licenses." Creative Commons, 2022. https://creativecommons.org/licenses/.

Harvard Center for the History of Medicine: Policies & Procedures Manual. "Guidelines for Inclusive and Conscientious Description." Harvard Wiki, January 20, 2022. https://wiki.harvard. edu/confluence/display/hmschommanual/Guidelines+for+Inclusive+and+Conscientious+Description.

Local Contexts. "Traditional Knowledge Licenses," 2022. https://local-contexts.org/licenses/traditional-knowledge-licenses/.

National Disability Authority. "What Is Universal Design." Centre for Excellence in Universal Design, 2020. https://universaldesign. ie/what-is-universal-design/.

Ochoa, Ellen. "WebAIM: Alternative Text." WebAIM, 2022. https:// webaim.org/techniques/alttext/.

Open Knowledge Foundation. "Open Data Commons Attribution License (ODC-By) v1.0 — Open Data Commons: Legal Tools for

Open Data." Open Data Commons, 2022. https://opendata-commons.org/licenses/by/1-0/.

The A11Y Project. "Home," 2022. https://a11yproject.com/.

W3C (World Wide Web Consortium). "Web Content Accessibility Guidelines (WCAG) 2.1." Web Content Accessibility Guidelines, June 5, 2018. https://www.w3.org/TR/WCAG21/.

Maintenance

General

- As new members join the project, do they understand and agree with the past decisions and policies made by previous members? Have the reasons for these decisions been explained and discussed?
- Will maintenance include editorial revision (e.g., to a controlled vocabulary) in response to feedback, or over time? This question should raise further questions about who our stakeholders are and what kind of consultation process we have.
- Do we have a mechanism / workflow / staff for dealing with inaccurate (or wrong) data?
- Do we have a mechanism / workflow / staff for dealing with take-down requests?
- Do we have a mechanism / workflow / staff for dealing with name, pronoun, or identity changes?
- If we are aware of other projects using our data, are they aware of its limitations and shortcomings?
- Do we have ongoing ethical sweeps of our data, policies, and procedures?
- Do we have regularly scheduled audits of past data, policies, or descriptions?

Accessibility

- Have we published mapping(s) to alternative models and vocabularies, including links to other ontologies/controlled vocabularies, to integrate our project with those of others?
- Do we have backups of these alternative models and vocabularies?
- Is there an up-to-date contact page for accessibility needs?
- Are our accessibility decisions (such as alt-text) regularly followed and/or audited?

Provenance, Sources, & Citations

- Are we providing transparency to changes made in the data?
- Has the source data changed? If so, do we have a mechanism for updating our linked data?

Oppression & Harm

- What problematic terminology exists in our system and how will we determine what to prioritize for our users or communities?
- Is our linked data up-to-date? Do we have scheduled audits and rechecking of data, understanding that terms are fluid and change?
- Do we allow ourselves to make mistakes and learn from those mistakes?
- Is there a clear method for audience(s) to point out and request remedies to mistakes?
- If the linked data uses historical terminology, is it properly contextualized?
- Does the linked data continue to use the person or group's preferred terminology?

- If the linked data (for example, knowledge panel data) is harvested by users or machines and recontextualized, could it harm the individual?
  Example:
    - If Wikidata data is harvested and displayed in another system, a qualifier regarding sourcing or veracity of the claim could be removed.

Inclusion & Diversity

- Is absence or omission flagged or highlighted? If so, how?
- Is there ongoing outreach and engagement with communities or individuals represented and not represented?
- What groups or individuals could be indirectly affected in significant ways by our data? Have their interests been protected? How do we know what their interests are, and have we consulted them?

Identity Management & Privacy

- Are there procedures in place to ensure that all personal data collected remains accurate and up-to-date?
- Is there a mechanism for take-down and editing requests? How is this communicated?
- Do our procedures for handling these requests include authenticating identities, responding to requests in a timely fashion, and/or allowing them to correct inaccurate data or delete the data entirely themselves?

Data Sovereignty & Intellectual Property

- Do we have a data retention plan? If there is unnecessary unpublished data, is there a deletion schedule? Who is responsible for disposing of this data?

- If our data contains personal information, what plans do we have in place in the event that this data is breached or stolen?
- Who owns the data and/or findings from our project? Does the licensing accurately reflect ownership?
- Do we have a mechanism through which an individual can request that their personal information be removed—known as the right to be forgotten?

Additional Maintenance Resources:

Cataloging Lab, and Violet Fox. "Problem LCSH." The Cataloging Lab, 2022. https://cataloginglab.org/problem-lcsh/.

Council on Publishing Ethics. "Update on COPE Guidance Regarding Author Name Changes | COPE: Committee on Publication Ethics." Council on Publishing Ethics, January 13, 2021. https://publicationethics.org/news/update-cope-guidance-regarding-author-name-changes.

Ganin, Netanel. "Every Occurrence of N4 in the Library of Congress Classification Scheme." I Never Metadata I Didn't Like (blog), March 26, 2016. https://inevermetadataididntlike.wordpress.com/2016/03/25/every-occurrence-of-n4-in-the-library-of-congress-classification-scheme/.

Tanenbaum, Theresa Jean, Irving Retting, H Michael Schwartz, Brian M. Watson, Teddy Goetz, Katta Spiel, and Mike Hill. "A Vision for a More Trans-Inclusive Publishing World: Guest Article." Council on Publishing Ethics, January 2021. https://publicationethics.org/news/vision-more-trans-inclusive-publishing-world.

The Trans Metadata Collective, Jasmine Burns, Michelle Cronquist, Jackson Huang, Devon Murphy, K.J. Rawson, Beck Schaefer, Jamie Simons, Brian M. Watson, and Adrian Williams. "Metadata Best Practices for Trans and Gender Diverse Resources." Trans Metadata Collective, June 22, 2022. https://doi.org/10.5281/zenodo.6756957.

About the Contributors

Sarah Ann Adams (she/her) is a Metadata Specialist in the Digital Research Division of the New York Public Library, working primarily on metadata for NYPL's Digital Collections. She is also a Research Fellow at the Semantic Lab at Pratt Institute. Adams holds a BA in the History of Art and Architecture from Boston University, and an MLIS from Pratt Institute, School of Information.

Stacy Allison-Cassin is a Citizen of the Métis Nation of Ontario. An Assistant Professor at the School of Information Management at Dalhousie University, Stacy engages in work and research related to metadata and Indigenous matters in libraries and the wider cultural heritage sector. Stacy is a passionate advocate for change in information structures and metadata systems within the library profession. She is the Chair of the International Association of Library Associations Indigenous Matters Standing Committee, the community chair for the Language Preservation and Instruction community, and a member of Council of the National Indigenous Knowledge and Language Association, an Indigenous-led association centered in Canada. Stacy also has extensive professional experience as a librarian, serving in a variety of roles, including music cataloguer, in the libraries at York University.

Kristi Bergland is the Music Metadata Librarian at the University of Minnesota Libraries. She received her MLIS from the University of Wisconsin-Milwaukee, and also holds a Master of

Music and a Doctor of Musical Arts, both from the University of Minnesota.

Previously the Collections Database Coordinator at the Snite Museum of Art, University of Notre Dame, **Hanna Bertoldi** is currently the Data Entry, Research, and Integrity Lead at Bowdoin College. She has a BA in Classical Archaeology and Ancient History from Franklin & Marshall College and an MA in Artefact Studies from the Institute of Archaeology at University College London. With years of professional work in database management, she approaches data projects with a commitment to increased accessibility of information by implementing strategies for clean, accurate, and ethical data.

Susan Brown is professor of English and holds a Canada Research Chair in Collaborative Digital Scholarship at the University of Guelph. Her research explores intersectional feminism, literary history, and online modes of collaborative knowledge production. She directs the Orlando Project in British women's writing, the Canadian Writing Research Collaboratory, and the Linked Infrastructure for Networked Cultural Scholarship. She collaborates with colleagues at Guelph in running The Humanities Interdisciplinary Collaboration (THINC) Lab, the DH@ Guelph Summer Workshops, and the major in Culture and Technology Studies.

Kathleen Burlingame (she/her) is Electronic Discovery and Access Librarian at the University of Pennsylvania Libraries and inaugural chair of its Diversity, Equity, and Inclusion in Discovery strategic team. Burlingame has worked on numerous linked data initiatives and co-founded the LD4 Ethics affinity group. She has a BA from Oberlin College, an MLS and MA in Literature from Indiana University-Bloomington, and a professional certificate in UX Design from the University of the Arts.

Erin Canning is the ontology systems analyst for the Linked Infrastructure for Networked Cultural Scholarship (LINCS) project, where they are responsible for defining the ontologies to be used by the project and overseeing the integration of datasets from researchers across Canada. Erin holds master's degrees in Information and Museum Studies from the University of Toronto, where they conducted research examining how information systems can be designed to accommodate affect as a fundamental way of knowing material culture.

Madison Chartier is the Metadata Librarian for Oklahoma State University's (OSU) Digital Resources and Discovery Services team. She holds a master's in library science from Indiana University Bloomington. As Metadata Librarian, Chartier oversees metadata creation and remediation for OSU's digital collections. She develops metadata application profiles and workflow documents to support efficient, high-quality metadata production. She also offers training on metadata practices to OSU faculty, students, and fellow librarians. In addition to her responsibilities at OSU, Chartier is a certified Data and Software Carpentries instructor and is involved with the Digital Library Federation's Assessment Interest Group's Metadata Working Group (MWG). A former co-facilitator of the MWG, she collaborates with other metadata professionals to develop resources concerning best metadata practices. She is also a member of the MWG's Metadata Quality Benchmarks subgroup and has helped analyze data and publish findings from a 2019 survey regarding current metadata quality assessment practices in digital libraries.

Zakiya Collier (she/they) is the Community Manager for the Documenting the Now project at Shift Collective. She is an archivist and memory worker whose work and research explore the role of cooperative thought and improvisation in the sustainability of im/material cultural memory, particularly in marginalized communities and cultural heritage institutions. They recently co-edited a special double issue of *The Black Scholar on Black Archival Practice*. Zakiya holds a BA in Anthropology from the University of South Carolina, an MLIS from Long Island University, and a MA in Media, Culture, and Communication from New York University, and is a Certified Archivist through the Academy of Certified Archivists (ACA).

Christine DeZelar-Tiedman is Cataloging Policies and Practices Librarian at the University of Minnesota Libraries. She has an MLIS from the University of Iowa, and has spent the majority of her career as a rare books and special collections cataloger.

Kate Dohe (she/her) leads the Digital Programs & Initiatives department in the University of Maryland Libraries. Kate's team oversees day-to-day activities related to digital content creation, access, and preservation, as well as digital library application services, web services, and discovery platforms. Select publications include "Care, Code, and Digital Libraries: Embracing Critical Practice in Digital Library Communities" (*In the Library with the Lead Pipe*), and "Linked Data, Unlinked Communities" (*Lady Science*). She holds an MLISc from the University of Hawai'i at Mānoa, and a BSEd in Speech and Theater from Missouri State University.

Peggy Griesinger is the Head of Metadata Initiatives at the University of Notre Dame's Hesburgh Libraries. She has an MLS and a BA in Classical Studies, both from Indiana University Bloomington.

Patrick Harrington is a Metadata Specialist at the University of Minnesota Libraries. He received a MLIS from the University of Illinois at Urbana Champaign and previously worked as the Metadata Librarian at the University of Wisconsin-Oshkosh.

James Kalwara is the Metadata Librarian at the William A. Wise Law Library at the University of Colorado Law School.

Cory Lampert is a Professor and the Head of Digital Collections at the University of Nevada Las Vegas University Libraries. She has over a decade of experience writing and administering grants and externally funded projects and her research interests focus on digital library best practices and linked open data for libraries, archives, and cultural heritage organizations. Recently she co-authored the ALA-published book, *Linked Data for the Perplexed Librarian*. She is also active in several service activities focused on libraries and open data, mentoring for cultural heritage professionals, and labor issues for contingent digital workers. She received her MLIS from the University of Wisconsin-Milwaukee.

Julie Pearson Little Thunder has been involved with the visual art scene in Oklahoma for nearly three decades. She has written numerous articles for *Southwest Art* magazine and *Oklahoma Today*, profiling individual artists and exploring various aspects of Native cultural production. Little Thunder was hired by the Oklahoma Oral History Research Program in 2010 to identify and interview Native artists from Oklahoma or those with Oklahoma roots. This resulting collection of oral history interviews with over 160 artists in a variety of media, has been used as a resource by the general public as well as academic researchers. Little Thunder drew upon some of this material for *A Life Made with Artists: Doris Littrell and the Oklahoma Native Art Scene*, published in 2015 by Roadrunner Press. In January 2020, Little Thunder began a new interview project, documenting the first-person oral histories of women artists in Oklahoma, with a particular emphasis on women of color, and has thus far completed half a dozen interviews for this series.

Megan Macken is the Assistant Department Head of Digital Resources and Discovery Services at Oklahoma State's Edmon Low Library where she oversees the metadata and cataloging units. Additionally, she serves as the liaison to the department of Art, Art History and Graphic Design and is a member of the implementation team for Experts Directory, Oklahoma State's research information management (RIM) system. Previously, she worked as a digital scholarship librarian and digital archivist. She has master's degrees in Library Science and the History of Art from Indiana University.

Kim Martin is an assistant professor of History at the University of Guelph, where she also co-developed the Culture and Technology Studies program. Her research investigates the role of serendipity in historians' information seeking and humanities researchers' use of linked data. She is the associate director of THINC Lab and the DH@Guelph Summer Workshops, and the LINCS Research Board Chair.

Darnelle Melvin is the Special Collections and Archives Metadata Librarian and an Assistant Professor at the University of Nevada, Las Vegas, where he is the lead metadata and Semantic Web strategist responsible for managing metadata activities, such as large-scale remediation projects, metadata workflows, and metadata documentation. He is co-author of *Linked Data for the Perplexed Librarian* and he researches metadata and resource discovery in digital libraries, ethical representation in public knowledge graphs, and data integration. His work explores linked data implementation, metadata remediation tools and services, workflow engineering and optimization, and system interoperability. Melvin received his MLIS degree from San José State University with a specialization in Information Organization, Description, Analysis, and Retrieval.

Daniele Metilli (they/them) is a research fellow in advanced data architectures for digital humanities at the Department of Information Studies of University College London, working on the Sloane Lab and Wikidata Gender Diversity projects. Daniele holds a BS in Computer Engineering from the Polytechnic University of Milan, as well as an MA in Digital Humanities and a PhD in Computer Science from the University of Pisa. They previously worked at the Institute of Information Science and Technologies of the National Research Council of Italy, where they contributed to several high-profile digital humanities projects (Mingei – Representation and Preservation of Heritage Crafts, Hypermedia Dante Network, Narratives in Digital Libraries, Linking Dante). Daniele's current research focuses on the intersections between knowledge representation, digital humanities, cultural heritage, gender, and ethics.

Sarah Milligan is Hyle Family Endowed Professor and Head of the Oklahoma Oral History Research Program at the Oklahoma State University Library. She is responsible for administering the production, access, and preservation of the OOHRP's 2,000+ interview collection. She has worked extensively in oral history throughout the U.S., and has served as the Oral History Association 2018 Principles and Best Practices Task Force co-chair and on the organization's governing Council. Milligan is a DPLA OKHub project lead and was the inaugural president of the OK Archivists Association.

Devon Murphy (they/them) is the Metadata Analyst at the University of Texas at Austin, with their work and research focusing on cultural heritage metadata, information ethics, and post-custodial workflows. Current and past projects include developing sustainable Spanish subject headings for digital collections in collaboration with partners at the University of Florida; creating new and updating harmful taxonomies for Texas Archival Resources Online (TARO); and developing best practices around trans and gender diverse materials with the Trans Metadata Collective (now the Queer Metadata Collective). They have an MLIS in Information Science and an MA in Art History, both from the University of North Carolina at Chapel Hill.

Mikala Narlock is the Director of the Data Curation Network based at the University of Minnesota. She has an MLS from Indiana University Bloomington and a BA in Interdisciplinary Humanities from the University of San Diego.

Chiara Paolini (she/her) is a PhD candidate in Linguistics at the Quantitative Lexicology and Variational Linguistics (QLVL) research group at KU Leuven. She obtained both her degrees in Digital Humanities (BA) and Applied and Theoretical Linguistics (MA) at the University of Pisa. She then worked as graduate fellow at the Institute of Information Science and Technologies "Alessandro Faedo" of the Italian National Research Council (ISTI-CNR) in Pisa, where she implemented and assessed the grammatical and semantic annotations of the digital version of Dante's Divine Comedy. Chiara's research interests include usage-based theories of language, distributional semantics, lexical semantics, and variational linguistics, as well as inclusivity and gender issues in language and linguistics.

Sam Popowich is an academic librarian in Canada and a PhD student in political science at the University of Birmingham. He is the author of *Confronting the Democratic Discourse of Librarianship: A Marxist Approach* (Library Juice Press, 2019).

Alexandra Provo (she/her) is Research Curation Librarian at New York University's Division of Libraries. A co-coordinator of the NYU/LIU Dual Degree Mentorship Program, she is also a Visiting Assistant Professor at Pratt Institute, where she teaches a course on metadata. Provo has been the project manager for two linked open data projects: Drawings of the Florentine Painters and the Linked Jazz Project. She has an MSLIS from Pratt Institute, an MA in interdisciplinary studies from NYU, and a BA in art history from Wesleyan University.

Erik Radio is the Metadata Librarian at the University of Colorado Boulder.

Sarah Roger is the LINCS project manager and an adjunct professor in English and Theatre Studies at the University of Guelph. Sarah's research is on Canadian literature and cultural concepts of reading. Her publications include *Borges and Kafka: Sons and Writers* (Oxford University Press, 2017) and the forthcoming *Future Horizons: Canadian Digital Humanities* (University of Ottawa Press, 2023).

Dorothea Salo is a Distinguished Faculty Associate in the University of Wisconsin at Madison's Information School. She has written and presented internationally on scholarly publishing, libraries in the digital humanities, copyright, privacy, institutional repositories, linked data, and data curation. As co-investigator for the IMLS-funded Data Doubles project, she is helping investigate undergraduate students' perceptions of privacy relative to learning analytics practices. Salo holds an MA in Library and Information Studies and another in Spanish from UW-Madison.

Ryan Shaw is an associate professor at the School of Information and Library Science at the University of North Carolina at Chapel Hill, where he teaches courses on the foundations, theory, and practice of information science and information organization.

Research-wise, he is interested in how information technologies are used to conceptualize and model our worlds and pasts. He is a member of the Organization Research Group (ORG).

Moritz Strickert is an ethnologist/sociologist and academic librarian at the University Library of the Humboldt-University Berlin as a staff member of the Specialized Information Service Social and Cultural Anthropology (FID SKA). He is currently working on a project that revises and supplements the Gemeinsame Normdatei (GND) and is active in the Thesauri Working Group of the Network for Sustainable Research Structures in Colonial Contexts.

Ruth Kitchin Tillman is the Sally W. Kalin Early Career Librarian for Technological Innovations at the Penn State University Libraries. She has written and presented on metadata encoding standards, library discovery, linked data, institutional repositories, and labor. She co-leads her library's Program for Cooperative Cataloging Wikidata Pilot Group and has contributed to the Art and Rare Materials BIBFRAME Extension, NISO's 2020 Linked Data Focus Group, and to other linked data and metadata efforts. Tillman holds an MLS from the University of Maryland.

Bri(an) M. Watson (they/them; @brimwats) is a disabled, white, queer & nonbinary settler living in Musqueam, Tsleil-Waututh, and Squamish. They are currently a Vanier Scholar at University of British Columbia's iSchool focusing on histories of information and the practice of equitable cataloging in libraries, archives, museums, and special collections. Watson is the Archivist-Historian of the American Psychological Association's Consensual Nonmonogamy Committee (div44cnm.org) and the Haslam Collection on Polyamory at the Kinsey Institute. They serve on the editorial board of Homosaurus (homosaurus.org), an international linked data vocabulary for queer terminology, and are the Director of HistSex.org, a free and open access resource for the history of sexuality. For 2022-2023, they are one of UBC Library's Equity, Diversity, and Inclusion (EDI) Scholars-in-Residence.

Index